PENGUIN BOOKS

BREACH OF PROMISE

After gaining a first-class honours degree in history at Reading University, Clive Ponting spent fifteen years in the Civil Service. He is now an author specializing in British politics and contemporary history and is an Honorary Research Fellow at University College, Swansea. His first book, *The Right to Know*, was the story of his own trial under the Official Secrets Act in 1985. He has also written two books about British government. His most recent book, *1940: Myth and Reality*, was published in 1990. He and his wife Sally now live in west Wales, where they also run an organic smallholding.

D1638604

BREACH
OF
PROMISE

LABOUR IN POWER 1964–1970

CLIVE PONTING

PENGUIN BOOKS

PENGUIN BOOKS

Published by the Penguin Group
Penguin Books Ltd, 27 Wrights Lane, London W8 5TZ, England
Viking Penguin, a division of Penguin Books USA Inc.
375 Hudson Street, New York, New York 10014, USA
Penguin Books Australia Ltd, Ringwood, Victoria, Australia
Penguin Books Canada Ltd, 2801 John Street, Markham, Ontario, Canada L3R 1B4
Penguin Books (NZ) Ltd, 182–190 Wairau Road, Auckland 10, New Zealand

Penguin Books Ltd, Registered Offices: Harmondsworth, Middlesex, England

First published by Hamish Hamilton 1989
Published in Penguin Books 1990
3 5 7 9 10 8 6 4 2

Copyright © Clive Ponting, 1989
All rights reserved

Printed in England by Clays Ltd, St Ives plc

To
Sally

List of Illustrations

Contents

Preface

This book is the first attempt to tell the inside story of one of the most crucial governments in modern British history. The focus is therefore deliberately on the internal decision taking of the Labour government rather than the public statements (already copiously available in Harold Wilson's memoirs) in an attempt to get behind the façade and examine how and why decisions were made. This is possible because of the unique sources available on the work of this government ranging from Wilson's own account to the Crossman, Castle and Benn diaries. This book also for the first time uses secret American material, some of it only obtained under Freedom of Information legislation, to provide radically new insights into British policy. The official British papers will not be completely available until 2001, and although these will provide more detail on policy making they will not reveal what was really said in Cabinet and will have to be read in conjunction with the vivid pictures of life in the Labour government drawn by the participants.

This book combines a chronological and analytical approach. Within a broad chronological framework each section begins with a survey of political developments and strategy, and each also has at least one chapter on economic policy. Other chapters deal with particular issues and problems, and are placed in the most appropriate section.

In the course of writing the book I have accumulated many debts of gratitude. The first is to my editor, Christopher Sinclair-Stevenson, and to Hilary Rubinstein, for encouraging me to write it in the first place. I am also grateful to Andrew Roth for lending me his collection of newspaper cuttings about Harold Wilson and also to my research assistant in the United States, Chris Wallace, who worked quickly to unearth vitally important material. I would also like to express thanks to the staff and students at University College, Swansea, and Birkbeck College together with the members of the Institute of Historical Research/Institute of Contemporary British History Seminar on Twentieth Century British History, all of whom heard early versions of parts of this book, and whose comments and criticism were invaluable.

I am also grateful to Hamish Hamilton for permission to quote from the Crossman diaries, to Barbara Castle for permission to quote from the Castle diaries and to Tony Benn for permission to quote from the first volume of his diaries.

My greatest debt of gratitude though is, as always, to my wife Sally who not only read the entire manuscript with a critical and perceptive eye but who also had to endure two years of discussions about the life and work of the Labour government.

PART ONE

GAINING POWER

1
Policies and Personalities, 1951–1964

Harold Wilson was elected leader of the Labour party on 14 February 1963. Just over eighteen months later on 16 October 1964 he became the youngest Prime Minister this century at the age of forty-eight. The interval between the two events was dominated by the general election and the requirements of electoral politics. Wilson had neither the opportunity nor the inclination to reshape the Labour party and its leadership in the brief period available to him. The party that he inherited and was to lead in government was heavily influenced by its experiences in opposition since 1951. Those years had been ones of bitter strife over the direction which the Labour party should take in its attempt to define the meaning of socialism in mid-twentieth-century Britain and, perhaps more important to its leaders, to win power. The battles over policy had been intertwined with personal rivalries and enmity between factions within the party and amongst its leaders. The thirteen years of opposition are of fundamental importance in understanding the stresses and strains that pervaded the life of the 1964–70 government. But the origins of many of these problems – the key to understanding the twin threads of policy and personality – can be traced back to the last crisis-ridden months of the Attlee government in 1951.

By 1950, after five years in power, the Attlee government had implemented many of the ideas which the Labour party had worked out during its long period in opposition in the 1930s. A free health service had been established together with a modern system of social security. The concept of 'planning' had been introduced, at least in outline, into the management of the economy. A major programme of nationalisation (the Bank of England, coal, electricity, steel and railways) had been carried through. The problem facing the government and the party was where to go next. One option, favoured on the left, was to keep controls over the economy and continue to extend the public sector by nationalising more industries, for example chemicals, armaments and sugar manufacture. An alternative was to consolidate the achievements

3

of the previous five years and move towards a more 'managerial' style, operating the existing system in a more egalitarian way but not seeking to extend the state sector. Although no formal decisions had been taken, the drift of the government was towards the 'managerial' option. These partially formulated alternatives were brought into focus by external events beyond the government's control.

As one of the victorious powers in 1945 the government had, almost without question, accepted the idea that Britain was, and would continue to be, a major world power. Security policy was based firmly on the alliance with the United States and, from the late 1940s, NATO. It was the North Korean attack on South Korea in June 1950 that triggered off a series of events leading to a crisis within the government. In July 1950 Britain agreed to send forces to fight alongside the US and other nominally UN forces to defend South Korea. However the United States regarded the attack as part of a major Communist offensive throughout the world and called upon its allies to undertake a massive rearmament programme. The Labour government's response was to plan for a doubling of defence expenditure in three years, with the share of national wealth devoted to defence rising from 8% to 14%, despite the impact this would have on Britain's precarious economic recovery since 1945. As envisaged, the programme was hopelessly unrealistic – the Churchill government after 1951 had to reduce it in scale and extend it over a longer period. And the consequences of this ill-thought-out scheme bedevilled the last year of the government.

In early 1951 the Chancellor of the Exchequer, Hugh Gaitskell, prepared the Budget. To balance the books, and pay for rearmament and higher pensions, without increasing taxes in what was likely to be an election year, he proposed to introduce charges for dental and optical work in the NHS. This precipitated a crisis within the government. The total money to be raised from charges was less than £20 million but it was an issue of principle over whether the NHS should remain, as it had been designed to be in 1948, a free service. After a long argument Nye Bevan, the architect of the NHS, resigned in April. He was joined by Harold Wilson (President of the Board of Trade) and John Freeman, a junior minister, both of whom placed more emphasis on the rearmament programme as the fundamental mistake. An increasingly tired and dejected government limped on until it was defeated in the October election.

On the surface, therefore, the 1951 crisis can be seen as a conflict of principles over policy, an argument about the long-term direction of the Labour party. Should priority be given to sound finance, rearmament and security questions, or to services like the NHS as being at the heart of a more 'socialist' approach? However, below the surface were powerful undercurrents of personal ambition. By 1950 the senior ministers in the government were old and tired, many worn out after ten years in office, including five gruelling years in the wartime coalition. Stafford Cripps and Ernie Bevin were dying, and others such as Hugh Dalton, Herbert Morrison and the Prime Minister, Clement Attlee, were clearly coming to the end of their political careers. Beneath them a new generation was manoeuvering for position.

The most rapid ascent had been made by Hugh Gaitskell. Educated at Winchester and Oxford, this former economics lecturer at University College London had risen through the Labour ranks under the patronage of Hugh Dalton. Appointed a junior minister in 1946, in 1950 he was still a junior minister at the Treasury. Yet in October 1950 he succeeded Cripps as Chancellor. He was typical of a new element in the Labour party (Douglas Jay, Patrick Gordon-Walker, Dick Crossman and, from a younger generation, Tony Crosland were other examples). Coming from a privileged background they lacked the radicalism of some of the older leaders, were interested in power and politics for their own sake, regarding the Labour party as an ameliorative force within existing society rather than a mechanism for transforming it. Gaitskell's rise had deeply offended Nye Bevan who, although a parliamentary rebel in the years up to 1945, had proved an effective Minister of Health under Attlee. He regarded himself, on the basis of seniority and experience, as the natural successor to Cripps and was never reconciled to the choice of Gaitskell. He was even more offended when he was passed over as the replacement for Ernie Bevin at the Foreign Office and had to settle for the Ministry of Labour. Although he was close to wealthy newspaper owners like Beaverbrook, Bevan still saw himself as a radical socialist. His problem was that although his Welsh oratory was effective he was unable to develop any coherent thought on the direction of socialism or a strategy for gaining support within the Labour party. His resignation over the NHS charges was heavily influenced by pique about his own position.

Harold Wilson was in many ways similar to Gaitskell, although he came from a northern, non-conformist background of modest means (his father was an industrial chemist and his mother a teacher). He too was an academic economist (at Oxford) and like Gaitskell had been a wartime civil servant, both at one time in the Ministry of Fuel and Power. As an undergraduate Wilson had been a member of the Liberal party (he only joined the Labour party in 1940) and it was not until 1943 that he decided to go into politics. He was elected in 1945 and immediately became a junior minister. In 1947, at the age of thirty-one, he joined the Cabinet as President of the Board of Trade. He believed that he was the natural successor to Cripps as Chancellor and, like Bevan, was not reconciled to the choice of Gaitskell, his junior in terms of experience and status. This was the main motivating force behind his resignation, but in order to assist his long-term ambitions he also needed to establish a clear identity, distinct from Gaitskell's. As President of the Board of Trade Wilson proved an effective administrator and so looked to be in much the same mould as Gaitskell. By resigning in 1951 he, for the first time, identified himself with the left (which was becoming increasingly important in the constituency parties) and placed himself in a stronger position for a period of opposition which he clearly thought was coming. Although Wilson was never particularly close to Bevan, it was at this time that he was first allied with members of the 'Keep Left' group formed in 1947. Some were to remain among his closest political friends for the next twenty years, in particular Dick Crossman, Barbara Castle (his parliamentary private secretary) and George Wigg.

During the period from 1951 until Wilson's election as leader in 1963 there was continuous dispute within the Labour party about policy. After the 1951 defeat and his earlier resignation, it was Nye Bevan who led the anti-leadership group within the party. Although strong in the party outside Parliament, they remained a minority within the Parliamentary Labour Party (PLP) and found little support in the trade unions, which were dominated by right-wing leaders. The Bevanites faced two fundamental problems. The first was Bevan's own unpredictable and inconsistent leadership, compounded by his inability to decide on a long-term goal or strategy. The second was the failure to produce a coherent programme of reform. The Bevanite group never developed an alternative economic or social policy – indeed Bevan himself was temperamentally incapable of the effort required to achieve such a policy. The Bevanite revolt in Parliament was therefore almost entirely confined to defence and foreign policy – issues such as German rearmament, British membership of the South East Asia Treaty Organisation and development of the H-bomb. The consequence of this lack of any carefully thought-out alternative was that the Bevanites became little more than a disruptive faction within the party, fighting increasingly obscure battles often for little apparent reason other than the sheer pleasure of fighting intra-party battles.

The dominant influence in the Labour party was the centre right and it was in this area that the main 'revisionist' thinking about its future took place. The most important tract on economic and social policy was Tony Crosland's *The Future of Socialism*, published in 1956. The core of Crosland's argument was that 'ownership' of economic assets (and hence nationalisation) was increasingly irrelevant under modern capitalism where managers and bureaucratic power were far more important. He argued that the Labour party should therefore concentrate on achieving greater equality (which he never defined) and social justice, together with enhanced personal and political freedom. In economic terms there would be more planning, not to replace the market, but to put increased emphasis on social costs. Economic growth was vital because redistribution of wealth would take place only by trying to ensure that the underprivileged received more of the benefits of growth, via government expenditure. Although Crosland's book became a standard text for revisionists it was honoured mainly by approbation. No attempt was ever made to work out its ideas in detail or examine how it could be translated into a political programme.

Revisionist thinking, though, did influence policy on nationalisation, where it was pushing at an already open door. There were widespread doubts, even on the left, about whether extension of conventional nationalisation was the right way forward. After limited proposals in the 1951 and 1955 manifestos, a new policy document from the National Executive Committee (NEC) in 1957 entitled 'Industry and Society' rejected nationalisation as an end in itself; in the 1959 manifesto only steel and long-distance road haulage (which the Conservatives had denationalised) were candidates for nationalisation. It was defeat in 1959, for the third successive time, that produced the most vociferous debate over party policy. Immediately after the election Douglas Jay, working closely with Gaitskell as leader, publicly advocated scrapping Clause 4 of the Labour party constitution (which committed them in theory to total state ownership) and even suggested changing the name of the party. Gaitskell tried hard to remove Clause 4 but within months widespread opposition within the party forced him to back down. Nevertheless, although Clause 4 might remain as a monument to the past, revisionist policies were dominant under Gaitskell's leadership.

Revisionist thinking was not confined to economic policy. A group led by Denis Healey rejected any idea of a specifically 'socialist' foreign policy (which the 'Keep Left' group had advocated in the 1940s) and argued strongly for support of NATO and the alliance with the United States. The main challenge to this policy came from the movement opposed to British nuclear weapons, which was an increasing force within the party following the creation of the Campaign for Nuclear Disarmament in 1957. The most spectacular defeat for the leadership came at the 1960 party conference when a resolution supporting unilateral nuclear disarmament was adopted. This provoked Gaitskell into making his famous promise to 'fight, fight and fight again to save the party we love'. The mechanism for doing this was the Campaign for Democratic Socialism (CDS), one of the most effective right-wing groups in that it was able to swing party policy back to a pro-nuclear stance within a year. It was led by some of the people (such as Bill Rodgers and Shirley Williams) who were to break with the Labour party over the identical issue in the early 1980s and form the Social Democratic Party.

Behind these arguments over policy there were bitter personality clashes too, usually driven by personal ambitions. Clement Attlee stayed on as leader after 1951 but gave no sense of direction to the party. His main reason for remaining was to ditch the chances of his deputy, Herbert Morrison, whom he had disliked for years. When Attlee finally resigned after his defeat in the 1955 election, Morrison was too old to take on the job and came a bad third in the poll. The winner was Hugh Gaitskell, who had carefully cultivated the right-wing trade union leadership and who was respected in the PLP as a politically competent, if unexciting leader. Bevan stood too, but received only half Gaitskell's vote. Even among his sympathisers he was widely regarded as too unstable and mercurial to make a competent leader; indeed earlier in the year he had had the Whip withdrawn for his constant revolts against party policy. Wilson was one of those distancing themselves from Bevan even before the 1955 election. The symbolic moment came in April 1954 when Bevan resigned from the Shadow Cabinet and Wilson took his place, a 'betrayal' the true Bevanites never really forgave. In 1955 he supported Gaitskell for leader and was made shadow Chancellor of the Exchequer, a post in which he was able to make his parliamentary reputation as an adroit tactician and brilliant debater.

Gaitskell's leadership remained problematic. His radicalism was suspect, and it was combined with an emphasis on 'responsibility' and an unwillingness to make policy without having access to all the information held in Whitehall. To these traits were added a temperament that did not relish compromises over policy but preferred instead to heighten differences. These were not ideal characteristics for the leader of any party in opposition, let alone the Labour party with its factions. Doubts about Gaitskell came to a head in the debate over unilateralism. Bevan had deserted his friends, and his earlier principles, when he supported the British deterrent at the 1957 party conference. After Gaitskell was defeated at the conference in 1960, Wilson (who had managed to steer clear of this argument) decided to stand for the leadership on a platform of supporting the party conference rather than on a unilateralist stance. He objected to Gaitskell's poor tactics and inability to unite the party. His other reason for standing was that Tony Greenwood threatened to do so as an out-and-out unilateralist and he wanted to preserve his nominal position as the leader of the 'left' in the party. Wilson was easily defeated, but had established the point that he was a potential party leader. He had done so, however, by alienating Gaitskell's supporters, who had never really trusted him in the first place. After 1960 the one identifying feature of a true Gaitskellite was a dislike of Harold Wilson. Gaitskell responded by shifting him from being shadow Chancellor to shadowing the Foreign Office.

The unexpected death of Hugh Gaitskell in 1963 (Bevan had died two years earlier) enabled Wilson to become leader far earlier than he could have hoped. His two rivals in that election – George Brown and Jim Callaghan – were to form, with Wilson, the inner triumvirate of the Labour government for its first three years in office; the rivalries between them were to shape its history. The problem for the Labour party in 1963 was that these men were seen as the only possible candidates, yet each had major drawbacks. Wilson was obviously competent but widely distrusted, even on the left where he gained most of his support. As Nye Bevan described him in 1958:

He's much more dangerous than Gaitskell because he isn't honest and he isn't a man of principle but a sheer, absolute careerist, out for himself alone.[1]

The problem for the Gaitskellites was that they could not find someone capable of mobilising their undoubted majority in the PLP in the fight against Wilson.

The obvious right-wing candidate was George Brown, who had been elected deputy leader in 1960. He came from a poor working-class background in London and had worked his way up through the Transport Workers Union to become an MP in 1945 and a junior minister at the end of the Attlee government. A man of undoubted ability and loyalty to the party, he was tragically flawed by his character. His emotional instability, made worse by his rate of alcohol consumption, led many of those who supported him on political issues to realise that he would be a disastrous leader. He was summed up by a senior member of the Attlee government, who had done much to promote his career, as 'very awkward, vain, sensitive and fundamentally self-seeking and unfaithful'.[2]

The alternative was Jim Callaghan. Like Brown, he too came from a poor working-class background, and had come up through the Inland Revenue Staff Federation to become an MP in 1945 and an unspectacular junior minister under Attlee. He was intensely ambitious, and worked hard at cultivating the party both inside and outside Parliament. He had gradually worked his way up until in 1961, as a reward for his loyalty, Gaitskell made him Shadow Chancellor in place of Wilson. Callaghan had always kept to the central, non-ideological section of the party. Many, though, interpreted this in a less than favourable light. One veteran of the party described him as 'too obviously a trimmer and doesn't seem to have any deep convictions'.[3] In a straight fight against Wilson Callaghan might have commanded more support but Brown would not stand down in favour of someone he regarded as his junior.

Wilson fought a clever campaign, guided by George Wigg and Dick Crossman, leaving Brown to make the mistakes. In the first ballot Wilson led Brown 115–88, with Callaghan eliminated after receiving forty-one votes. This was only eight votes short of an overall majority and Wilson easily won the second ballot a week later by 144–103. Brown was asked to stay on as deputy leader, but in the immediate aftermath of defeat he refused to say what he might do. In private Wilson had other plans, as he told his friends on the night he was elected:

> He will have to go in the end, but it will have to be at a time of our making, when it suits us. And when we do drop him, you won't even hear a splash.[4]

Eventually Brown accepted the deputy leadership, but Wilson refused to make him shadow Foreign Secretary as he wanted. It was left unsettled exactly which post Brown would fill.

Much the same mixture of policy and personality persisted within the Labour party under Wilson's leadership. However, Wilson's style of leadership was very different from Gaitskell's, emphasising consensus at the expense of conflict. In this he was helped by the wider political situation. The Conservative government was deeply unpopular and seemed to be heading for defeat. An election might be called in the autumn of 1963 and Labour MPs, desperate for office after years in the political wilderness, had every incentive and little alternative but to unite behind Wilson's leadership.

Wilson also benefitted from the fact that certain political issues where Labour was divided or weak became less important. As we have seen nationalisation was no longer a major issue and EEC entry, over which the Labour party was divided, went dormant when, just before Wilson was elected as leader, de Gaulle vetoed the British application. On defence, after the battles over unilateralism, the party was desperate to find a compromise. There were signs that this was beginning to emerge even before Wilson took over, and he rapidly developed a line that satisfied both the left and the right of the party. The left was mollified by a series of denigrating remarks about the lack of a truly independent British deterrent following the choice of the US Polaris system in 1962. The right was satisfied because no firm commitment was ever given to scrap Polaris.

Wilson's approach was to put on one side the divisive issues and project new ideas, less controversial and less ideological, around which the party could coalesce. In this he was aided by a growing mood in the country that Britain was falling behind its rivals, that its ideas and institutions were outmoded, incapable of dealing with the challenges ahead. Wilson emphasised the themes of modernisation and progress, based on his study of John Kennedy's successful 1960 campaign for the Presidency. Labour was portrayed as the party that was not tied to the past, like the Conservatives, a party that wanted to bring Britain up to date. In a series of speeches Wilson built on these themes, in particular the need to modernise institutions and adapt to rapid economic, social and scientific change. It was a message that bypassed rather than resolved the ideological arguments that had long divided the party but it was one they readily accepted because of its electoral appeal and promise of power.

11

Although these policy issues were defused in the short term, the old divisions and personal ambitions remained just below the surface. Wilson inherited a shadow Cabinet composed almost entirely of Gaitskell supporters, many of whom were his political enemies. Indeed only one of them, Fred Lee, had voted for him as leader. The autumn 1963 elections for the Shadow Cabinet, the first under Wilson's leadership, did not change this picture. Wilson had no choice but to work with this group while introducing one or two friends into fringe positions, such as Crossman as spokesman on science matters. Wilson made few changes in responsibilities apart from moving Gordon-Walker to take over the role of shadow Foreign Secretary, replacing him with Healey as defence spokesman.

Wilson's most difficult problem was what to do with George Brown, both immediately and if he had to form a government. As deputy leader he had to be given an important post but none seemed to be available. Wilson would not make him Foreign Secretary, partly because Brown wanted the post, and partly because of doubts about his behaviour and how the Conservatives could exploit the issue. Callaghan, firmly in place as shadow Chancellor, refused to move and after his respectable showing in the leadership election Wilson could not force him out. For some time the Labour party had felt that the dominance of the Treasury over economic policy ought to be reduced by the creation of a new department that would be responsible for planning the economy in a more modern way, that would emphasise growth and real resources, rather than fiscal and financial matters. Brown was persuaded to take on this job. It was a neat solution to Wilson's dilemma: not only did it provide a suitable job for Brown, it also placed Wilson's two main opponents as rivals over economic policy. Their continual arguments, particularly once they gained power, were a major feature of the life of the new government.

Although he had to accept the colleagues he had inherited, Wilson never forgot who were his friends and who were his enemies. Some of the latter, such as Roy Jenkins, had to be promoted because of sheer competence, while others such as Tony Crosland were less favoured. One incident late in the life of the government illustrates just how long Wilson's memory was. In February 1969 Crossman was looking for a new Minister of State to run the Social Security side of the giant DHSS. He asked Wilson for either Roy Hattersley, Shirley Williams or Dick Taverne, all of whom Crossman regarded as immensely competent. Wilson rejected the first two immediately because he thought they were disloyal and then said to Crossman:

> Have you lost all your political antennae? Dick Taverne, he is a silken, treacherous member of the CDS group . . . If you have him it will be a betrayal of all we stand for. I am amazed at your forgetting.[5]

As newly elected leader Wilson inherited a favourable political position in early 1963. The Conservatives, having won the 1959 election with an overall majority of 101, remained popular until the latter part of 1961. Then the effects of a deflationary Budget and additional July measures (a 'pay pause' in the public sector, cuts in public expenditure and Bank Rate up from 2% to 7%) were beginning to be felt. The immediate beneficiaries were not Labour, but the Liberals who took second place at a series of by-elections and won Orpington in March 1962. Their standing in the opinion polls rose from about 8% in 1960 to around 20% by mid-1962. After the Liberals had forced the Conservatives into third place at Leicester North-East (a Labour-Conservative marginal in 1959) Harold Macmillan sacked a third of the Cabinet in an attempt to improve his standing.

However, the Conservative position did not pick up and, as the Liberals started to decline, Labour moved into a strong position. By the end of 1962 they were about 6–7% ahead in the polls. In January 1963 the Conservatives suffered a major blow with the collapse of the application to join the EEC. Immediately after his election Wilson found that events played into his hands. The government was beset by a series of scandals, the most important of which led to the resignation of John Profumo, the Secretary of State for War, who admitted lying to the Commons over his affair with Christine Keeler. Wilson played these questions with a sure political touch and reaped the benefit. For most of 1963 Labour was ahead in the polls by over 10%.

An expansionary, tax-cutting Budget in 1963 kept open the option of an autumn election in which Macmillan was determined to lead the Conservatives. But Labour's steady lead in the polls made an election increasingly unlikely and Macmillan's sudden resignation on the eve of the Conservative conference because of illness made it impossible. The Conservative conference was turned into something resembling an American political convention as rivals scrambled for position. This was the last occasion on which the Conservatives did not hold an election for leader and a hereditary peer, Lord Home, emerged through the 'usual channels' of consultation as the compromise choice. He promptly resigned his peerage but obviously needed time to establish himself before calling an election.

The Conservatives had a difficult choice in deciding when to go to the country. The first possibility, March, was ruled out because Labour was too far ahead in the polls. May or June was an attractive option before a rapidly overheating economy ran into serious trouble, but was rejected because Labour was still ahead in the polls. In April Sir Alec Douglas-Home announced that the election would be held at the last possible date – October. The Conservatives were hoping that the economy would stagger on and that the normal government recovery during the quiet summer months would help their position.

Wilson, half expecting a May or June poll, had started the Labour pre-election campaign in January with a series of speeches on the theme of modernisation and he kept going for the next ten months. The main feature of the period was a declining Labour lead in the polls after a peak at around 10% in April and May when Labour swept to victory in the first elections for the Greater London Council, winning sixty-four of the 100 seats and capturing two-thirds of the London boroughs. By September when the official campaign began their lead was down to about 2%. The Conservative manifesto, 'Prosperity with a Purpose', proposed little that was new and was essentially defensive about achievements. In late 1963 the party had tried to compete with Labour on the issue of modernisation but this had proved unsuccessful and was hurriedly dropped. The Conservative campaign was uncertain, Douglas-Home's performances were no more than adequate and in the end they concentrated on attacking Labour's proposals rather than proposing their own solutions.

Although there had been plenty of time in which to prepare, Labour's campaign was largely unplanned. Indeed the manifesto was completed in such a rush that only when Jim Callaghan woke up in the middle of the night as it was about to go to the printers was it realised that nothing had been included about either Scotland or Wales. The manifesto, with its last-minute additions, boldly grasped at the theme of modernisation. Entitled 'Let's Go with Labour for the New Britain', it claimed that the Labour party was 'restless with positive remedies for the problems the Tories have criminally neglected'. It went on to describe Labour's 'New Britain' mobilising the resources of technology under a national plan; harnessing the nation's wealth in brains, scientific research and medical discovery; 'reversing the decline of thirteen wasted years' and surpassing the progress of other western powers. The whole approach was put across in ringing terms by Wilson himself when he launched the Labour campaign on 12 September:

> Those who are satisfied should stay with the Tories. We need men with fire in their bellies and humanity in their hearts. The choice we offer . . . is between standing still, clinging to the tired philosophy of a day that is gone, or moving foward in partnership and unity to a just society, to a dynamic, expanding, confident and above all, purposive new Britain.

Polling was on 15 October and the early results suggested a Labour win with a majority of about twenty. However, they failed to gain a number of key marginal seats and it was not until well into the afternoon of 16 October that they secured a narrow majority. The final result gave them an overall majority of five and a majority of fourteen over the Conservatives. Labour gained sixty-one seats on an average swing of 3½%, the largest since 1945. But results were very variable across the country with an 8% swing to Labour in Liverpool and Conservative gains at Smethwick (7% swing), Birmingham Perry Bar and Eton and Slough, all heavily influenced by anti-immigration campaigns.

The result was hardly an overwhelming endorsement of Labour. They obtained slightly less votes than in 1959 when they lost by a majority of 100. Their victory was the result of two factors. The Conservative vote fell by 6% compared with 1959, the largest drop for any major party since 1945. Most of these votes went to the Liberals, who polled three million votes, their highest since 1929 and almost double their tally in 1959. It was this shift of support that enabled Labour to scrape home. Overall they won just over 44% of the votes cast – the lowest share obtained by any majority government since 1922.

Wilson had promised 'a hundred days of dynamic government' and as part of this process he announced the first six appointments to the Cabinet on the night after the election. Wilson, though, had little room for manoeuvre in choosing his Cabinet; he told one close supporter four months before the election: 'My real Cabinet will be made in 1966 – just as Clem's was made in 1947.'[6] The key jobs went exactly as expected. Brown took on the new Department of Economic Affairs with the title of 'First Secretary of State' and a position as effective deputy to Wilson. Callaghan became Chancellor and the dour, uninspiring Gordon-Walker went to the Foreign

Office. Denis Healey, who had specialised in defence matters, became Defence Secretary and Bert Bowden, the Chief Whip, was made Leader of the House of Commons.

Among the remaining appointments made over the weekend there were only two surprises at Cabinet level. Dick Crossman had expected to be made Education Secretary, but at the last minute he was swapped with Michael Stewart, who had been Shadow spokesman on Housing. During the summer Wilson had persuaded Frank Cousins, the leader of the Transport and General Workers Union, to accept office. Wilson's original intention had been to make him Minister of Transport but the Shadow spokesman, Tom Fraser, had insisted on keeping the job and Cousins was given the herculean task of setting up the new Ministry of Technology. Wilson just managed to squeeze in some of his close political supporters. Barbara Castle was put in charge of the new Ministry of Overseas Development and Tony Greenwood became Colonial Secretary, a post that under the Conservatives had been combined with the Commonwealth Office.

The final Cabinet of twenty-three was, not surprisingly after thirteen years in opposition, marked by two features – age and inexperience. Despite Labour's claims about moving into a dynamic new Britain the average age of the Cabinet was fifty-seven, six years more than that of the outgoing Douglas-Home Cabinet. Only three members – Wilson, Gordon-Walker and Jim Griffiths – had been in Cabinet before and none of them had held a key ministry. In total only half the Cabinet had even held ministerial office. In political terms Wilson and his supporters were outnumbered (only six of the Cabinet had voted for Wilson in 1963) and the right-wing domination of the Shadow Cabinet was repeated. The right held all the key posts on the economic side (Brown, Callaghan and Jay) and on the foreign and defence fronts (Gordon-Walker, Healey and Bottomley). Wilson's supporters were away from the centres of power and unable to influence the central strategy of the government, although some, such as Crossman in charge of the housing drive, held important posts.

Outside the Cabinet some of the younger up-and-coming politicians, such as Roy Jenkins, Tony Crosland and Tony Benn, were given their first experience of office (at Aviation, DEA and the Post Office respectively). Some new posts were also created to help promote the image of an innovative, dynamic government. Alun Gwynne-Jones, the defence correspondent of *The Times*, was, as Lord Chalfont, made Minister for Disarmament within the Foreign Office. Jennie Lee, Nye Bevan's widow, was appointed

Minister for the Arts, a post she was to keep until 1970. Dennis Howell became Minister for Sport. Lord Caradon as Ambassador to the UN was also made a minister at the Foreign Office to enhance the status of the post. C. P. Snow, scientist and novelist, joined Cousins to run Mintech and Lord Bowden, scientist and academic, joined the Ministry of Education to oversee policy on higher education. And there were new jobs at the Ministry of Labour for industrial training (Dick Marsh) and at Housing for London housing (Bob Mellish).

Although one of Wilson's closest allies, Dick Crossman, temporarily left the inner group to run his own department Wilson kept around him some of his oldest confidants. One of the closest was George Wigg, who had been on the left of the party in the 1940s and as PPS (parliamentary private secretary) to Manny Shinwell had come to hate Gaitskell from the time he displaced Shinwell as Minister of Fuel and Power after the catastrophic winter of 1946–7. He had been close to Wilson since the mid-1950s and supported him against Gaitskell in 1960. In the 1963 contest he served as Wilson's campaign manager and took much of the credit for a shrewdly judged, low-key campaign. Wigg had long been involved in defence matters and from the late 1950s he had taken an increasing interest in security affairs. In 1963 he dominated the discussions about Labour's tactics over the Profumo affair and successfully steered a difficult course by keeping to security rather than moral questions. In the new government he became Paymaster General, a purely nominal post that enabled him to act as general adviser to Wilson on political affairs and security matters.

On economic matters Wilson's closest adviser was Tommy Balogh. He was a Hungarian who had emigrated to England in 1930 and after a spell as a banker had become an academic at Oxford. From the early 1950s he had been an unofficial adviser to the 'Keep Left' group and the Bevanites who used to meet weekly at Dick Crossman's house. There he had become closer to Wilson and was to remain loyal to him. He used to meet Wilson about once a week to discuss not just economics but also politics, and was with Wilson and Crossman on the night that Wilson decided to run for the leadership in 1963. From 1964 until 1967 he was, according to his title, Economic Adviser to the Cabinet, although in practice he remained economic adviser to Wilson and also political confidant.

The most controversial member of what came to be known as the 'Kitchen Cabinet' was Marcia Williams, Wilson's secretary. After leaving university she had become secretary to Morgan Phillips,

17

the General Secretary of the Labour Party. She had first got to know Wilson when he began an enquiry into Labour party organisation after the 1955 defeat and became his secretary in October 1956. Originally she worked at his office in the firm of Montague Meyer where he was a consultant and moved into the Commons when Wilson became chairman of the Public Accounts Committee in 1960. After his election as leader she rapidly replaced the secretary who had acted for both Attlee and Gaitskell. There were plenty of unfounded rumours about her relationship with Wilson. Her role, though, was political. Totally loyal to Wilson and with a shrewd political mind, she was someone on whom he could rely absolutely in dealing with any threats to his position. In return for this loyalty and advice he was prepared to put up with her often tempestuous moods. Other members of Marcia Williams' family were also part of Wilson's personal entourage. Tony Field, her brother, was Wilson's driver during the 1964 campaign and later became a not very effective office manager. Peggy Field, Marcia's sister, was personal secretary to Mary Wilson. And Marcia's father even cooked the first meal that the Wilsons ate at No 10 after the election.

Marcia Williams' role as political loyalist and confidante was particularly important to Wilson because of his wife Mary's attitude to politics. When she married Wilson in 1940, he seemed destined to become an economics don at Oxford and she was never reconciled to his political life. When he was a junior minister in the Attlee government, she continued to live in Oxford and even after she finally moved to London for a long time she refused to allow him to bring his political friends home. On the night Wilson was elected leader she told Dick Crossman:

> The only thing I have ever dreamt of is living as the wife of an Oxford don and that is the only thing I want today.[7]

In this atmosphere so deeply antipathetic to politics Marcia Williams was someone with whom Wilson could discuss endlessly his one obsession – politics.

After thirteen years in opposition the Labour party had at last regained power. That was a major achievement for Wilson and the party. They had fought the election and received a mandate, on a programme of change in all aspects of British life – some of that change even promised to be radical. But in trying to carry out that mandate the experience of the previous thirteen years could not be forgotten. During that period the party had been divided between a left-wing minority, unable to construct a coherent alternative policy, and a larger group of right-wing revisionists who had been able to construct at least the outlines of a policy. That policy had been partially accepted, but the internal debate in opposition about the long-term objectives of the Labour party had never been satisfactorily resolved. Wilson did not see this as a problem. He turned the party towards the simple goal of gaining power through a series of essentially non-ideological appeals. This left a large question mark over the purpose for which power had been gained which was to underlie much of the internal debate in government. Moreover, the party remained deeply divided by personal rivalries and ambitions. A superficial unity only had been established after Wilson's election as leader, mainly because no alternative was available immediately and an election was rapidly approaching. It remained to be seen how long those rivalries, and in particular those between Wilson, Brown and Callaghan, who constituted the core of the government, would remain below the surface.

The result of the 1964 election, though far from a ringing endorsement of Labour, did mark an historic change. It was only the third non-Conservative government this century with a parliamentary majority and so far the only occasion on which Labour has won an overall majority directly from the Conservatives in peacetime. Although the majority was small it provided enough time to take the political initiative, and with luck dictate the timing of the subsequent election and the chance to gain a majority for a full Parliament. Harold Wilson and the Labour government had therefore been given a great opportunity to achieve the aims that had been so often discussed on the left of British politics.

PART TWO

A WAFER-THIN MAJORITY

OCTOBER 1964–MARCH 1966

The Cabinet

(October 1964)

Prime Minister	Harold Wilson
Frist Secretary at DEA	George Brown
Lord President of the Council and Leader of the House of Commons	Herbert Bowden
Lord Chancellor	Lord Gardiner
Lord Privy Seal and Leader of the House of Lords	Lord Longford
Chancellor of the Exchequer	James Callaghan
Foreign Office	Patrick Gordon-Walker
Home Office	Frank Soskice
Agriculture, Fisheries and Food	Fred Peart
Colonial Office	Anthony Greenwood
Commonwealth Relations Office	Arthur Bottomley
Defence	Denis Healey
Education and Science	Michael Stewart
Housing and Local Government	Richard Crossman
Labour	Ray Gunter
Chancellor of the Duchy of Lancaster	Douglas Houghton
Overseas Development	Barbara Castle
Power	Fred Lee
Scottish Office	William Ross
Technology	Frank Cousins
Board of Trade	Douglas Jay
Transport	Tom Fraser
Welsh Office	James Griffiths

Changes on 22 January 1965

Foreign Office	Michael Stewart
Education and Science	Anthony Crosland

Patrick Gordon-Walker resigned.

Changes on 23 December 1965

Lord Privy Seal Home Office	Frank Soskice
	Roy Jenkins
Colonial Office and Leader of the House of Lords	Lord Longford

Overseas Development   Anthony Greenwood
Transport   Barbara Castle
Tom Fraser resigned.

2
The Politics of Tightrope Walking

The dominating feature of the life of the new Labour government from October 1964 till its triumph at the polls in March 1966 was its narrow parliamentary majority of five, reduced to three within three months. The overriding concern of the government was the need to preserve that majority long enough to fight the next election at a time of its own choosing.

These eighteen months were a time of mixed fortunes for the government falling into four main phases. The first lasted until the end of January 1965 and the loss of the Leyton by-election. It was marked by economic crisis. Yet it was also the period of the promised '100 days of dynamic action' (plagiarised from John Kennedy) and in what is often a honeymoon period for any new government Labour remained well ahead in the opinion polls by about 10%. The second phase after the defeat at Leyton was a difficult period. The long fight to enact the Finance Bill, an extended pay dispute with the doctors, and the dramatic debate and narrow escape from defeat over steel nationalisation all sapped the government's standing and morale. Yet the Conservatives were not able to take full advantage of these problems and the departure of Sir Alec Douglas-Home seemed only a matter of time. The third phase from May to August 1965 was the worst time for the government. The Conservatives elected Ted Heath as their new leader in July and surged to a 9% lead in the polls. Labour morale plummeted after the deflationary package in July and the White Paper proposing immigration restrictions in August. The last phase began in September when Labour took a 6% lead in the polls and never fell behind before the election. The Conservatives could make little impact and were themselves in trouble when they split three ways in a vote on Rhodesian sanctions in December. By the time Labour won the by-election at Hull North at the end of January 1966 with an increased majority over the October 1964 result there was little doubt that an election would be called soon and that Labour would win.

In retrospect Labour's progress to ultimate victory seems inevitable but it required a degree of luck, careful management and a cool head to transform a toe-hold on power into a firm footing. The primary aim of the government was to deal with two contradictory factors. The government needed time to establish itself in the public mind as competent to govern after thirteen years in opposition and also to implement some of the promises made at the election and develop policies that would form the basis of their appeal at the next. But they could not sustain indefinitely the difficult economic situation inherited from the Conservatives, notably a balance of payments deficit of over £700 million. With deflation and devaluation ruled out because of the overriding political requirement, for eighteen months the government had to steer a difficult course trying to keep the balance of payments and sterling reasonably stable without taking economic measures that might damage their electoral prospects.

In walking this tightrope the government had a number of advantages. They were fresh in office, superficially united in dealing with the immediate problem of survival, buoyed up by the delights of power after thirteen years in the wilderness – unlike the last year of the Attlee government, which had disintegrated under the strains of a small majority mainly because ministers were disunited, tired and demoralised. The Whips also found the parliamentary party easy to manage, their minds concentrated by the narrow majority and unwilling to risk that majority with a back-bench revolt. Labour at last had the great advantage, available to all governments, of setting the political agenda and holding the initiative. By careful selection of issues the government could pose a difficult choice for the Conservatives between opposing popular measures or agreeing with the government. In this area Wilson, who had always shown a flair for the intricacies of day-to-day parliamentary tactics and creative use of the media rather than longer-term political strategy, was in his element.

The Conservatives themselves had plenty of problems. They were still saddled with their record in office and in particular it was difficult for them to escape the blame for the state of the economy. Their morale was low after the election defeat and the shock of sitting on the opposition benches after their long period in power. They were also disunited over the leadership and, although Sir Alec Douglas-Home was judged to have done reasonably well in the campaign, it was accepted that he would have to go before the next election, particularly since he was unable to match the performance of Harold Wilson in the House of Commons. The problem was the timing of his removal. If an election was expected shortly he would have to stay, since the new leader would need time to establish himself. Wilson exploited this dilemma ruthlessly: by keeping rumours of an imminent election circulating until June 1965 he helped to ensure that Douglas-Home was not removed until July of that year. By the time the Conservatives had a new leader Parliament went into recess almost immediately and when it reassembled Labour was again leading in the polls. This latter factor was vital. For all the superficial noises from the opposition about their desire to defeat the government they had no incentive to do so when Labour was ahead in the polls and defeat in the ensuing election seemed likely. At the time when the fortunes of the government were at their nadir in the summer of 1965 the Conservatives were electing a new leader and didn't want an immediate election. By the autumn, when Parliament reassembled, it was too late.

The ultimate test for the government was its ability to maintain its majority in the House of Commons, since only there could it be forced into an election against its wishes. The majority could only disappear through losses at by-elections, the death or illness of MPs or failure to mobilise all the government's supporters. The only by-election lost was at Leyton in January 1965, reducing the majority to three and giving the government less room for manoeuvre. The Whips were able to maintain the flow of ill, even dying MPs, through the lobbies even when the theoretical majority twice fell to two after the death of an MP and before a by-election could be held. Only once, over steel nationalisation, did it seem at all likely that a backbench revolt would deprive the government of its majority. Throughout this period the government was helped by the fact that, although its overall majority was tiny, its majority over the Conservatives was fourteen and only when the Liberals voted against them was the government in any real danger. In practice the nine Liberals were not consistent opponents. By July 1965 they had voted against the government eighty-five times, supported it on forty occasions and abstained three times. Thus although the parliamentary position was difficult it was not impossible and the government knew that with caution it could be sustained, if not indefinitely, at least long enough for them to meet their major objective of buying enough time to establish their competence and be able to choose the date for the crucial electoral test.

At the first Cabinet of the new government four days after the election Wilson laid out the underlying plan. The government would work as though it had a full majority and would plan on one full session of parliament (i.e. until autumn 1965) with the possibility of one or perhaps two more after that. The differing views on how this bold general approach should be interpreted were apparent when the Cabinet next met on 22 October to consider the Queen's Speech and the content of the legislative programme. The topic that was to cause a continual problem for the next eighteen months – nationalisation of steel – was the main item for discussion. The Cabinet was never to resolve two conflicting desires. On the one hand it felt that, since the proposal was in the manifesto, it should proceed and it did not want to be seen to give in to pressure to postpone. On the other hand it knew that the proposal was not a vote winner with the public at large, although it had become a shibboleth for the Labour party since the industry's partial denationalisation in the early 1950s. It did not want to be defeated on the proposal and thus have to fight an election at least partially on the issue. The minister in charge, Fred Lee, argued that it should be postponed for a year, partly on grounds of the difficulty of drafting the bill and partly on grounds of expediency. But George Brown argued strongly that it needed to be taken at the beginning to show determination and with only Douglas Houghton supporting Lee, the bill was included in the Queen's Speech. A month later the Cabinet thought they had found a clever tactical device to minimise trouble in the Commons and agreed to run the steel bill and the much more popular bill controlling rents for private tenants on a single guillotine motion. Unfortunately this bright idea came to nothing when the steel bill could not be drafted in time.

In accordance with their general aim of seizing the initiative, particularly on the economic front, the government introduced an October package to try and deal with the balance of payments problem, followed by a November Budget including not only tax rises but also major pension increases. Talking to Frank Cousins and Dick Crossman in the House of Commons early in November, Harold Wilson elaborated on how he saw his approach operating on all fronts:

> My strategy is to put the Tories on the defensive and always give them awkward choices . . . . They have an awkward choice voting for or against the pension increase. We have given them an awkward choice on office building and, Dick, you'll be giving them an awkward choice with your Bill for preventing evictions. Whatever we do we must keep the initiative and always give them awkward choices.[1]

28

By early January, with the government over 10% ahead in the opinion polls, an early election must have seemed tempting. But Wilson admitted that the rumours were only tactics to keep the Labour backbenchers under control and give the Conservatives problems. On 14 January he confirmed to the Cabinet that he had ruled out a spring election but that a summer or autumn one was still a possibility, though they were to go on planning for a longer period.

This sense of optimism rapidly evaporated after the Leyton by-election on 21 January. When Patrick Gordon-Walker had lost his Smethwick seat at the election he had still been appointed Foreign Secretary but a new seat had to be found for him rapidly. He wanted a seat near Westminster and his home in Hampstead, and the short straw was eventually drawn by seventy-three-year-old Reg Sorensen, MP for Leyton since 1935. After a great deal of pressure Sorensen was persuaded to take a peerage. In spite of local resentment and his image as a loser, Gordon-Walker was duly selected as candidate. At the same time the MP for Nuneaton was eased out to make room for Frank Cousins, who also needed a seat. Although Labour was well ahead nationally in the polls, Cousins only just scraped home, with a 4.9% swing to the Conservatives, and after a recount Gordon-Walker was defeated on a 8.7% swing. The government's overall majority was down to only three.

The honeymoon period was over. At the Cabinet meeting the week after Leyton the civil servants were asked to leave so ministers could talk frankly about their political strategy. Jim Callaghan, who had already adopted the mantle of the Cabinet's Jeremiah, said that he was 'all in favour of blood, sweat and tears' but George Brown argued passionately that they had been guilty of too much morality and not enough politics, nearly causing Lord Longford to swoon. His limp intervention (perhaps he had misheard the First Secretary) was waived airily aside and Brown continued to assert that the government now had to make a short-term calculation and dispense with the assumption that it was going to stay in office for three or four years. 'We must now have nothing but short-term tactics and prepare an offensive to put the blame back on the Tories.'[2] Agreeing on the need to court popularity, the Cabinet decided to introduce 100% mortgages and cut the cost of conveyancing. Meanwhile relations with Transport House and the Labour party organisation would be improved, and Harold Wilson suggested that he would in future spend less time on foreign affairs 'on public image grounds'.

Again the difficult issue that had to be confronted was steel. Having taken the decision to press ahead with the bill there were increasing signs of unease amongst Labour MPs. At the Cabinet on 18 March the civil servants were again asked to leave whilst political tactics were discussed. The Prime Minister announced that Manny Shinwell (Chairman of the PLP) had been to see him carrying the message that MPs did not want to be defeated on the steel issue. He admitted that the subject didn't interest the country as a whole but argued that because the proposal was in the manifesto something would have to be done, particularly since the government could not be seen to give in to the pressure groups opposed to nationalisation. The other problem was that a long and complex finance bill meant that there was little spare space for legislation. Wilson came up with one of the standard devices for getting out of a difficult corner. He proposed a White Paper setting out the proposals and stating that the industry would be national-ised in that session (even though it wouldn't be). The Cabinet agreed to this disingenuous proposal on the basis that any defeat on the White Paper could be reversed on a vote of confidence.

Defeat on the White Paper seemed a distinct possibility be-cause of the attitude of two Labour MPs – Woodrow Wyatt and Desmond Donnelly, both eccentrics on the right wing of the party. Despite the 1964 manifesto commitment they now decided that they could not support nationalisation and proceeded to exploit the government's narrow majority to achieve a brief mo-ment at the centre of the political stage. They worked closely with the steel owners and argued for an arrangement short of total government control but with the government taking a 51% share-holding in the steel companies. Long negotiations were put in train with the two rebels, mainly undertaken by their closest friend in the Cabinet, George Brown, although they also met Wilson. These talks reveal the way such problems can be tackled when in office. Wyatt claims that the Chief Whip, Ted Short, offered him 'a good job' or an all-expenses-paid trip abroad if he would vote for the White Paper.

During Brown's winding up speech in the debate on 6 May a carefully staged intervention was made by Wyatt to ask whether the government would listen to the steel owners if they conceded control but not total government ownership. To which Brown replied, 'Listen is the word. Listen, certainly.' On this basis the government secured the two critical votes and endorsement of its White Paper by 310 to 306. But did Brown have any authority to make a concession which seemed to imply that the government's proposals were negotiable? Certainly he had not consulted Fred Lee, the minister actually in charge of steel nationalisation. Other ministers reacted strongly: 'I was flabbergasted';[3] 'The worst blow yet for the Government'.[4] Brown had consulted Wilson, at least in general terms, although the latter was to write that Brown 'appeared to incline more to their views than anyone expected'.[5] Shortly after the debate, however, Wilson told two Cabinet colleagues that he 'intended to hold a Lobby conference that day in which he would explain how George Brown had done it all entirely on his own and how he himself had nothing to do with it'.[6] At the Cabinet meeting on 11 May, Brown apologised for what had happened but other ministers were not prepared to criticise – the White Paper had after all been approved. Wilson explained that there would be no change in policy, that the White Paper would stand, that the bill would be introduced late in the summer but that because of the full legislative programme it would have to be reintroduced in the autumn when the Cabinet would reconsider its tactics. Brown's exact motives in the episode are unclear. Even after the 1966 election he, and Callaghan, were to argue that the government should go for something less than 100% state ownership. The suspicion must be that he was opposed to nationalisation, that he first suggested the Bill should proceed so that it was taken in the most unfavourable circumstances and then, in conjunction with Wyatt and Donnelly, tried to force a change of policy.

So ended the episode which came nearest to ending the government's fragile majority. They had not conceded any principle, the White Paper had been endorsed and the form of words used by Brown was virtually meaningless. Certainly the steel owners had no intention of negotiating since they hoped the Conservatives would win the next election. The government had achieved its aim of appearing to make progress on steel nationalisation whilst not taking any concrete steps.

The three following months were the most difficult and harrowing period of all. Parliamentary time was largely devoted to passing the Finance Bill with its ninety clauses and twenty-one schedules. This long grind of all-night sittings and endless divisions was at that time still taken on the floor of the House rather than in Committee. Wilson admitted to his colleagues that the main aim was to prove that the government could legislate and thus increase its prestige. But it was a long and bruising battle and morale suffered. The Conservatives were ahead in the opinion polls and the local elections had gone badly for Labour. The government was under pressure and as so often at the end of a long parliamentary session ministers were tired and irascible. Worried about the state of the government, some were pressing Wilson for an October election. But Wilson remained calm. He told the Cabinet in June:

> There was no reason for desperation . . . Once we got into the summer recess and could have two months ahead with no Parliament we should be able to recover.[7]

Even under pressure he was still able to play politics astutely. For most of the year he had been allowing rumours of an imminent election to circulate, sometimes deliberately fostering them himself. Now with the government in trouble and behind in the polls he announced on the 26 June that it was not his intention to have an election that year. This was the green light for the Conservatives to remove their leader. On 22 July Sir Alec Douglas-Home resigned to be replaced, six days later, by Ted Heath. Now the Conservatives needed time for Heath to establish himself and the parliamentary recess was rapidly approaching.

Wilson's sense of political timing was demonstrated again when on 27 July the government announced a package of deflationary measures, including the abandonment of a number of election pledges, well timed to coincide with the result of the Conservative leadership election. Almost immediately the Conservatives gained a 9% lead in the opinion polls and Labour MPs' morale sank to rock bottom as Parliament rose for the summer recess. As one Cabinet Minister commented:

> We have taken a terrible beating; and our own people are disheartened and the press is utterly vicious. Terrible times. We can still pick up but I am pretty sure we wouldn't be able to pick up after the next package Callaghan wants to put through in defence of sterling.[8]

On 2 September the Speaker of the House of Commons, Sir Harry Hylton-Foster, died. The Conservatives, who already supplied two of the three occupants of the Chair, refused to replace Hylton-Foster. If Labour had to provide two, instead of their current one (Horace King, the Deputy Speaker), then its majority would fall to one. To many it seemed like the end of the government but Wilson was imperturbable. He quickly devised a scheme to move Horace King to the Chair and promote the existing number three to number two. He then had to persuade someone to serve as deputy chairman of Ways and Means. Privately he knew that a Conservative backbencher was prepared to break the party line and accept because he was so keen for the honour. However, Wilson's preferred solution was to select a Liberal, Roderic Bowen, for the job and another potentially disastrous problem was resolved.

Before turning to the recovery in the government's fortunes and the run-up to the 1966 election we need to investigate how Cabinet government functioned in the early days of the administration, and look at the relative positions of the main ministers within the Cabinet and the two reshuffles that took place in the first eighteen months. Harold Wilson was the dominating force in the government not just because of his position as Prime Minister but also because he was one of the handful of ministers who had real government experience. He decided tactics and what strategy there was with little consultation. Certainly the Cabinet was not a major force in policy making. In the first months it had no influence over economic policy and only on two issues – pensions and MPs' pay – was its voice decisive. In July 1965 the economic package was dumped without warning on the Cabinet table the morning it was due to be announced and ministers were given three hours to discuss and agree it. Similarly on defence and foreign policy Wilson had the decisive voice, formulating the approach and personally negotiating understandings with President Johnson.

The number two in the government without doubt was George Brown, who in practice functioned as 'deputy Prime Minister'. Relations between Wilson and Brown had always been bad; both before and after the 1964 election Wilson commented that Brown would have to go within the first six months. But somehow they managed to patch together a working relationship and Brown was regularly consulted on major aspects of policy. Brown carved out an impressive public position for himself through his dynamic handling of the Department of Economic Affairs and the first stages of evolving a National Plan and the voluntary prices and incomes policy. Wilson found himself unable to sack such an apparently successful minister with a strong standing in the parliamentary party and he had to wait for Brown to destroy himself. Already within the first few months of the government there was every sign that Brown would do just that sooner or later.

Brown had long been known for his volubility and rapid changes of mood, combined with a sometimes shrewd political judgement and an ability to get the best out of people. But under pressure and the effects of drink his behaviour became increasingly unstable. The first real flare-up came on 13 April over a minor proposal by Denis Healey to call up 175 army reservists for service in Aden. At an evening meeting of the Overseas and Defence Policy Committee (OPD) Brown was described by Barbara Castle as 'in a strange state – I wouldn't have said intoxicated (though Ted told me he was roaring tight in the House later that night) so much as auto-intoxicated'.[9] After keeping up a one-and-a-half-hour monologue Brown was finally persuaded by Wilson to agree to the proposal. A few hours later he told Wilson that he couldn't accept the proposal and would resign if it wasn't rescinded. As Wilson recalls, 'This was the first of many threatened resignations.'[10] After a number of visits and telephone calls Brown was demanding that Wilson's visit to the United States the next day be cancelled. But a night's sleep swept away the problems and life continued as before.

A month later, after Brown had been 'drunk as a coot' at a Cabinet committee meeting, Barbara Castle suggested to Wilson that he should get rid of him, but found that the time was not yet right:

> H[arold] said that the main worry was when he was on television. People who had voted for George were now coming and asking him to sack him. 'If I did he'd only make cause with Wyatt and Donnelly to destroy us.'[11]

Altogether Barbara Castle and Dick Crossman record thirteen separate occasions in the first few months of the government when George Brown was so drunk as to be incapable. By late 1965 Wilson was becoming increasingly tired of accommodating the violent swings of mood of his deputy. Brown was not consulted over the Cabinet reshuffle in December, which left him in a furious mood, and by March 1966 Wilson had suggested that Brown should leave the Department of Economic Affairs and become merely a minister without portfolio whilst remaining, at least in name, deputy Prime Minister. Brown showed little enthusiasm for the idea and remained at the DEA until his spectacular near-resignation in July 1966. Similarly, Brown made his views clear, as Cecil King wrote after lunch with him in October 1965, '[he] doesn't like Wilson and makes no attempt to hide his feelings.'[12]

Below George Brown the central minister in the Cabinet was Bert Bowden, the largely unknown Leader of the House of Commons. His main role was to chair key Cabinet committees, in particular Home Policy, in preference to the ailing and incompetent Home Secretary, Frank Soskice, Legislation and the Immigration Committee. He was unspectacular but a steady and reliable politician on whom Wilson could depend to ensure that there were no major disasters. Douglas Houghton, Chancellor of the Duchy of Lancaster, performed a similar role in the field of social policy. On the economic front the key ministers were Wilson, Brown, Callaghan and Jay, who acted as an inner group deciding on major policy moves, usually on their own, occasionally consulting the Cabinet in a perfunctory way. The inner group on defence and foreign policy, far more important than OPD, consisted of Wilson, Brown, Callaghan, Healey and Gordon-Walker, and later Stewart.

Apart from George Brown the main misfit in the government was Frank Cousins. Although he, and perhaps Wilson, saw his role as being the Ernie Bevin of the Wilson government, dominating its discussions with his earthy, working-class common sense, he never adapted to life in government or Parliament. He was given a tough job creating a ministry out of nothing, but within a year the new Ministry of Technology was functioning well and even had a few minor policy initiatives to its credit. Cousins never became one of the inner group of ministers. He was offered a place on OPD but turned it down because he disagreed with the government's defence policy. Similarly he would have nothing to do with the atomic weapons' side of the work of the Atomic Energy Authority. Cousins was frustrated by the lack of radicalism, drive and determination in the Cabinet, and as early as March 1965 he was telling colleagues that he might resign because Wilson was surrounded by right-wingers and he didn't expect the government to last long. He had major rows with George Brown over the voluntary incomes policy, which his own union also opposed, and his total opposition to any form of incomes policy left him in a minority of one inside the Cabinet. Several times in 1965 he asked Wilson to 'release' him but he was still torn by the thought that Mintech might achieve something and Wilson played on this assiduously by steadily enlarging its functions to show his faith in Cousins.

At a strategy session on 12 September Cousins told the Cabinet that he ought to resign now it was clear that the prices and incomes policy was going to have some form of statutory backing. From then on Wilson's aim was to stop him resigning before the election. Cousins claims Wilson told him that the policy was only window dressing to impress the foreign bankers and that with a big majority everything would be different. Wilson also carefully ensured that Cousins accompanied him on his visit to Moscow at the end of February 1966 when the Prices and Incomes White Paper would be published. By then Cousins had in fact already taken his decision to quit at a family conference on 19 February. But Wilson had won the most important battle; Cousins had decided to go, but only after the election.

There were only two reshuffles of the government before the 1966 election and the first of these in January 1965 was unplanned. After his defeat at Leyton Gordon-Walker had to resign as Foreign Secretary, a move which seemed to give Wilson few regrets. As Dick Crossman commented, 'He obviously felt, as I did, that he really had been no good as Foreign Secretary and no great strength in the Government.'[13] Wilson briefly considered Denis Healey as his replacement but rejected him on the grounds that he 'wouldn't trust Healey in the Foreign Office with all those professionals. And anyway we can't let him run away from the Defence job.'[14] Wilson chose the dour, right-wing Education Secretary, Michael Stewart, to replace Gordon-Walker. The other candidate had been the rising star amongst non-Cabinet ministers, Roy Jenkins, who had been a great success at the Ministry of Aviation. Instead of the Foreign Office Jenkins was offered Stewart's old job at Education and Science but in what Wilson described as 'a brave decision' he turned down the opportunity of a Cabinet post because his aim was to replace Soskice at the Home Office. Jenkins, though, did tell the whole story to the media through the Lobby to secure his personal position. The choice of a replacement for Stewart was made at a meeting in the House of Commons between Wilson and his two old cronies, Crossman and Wigg. Reg Prentice was rejected on the grounds that 'it's too big a job for the boy' and Tony Greenwood likewise because he too was not up to the job. Then George Wigg suggested Tony Crosland and Wilson quickly agreed: 'That's the right choice. He's got a good brain, he's written well about education and he will be a positive addition to the Cabinet.'[15]

Roy Jenkins was to get his chance to replace Frank Soskice at the Home Office as part of the second reshuffle in December 1965 (though only after Michael Foot rejected the offer because of his opposition to the government's policy on Vietnam). Soskice was persuaded to move on grounds of ill health, although incompetence was the real reason. Wilson had earlier tried to persuade Soskice to retire at the Labour Party Conference that autumn but he had refused to go to the backbenches and threatened to resign and force a by-election if Wilson insisted. Wilson gave into this pressure and Soskice became Lord Privy Seal, replacing Lord Longford, who remained Leader of the House of Lords and became Colonial Secretary, even though Wilson had earlier described him as 'quite useless – mental age of twelve'.[16] Wilson offered Cecil King of the *Daily Mirror* a peerage and a post as Minister of State at the Board of Trade in charge of the export drive. This was a subject about which King admitted he knew nothing and he turned down the offer.

The only other significant change in this second reshuffle was the promotion of Barbara Castle to the Ministry of Transport from Overseas Development. She replaced Tom Fraser, who had been a disaster, as Wilson admitted: 'I always knew Tom was weak, but I was saddled with a Shadow cabinet, every one of whom expected a job.'[17] Fraser had been dominated by his civil servants, particularly his permanent secretary, Sir Thomas Padmore, and had infuriated his colleagues by proposing to stop the nationalised industries from diversifying into new areas, a direct contradiction of the election manifesto. It had taken a revolt at EDC to overturn his proposals. Castle was told her main task was to devise an integrated transport policy. In return Wilson allowed her to choose her successor at Overseas Development. She rejected Fred Lee and settled for Tony Greenwood, even though Wilson's views of him were plain:

> 'Tony,' he said in tones of contempt, 'has no brains. I soon realised that all he is good at is public relations.'[18]

Wilson's common sense and coolness had been important in seeing the government through a difficult patch in the summer of 1965, and his optimism that their fortunes would improve during the holiday season with Parliament on holiday was justified. By September Labour was back in the lead in the polls, a lead it was to maintain until the election. The final run-up to that election was already starting to preoccupy Wilson. At the beginning of September he asked Dick Crossman, his old propaganda expert, to take over from George Wigg as linkman with the party organisation. At a strategy session at Chequers on 12 September the Cabinet discussed the way ahead. It was Jim Callaghan who first suggested that the theme should be 'our uncompleted mission', a theme that was to dominate the next six months. Wilson's campaign advisers – Dick Crossman, Tony Benn, Peter Shore and Tommy Balogh – were already meeting, with Wilson's knowledge, to discuss an outline manifesto. And after the launch of the National Plan on 22 September Crossman was even deputed to put the case for an early election in October but Wilson rejected the thought. As Denis Healey commented:

> [The Cabinet] would like to have an election now when their stock is high, but don't feel that any plausible excuse is apparent and to have an election purely to increase their majority might be badly received.[19]

Even though an immediate election had been rejected, the thought was never far from ministers' minds. On 21 October the Cabinet were discussing what to do about the grossly oversubscribed legislative programme for the forthcoming session. Wilson clearly regarded the run-up to the election as much more important than purely practical considerations, arguing:

> We need not cut the programme back since even if the Bills got no further, a number of Second Readings would be useful in the election manifesto.[20]

By December, when the government had been ahead in the opinion polls by about 5% for four months, the question of timing was becoming acute. Early in the month the strategy group met to discuss possible dates to put to Wilson. They considered several options: March (before the Budget), May (after the municipal elections) or October. Benn and Marcia Williams strongly favoured October, with Crossman and Balogh suggesting March before a tough Budget. At that stage Wilson didn't want a spring election, a view shared by George Brown. Exactly when he changed his mind is not clear. Marcia Williams says that it was over Christmas at her house in Golders Green. Wilson says it was after his return from the Commonwealth Prime Ministers' Conference in Lagos in mid-January. That was certainly the impression gained by Crossman who discussed timing with him on 23 January:

> He seems to be moving round more and more to the feeling that things are crowding in dangerously upon us, that the prices dam is going to break and that the position he has built up in Rhodesia is strong enough to risk an election . . . we are able to divert attention to Rhodesia, where we are being successful, from the home front where we are not.[21]

Wilson was inclining towards March rather than April, when 'the rate demands will already be in people's hands and that will cost us votes'.[22]

The result of the Hull North by-election on 27 January was decisive. The seat had been gained by Labour in 1964 by just 1100 votes but seemed likely to be a Conservative gain, since an anti-Vietnam war candidate would split the Labour vote. In fact Labour won with a 4.5% swing in their favour, the largest pro-government swing in a by-election since 1924. With two Labour MPs in marginal constituencies, Harold Hayman (Falmouth) and Megan Lloyd-George (Carmarthen) dying there was little to be gained by hanging on any longer. Five days later over dinner at No 10 with his closest advisers Wilson was discussing who would do what in the campaign. He had already decided that his own role should be as a 'doctor figure', an essentially non-party leader who would appear as the safe and comfortable Prime Minister of the nation as a whole in the Stanley Baldwin tradition. On 6 February Wilson asked Crossman and Shore to start drafting the manifesto which was discussed a week later. At the same time Wilson, Callaghan and Crossman agreed to subsidise council rents that year in view of the forthcoming election. The Cabinet were finally told of the date on 28 February, the day of the announcement.

Although the government were well ahead in the polls and a large victory seemed certain, ministers, despite their optimism in public, were far from sanguine. As Crossman wrote:

The main trouble is that we haven't delivered the goods; the builders are not building the houses; the cost of living is still rising; the incomes policy isn't working; we haven't held back inflation; we haven't got production moving. We are going to the country now because we are facing every kind of difficulty and we anticipate things are bound to get worse and we shall need a big majority with which to handle them.[23]

3

The American Connection

A newly elected government does not find when it takes office a blank sheet of paper on which it can devise new policies from scratch. As well as all the problems its predecessors have left behind it inherits a wide range of existing institutions and pressures that restrict its freedom of action. This was particularly the case for the Labour government in 1964, given Britain's central position within the various organisations and methods of working that had been devised after 1945 to link the strategic, economic and financial policies of the western world. This situation was accepted as perfectly natural by the new ministers. Some had been in the Attlee government that had participated in the formation of many of these institutions, and in opposition they had also been drawn into this nexus of relationships through briefings, conferences and meetings with politicians and leaders in other countries who similarly accepted the established framework. The new Labour government never even considered questioning the structure or the way in which it was expected to operate within it. The key factor was the role of the United States. Ever since 1940, the UK's strategic, foreign and economic policy had been built around what the British called the 'special relationship'. It was this relationship that was to be of major importance in the life of the new Labour government and at crucial moments dictate many of its policies.

What was the structure that the new Labour government inherited? The Bretton Woods conference in 1944 devised the framework for the post-war operation of the Western international financial system, including a scheme of fixed exchange rates and methods for controlling fluctuations. The International Monetary Fund (IMF) was set up to maintain international liquidity, act as a lender to governments in economic difficulties and, through its various sub-groups and separate meetings of the most powerful countries (including the UK), serve as a mechanism to integrate the policies of the participating countries. Similar, but more technical operations were conducted through the relationship between the central banks in each country and their international organisation – the Bank for International Settlements. Economic policies were discussed and co-ordinated in the Organisation for Economic Co-operation and Development (OECD). Here too various subgroups and meetings of officials attempted to keep all the economies moving in the same direction and ensure that no country stepped outside the existing consensus. Trade policy was discussed in the General Agreement on Tariffs and Trade (GATT) where the aim was to reduce barriers to free trade.

In the strategic field the most important organisation was NATO, which had been the central pillar of the UK's defence policy since its foundation in 1949. It provided an integrated military structure and forum for common planning and collaborative efforts particularly on weapons procurement. In 1964 the UK had almost as many troops in the Far East as in Germany and there it was a member of the South East Asia Treaty Organisation (SEATO). It was also a member of the Central Treaty Organisation (CENTO) which carried out the same function as SEATO in the Near East.

In all of these organisations the relationship with the United States was fundamental. Ever since the Second World War the UK had seen its role as an important, albeit junior, partner of the United States throughout the world. Even if Britain no longer had the resources available to act as a great power on the scale of the US or the USSR, there remained an underlying assumption in British policy that it did have a major role to play as the United States' most reliable ally, ranking well above the other allies in Europe – France and Germany – and elsewhere – Australia, Japan and others. With its greater experience of world affairs Britain saw itself acting as the guide and mentor of the brash and inexperienced Americans in the complexities of world affairs. Or, to use Harold Macmillan's phrase, the British were the Greeks to the American Romans. Although by the 1960s the UK had been overtaken by Germany and France as the biggest economy in Europe, because of the reserve currency role of sterling it still saw itself as the second power in Western economic affairs and therefore as a close confidant of the Americans in managing the international financial system. Within NATO Britain saw itself as the second strongest power and therefore acting as the link between the United States and the Europeans rather than being a power equivalent to France and Germany. Similarly East of Suez Britain felt it had to continue to bear much of the Western 'burden' in areas where the United States was a relative newcomer. The basis of British foreign and defence policy was therefore to consult and inform the Americans on every possible occasion and to assume that only in very rare instances would there be any real divergence between the two national interests. This approach fulfilled three purposes. It involved the United States in British problems, hopefully as a strong supporter and backer of the British position. It also helped to put the UK in a position to influence American policy and where necessary 'restrain' it (as Whitehall saw it). Finally it also served to reinforce the illusion that Britain was still at the centre of world affairs.

There were two particular areas of collaboration (intelligence and nuclear weapons) between Britain and the United States, both of which dated back to the Second World War, which Britain saw as confirming its claim to a 'special relationship' with the Americans. To all governments since 1945, including the new Labour government, the maintenance of these links was of fundamental importance. In the middle of the war Britain and the United States had established a system for the free flow of intelligence information and this was continued after 1945. MI5 worked closely with the FBI and MI6 with the CIA but perhaps the most important relationship was between the British signals interception organisation, GCHQ, and its American equivalent, the National Security Agency (NSA) and the CIA. Britain maintained a number of key intelligence stations around the world, particularly in Hong Kong and Cyprus, which provided important capabilities not otherwise available to the Americans and in return for these facilities received access to high-level American intelligence shared with no other country. This information was regarded as of the utmost importance within Whitehall as an aid to policy making and Britain was prepared to pay a high price to ensure that this information continued to flow from the Americans.

Collaboration on nuclear weapons had also begun during the war when Britain had provided vital theoretical insights on the feasibility of producing nuclear weapons and worked closely with the Americans on the design and production of the first atomic weapons. Collaboration was unilaterally ended by the United States in 1946 and Britain had gone on to build its own weapons. It was Macmillan, working with his old wartime friend President Eisenhower, who re-established the nuclear relationship with the Americans in 1958. A whole series of new agreements were reached on the exchange of design information, theoretical work and the swapping of various materials vital for the nuclear programmes, such as British plutonium in return for American highly enriched uranium. The US also supplied the design of the reactor to power the UK's nuclear submarines. In 1962 the government decided to buy the US Polaris as the future strategic nuclear system. Only the warhead was of British design and in other areas the UK relied on the US for the supply of the missiles and spare parts and for the design of the vital centre section of the submarine that contained the launch tubes and control systems. There was also joint US-UK planning over nuclear submarine operations. After the Partial Test Ban Treaty of 1963 the UK was also dependent on US facilities to test its nuclear warheads. The British nuclear programme simply could not continue without American assistance. In return the UK provided important nuclear bases for the United States. These were the various US Air Force bases and the facility at Holy Loch for the operation of the United States Polaris submarines.

The UK was therefore highly dependent on the United States in two key areas – intelligence and nuclear matters. This dependence, combined with the US dominance of the multilateral framework, set strict limits to the ability of any British government to institute independent policies and reduced the British role to one of junior partner to the Americans. To help disguise this dependence the myth of the 'special relationship' was assiduously cultivated in an effort to believe that the wartime relationship was still in existence. If the British believed in the 'special relationship' then the United States by the 1960s did not. They regarded Britain as a useful ally but no more. Japan and Germany were more powerful economically and Germany was equally important in European defence. If the British were prepared to help the United States in various areas of the world that was fine and in return the US would take some account of British interests, but the Americans had a much more realistic picture of the true relationship. As Henry Kissinger was to write of the late 1960s:

> We do not suffer in the world from such an excess of friends that we should discourage those who feel that they have a special friendship for us.[1]

In private the US Ambassador in London for most of the 1960s, David Bruce, was to tell the State Department in 1967:

> The so-called Anglo-American special relationship is now little more than sentimental terminology.[2]

When the new ministers took office a large proportion of their time was spent in talking to and corresponding with their opposite numbers in Washington. Inevitably they started to place more emphasis on these relationships than with those outside this world of power. Wilson was in constant touch with the President through the special telecommunications link between No 10 and the White House, and he was to make much of his relationship with President Johnson. Gordon-Walker, and later Stewart, were keen on their links with the State Department and Dean Rusk (Secretary of State). Jim Callaghan at the Treasury was similarly close to the US Treasury and Henry Fowler (Secretary of the Treasury).

The first action of the new government in the foreign policy field was to send Gordon-Walker to Washington within ten days of taking office. The purpose of the visit was twofold, as Dean Rusk told President Johnson:

He will . . . wish to assure you that the United Kingdom does not plan any radical foreign policy initiatives embarrassing to the United States. Finally he wishes to meet you as a tangible demonstration that the United States continues to value its association with Britain now that Labor is in control.[3]

Both objectives of the visit were attained. Indeed the overwhelming impression of the first few months of the new government is that it actively sought to increase British dependence on the United States and develop its relationship with the American administration into the central pillar of its policy in the strategic, foreign, defence and economic fields.

In the key areas of bilateral cooperation there was no change. At the highest strategic level the arrangements for intelligence collaboration remained the same. But Wilson was worried about the rising cost of GCHQ and the price of maintaining the relationship with the US, particularly now that the Americans were moving into intelligence-gathering satellites. Burke Trend called in a wartime codebreaker, now an academic at Oxford, Sir Stuart Hampshire, to conduct a full-scale review of GCHQ and the relationship with the Americans. A high-level review concluded that the UK had to maintain the links with the US but that this could probably be done at lower cost without involving the UK in a joint satellite programme. On this basis the exchange of information continued.

Anglo-American intelligence activity took many forms. Sometimes it could be relatively mundane. For example, in May 1965

British intelligence sources discovered that some of the opposition to the recent US invasion of the Dominican Republic had been 'trained in the technique of armed revolt'. This information was passed to Johnson who asked for it to be published. In less than a week Michael Stewart had made a statement in the Commons which contained the information.[4] At other times it could be of fundamental importance. In Latin America Britain regarded US interests as paramount and when the possible election of the left-wing Cheddi Jagan as Prime Minister of British Guiana before independence created major concern in Washington Britain had to decide how to help. In Opposition, Labour had been strong supporters of Jagan but in December 1964 US and UK officials met in London to decide how to counter the 'threat' from Jagan. They agreed on a programme of joint intelligence activities in British Guiana, including covert assistance to the anti-Jagan parties in an attempt to get them elected. The Colonial Secretary, Tony Greenwood, was at first reluctant to agree to this anti-democratic activity but eventually gave in. In July 1965 agreement was reached on a joint programme that was successful in excluding Jagan from power.[5]

Similarly the Anglo-American nuclear relationship was preserved. The exchange of information and materials continued, and Wilson rapidly accepted the terms of the Nassau agreement (negotiated by Macmillan in 1962) for the purchase of Polaris. The attempts to change the arrangements for controlling Polaris in fact all came from the American side: Wilson resolutely opposed American attempts to incorporate the British deterrent into an alliance force (the Multi-Lateral Force) and later resisted their efforts to get Britain to assign Polaris permanently to NATO with no right of withdrawal.

In the financial field relations were also close. Apart from the normal multilateral contacts the new government went to great lengths to maintain the tradition of consulting the Americans over major changes of policy and keeping them informed of policy developments. The Americans were normally consulted before any raising of British Bank Rate. In the November 1964 crisis, for example, Wilson sent the head of the DEA, Sir Eric Roll, and his own Private Secretary, Derek Mitchell, to Washington over the weekend to consult the Americans about a possible 2% rise. Callaghan as Chancellor was prepared to go even further and gave detailed and highly confidential information about British policy to the Americans. Walter Heller, Chairman of the Council of Economic Advisers, told Johnson:

in spite of the British secrecy, Jim Callaghan told me last November
7 – for your eyes only – what was going to be in their Budget a few
days later.[6]

Callaghan therefore told the Americans the details of his first
Budget four days before it was made public and three days before
he told the Cabinet of its contents. A previous Labour Chancellor,
Hugh Dalton, had had to resign when he mentioned a few details to
a journalist just minutes before his speech in the Commons. Later
Callaghan was to tell the Cabinet that informing them in advance
about the Budget would be 'subverting the Constitution'. Presumably these strictures did not include the Americans. Wilson too
kept the Americans in close touch with British economic policy.
The US Ambassador, for example, was told the details of the July
1965 deflationary package the evening before the Cabinet had their
only meeting on the subject.

In foreign policy there was the closest possible contact and
continuous consultation with the Americans. This was on a day-to-
day basis between the Foreign Office and the State Department at
both ministerial and official level. For example at the meeting
between Michael Stewart and Dean Rusk in Washington in the
spring of 1965 the agenda covered nearly twenty items ranging
from such obvious topics as East-West relations and problems
within NATO to obscure issues such as joint assistance to Sri
Lanka. In each case during these consultations there was a careful
trading of interests where help in one area was expected to produce
a similar response somewhere else without anything ever being
consciously described as a 'deal' or 'agreement'. The UK would
consult the US whenever American interests were at stake. Similarly the US did consult Britain, for example when they intended to
invite President Suharto of Indonesia to Washington but wanted to
take account of British sensitivities because of the Indonesian
'confrontation' with Malaysia involving British troops. On other
occasions the US might be less helpful. When the UK asked for
assistance over the dispute with Spain about Gibraltar, the US
refused because they did not want to take sides between two of
their allies.

Perhaps somewhat more surprising were the close relations
between the US and UK over Rhodesia. Although this was a
dispute between Britain and one of her last remaining colonies, the
Americans were drawn in at every stage. When Wilson visited
Rhodesia in an attempt to stop UDI in October 1965 the Americans were given special daily briefings in Salisbury on the progress

of the talks and the positions taken by each side. Immediately after UDI joint talks were held on how to assist Zambia and, more importantly, on how to implement oil sanctions where the UK would not make any move without US agreement. The closeness of the relations between Britain and the United States over Rhodesia can be judged by two factors – the frequency of the messages between Wilson and Johnson, and the information exchanged. For example, in the five days after 8 January 1966 Wilson sent four personal messages to Johnson about Rhodesia and in the sixteen days after 11 November 1966 (the run-up to the *Tiger* talks) he sent thirteen. Apart from these personal messages the UK was also giving the Americans copies of the correspondence between the British and Rhodesian governments over the possible terms for a settlement within a day of the Rhodesian replies being received in London (information which was not circulated to the British Cabinet).[7]

In the defence field not only did the Labour government accept all the existing US bases in the UK but it did everything possible to help develop worldwide US military capabilities. In 1965 a new colony in the Indian Ocean was created solely to enable it to be leased to the Americans as a military base. The inhabitants were simply removed from the islands. In one area the Labour government deliberately increased British dependence on the United States – the supply of military aircraft. Having decided to hold defence spending at about its 1964 level the government found that it could not afford to continue with a number of British military aircraft programmes which were expensive, late and not as technically advanced as similar US projects. In December 1964 Denis Healey agreed with his US opposite number, Bob McNamara, on a programme of weapons collaboration. In practice this meant that the UK would buy US aircraft – the C-130 Hercules as a transport, the Phantom as a fighter and the F-111 to replace the TSR-2 as a strike-attack aircraft.

Wilson made his first visit to Washington as Prime Minister in early December 1964, only six weeks after taking office. He was determined to use the visit to establish a close relationship with President Johnson. Much of the time was taken up with a discussion of nuclear affairs within NATO but Johnson raised an issue that was to figure in most of the subsequent talks – Vietnam. The US was already fully committed against the Vietcong guerillas and the North Vietnamese fighting to reunify the country but had stopped short of full-scale deployment of army combat forces. Johnson asked for a UK military commitment in Vietnam, though he clearly did not expect Wilson to agree. Wilson, well aware of opposition within the Labour party to any support for the Americans and the fact that Britain had virtually no spare forces available, refused. Instead he offered training facilities in counter-insurgency warfare and jungle operations. Two months later Wilson tried to intervene with Johnson, via a late-night telephone call on the 'hot-line', to limit American retaliation after a Vietcong attack on US personnel. When he suggested he fly to Washington to give his advice at first hand, Johnson told him that since he had no troops in Vietnam he could keep his opinions to himself.

However, in the spring of 1965 a general 'understanding' was reached between Wilson and Johnson over what the UK could do to help. Britain agreed to give support to US actions in Vietnam but not provide direct military assistance, apart from some arms sales. For its part the US agreed to keep the British informed of its policy but stopped short of any commitment to advance consultation. The Americans reluctantly accepted that the best way Britain could help was through its role as co-chairman of the Geneva conference on Vietnam. Here it had a channel of communication with the Russians and was also able to use its diplomatic position to put forward possible ideas for peace (though these would always be cleared with the Americans beforehand and be subject to their agreement). Although the Americans often suggested that they could be even more co-operative if British troops were sent to Vietnam, they generally accepted that it was not politically possible for Wilson to do this. Johnson was often to moderate the demands of his more hawkish advisers, particularly Bundy, and in the end did not make help in Vietnam a condition for US assistance to the UK. Instead, they had other demands to make of the British.

Relations between Britain and the United States had a dominating influence over the policy of the Labour government, particularly in its first three years in office. Previously secret American documents reveal that in the course of 1965 the Labour government reached a series of 'understandings' with the United States. What was agreed has never been made public, yet these unwritten agreements fundamentally shaped both British domestic and strategic policy over this period. When sections of the government's policies are re-examined against the background of the deal made with the Johnson administration the priorities and concerns of the government can be seen in a new light. The key players on the British side were Wilson and Callaghan, although Brown too was aware of what was happening. The Cabinet was neither consulted nor told about what had been agreed, although individual members had their suspicions about what had been going on behind their backs as the consequences made themselves felt in the subsequent development of policy.

The reason why the United States was in a position to make policy demands on the British was the weak position of sterling. The US Federal Reserve Bank had taken part in a major rescue operation mounted by the central banks in November 1964 but this had not involved the US government directly. By the spring of 1965, when this rescue had proved only temporary, the US government was seriously worried that devaluation of sterling was imminent. In March, before the UK Budget, there was a mild panic in Washington and Johnson's economic advisers demanded that he intervene with Wilson to stop devaluation. That panic passed, but the US fear of a UK devaluation remained. Within the tightly linked world of Western international financial arrangements the pound was seen as the first line of defence for the dollar. By the mid-1960s the dollar was no longer pre-eminent and strong, and the US was running a major balance of payments deficit. In the interests of stability within the system and of protecting the dollar the US wanted to help support the pound against the speculators. They believed that if the pound were to be devalued then the dollar would be next in line and might go the same way. By the early summer of 1965 the Americans again expected a major speculative attack on sterling to start soon and they anticipated that the UK government, with inadequate resources to defend the pound, would have to turn to them for help. At the end of June Callaghan was due in Washington to discuss support for the pound. Early in June the American administration began to consider the terms on which it would make help available.[8] From the start the US government saw this as an opportunity to do a deal that would be both far-reaching and high-level. Bundy reported to President Johnson:

We had a full discussion on the British problem in Joe Fowler's office and we are all agreed that we should not make any deals with the British on the Pound alone. Any deals we make should be put together in terms of our overall interests – political and economic, as well as monetary. None of us expects this kind of deal can be made with Callaghan. It will have to be a bargain at a higher and broader level.[9]

Callaghan was told that the US would not give support unless the UK economy was put in order and that this meant, in the first place, restraining the high level of demand and reducing the rate of growth. Immediately on his return Callaghan gained Wilson's approval for work to start within Whitehall on a deflationary package that was announced on 27 July. During the intervening period the Americans had time to develop their position.

The Americans found the British unprepared at first to see that they had to agree to a fundamental economic and political deal. The hawkish Bundy was worried by this attitude, as he told Johnson on 28 July:

> We are concerned with the fact that the British are constantly trying to make narrow bargains on money while they cut back on their wider political and military responsibilities. We want to make very sure that the British get it into their heads that it makes no sense for us to rescue the Pound in a situation in which there is no British flag in Vietnam, and a threatened British thin-out in both east of Suez and in Germany.[10]

By this date the US administration was agreed that ideally what it wanted from Britain was no devaluation, no defence cuts in Germany or East of Suez, internal measures to deflate the economy (preferably including a six-month wage and price freeze) and possibly UK troops in Vietnam in return for US help in putting together a multilateral rescue package for sterling.[11] The key decision-makers recognised that the US was unlikely to achieve all of its aims. What then were its priorities? The main US concern was to maintain the value of the pound because of the effects any devaluation would have on the dollar. On 28 July Henry Fowler (Treasury Secretary), George Ball (State Department), Henry Martin (Federal Reserve) and Bundy (White House) met and agreed

> that the UK should be told that under any and all circumstances devaluation of the pound is unthinkable and cannot be permitted.[12]

Their negotiating strategy was to try and ensure that devaluation was avoided and then that their other aims were achieved. They recognised that how much they could obtain would depend on how far Wilson was prepared to go to keep sterling at its existing level. As one White House aide summed up the US calculations:

The premise . . . is that, for Wilson, there are some things worse than devaluation. If I'm wrong – if he makes an absolute objective of $2.80 – then of course we are in the saddle and can impose whatever terms we wish when he comes for help.[13]

Wilson did give absolute priority to the value of sterling and this did mean that the US could impose tough terms for their help. The issue that created major debate within the administration was whether they could, or should, insist on a UK presence alongside the US in Vietnam as part of the price for assistance. As we have seen, some in the US administration, in particular Bundy, did want to make this a condition, but Johnson decided against it. He realised that Wilson simply would not be able to deliver such a commitment and that to try and force him down this road might well mean that Britain would decide that devaluation and withdrawal from East of Suez was a preferable alternative.

The crucial meeting in developing the outlines of the deal was between Burke Trend, Secretary to the Cabinet, and Mc George Bundy, Johnson's principal aide, at the end of July. At that meeting, as Bundy told President Johnson:

In accordance with your instructions, I kept the two subjects of the pound sterling and Vietnam completely separate.[14]

(Instead the US made a separate high-level approach to Wilson for help on Vietnam which he effectively turned down.)[15] At the Bundy-Trend meeting the British were told first that devaluation was unacceptable as too damaging both to Britain and the US, as well as to the world financial system. They were also told that any rescue for the pound would not be a unilateral American operation but would have to be a multilateral package involving European central banks. This latter condition inevitably meant that further measures, going beyond the deflationary package just announced, would be needed to tighten control over the British economy in order to convince the bankers to participate in the rescue operation.

The immediate British response was to ask for an open-ended declaration of US support for the pound. The Americans briefly considered the idea, and agreed amongst themselves that the British would have to turn over all their remaining gold (worth $2 billion) to the United States. They realised that such a demand would be unacceptable to the British and so rejected the UK request.[16] With the pound under heavy pressure at the beginning of August and with the foreign exchange reserves in a weak position the British were in no position to argue – if they wanted more support for the pound they had to accept the US conditions. The first step was for the heads of the two central banks – Lord Cromer and Henry Martin – to agree on the technical arrangements for the support of sterling. Within days this phase of the negotiations was successfully concluded. But the Americans still had to decide on their exact terms for implementing the Martin-Cromer plan. On 6 August George Ball of the State Department told President Johnson that

> We should place two *firm* conditions on our support:
> a. That the British agree to maintain fully their worldwide defense commitments;
> b. That they agree to take whatever additional internal measures are necessary to make possible multilateralizing a rescue effort.[17]

By 9 August the US conditions for accepting the Martin-Cromer plan were refined still further, as Gardner Ackley of the Council of Economic Advisers told Johnson:

> The price for our help in selling this plan to the Continent is (a) maintenance of UK defense commitments; and (b) Wilson's public commitment to a wage-price freeze.[18]

When these terms were received in London, Wilson decided to send Callaghan to Washington to negotiate with Fowler over the economic side of the package. The US terms were stiff and he was worried that with an election due within months the government simply could not afford to implement a freeze (although Callaghan personally favoured the idea). The outcome of the Chancellor's talks with Fowler was that there would be no devaluation and that, despite the deflationary Budget in April and the July measures, the British economy would not be reflated in the near future. In addition the existing voluntary, and largely ineffective, prices and incomes policy would be given a statutory basis. These internal measures were just enough to persuade the Americans to mobilise a rescue effort: Fowler agreed to travel to Europe and negotiate arrangements with the central banks in line with the Martin-Cromer plan. In Britain the Cabinet was summoned to an emergency meeting on 1 September at which they agreed to introduce a statutory incomes policy. George Brown, after a mammoth negotiating session, obtained the TUC's agreement for the prior notification of wage and price rises and powers for the government to delay increases. Fowler also successfully completed his mission to Europe, and on 9 September the Bank of England and Callaghan finalised the arrangements with the other central banks for support of the pound.

The other half of the bargain still to be delivered by Britain was the commitment on defence policy. George Ball was sent to Britain in early September to gain British agreement to not cutting any defence contribution whilst US support for the pound lasted. He saw Wilson on 8/9 September. The US records of those talks are still classified as 'Secret' but Bundy gave Johnson a summary of what had taken place:

> The . . . cable from London shows how George Ball really put it to the British on Singapore and our support of the pound . . . You will notice that it took two talks for Wilson to agree to the association between our defense of the pound and their overseas commitments. The one thing which he was apparently trying to avoid was a liability in Vietnam.[19]

Once the various elements of the deal were in place the tangible benefits for the pound were rapidly experienced. Within a day of the completion of the Ball-Wilson talks and final agreement on the rescue package for sterling there was massive co-ordinated buying of the pound on the foreign exchange markets by the central banks. This had the intended effect of severely damaging the speculators and restoring confidence; it ensured that the pound remained stable and relatively strong until well into 1966.

Why did Wilson accept a deal that allowed American dictation of British policy? Clearly of prime importance was the fact that the 'understanding' was secret. Not even the Cabinet, let alone the public, was aware of the commitments that were made. In entering into these commitments to what extent were Wilson, and his close colleagues, being forced down paths they did not want to tread? Given Wilson's personal commitment to maintain the value of sterling, he had little alternative but to turn to the Americans when the UK was no longer able to cope unaided. He saw no problem in giving the Americans the assurance they were seeking that Britain would not devalue because it was the one thing he himself was determined to avoid. Deflation of the economy in July 1965 and the commitment not to reflate in the near future also fitted in with the Chancellor's and the Treasury's view of how to run the economy, and so caused no major problems. The idea of a wage-price freeze was, however, carrying this approach too far, partly because the government itself was not united (George Brown strongly opposed a freeze) but mainly because of the political problems involved with an election rapidly approaching. But the acceptance of a statutory basis for the prices and incomes policy was an important first step towards the July 1966 freeze. The agreement not to cut military commitments around the world, and particularly in the Far East, fitted in with Whitehall's own preferences. Wilson was keen to stay East of Suez, as was the defence and foreign policy lobby. There were, moreover, doubts about how quickly the UK could withdraw anyway. Wilson seems to have regarded it as a small price to pay for rescuing the pound. It was the rescue of the pound that was the key. With an election rapidly approaching Wilson wanted a period without sudden runs on the pound and perhaps panic economic measures. He wanted to create the impression that the government had virtually solved the problem and if that required conditions dictated by the Americans and the central banks it was a price he was willing to pay – behind the scenes – for electoral success. The problem was that the deal also enabled the government to go on without having to face up to the difficult policy choices that needed to be made on both economic and defence policy. It merely put off the day of reckoning.

The full extent of the deal with the United States remained a closely guarded secret and Wilson did not tell the Cabinet about it. Nevertheless, for the next eighteen months the government was to live up to the commitments that had been given and the United States continued its support for the pound.

The first crucial test came with the final decisions on Britain's defence review which had started in the spring of 1965 and was due to be completed by early in 1966. Wilson gave Johnson a commitment that the Americans would be consulted about the results before any final decisions were taken. He briefed Johnson on the first outlines of the results of the review during his visit in December 1965 – reductions in forces in the Far East after the end of 'confrontation' with Indonesia but withdrawal only from Aden when it became independent. Early in January a full-scale British team was sent to Washington to brief the Americans in more detail. After the US confirmed that they were satisfied about British intentions, the Cabinet had their one meeting on the review in February. It was at this meeting that Wilson came nearest to admitting the deal he had done with the Americans when he warned his colleagues somewhat cryptically:

Nevertheless, don't let's fail to realise that their financial support is not unrelated to the way we behave in the Far East: any direct announcement of our withdrawal, for example, could not fail to have a profound effect on my personal relations with LBJ and the way the Americans treat us.[20]

American pressure explains the nature of the 1966 defence review. It was the last of a series of attempts to maintain a world-wide military role but without the resources to finance a realistic military capability. If defence spending had to be reduced and the Americans placated by keeping forces in the Far East, then there was no alternative but to keep the commitments and try and find cheaper ways of carrying them out.

During Wilson's visit to Washington in December 1965 another item was on the agenda – Rhodesia. Britain wanted US support for oil sanctions against the illegal regime in Rhodesia and in previous weeks there had been detailed talks between officials. Johnson decided it was time to reinforce the bargain that had been made back in the summer. According to Crossman, Wilson told the Cabinet on 21 December:

He got . . . an understanding that if we stood firm in the Far East the Americans would back the oil sanctions.[21]

The deal was next put to the test in the July 1966 crisis. Wilson was still strongly opposed to devaluation. The Americans still regarded devaluation as the worst possible outcome. Indeed so strong was this determination to resist devaluation that some within the administration – Fowler, Ball and Dean Acheson – gave this a higher priority than the UK keeping its East of Suez presence.[22] Nevertheless, Johnson kept Wilson to the 1965 deal of no devaluation, no cuts in military commitments and deflation at home to maintain confidence in the pound, as John Stevens, the Treasury representative in Washington, explained:

Johnson had made it clear to Wilson that the pound was not to be devalued and no drastic action east of Suez was to be undertaken until after the American elections in November. In return the pound would be supported to any extent necessary.[23]

The outcome of the July crisis – rejection of devaluation, a major deflationary package and a wage and price freeze but no cuts in Britain's overseas commitments – reflected American demands.

At the height of the crisis the US administration decided that Britain should be told that their performance since September 1965 had been 'disappointing', that reserves accumulated with outside help were being dissipated, and that avoidance of devaluation and the maintenance of the reserve role of sterling required 'some compression of demand [and] the prompt inauguration of an effective incomes policy'.[24] Both of these policies were duly implemented. Johnson once again asked for a British force in Vietnam – this time he would be content with a token gesture – but again Wilson refused. Once again the British economy was deflated, far more severely than a year earlier, to try and maintain the value of sterling. Wilson forced the Cabinet into line behind this policy and stuck to the deal he had made with the Americans in the previous autumn. As George Brown told one of his colleagues Wilson was 'bound personally and irrevocably to President Johnson and had ceased to be a free agent'.[25] In return for this co-operation Johnson gave Wilson a eulogy at a lunch in his honour during his visit at the end of July. After comparing Wilson to Churchill, Johnson went on:

> I must say that England [*sic*] is blessed now, as it was then, with gallant and hardy leadership . . . Your firmness and leadership have inspired us deeply in the tradition of the great men of Britain.

But whatever the fine words another opportunity to confront the major decisions that had to be made about the role of sterling and Britain's worldwide commitments had been avoided.

The July 1966 measures mark the last phase of the deal made with the Americans in 1965. In early 1967 a new British policy, less dependent on the Americans, began to emerge. In the early autumn of 1966 Wilson authorised Healey to start work on another defence review. When the results were ready at the end of October Healey admitted to the inner group of seven ministers on defence policy that intellectually the right solution was to pull out from East of Suez but that the Americans would not allow this. Instead he proposed the old solution of thinning out forces in every area with a study on possible withdrawal from the Middle East but not the Far East. At OPD in December, however, other ministers insisted on a study on possible withdrawal from the Far East.

The Americans may well have been aware of this work because in February 1967 they proposed to place the 1965 understandings on a permanent basis. They suggested a twenty-five-year multi-billion-dollar US loan to fund the sterling balances, stabilise the pound at its existing level and create a joint sterling-dollar area to protect both currencies and the position of gold. In return the UK would undertake not to withdraw from the Far East and to maintain a major strategic presence in the area. This proposal was rejected for a number of reasons. The 1965 understandings had been secret, even from most of the Cabinet, and Wilson must have doubted whether he could ever sell a long-term agreement with the Americans, which would have turned Britain virtually into an American dependency, to the Cabinet, the PLP or the public. Acceptance would also have ruled out British entry into the EEC on political and economic grounds. Wilson and Callaghan believed, however, that they could survive without such a new deal. Their aim was to keep the economy deflated, hoping that this would avoid the worst balance of payments problems and that increasing savings in overseas defence expenditure would also help to keep the balance of payments just in surplus until the next election, thus avoiding devaluation. With the rejection of the US offer Wilson also regarded himself as released from the deal made in September 1965.

In April 1967 the Cabinet was considering proposals to withdraw from Singapore and Malaysia by 1975, with the rundown starting much earlier. George Brown, visiting Washington as Foreign Secretary in May, had a rough time as Dean Rusk, the Secretary of State, put on considerable pressure to try and keep Britain on the mainland of South East Asia. Wilson was subjected to similar pressure during his visit at the beginning of June but he too was immovable. Although the Americans were obviously for their own reasons trying to keep Britain in the Far East, they too were beginning to realise that the sort of policy they wanted from the British was not realistic. The briefing for President Johnson for Wilson's visit in June argued that without a $3–5 billion loan Britain was going to devalue in the near future and that

> In a siege environment – with economic stagnation at home and no progress towards Europe – it would be exceedingly difficult for any elected politician to do all the things we would like Harold Wilson to do:
> – stay in the Far East;
> – back us on Vietnam;
> – avoid balance of payments trouble and any risk of devaluation (whatever the costs in domestic deflation);
> – maintain a constructive stance vis-a-vis Europe (no further cut-backs in the BAOR, no giving up on entry to Europe etc).

Taken together, all this simply does not add up to a workable platform for Wilson's 1969–70 elections.[26]

It certainly didn't: Wilson realised that he could not deliver what the Americans wanted and survive. He chose survival. Later that month the government announced that a final date had been set for the withdrawal from the Far East. A symbolic point had been passed as the Americans realised.

In November 1967 the decisive crisis for sterling arrived. With reserves low, unemployment rising and no prospect of any improvement in the balance of payments in the foreseeable future, the government finally appreciated that devaluation was inevitable. The Americans were consulted and they too accepted that the end of the road had been reached. They made an effort to construct a rescue package with the European central banks but the British government never had any real intention of accepting another attempt to rescue the pound because the terms involved would have been politically unacceptable. Wilson in particular had convinced himself that devaluation would represent an opportunity to 'break free' from the past and start on a new course. It was only later that the difficulties involved in devaluation became apparent. Devaluation did have the effect the Americans had always feared. The pound remained weak but speculative attention turned to the dollar and in particular the fixed price for gold. By March 1968 a new financial crisis involved closing world gold markets and devising a new agreement to keep the international financial system working.

The consequences of devaluation in Britain were also fundamental. The Cabinet agreed on massive public expenditure cuts to try and make devaluation work. For political reasons they decided that half the cuts must come from the defence programme. The decision was taken to withdraw not only from the Far East but also from the Gulf and the date of withdrawal was brought forward to 1971. The purchase of American F-111 aircraft was cancelled. George Brown was once again sent to Washington to tell Dean Rusk of the British intentions. Rusk complained of 'the acrid aroma of *fait accompli*' and accused Britain of 'opting out', describing it as the 'end of an era'.[27] Johnson threatened Wilson with retaliation for the cancellation of the F-111 order but Wilson, in a complete volte-face from his position two years earlier, told the Cabinet that he wasn't worried by Johnson's threats and that Britain should look after its own interests.

By early 1968 the relationship between Johnson and Wilson, and between Britain and the United States, had greatly altered. The pound had been devalued, the sterling area was being run down and Britain was withdrawing from any remaining responsibilities outside Europe. Although British policy makers believed that they had maintained the 'special relationship' with the United States, the Americans regarded the British as no more than one of the many regional powers with whom they had ties. Whatever its public posture the US administration was ruthlessly realistic in its assessment of the UK's position once the last elements of its world power role were being wound up. As Dean Rusk told the US National Security Council in June 1968:

Operationally the US and UK are working on fewer real problems. The concept of Atlantic cooperation could replace the special relationship.

And as the Secretary for Defense, Clark Clifford, added,

the British do not have the resources, the backup, or the hardware to deal with any big world problem . . . they are no longer a powerful ally of ours because they cannot afford the cost of an adequate defense effort.[28]

By June Johnson's time as President was already drawing to a close and Wilson never established a close rapport with his successor, Richard Nixon, who, according to Kissinger, distrusted Wilson. Nixon visited London in 1969 (as part of his European tour – something Johnson had never done) but little was achieved and the main event of the visit was a ghastly mock Cabinet meeting put on to impress the visiting Americans. When Wilson visited Washington in early 1970 Nixon reciprocated by inviting him to a meeting of the National Security Council. Wilson says that this was 'a unique occasion . . . not an event staged for our benefit'.[29] Kissinger says that 'both events were part charade'.[30] Even if British decline meant that they had little to contribute to world problems they could still keep up appearances, as Kissinger commented during the Nixon visit in 1969:

Harold Wilson greeted Nixon with the avuncular good will of the head of an ancient family that has seen better times but is still able to evoke memories of the wisdom, dignity and power that had established the family name in the first place.[31]

Awareness of the American connection – in its overt form of the much-vaunted special relationship, and the multifarious bilateral and multilateral contacts between the two governments, and especially in its covert form of the deals deliberately kept secret from most of the British government, let alone Parliament and the people – is essential to understanding the way in which British policy evolved in the economic, financial, foreign and defence fields in the period between 1964 and 1967. The next two chapters will examine the specific effects in more detail. There were two phases in US–UK relations during the life of the Labour government and the American connection was not the same at the end as at the beginning. Wilson and the senior members of the government came in with something to prove to themselves, the Americans, the Conservative opposition and the British electorate – namely, that Britain under a Labour government was a responsible partner in world affairs, and a faithful and reliable ally of the United States. This keenness added another dimension to the close links already existing. For the first two and a half years of its life the Labour government actively sought to deepen the relationship with the Americans and turned to them for help, even though after September 1965 a major price had to be paid in terms of Britain's ability to determine its own policies. After 1967 this relationship could not be sustained. The period from 1964 to 1967 was Britain's last-gasp effort to continue as a world power in both the military and economic spheres. This desire was egged on by a United States eager for help in defending the overexposed dollar, and its military and diplomatic posture in the Far East. The period after 1967 is one of the British beating retreat – not just from East of Suez but in economic terms too. It was accompanied by a ruthlessly honest appraisal by the Americans of Britain's reduced status – even if the British were more reluctant to accept the new reality.

4
Defending the Pound:
Economic Policy 1964–66

I myself have always deprecated . . . in crisis after crisis, appeals to
the Dunkirk spirit because what is required in our economic situation is not a brief period of inspired improvisation, work and
sacrifice . . . but a very long, hard prolonged period of reorganisation and rededication. It is the long haul, not the inspired spirit,
that we need.

Harold Wilson, House of Commons, 26 July 1961

I believe that our people will respond to this challenge because our
history shows that they misjudge us who underrate our ability to
move, and to move decisively, when the need arises. They misjudged our temper after Dunkirk, but we so mobilised our talent
and untapped strength that apparent defeat was turned into a great
victory. I believe that the spirit of Dunkirk will once again carry us
through to success.

Harold Wilson, Labour Party Conference, 12 December 1964

The immediate problem facing the new Labour government, and
one that was to dominate its life for the next six years, was the state
of the economy and in particular the balance of payments. In
the spring Budget of 1963 the Conservative Chancellor of the
Exchequer, Reginald Maudling, launched a policy of expansion:
his tax cuts and increases in government spending were designed,
so he claimed, to break through the barriers to growth in the
British economy. Previous attempts to increase the rate of growth
had always run into the problem of a rapidly deteriorating balance
of payments as imports rose faster than exports. Now Maudling
asserted that he was prepared to get through such a period in order
to reach a new level of economic activity where he thought exports
would pick up and Britain would become a more dynamic economy. There was little evidence to back such a 'theory' and the
government's advisers were dubious in the extreme about the
outcome. In fact, the main motivation behind the policy was, as so
often in the past, to engineer a pre-election boom. When Maudling

61

had opted for rapid expansion a general election seemed likely in the autumn of 1963 but the resignation of Harold Macmillan, the battle for the leadership and Labour's continued strength in the opinion polls caused the Conservatives to put off the election till the last possible date. As a result there had been eighteen months of unrestrained pre-electoral boom by the time Labour took office.

The full extent of the problems the Conservatives had deliberately created did not become apparent before the election. On the day after the election, Friday 16 October, Wilson, Callaghan and Brown were handed alarming briefs by officials which set out the scale of the problem and the need for urgent action. In 1963 exports had increased rapidly (by 7½%) as the slack in the economy was taken up but by 1964 real problems were emerging. In the first half of the year industrial output remained roughly stationary and exports rose by only 1% because the economy was working at almost full capacity. All the pre-election boom was doing was drawing in imports, which went up by 13%. By the summer of 1964 private estimates within the Treasury and the National Economic Development Council were forecasting a balance of payments deficit of £750–800 million compared with a figure of £35 million in 1963. Preparations had already begun, with Maudling's approval, for a post-election package to deal with the impending crisis. However, the way in which the new ministers responded to this crisis cannot be understood without some appreciation of the constraints on economic policy. In particular this involves the role of sterling and the powerful symbolic importance it had acquired in the minds of policy makers, as well as the technical constraints associated with its use as a reserve currency and the operation of the sterling area.

After 1914 sterling lost its position as the pre-eminent currency in the world to the dollar but successive British governments were to attempt, for nearly the next sixty years, to preserve the tattered remnants of its role as a reserve currency for the conduct of international trade and finance. The City of London, the Bank of England and the Treasury were agreed that one of the major symbols of Britain's position in the world was the role of sterling, hence the importance of maintaining its accepted place and its value. In 1925 the gold standard was disastrously re-established at the 1914 level, leading to severe depression in the domestic economy because of overpriced exports and cheap imports. After Britain left the gold standard in 1931 the sterling bloc slowly emerged, reaching its peak during the Second World War. It was in effect a highly discriminatory financial union run by London.

Members (mainly the Empire and Dominions) operated fixed exchange rates and there was a common currency reserve held in London which, protected by draconian foreign exchange controls, was not freely convertible into dollars. When in 1947, under US pressure, convertibility was restored there was a massive outflow of funds into dollars, the proceeds of a substantial US loan were frittered away in weeks and foreign exchange controls had to be reintroduced.

The policy of the Conservative government from 1951 was to re-establish sterling as an international currency and restore London's role as a world financial centre. The London international market for foreign exchange was reopened, as were the gold and commodity markets. In a momentous decision they introduced full convertibility of sterling for non-British residents in 1958 (essential if sterling was to be a reserve currency). This meant that holders of sterling (mainly Australia, Malaysia, Kuwait, Libya, Hong Kong and Eire) were free to sell their holdings and buy other currencies at any time. This freedom entailed severe restraints on economic policy making in Britain.

A reserve currency needs the backing of a strong domestic economy and substantial financial reserves to cope with market fluctuations. Britain had neither. Low investment, poor productivity and a falling share of world markets were part of a vicious circle of declining economic performance. When the economy expanded imports always rose faster than overpriced exports producing a balance of payments crisis. The inevitable reaction was to deflate the economy and reduce demand for imports. (However these actions also reduced investment, making the economy more inefficient in relation to Britain's competitors.) The balance of payments problems were exacerbated by large government expenditures overseas, mainly from keeping large forces in both Germany and the Far East. Net government spending abroad rose by over 200% from £147 million in 1957 to £499 million in 1967 largely from this cause. From the mid-1950s Britain suffered from an almost permanent balance of payments crisis which continually raised questions about whether the value of the pound could be maintained in the long term. These doubts were compounded by inadequate reserves of gold and foreign currency available to the Bank of England to support the pound against movements in the world markets were and sustain sterling as a reserve currency.

The room for manoeuvre in British domestic economic policy was therefore very limited. In a system of fixed exchange rates the foreign exchange reserves had to be used to maintain sterling within a very narrow band of its value of £1=$2.80. Because of the limited reserves available Britain could not counter major selling of sterling and therefore maintaining international 'confidence' was of vital importance. Actions which might alienate foreign holders of sterling had to be avoided and the domestic economy restrained to try and avert major balance of payments deficits. Any hint that British reserves might be inadequate to sustain pressure on the pound would only increase speculation about possible devaluation. In the worst case this could become a self-fulfilling prophecy as people with doubts about the pound sold it before a possible devaluation, thereby increasing pressure which the Bank of England could not resist, resulting in devaluation. During the 1960s public and media attention focused on the monthly balance of payments figures and the state of the reserves to an unprecedented extent. Even quite small movements in the figures could have major consequences.

When the new ministers studied their official briefs on the night after the election they found that the situation was even worse than they had been claiming during the election campaign. The likely balance of payments deficit was expected to be the largest since the war, the economy was overheated (with unemployment at just over 350,000) and the secret figures for the foreign exchange reserves showed that they were inadequate to defend sterling. What were the policy options open to them and how did they respond?

In Downing Street there was a sense of crisis from the start. Wilson, Brown and Callaghan met to discuss the economic situation on the morning of Saturday 17 October, just over twelve hours after taking office. They briefly considered, and immediately rejected, the possibility of devaluing sterling. There were many reasons for the decision. Callaghan represented the Treasury view (which reflected that of the Bank of England, the City and the international financial community) that it was almost a moral question. Devaluation would not only signal a decline in the status of Britain, it would also mean reneging on Britain's obligations to the holders of sterling. Since the stability of the international financial system depended on fixed exchange rates there was a strong feeling that no country should change the value of its currency without doing its utmost to maintain the existing parity. If one country devalued others might follow (thereby negating many of the gains of devaluation) and pressure might then concentrate on another country (a point that particularly concerned the Americans). Callaghan as Shadow Chancellor, during a visit to the

United States in May 1963, had told both Al Hayes (Chairman of the Federal Reserve Bank of New York) and Henry Fowler (the Secretary of the Treasury) that a Labour government would not voluntarily devalue. George Brown took a more practical view. He thought that devaluation, with its consequential rise in import (particularly food) prices, was an attack on working-class standards of living and therefore to be resisted.

Wilson shared Callaghan's views but had additional reasons for his opposition to devaluation. He had been on the fringes of the decision by the Attlee government to devalue in 1949 and had supported that decision but later blamed it for Labour's defeat in 1951. Ever since he had been a strong supporter of maintaining the value of sterling, as he told the Commons in 1958:

> The strength of sterling must be our first and primary consideration
> . . . the strength of sterling and all that depends on it must take
> priority over all other considerations.[1]

He was also influenced by his personal economic adviser, Tommy Balogh. A firm believer in 'planning', Balogh disliked devaluation which he saw merely as a price mechanism to try and bring about changes in the economy by making exports cheaper and imports dearer. He preferred, as did Wilson, to try and operate directly to improve economic performance. There was considerable evidence to support Balogh's view that the balance of payments deficit was a symptom rather than a cause of Britain's economic difficulties. Unless industrial performance, innovation and productivity were improved, then any devaluation would at best be only a temporary respite. However, this argument did neglect the fact that British exports were 20% less competitive in 1964 than in 1955; without devaluation it was difficult to see how exports could overcome such a disadvantage. And it was clear that the structural problems for the British economy were becoming worse. The deficit on the current account in 1964 was about £400 million but this compared with deficits of £150 million in 1955 and £250 million in 1960 at previous peaks of the economic cycle.

It is virtually certain that Wilson, Brown and Callaghan had agreed before the election to reject devaluation as an option. Certainly none of the papers they saw on taking office would have encouraged them to change that position. There was, however, one other factor that made the case against devaluation over-whelming in October 1964, and that was political. With a majority of five the government had to plan on another election within a year or so and it was therefore in no position to sustain the difficulties associated with devaluation. Even though it would have been possible for them to blame the Conservatives, Wilson was convinced that devaluation itself – as well as the accompanying deflationary package that would be necessary – would be highly damaging to Labour's prospects.

After their initial private meeting Wilson, Brown and Callaghan held another with four key civil servants – Burke Trend (Cabinet Secretary), William Armstrong (Head of the Treasury), Eric Roll (Head of the DEA) and Donald MacDougall (Director General of the DEA). Wilson told them that 'We three have decided that the exchange rate should stay where it is.' Only MacDougall dissented from that view and argued briefly for devaluation. Having ruled out devaluation as an option ministers now had to decide what other course to take in dealing with the economic crisis.

The brief prepared by officials suggested two possible options for dealing with the balance of payments. Both originated from the work that Maudling had started before the election. The first was to impose import quotas. These would require an elaborate administrative structure to implement but were in line with Labour's commitment to 'planning'. The alternative was an import surcharge, in effect a tariff. Although indiscriminate in its effects it had the advantage that it could be introduced more rapidly and easily than quotas.

The first discussion took place on 17 October between Callaghan, Brown, Jay, Crosland and three civil servants – Armstrong, Roll and Cairncross (Chief Economic Adviser). Jay pointed out that the surcharge was illegal under the rules of both GATT and EFTA (the European Free Trade Association). However, the officials argued strongly for the surcharge because of the administrative difficulties of introducing quotas. The next day at a meeting with Wilson at No 10 the same arguments were repeated. Wilson, who, as President of the Board of Trade in the 1940s, had been responsible for dismantling many of the wartime controls over the economy, came down in favour of the surcharge. By Tuesday 20 October the inner group of ministers had agreed on a surcharge of 15% on imports other than food and raw materials, and an export 'rebate' of 1½% through refunds on certain indirect taxes (the same choice Maudling would have made). Although at their first meeting on 19 October the Cabinet had readily agreed that the inner group of ministers should work out policy, they were surprised to be left completely in the dark about what was happening at their next meeting on 22 October. As one member described the scene:

> It really was an absolute farce to have George Brown saying, 'Naturally you won't want to be told, for fear of the information leaking, how serious the situation is. You won't want to be told what methods we shall take but we shall take them.'[2]

The import surcharge and the estimated size of the balance of payments deficit were announced jointly by Brown and Callaghan on 26 October. Although this linkage was a clever move politically to place the blame for the situation on the Conservatives and justify the surcharge, it had unfortunate consequences. It immediately created a sense of crisis. From this point on the government was under considerable pressure as was the pound on the foreign exchange markets.

The import surcharge provoked almost universal hostility abroad and threats of retaliation. The most difficult moment came at an EFTA meeting in Geneva in mid-November, when the other members threatened to impose a 15% surcharge on all British exports. After an all-night session Jay and Gordon-Walker had to promise that the surcharge would only be temporary and last for 'a matter of months'. Just before the next meeting of EFTA in February 1965 the Cabinet hurriedly agreed to cut the surcharge from 15% to 10% before it was finally abolished in 1966. The surcharge probably saved about £150 million of imports a year while it lasted but it also reduced demand in the economy by raising import prices. It was therefore a useful tool for domestic economic management and it was here that the government had a difficult, narrow path to tread.

As we have seen, the economy was running at full capacity and the unresolved structural problems were becoming worse. Yet the government was not in a political position to take any far-reaching measures. Because of the need to fight another election within a year or so it did not want to deflate the economy and increase unemployment. Yet somehow it had to ensure that the balance of payments did not worsen and cause an economic crisis through a run on the pound. So it had to live from hand to mouth hoping to sustain employment without a financial crisis. For the next eighteen months it was to take a series of *ad hoc* decisions to try and cope with particular problems as they arose without any clear idea of long-term strategy. The import surcharge was the first of these measures.

The next was to introduce an early Budget in November. Labour's election manifesto committed the government to abolishing prescription charges and increasing pensions and social security benefits. The question they had to settle was whether the economic situation allowed this pledge to be carried out and if so on what scale. A Cabinet committee chaired by Jim Callaghan considered the problem on 27 October. He proposed a compromise: pensions and benefits would rise by 50p* a week but prescription charges would not be abolished. The other members of the committee wanted both abolition and a rise of 62½p a week. No agreement could be reached and the matter was discussed next day in Cabinet. Only Lord Longford supported Callaghan, with the other ministers feeling that they should stick by their commitments. Wilson joined the majority and Callaghan was overruled. When the Budget was announced on 11 November these increases (payable from April 1965) were balanced by an increase of 2½p in the pound on income tax and a similar amount on petrol. Callaghan also announced his intention to introduce both Corporation Tax and Capital Gains Tax in the spring Budget without specifying possible rates. Although the overall effect of the Budget was mildly deflationary by about £100 million a year, the government had stuck to its election pledges. The Budget, in conjunction with the import surcharge, also met their aim of taking some of the pressure off an overheated economy without starting a recession.

The day after the Budget the Cabinet had to decide how to deal with a report on MPs' pay that had been commissioned earlier in the year on the understanding that whichever party won the election the recommendations would be implemented. Faced with the report's recommendations for an 85% increase Wilson proposed that the rise for MPs should be approved but that those for ministers should be halved and not implemented before the next election. He was supported by seven ministers, including Callaghan. The opposition came from Brown who, though content to accept only half the recommended increase for ministers, wanted it paid from 1 April 1965, the date agreed for the pension increases. Brown was supported by a majority of the Cabinet and Wilson was defeated.

However, the Cabinet had not discussed the proposal to backdate the increase for MPs to the start of the Parliament on 16 October. When the increases were announced this proposal created outrage among Labour backbenchers over the different

---

* All figures have been converted into decimal currency.

treatment accorded to pensioners. At the Cabinet meeting on 19 November the main subject was the pensions increase. The administrative difficulties of raising all pensions before April were judged to be too great and so it was agreed instead to pay a lump sum of £4 to everybody on National Assistance, a move which could be done relatively quickly. The fact that most pensioners did not receive National Assistance was brushed aside in the desire to do something to placate the backbench revolt. However, by the time Peggy Herbison, Minister for Pensions, came back to the Cabinet on 24 November with a scheme for paying out the lump sum, the government was caught up in a major economic crisis and a run on the pound. With virtually no discussion the whole idea was dropped. At a PLP meeting later that day MPs were told that the economic situation was too desperate to do anything for the pensioners and the poor.

The situation had been brought about by the reaction of the international financial community and the City to the Budget on 11 November. Despite its slightly deflationary effect, they chose to regard the Budget as grossly irresponsible, given the balance of payments deficit. Lord Cromer, the Governor of the Bank of England, was arguing that, because major selling of the pound was underway, the government would have to restore confidence through cutting public expenditure (especially on social programmes), dropping any curbs on overseas investment and raising Bank Rate by 1%. During the week after the Budget Wilson, Callaghan and Brown were divided over what to do about Bank Rate. Callaghan was tending towards accepting Cromer's advice, Brown was undecided and Wilson opposed, mainly because there had not been time to consult the Americans. When the rate was not raised on the Thursday, the normal day for such action, this failure to act only increased pressure on the pound. By the Friday it had fallen to just above $2.78, the lowest level it could go under the fixed exchange rate system.

Ministers were meeting that weekend at Chequers for a major conference on defence strategy, but they began by discussing how to stop the run on the pound. The mood was grim and Callaghan in particular was showing signs of the pressure that was threatening to force their hand after only weeks in office. George Wigg remembered the scene at Chequers:

> Jim Callaghan's lips quivered, his hands shook, he had no idea what hit him. I remember vividly Callaghan mumbling 'We can't go on. We shall have to devalue.'[3]

69

The next day Dick Crossman found him

> Heavy and gloomy as ever. 'I am the Selwyn Lloyd,' he said, 'of this Government.' He was obviously overawed by the situation and full of self-pity . . . He was in a terrible state.[4]

And Wilson too confirmed this picture:

> I'm having to hold his hand. His nerve isn't very good these days.[5]

The immediate decision taken that weekend by the inner group of Wilson, Brown and Callaghan was that, having failed to raise Bank Rate by 1% on the Thursday, they would now take emergency action to raise it by 2% on Monday in an attempt to demonstrate 'firmness'. Wilson's private secretary, Derek Mitchell, was despatched across the Atlantic to brief Sir Eric Roll on the situation before Roll consulted the Americans to ensure that they supported the British action. When Bank Rate was raised by 2% (to 7%) on Monday 23 November it was interpreted not as a sign of 'firmness' but as a last-minute panic measure to save the pound. During Tuesday mass selling of the pound was under way and by the end of the day the Bank of England had spent £280 million (over 30% of the available foreign exchange reserves) in supporting sterling. That evening Lord Cromer and his deputy saw Callaghan, and then together with George Brown they went to see Wilson.

The situation they faced was critical. The foreign exchange reserves were already below £600 million and the Bank of England had only a limited amount of international assistance on which to draw. There was a swap agreement with the US Federal Reserve, which had begun in 1962 at just £18 million but had been extended to £180 million in May 1963. A second swap agreement for a similar amount existed with the European Central Banks through the Bank for International Settlements in Basle. By October the Bank of England had already borrowed £100 million from these two sources, leaving some £250 million still available. At best, therefore, the Bank of England had only about £800 million left to support the pound and on current trends that might only last a couple of days. Immediate action was required to avoid enforced devaluation of sterling.

Lord Cromer tried to exploit the situation to get the changes in the Labour government's economic policy he had argued for since the election. In his memoirs Wilson gives a touching account of how he fought the bankers, arguing that democracy in Britain was not dead and that rather than give in he would call an election, devalue the pound and come back with a huge majority. But these were only words to impress Cromer. Earlier that evening Crossman had tackled him privately in the Commons to argue for devaluation and Wilson had replied:

> You're talking nonsense . . . devaluation would sweep us away. We would have to go to the country defeated. We can't have it.[6]

In a more pragmatic vein Wilson's tactics with Cromer were to bring him round to see that the international financial community, and particularly the Americans, had a direct interest in the stability of sterling. By the end of the meeting Cromer agreed to try and organise an international package to rescue the pound. In less than twenty-four hours he raised over £1 billion from other Central Banks (a third of it from the US Federal Reserve). When this was announced the immediate pressure was taken off the pound. Wilson's judgement proved sound: the other Central Banks were prepared to help because they felt that speculation against sterling endangered the whole international financial system. In particular the United States authorities saw the pound as the first line of defence for the dollar:

> With the US and the UK, the two major countries with balance-of-payments deficits, and the rest of the world wondering whether we will be able to solve our problem without devaluation, it is possible that a devaluation of sterling would spread feeling that the dollar will also have to be devalued, and lead to further cashing in of dollar holdings for gold, and to balance-of-payments crisis for the US.[7]

Although the immediate problem was resolved in November 1964, the cost of defending the pound was substantial. Nearly £600 million had to be spent in the last three months of 1964 in keeping the pound at its $2.80 level. This was financed from swap agreements but they had to be repaid within three to six months. The only way this repayment could be financed was through using an IMF standby, although taking this up would allow the IMF to monitor British economic performance. The £360 million standby facility with the IMF was drawn in December 1964 and a further £500 million in February 1965. In addition the annual repayment on the 1947 loan from the US had to be deferred (as it was again in 1965).

The price of accepting this support gradually became apparent.

It was not that strict terms were imposed but rather that the government recognised they would have to be 'responsible' and not embark on programmes that alienated the international financial community. Already a £4 payment to all those on National Assistance had been rapidly abandoned at the height of the crisis, and over the next months we shall see the continuing influence of the United States and others over both economic and foreign policy. These powerful constraints on an independent domestic programme were anticipated by Harold Wilson in a speech he made in Edinburgh just before the 1964 election:

> You cannot go cap in hand to the central bankers as they [the Conservatives] have now been forced to do, and maintain your freedom of action, whether on policies maintaining full employment here in Britain or even on social policies. The central bankers will before long be demanding that Britain put her house in order.

After the November crisis the government could at least congratulate itself that it had survived without having to take either of the two courses it was trying so hard to avoid – devaluation or deflation. The pound had been saved (at a price), the import surcharge ought to reduce the balance of payments deficit and some popular measures had been included in the November Budget. But the underlying problems had not been tackled. The economy was still operating at full capacity – unemployment was to drop another 50,000 to just over 300,000 on average in 1965 (unfilled vacancies were about 400,000) and inflation was picking up from 3% in 1964 to 4.8% in 1965. Yet Wilson could still talk of the Dunkirk spirit and claim that the problems had been solved, as when he addressed the PLP on 4 February 1965:

> The economic crisis, with the unpopular measures it has demanded, is now virtually over. The future is bright with promise.

In the short term there was some improvement. In the first four months of 1965 the average trade deficit was only £17 million (overall imports rose by only 1% and exports by 5%) and the year as a whole was to show a current account deficit of only £52 million.

The next hurdle was the spring Budget. The question was how to maintain the difficult balancing act of satisfying both electoral requirements and the desire of the international financial community for tough action to defend sterling. Lord Cromer was continuing to demand massive cuts, particularly on social spending. The Americans too were becoming worried about the future of the pound. They were not impressed by the October 1964 measures, which the US Ambassador in London described as 'modest' given the scale of the problem; they believed major policy changes were required in the forthcoming Budget.[8] At the end of March the Chairman of the US Federal Reserve, together with other key advisers, asked President Johnson to tell Wilson that

> there is very real uneasiness and a great deal of apprehension that your budget will be inadequate . . . It seems very important that your budget, which is being watched very carefully, should be a tight one . . . and that your Government advertise it to be one designed to achieve confidence in your currency.[9]

Callaghan was well aware of these pressures as he prepared the Budget. He told colleagues that anything less than £100 million in extra taxes would cause a run on the pound. The choice was stark:

> So we had got to make up our minds: either an election before the Budget or one immediately afterwards in which we could gamble by introducing a soft Budget for electoral purposes. Otherwise, we would have to sit tight and sweat it out. But if we were going for the long term [we] could only weather it by being tough.[10]

Wilson's political objective was, as we have seen, not to go to the country until the autumn of 1965 at the earliest and preferably later. The April Budget was not a 'soft' one for electoral purposes. The centrepiece was the introduction of Corporation Tax and Capital Gains Tax, as promised in November. In addition there were increases in duty on beer, spirits, tobacco and motor licenses. To balance these unwelcome increases politically, Callaghan introduced restrictions on overseas investment and abolished allowances for business entertainment. In total, taxation increased by £475 million with the bulk, nearly £350 million, coming from the taxes on personal consumption. Although there was much in the Budget that the City and similar institutions abroad would not like, it was clearly an attempt to placate their views without doing too much damage to Labour's electoral chances.

By the spring of 1965 the government had also been able to construct a voluntary prices and incomes policy. Action on prices and incomes had become an important part of economic policy before Labour came to power. In 1961 the government had, for the first time since the war, taken direct powers to control wages with a 'pay pause' followed by a 2½% 'norm'. This was a one-sided policy, since no powers were taken to control prices, dividends or profits. In 1962 the Conservative government announced a National Incomes Commission to try and keep wage rises in line with productivity increases. The TUC refused to cooperate and the NIC never got off the ground. The formation of the National Economic Development Council in 1962 was also an attempt to develop through consensus an economic strategy that would necessarily include wages but no agreed policy had emerged by 1964.

The Labour government, largely through the hard work of George Brown, established a new approach to the question. Within two months of taking office Brown had persuaded both the employers and the TUC to sign a 'Declaration of Intent', covering productivity, prices and incomes. By April 1965 he had turned this into a 'Joint Statement', which was to form the basis for a new voluntary approach to prices and incomes policy. All three sides agreed on the unexceptionable goals of a rapid increase in output and real incomes linked to full employment. But the two crucial elements of the new policy were redistribution of the benefits of growth so as to achieve greater social justice and linkage of the rise of money incomes with increases in output. At a special TUC conference at the end of April Brown made an emotional speech, stressing the government's determination to achieve greater social justice, and persuaded the trade unions to accept the agreement. A National Board for Prices and Incomes (NBPI) was established but its powers were limited. It could investigate price and wage increases but its reports had no statutory force and its recommendations had to be negotiated with the parties concerned. Not surprisingly its impact was also limited.

Shortly after the April 1965 Budget the government came the nearest it ever did before November 1967 to having a debate about devaluation. At no time was the Treasury ever officially asked for its views and it never formally set them out. Indeed Wilson had formally prohibited discussion of the subject. Instead the work was done by the group of outside economic advisers. MacDougall, who had spoken up for devaluation in October 1964, decided to reopen the question by writing a private note to his boss, George Brown, arguing why devaluation was necessary. Before sending it he discovered that Robert Neild and Nicky Kaldor had independently produced a separate note coming to the same conclusion. They collaborated on a single paper which was sent to Wilson, Brown, Callaghan and their permanent secretaries. Brown was open-minded and soon converted to devaluation as the right course. Callaghan remained unconvinced while Wilson reacted strongly. He ordered all the relevant papers to be destroyed and the discussion to cease.

At the end of May ministers were optimistic about the economic situation and Wilson wanted to find some way of signalling an improvement so as to try and halt the decline in the government's political standing. At a late-night meeting with Brown and Callaghan on 26 May, he argued for a 1% cut in Bank Rate. Callaghan explained that the Treasury was opposed to the move, though he personally was in favour, and Lord Cromer would only agree if restrictions on hire purchase were drastically tightened so as to impress the international bankers. Brown was strongly against accepting such a deal but was talked round by his two colleagues. The Cabinet was consulted on 3 June. Despite persistent doubts from Brown and opposition from Crosland, most of the Cabinet were inclined to support the idea. Wilson was quite frank about the motives for the move, as Barbara Castle recorded:

We were in a rut, groove, corner: no room for manoeuvre: and the time had come to break out. If we did not lower bank rate now, we should probably never have another chance . . . If the whole thing went wrong, we should be in a mess. He did not underestimate the risk. But there was a sporting chance that it would enable us to break out, politically as well as economically.[11]

After a rushed discussion the Cabinet decided to go ahead.

Within a month it was clear that the gamble had failed. The international bankers were starting to ask Britain to put her house in order, as Wilson had foreseen. In May, when the UK had taken out a further £500 million loan from the IMF (to repay the short-term swaps used in the November crisis), Callaghan had to go beyond his public commitment in the Budget to achieving balance of payments equilibrium by the second half of 1966 and give a private undertaking to the IMF that the government would 'take such further action as may be necessary should existing policies not succeed'. In early May, at a meeting of OECD Working Party 3 in Paris (the little-known key group for co-ordinating international economic policy composed of senior Treasury officials from member countries), serious doubts were expressed about the British position. UK policy was cuttingly described as 'not clearly inadequate' and the margin for safety as 'extremely small'.[12] This virtual vote of 'no confidence' was echoed in Washington. The US authorities saw the British economy as expanding too fast in all areas, with an ineffective incomes policy and felt that 'unless there is a general tightening of the screws still further' the balance of payments target for 1966 would not be met. They also believed a major speculative attack on sterling was likely within the next few months and feared the British might be unable to resist the pressures.

Callaghan went to Washington at the end of June for talks ostensibly about international liquidity but in practice about assistance for the pound.[13] As Treasury Secretary Fowler told President Johnson before seeing Callaghan:

> The outlook is not very promising in the absence of more decisive British measures to correct its position [sic].[14]

Callaghan's visit was seen as an opportunity to put pressure on the British to take those decisive measures. The US Treasury prepared a list of forty-six detailed questions on the way the government was managing the British economy to put to the Chancellor. The aim of the meeting from their point of view was to explore

> the further actions which the UK could take to reduce the domestic demand pressures and restore confidence.[15]

When Callaghan discussed the idea of major long-term assistance for sterling with Henry Fowler, the message was clear. Assistance would have to be not just from the US but multilateral and before any was forthcoming the UK would have to take steps to deflate its economy. Early in July, at a meeting of OECD Working Party 3, other countries put more pressure on the British to take action. A note of the meeting recorded that

> Basing their conclusions in part on the obvious lack of confidence of the private financial community in the outlook for sterling, Working Party members were unanimous in asking the UK to consider further action to achieve its balance of payments objectives.[16]

After Callaghan's return from the United States work started on a deflationary package. Wilson told Barbara Castle a few days later:

> The Treasury was in a panic mood . . . they were overdoing it, but Jim had come back from Washington very depressed.[17]

Wilson too was affected by the same mood: two days before he made that comment he had issued instructions for officials to examine a possible total moratorium on all new government contracts for three months in an attempt to cut expenditure. As one of the ministers involved commented:

> Talk about 'stop-go'. This was the most violent, primitive, stupid form of 'stop-go' ever thought of.[18]

Work on the package was supervised by the inner group of four – Wilson, Brown, Callaghan and Jay, who met six times in the week from 11–18 July. They decided to include a series of planned public expenditure cuts nearing completion as the package was being discussed. The cuts stemmed from a review the Cabinet had put in hand when they had their first discussion on public expenditure plans at the end of January 1965. Callaghan had explained that the economy might grow at about 3.5% a year and this, together with the need to avoid massive increases in taxation, meant that public expenditure could not grow at more than 4.25%. The plans Labour had inherited from the Conservatives, plus their own commitments, required growth of over 5% a year. Defence would provide some savings but the message was clear – cuts were also required elsewhere. By June a Cabinet committee (Public Expenditure Survey Committee), chaired by Callaghan and Brown and composed mainly of non-spending ministers (Cousins, Houghton and Gunter), was arbitrating various departmental claims. The cuts agreed by that committee – in local authority mortgages, postponement of the plans for income-related benefits for the low paid and for cheap mortgages, removal of remaining NHS charges plus a saving of £100 million in planned defence spending – were adopted as part of the deflationary package. The remaining items were the moratorium on government contracts (which was now to last for six months but to exclude industrial building, housing, and school and hospital building), a tightening of hire purchase restrictions and further controls on bank credit and foreign exchange transactions.

Once the group of four had decided on the main features of the package on 18 July, officials worked out the details and ministers involved in the cuts discussed the proposals at a meeting at No 10 on 26 July. The final details were settled late that night between Wilson, Brown and Callaghan. The Americans had already been alerted and Wilson gave Bruce, the US Ambassador, a full briefing that evening.[19] Only then were the details circulated to the Cabinet which was to meet the next morning. The fact that a package was to

77

be announced had already been leaked to the press and Wilson was determined on an immediate announcement to coincide with the declaration of the result in the ballot for the Conservative leadership.

The Cabinet met at 9.30 on 27 July knowing that a statement was to be made in the Commons that afternoon. As one member commented:

> What happened then was as near to central dictatorship as one is likely to get in a British Cabinet. At Cabinet we were not given the time either to discuss the underlying strategy or even to consider the document as a whole.[20]

Callaghan tried to frighten his colleagues by saying that the foreign exchange reserves had fallen by £200 million in the last week, warning them that devaluation would follow without the package and hinting that he wanted a stiffer package, including a 10% increase in indirect taxation. The most coherent critique of the proposals came from Tony Crosland. He recognised that action was probably inevitable but felt that the Cabinet

> ought to recognise where it was leading . . . straight into stagnation and Tory policies. There was no guarantee these steps would do the trick and the Chancellor might have to come back for another dose before very long.[21]

Privately Crosland favoured devaluation but he had agreed with Callaghan beforehand not to raise the subject. In his opposition to the package he was joined by Castle and Cousins. Others too were unenthusiastic but there was no time to develop any alternative. By 12.30 they agreed to go ahead. There followed half an hour's discussion of the contents of the package which, not surprisingly, went through unamended. Then the question of who should make the statement in the Commons came up. Wilson declined, saying that he

> didn't think he was the right person to make a Statement which included the abandonment of so many promises and pledges. He couldn't possibly do this.[22]

That left Callaghan but he too was reluctant. Eventually after twenty minutes of argument Wilson took a vote of the whole Cabinet which revealed a two-to-one majority for handing

Callaghan the short straw. The majority against Callaghan probably reflected something of Crossman's personal determination

> to nail him to our cross – after all he had been mainly responsible for constructing it.[23]

The July measures did not buy even a temporary respite. Pressure on the pound in the early days of August was almost as great as during the worst days of the November crisis. On 5 August there was a crisis meeting between Wilson, Callaghan and Cromer at No 10. The situation facing them as they studied the secret figures on Britain's financial position was grim indeed. In the most favourable possible circumstances and assuming the objective of a neutral balance of payments within a year was achieved, at least £325 million was needed just to fund the interim deficit. The total external debt was £5.7 billion (including £2.85 billion of sterling reserves which could easily be moved out of London). To meet these liabilities the foreign exchange reserves stood at about £650 million at the beginning of August. In addition there was a portfolio of dollar securities worth about £430 million (which might be sold in the medium term), plus unused lines of credit with the US worth about £350 million. In total, therefore, the UK had available reserves of about £1.4 billion but only about £700 million in readily realisable assets (after taking account of the need to fund the balance of payments). Yet recent experience showed that amount could easily be lost in a bad week, and devaluation would have to take place long before the reserves were exhausted. As Henry Fowler commented a few weeks earlier:

> The British have, for all practical purposes, exhausted their recourse to the International Monetary Fund and have been told by European officials that it would be politically impossible for them to extend further credit under present circumstances.[24]

The British government had borrowed nearly £1.5 billion from the IMF in the previous nine months; it had exhausted all its short-term swap arrangements and liquidated part of its remaining dollar holdings. Yet sterling was still as weak as it had been in November 1964.

At the meeting on 5 August, with devaluation still the unmentionable alternative, Wilson, Callaghan and Cromer hoped that the July measures had reassured other countries that the government was serious in its attempts to defend the pound and that another international rescue package could now be negotiated. They decided to keep calm. Talks between Cromer and Martin of the US Federal Reserve had outlined a possible support operation. Wilson ordered Cromer to go on holiday rather than risk provoking a panic by cancelling his plans. Wilson himself, though, made contingency arrangements to fly to Washington. They agreed that Callaghan would go to Washington to see whether the Americans would save the pound yet again. Meanwhile they hoped that August would be a quiet month on the foreign exchanges because of the holiday season and that they would have time to organise further international support.

Since Callaghan's earlier visit at the end of June, the Americans had been working out the terms on which they were prepared to help Britain. This time there was no question of unconditional support as in November 1964, nor of unilateral American assistance. The deal was to be multilateral because the crucial element would be a network of support between the central banks to coordinate market operations and act together in support of sterling on the foreign exchanges. Even though the operation was multilateral, as we have seen the Americans were determined to use the leverage they had over Britain to obtain some of their objectives. On the strategic front this meant Britain staying in the Far East. They also wanted Britain to adopt what they regarded as a 'more realistic' economic policy that would help in the defence of sterling and convince the international bankers to back a rescue package. Callaghan's visit to Washington in August was crucial in setting the framework for the 'understanding' that was reached between the two governments. Although there was no signed agreement, Wilson and Callaghan understood what they had to do in order to obtain US support for a major deal to support the pound.

The Americans insisted that the UK continue a generally deflationary policy. Douglas Jay, one of the inner group of four on economic policy and therefore privy to this part of the understanding with the Americans, accidently blurted out this part of the deal to the Cabinet in the middle of September 1965:

> We can't reflate this autumn without breaking the pledges which James Callaghan made to Fowler in Washington.[25]

Callaghan tried to deny that 'pledges' had been given but other members of the Cabinet had their suspicions about what had been going on. Tommy Balogh, Wilson's economic adviser, privately confirmed the deal to Crossman when he told him that 'Callaghan had made a series of firm commitments to Fowler in return for strong American backing'.[26] A few months later George Brown also confirmed to Barbara Castle that a deal had been made.[27] The Americans asked for, and obtained, postponement of the publication of the National Plan until the new support for sterling was in place.[28] They also wanted a tougher prices and incomes policy (originally a freeze but later a statutory policy). Neither of these aspects of the economic side of the deal (like the strategic side) was revealed, even accidentally, to the Cabinet.

The voluntary prices and incomes policy negotiated by George Brown had made no noticeable impact on either prices or incomes. An 'indicative norm' for wage rises of 3–3½% had been set (in line with productivity growth) but in practice weekly wage rates rose at over 4½%, and the general growth of wages and salaries in 1965 was nearly 6½%. Almost as soon as the voluntary system was in place some members of the government were advocating something much more dramatic. In mid-June Callaghan told the Cabinet that he favoured a one-year freeze. The Americans too were worried, as the Treasury Department brief for the discussions with Callaghan at the end of June commented: 'It is . . . obvious that Britain's incomes policy is not yet effective.'[29] Callaghan himself said that during his discussions with the Americans,

> Joe Fowler began to ask questions about the prospects for our voluntary policies which I found increasingly hard to answer.[30]

Wilson was more blunt in his description of what took place:

> The Americans were insisting that we should introduce a statutory P and I policy. Jim Callaghan . . . had caved in and sold out to the US Secretary to the Treasury, Fowler.[31]

When Callaghan returned from the United States with the American terms for the deal he consulted Wilson, who was on holiday in the Scillies, and George Brown was recalled from holiday in France. After they had discussed the situation the Cabinet was recalled from holiday for an emergency meeting on 1 September.

At that meeting the inner group was careful not to tell the rest of the Cabinet that a new prices and incomes policy was being introduced at the wish of the Americans. The inner group had already decided against a completely statutory policy. They proposed instead that the NBPI should become a statutory body with the power to collect information and summon witnesses. There would also be a power for the government to compel advance notification of pay or price increases and to hold up their implementation until the Board had reported. But there would be no centrally imposed 'norm' for increases. The proposals had an easy passage through the Cabinet. Crossman, Castle and Greenwood tried to raise the question of overall economic strategy and where the measures were leading, but they were brushed aside by Wilson. Callaghan hinted that he would have preferred a fully statutory policy but Brown interjected:

> I want to make it clear that I am only introducing these proposals on the strict understanding that this is *not* the first step to statutory wage control.[32]

Wilson backed Brown, saying that a statutory system hadn't worked in wartime and wouldn't work now. The proposals were agreed. Brown went off to the TUC conference at Brighton and after a mammoth twelve-hour negotiating session persuaded them to accept the new powers. George Woodcock, the General Secretary, went further and announced that while the statutory powers were being implemented the TUC would institute its own system of voluntary notification of wage rises. This was eventually endorsed by the conference, no doubt in the hope that it might persuade the government to postpone the proposed statutory powers.

Whilst the British government had been working out how to respond to the American demands on economic policy, the contents of a package to support the pound were being discreetly negotiated. The outlines of the multilateral package had been agreed between the two central banks – Cromer at the Bank of England and Martin of the Federal Reserve. The details were settled between the US Treasury, the British Ambassador and John Stevens, the Treasury representative in Washington.[33] Once the package was agreed – as it had been by the third week of August – the British insisted that the Americans should take on the task of selling the proposal to the other countries involved in the operation. The Americans agreed and Joe Fowler travelled to Europe, ostensibly to discuss international liquidity, but in reality to protect the pound. By the end of the first week of September the negotiations over the various parts of the deal were reaching a climax. The British had already made it clear they would keep to a generally deflationary stance, and on 8 September the new prices and incomes policy was agreed by the TUC. Wilson also agreed to American demands to keep British forces in the Far East. The last part of the deal was the multilateral package. This was finally completed late at night on 9 September after a marathon negotiating session involving the Bank of England, Jim Callaghan and the European central banks (who had been put under pressure from Fowler during his trip round Europe). The agreement that emerged was for a £350 million package to support sterling (40% of which came from the Americans).[34] More important than the sum of money involved was the commitment of the central banks to support sterling on the foreign exchanges.

The next morning the Federal Reserve and the other central banks simultaneously placed massive orders for sterling at the prevailing rate. The impact on the market was stunning. Most dealers were expecting the price to fall (or even devaluation) and they lost large sums of money. The shock of this unexpected operation, together with the clear evidence of coordinated central bank operations, powerfully influenced the market and its expectations. For the next nine months there was very little speculation against sterling.

The inner group of ministers had set their objective from the start – no devaluation and no severe deflation. They achieved that aim and by the autumn of 1965 could look forward to a stable pound in the run-up to the election. But their objective could only be met at a price, given the weaknesses of the British economy. And the price rose steadily, from central bank arrangements in November 1964, through IMF borrowings in the winter and spring of 1964–5, and American- and OECD-requested deflation in July 1965, to the far-reaching deal with the Americans in the September. The latter deal placed significant constraints on British policy not just in the economic field but also in foreign and defence policy. Wilson and his close colleagues could live with this deal because it was secret and because it gave them a secure position on the pound in the run-up to the election. The danger was that this policy of short-term expedients and help from the Americans was not a long-term solution to the problems of the pound and the British economy. Although Wilson could keep the cost of this support secret, a bigger price had to be paid in July 1966 when the room for manoeuvre in British economic and defence policy remained constrained by the Americans. Even though the political case against devaluation in October 1964 was strong – although it would have been possible to put the blame on the Conservatives – it is clear that Wilson was determined to avoid devaluation at any cost. The weakness in the government's strategy (if it had a strategy) was not even to consider alternatives or realise that they were engaged in an ultimately vain attempt to defend an increasingly indefensible position.

5

A New Defence Policy?

In its first two and a half years in office the Labour government had to take a complex series of decisions on defence policy. All of these decisions raised fundamental strategic and political problems about Britain's policy, its position within the NATO alliance and its wider world role. The new government had to determine the priority to be given to defence spending and decide whether Britain should be an 'independent' nuclear power, what its attitude should be to the possibility of a NATO nuclear force, and whether an effective strategic role could and should be maintained throughout the world, and in particular East of Suez. The government also had to make decisions on a number of defence projects which the Conservative government had been unwilling to take before the election. These various issues were not just about defence in a narrow sense; they also raised questions about the future of relations with the United States and with the rest of Europe. British defence policy since 1945, like foreign policy, had been essentially bi-partisan and the government had to decide whether it wanted to stay within this mould or whether they wanted to develop a different approach.

I. NUCLEAR POLICY

The Attlee government in the 1940s had taken the fundamental decision to produce an A-bomb and the aircraft to deliver it – the V-bombers. The Conservatives in the 1950s had authorised production of an H-bomb but the delivery system to replace the V-bombers was to remain a problem for years. The attempt to produce a British rocket capable of reaching Russia (Blue Streak) had collapsed in the late 1950s because of concern about its vulnerability and soaring costs. As an interim measure Britain decided to buy the US Skybolt system, which would extend the range of the V-bombers and keep them operational until a completely new system came into service. In 1962 the Americans, without warning, cancelled Skybolt. This faced the British government with an acute dilemma. Although Britain could manufacture its own nuclear warheads it had no delivery system; without one the British deterrent would inevitably end when the V-bombers became obsolete about 1970. The only option was to try to purchase an existing American system. But this raised the question of the terms on which the United States would be prepared to make it available.

The crucial negotiations took place between Harold Macmillan and President Kennedy at Nassau in the Bahamas in December 1962. The US agreed to sell the new Polaris submarine-launched missile, together with the related design for the crucial part of the submarine. The warheads on the missile would be British. The key question was who could authorise the missiles to be fired. The US insisted, and Macmillan agreed, that the submarines would normally be under NATO command. But Macmillan was able to secure a clause that allowed for British control in cases 'where Her Majesty's Government may decide that supreme national interests are at stake'. Since it was difficult to imagine circumstances when the government would wish to fire the missiles except when 'supreme national interests' were at stake Macmillan had obtained enough to be able to claim that Britain would retain an independent nuclear deterrent.

It was the purchase of Polaris that the Labour party scornfully dismissed during the 1964 campaign alleging 'it will not be independent and it will not be British and it will not deter'. As we have seen in Chapter 1 the Labour party was deeply divided over the future of Britain's nuclear weapons. Although the unilateral disarmers had been defeated in 1961 a definitive policy statement had not emerged. The Labour party was committed to remaining in NATO and to the United States retaining nuclear weapons and bases in Europe. It seemed willing to maintain the V-bombers but not to replace them (the conference rejected Polaris in 1961). Even Gaitskell and Healey were prepared to endorse an NEC document in 1961 which stated that the UK 'should cease to attempt to remain an independent nuclear power, since this neither strengthens the alliance nor is it a sensible use of limited resources'.

In the early 1960s Wilson's own position had been firmly anti-nuclear. In 1961 he proposed a defence plan to the NEC that advocated 'permanent rejection' of an independent British deterrent and no foreign nuclear bases in Britain. During his campaign against Gaitskell for the leadership in 1960, after the unilateralist victory at the Scarborough conference, he stated publicly:

> I believe the crisis of confidence arises from the feeling that some of our leaders do not unequivocally reject the idea of the independent British bomb, and that they are waiting for Skybolt or Polaris to come along, with the idea of returning to the notion of a separate British deterrent with an American rocket to deliver it. I believe it is essential that the leader of the party states beyond all doubt that . . . he accepts that there will be no British H-bomb.[1]

When Wilson became leader the Polaris deal had already been agreed and the Labour party had to decide whether it would continue with the project if it gained office. Wilson faced pressure from the left, who wanted cancellation, but also from the right (the dominant element within the Shadow Cabinet) who wanted to retain the deterrent. His policy (or substitute for one) was to placate the left with a series of sarcastic remarks about Polaris and the right by stopping short of an outright pledge to cancel the programme. In private with the Americans Wilson was far less ambivalent. When he paid his first visit to Washington as leader in March 1964 he saw the US Defence Secretary, McNamara. According to the minutes of that meeting he 'reiterated Labour's intention to do away with the UK's nuclear force' and planned to use the money saved to increase expenditure on conventional defence. Despite his 1961 view that nuclear bases should be removed from the UK he told the Americans that he unequivocally supported the Holy Loch agreement (which provided a base for US Polaris submarines in Scotland) although a Labour government 'might favour labelling Holy Loch a NATO installation (solely for US use, of course) but that was merely a matter of nomenclature'.[2] The Americans were given similar messages on Labour's intention to end British nuclear weapons when Healey (Shadow spokesman on defence) and his deputy, Fred Mulley, visited Washington in March and February 1964.[3]

The 1964 manifesto was ambiguous: Polaris was ridiculed, but the only pledge was that 'we shall propose the renegotiation of the Nassau agreement'. While this deliberately cautious wording implied that Polaris would be cancelled, it committed the government to no more than raising the subject with the Americans and said nothing about the possible outcome. The private understanding within the leadership of the Labour party seems to have been that they would wait until they secured power before deciding what to do.

Within days of taking office the Labour government decided to keep Polaris. This decision was taken by Wilson, Healey and

Gordon-Walker without consulting any other Ministers. Within ten days of becoming Foreign Secretary Gordon-Walker visited Washington and told both Secretary of State, Dean Rusk, and the Defence Secretary, Robert McNamara, that the Labour government wanted to continue the Polaris programme.[4] Long after the event this decision was ritually endorsed by OPD and the Cabinet. The only change made in the programme was to cancel the plans for a fifth submarine. In fact there was no clear military requirement for this extra boat and it had only been included in the programme by the Ministry of Defence so as to give an incoming Labour government something visible to cut.

Why did they decide to keep Polaris? Wilson says that it could only have been cancelled at 'inordinate cost'. That argument is not supported by the facts. Denis Healey let slip the true position three years later when he told the Cabinet that 'it would have made economic sense to cancel Polaris when we came in'.[5] The programme was only a little over eighteen months old in October 1964 and the first submarine was not due to become operational for another three years. The Treasury, expecting a Labour government to cancel the project, had deliberately refused to sanction major expenditure. Internal Whitehall estimates put the cost of cancellation at about £40 million out of a projected total cost of over £300 million. Early cancellation would thus have produced substantial savings. Costs were not, therefore, the reason.

The pressure within Whitehall for continuing was massive. The military, the Ministry of Defence, the Foreign Office, the scientific advisers and the large nuclear lobby formed a powerful united front in favour of Polaris. They argued that Nassau was a very good deal for retaining an effective deterrent at minimum cost (which indeed it was). Both Healey and Gordon-Walker were strong proponents of the deterrent, saw no reason for cancellation and were happy to argue that it was too late to cancel. The rapid decision taken once in office suggests that there had never been a very serious intention to cancel within the leadership of the party despite what was said in opposition. Many of them, Wilson included, were believers in Britain's great power role and in office appreciated the status that the possession of nuclear weapons was supposed to confer. The narrow parliamentary majority was also a factor. Wilson did not want to create a political issue for the Conservatives to exploit, particularly because Douglas-Home had run a strong campaign on retention of the deterrent and this was widely reckoned to be the issue on which he was most effective. There was no agonising reappraisal of Britain's future role – the decision on Polaris was taken quickly and painlessly. However, there were other difficult decisions ahead on nuclear affairs.

In 1964 NATO was in the throes of a prolonged and highly charged political and military debate about the possession and control of nuclear weapons within the alliance. NATO strategy was based on the possession of nuclear weapons but effective control of these weapons lay outside the alliance framework in national hands, mainly those of the United States but there were small separate British and French nuclear forces. By the late 1950s there was increasing pressure within the alliance from its non-nuclear members for some degree of control over nuclear policy. In addition the Germans were keen to have their increasing import-ance within the alliance, and their rehabilitation after the war, finally ratified by a new structure that gave them some say in the possession and control of nuclear weapons. There were two responses to these various demands from the existing nuclear powers, in particular the UK and US. The first was to develop a consultation process about nuclear strategy through a series of committees that led to the establishment of the Nuclear Planning Group in 1966. The second response was a US initiative to estab-lish an alliance nuclear force. This had first been suggested by the Eisenhower administration in 1960 but the incoming Labour gov-ernment had to deal with the proposal made by the Americans in 1963 for the creation of a Multi-Lateral Force (MLF). This was to comprise two elements. The first was a surface fleet of 200 Polaris missiles on twenty-five ships which would be jointly owned, oper-ated and manned by the alliance. The second involved a number of national systems, in particular the UK's V-bombers and later Polaris boats, which would be permanently assigned to NATO. Although these proposals posed controversial questions about command and control, and the political veto over firing the mis-siles, the crucial point was that under the American plan no system could be withdrawn for independent national use. The debate within the alliance over MLF was reaching its height in the autumn of 1964 just as Labour took office.

Britain had been opposed to the concept of the MLF from the start and Labour in opposition had taken a similar view. The reason for these objections can be seen from recently declassified American documents. These papers make it clear that the US realised very quickly they had gone too far at Nassau in giving Britain what amounted in practice to a nuclear force of its own. The MLF was therefore seen as a means of recovering some of the lost ground by incorporating the UK Polaris into a purely alliance deterrent. The brief for President Johnson for his first meeting with Wilson in December 1964 makes the US motives clear in defining one of the aims of the MLF, namely:

> To set a pattern for the management of atomic weapons by collective action rather than by the proliferation of individual national deterrent systems.[6]

The other crucial aim of the MLF was to incorporate Germany firmly into NATO by giving it a role in nuclear affairs and removing any sense that it was being treated as a second-rate member of the alliance. But this had implications for Britain's position as the Americans were well aware. They were determined that the UK was to have 'no special position' and that

> In dealing with the British we must impress upon them that the final scheme must be so arranged that their participation is on a parity with the Germans and other Europeans rather than with the United States.[7]

This new British position was to be achieved through two routes. First, the Polaris force would be fully incorporated into the alliance and could not be withdrawn for any reason. Indeed the submarines might be owned by the alliance, fly a common flag, with the crews wearing a NATO uniform and in the long term other nations might be involved in providing part of the crew. Second, Britain was to contribute to the surface fleet of missile-firing ships on exactly the same basis as Germany and Italy. There was also to be no UK veto over any decision to fire the missiles.[8]

Any such proposals struck at the heart of what the British defence and foreign policy establishment still regarded as the 'special relationship' with the United States and threatened to undermine Britain's position as second only to the US within the alliance. They also spelt the end of the 'independent' deterrent. Labour's opposition to MLF was, therefore, closely bound up with the desire to preserve Britain's status and existing relationships within the alliance. But the new government brought two elements into British thinking. The first was opposition to any real involvement of other NATO countries in nuclear planning. Mulley told the Americans before the election that he did not want any increased participation in US strategic planning:

Rather, he seemed to have in mind some sort of machinery, which he referred to as 'window dressing', that would not in any way dilute the ultimate US control of the US strategic deterrent, but that would provide the appearance of greater alliance consultation.[9]

The second was total hostility to any German control over nuclear weapons, however indirect. The prospect that if the UK failed to agree to the MLF the US might go ahead with the Germans alone provoked Mulley to say that it would

compel the British Labour government to examine the whole question of its commitment to NATO. He also emphatically stated his opposition to any formula that would give the Germans a greater degree of control even after a number of years.[10]

This anti-German stance was another indication of Labour's intention to retain the traditional role of Britain within the alliance and ensure that the Germans did not obtain equality of status. In its vehement opposition to the MLF the Labour government was being both highly conventional and chauvinistic in its views about Britain's status, the preservation of the 'independent' deterrent and the balance of power within NATO.

When Labour took office the United States told them that decisions on the MLF were required rapidly and that Wilson's first meeting with Johnson in December would be crucially important. A variety of Americans were despatched across the Atlantic to bring this message home to the British.[11] British officials were, however, before October, already engaged in devising an alternative to the MLF. A new 'multilateral' scheme, known as the Atlantic Nuclear Force (ANF), was agreed by ministers at a major defence conference held at Chequers on 21–22 November. This proposal removed all the features of the MLF which were objectionable to the British. The ANF would consist of the British V-bomber and Polaris forces together with a matching number of US Polaris submarines and whatever the French wished to contribute. Although nominally allocated to NATO, these forces would remain under national command and could be withdrawn if necessary. The non-nuclear powers were to be allowed to run a mixed-manned force of land-based nuclear missiles and aircraft. Any country that currently owned nuclear weapons would have a veto over changes to the system of control. The ANF was therefore designed to maintain Britain's 'independent' deterrent in exactly its post-Nassau position; it safeguarded Britain's position as the senior NATO partner in Europe, permanently relegated Germany to a subordinate position through participation in the second-rate mixed-manned force (which had no British participation) and maintained a British veto over German nuclear aspirations.

The British proposal also fulfilled two other functions. The first was to exploit the growing differences within the American administration over the MLF. The advocates of MLF were losing ground and Johnson losing whatever enthusiasm he had for the scheme in face of the major practical difficulties inherent in setting up and operating the force. As Denis Healey admitted:

> We devised the ANF as a means of scuppering the MLF. The Ministry of Defence was totally opposed to MLF and the Foreign Office wasn't terribly keen on it, but felt that our relationship with the Americans required that we should put it to sleep quietly, rather than directly oppose it.[12]

The second function of the ANF was to enable Wilson to claim that Labour's election manifesto commitment had been carried out. As he wrote:

> This was our answer to the controversial Nassau Agreement, which we had said we should 'renegotiate'.[13]

In fact of course the Nassau agreement was being reconfirmed, not renegotiated: the ANF proposal provided for exactly the same arrangements for the supply of Polaris and retained British control over the system unchanged. A few multilateral frills were simply stitched on to dress it up.

Wilson's visit to Washington in early December 1964 marked the end of the MLF. British opposition and the ANF proposal enabled the opponents of MLF within the American administration to gain the upper hand. In the middle of the visit there was a meeting of key US advisers with Johnson which agreed to consider the ANF and remit it for a full-scale NATO study. Although the idea of a NATO nuclear force lived on in some quarters in Washington, by the time the NATO bureaucracy had completed its work during 1965 MLF was no longer on the political agenda and died an obscure and largely unlamented death.

The British Polaris programme is often cited as proof of the closeness of US–UK relations and the US desire that the UK should remain an independent nuclear power. Behind the public posture the US administration's attitudes and motives in the mid-1960s belie this picture. In private the US administration remained convinced that the 'independent' British deterrent should not continue and were keen to devise ways of bringing it fully within the NATO framework. A major effort was made with Wilson during his third meeting with Johnson in December 1965. As Bundy told Johnson:

> The essence of our position is to encourage the British in any action which 'lowers the status' of their 'independent' deterrent . . . the further he (Wilson) is willing to move the better for us.[14]

The US proposal was that the UK should assign the four Polaris submarines to NATO 'irrevocably for the life of the alliance' with no right of withdrawal as provided in the Nassau agreement. As a sweetener the US would do the same for four of their submarines. The American aim was clear:

> This could be represented as taking the British out of the possession of a national nuclear deterrent and would be a real breakthrough toward non-proliferation.[15]

Here was a real opportunity for Wilson to implement the ideas he had advocated in opposition only five years earlier, to 'renegotiate' the Nassau agreement with American assistance and commit Polaris to NATO with respectable multilateral cover from the Americans. He chose instead to maintain the 'independent' deterrent as negotiated by the Conservatives. He had little problem in dealing with the US pressure to give up the deterrent because he knew that they were unwilling unilaterally to tear up the Nassau agreement. On this issue he therefore resisted the US pressure and secured the future of an 'independent' Polaris. There was no discussion in Cabinet on whether to accept the US offer.

The government, however, went further than securing the immediate future of Polaris. They decided, in absolute secrecy, to start a new programme. The long-term effectiveness of Polaris could only be secured if it was kept up to date and even before it came into service a small group of ministers was deciding how to modernise it. This group (Wilson, Healey, Brown, Callaghan and Benn) was so secret that it was omitted from the official list of Cabinet committees in order not to alert possible opponents to what was happening. One option they considered was to purchase, in the mid-1970s, the US Poseidon system, a longer-range missile compatible with the Polaris submarines. This was rejected in favour of a British development programme for the warhead of the Polaris missile. One of the main reasons for this decision was the need to find work for the design teams at the Atomic Weapons Research Establishment at Aldermaston, which had completed work on the warhead for Polaris and which, without a new project, might well disintegrate. In February 1967 this small group of ministers agreed to start work on a new triple-warhead system for Polaris together with penetration aids to enable it to defeat possible Russian anti-ballistic missile systems around Moscow. This was to become the Chevaline system, which was eventually deployed in the early 1980s after huge delays and at a cost of £1 billion. Within three years of taking office the Labour government, which had appeared to favour the cancellation of Polaris and the end of the British deterrent, had not only decided to continue with the project but had also resisted US pressure to assign it permanently to NATO and embarked on a costly new modernisation programme to ensure its future until the 1990s.

II. THE AIRCRAFT DECISIONS

Before Ministers could begin to examine the future of British military commitments around the world they were faced with pressing decisions on a number of aircraft projects involving a difficult balance between military requirements, cost considerations, industrial and employment consequences. The particular problem they faced was that the Conservatives had been unwilling to take difficult decisions before the election. This meant that too many projects of doubtful value had been kept going because they generated jobs in key constituencies and kept aircraft firms in business. The whole future of the aircraft industry was also ripe for review. It took up 25% of the government's total expenditure on research and development, yet generated only 2½% of Britain's exports and too many projects had been started that could never be brought to fruition. The projects in question were the TSR-2, a new long-range strike aircraft for the RAF, the P-1154, a replacement for the Hunter and possibly for use on the Navy's aircraft carriers, and the HS-681 transport aircraft.

Decisions were taken on the basis that existing defence commitments would continue and so Ministers looked for different ways of meeting the various requirements rather than questioning whether these roles had to be carried out at all. At the defence policy meeting at Chequers over the weekend of 21–22 November

1964 the drift of the discussion was towards cancellation of all three projects, but the problem was what to put in their place. The government's solution was to plump for a series of major purchases from the United States. One of the main reasons was cost. At the meeting ministers decided that, although the defence budget would not be cut, it would not be allowed to rise above its existing level of about £2 billion a year. Continuation of all three British projects would cost about £1.2 billion, whereas purchase from the US would cost only half that sum. During his visit to Washington in February 1964 Fred Mulley had already hinted that the Labour party would opt for the US purchases but the outline of the deal was devised when Healey accompanied Wilson to the United States in December 1964. Healey agreed with McNamara that there should be what was grandly described as a 'pooling' of research and development effort. In practice this meant that the UK would buy from the US with virtually no reciprocal gestures. Immediately after the Healey visit a team of over twenty officials was despatched to Washington to establish the terms on which the UK would buy US aircraft. American officials were surprised that the 'UK team appeared less interested in production sharing programs than they were in straight procurement from the US'.[16]

In mid-January 1965 the leaders of the aircraft industry were told at a dinner at Chequers with Wilson and Jenkins (Minister of Aviation) that all three projects were likely to go. The fate of two of the three projects was soon determined. Cancellation of the P-1154 and its replacement with a purchase of more US Phantoms (with a British engine to give work to Rolls-Royce) caused no major difficulty. There was a slight flurry in Whitehall over cancellation of the HS-681 and its replacement by the US Hercules when the British manufacturers came up with a last-minute offer to save the project. Jenkins described this offer to the Cabinet on 8 February as 'almost embarrassingly good' in that costs were cut to US levels, although it would still take two years longer to be operational than the Hercules. There was pressure from Cousins and Crossman, MPs for the workers involved, to consider the new offer. But Healey weighed in, saying,

> if we wanted the American package we couldn't go back on it and start thinking about making one British plane which would upset the whole deal.[17]

Purchase of the US aircraft was agreed.

The final question to be resolved was the future of the TSR-2.

Prototypes were already flying but costs were escalating wildly as the industry tried to develop a new airframe, a new engine and new avionics in parallel. Yet it was the centrepiece of the RAF's future force and British industry's attempt to stay in the forefront of modern technology. In addition a large number of jobs were at stake. The fate of the TSR-2 was sealed by two factors. First, its performance was barely adequate for operations in the European theatre against the Warsaw Pact, and second, the minimum purchase of 150 aircraft was estimated to cost £750 million which could not be found within the newly imposed defence budget ceiling. The only alternative was the US F-111 fighter-bomber, more advanced technically than the TSR-2 and about to go into production.

The government put off a decision in the early months of 1965 and kept development work going on the TSR-2 while they considered what to do. The question was whether the Cabinet could be persuaded to go along with the last part of the package deal with the United States. The final decision was taken by the Cabinet during two meetings on 1 April. The first, in the morning, was inconclusive, with Ministers divided into four camps. Callaghan was largely isolated in arguing a predictable Treasury line in favour of cancellation but against purchase of a replacement. Healey wanted to cancel and buy the F-111 immediately. Jenkins and Brown favoured cancelling but replacing the TSR-2 with a cheaper British alternative. Another group, led by Wigg and Crossman, wanted to postpone a decision until after the major review of defence strategy then about to start. When the Cabinet resumed discussion at 10 pm, Healey strongly influenced the outcome by arguing that it was possible to take out an option to purchase the F-111 without this constituting a binding commitment. This united Callaghan, Brown and Jenkins in agreeing to immediate cancellation as long as there was no final commitment to buy American. After two and a half hours the Prime Minister's summing up set out three options: cancel and take up the F-111 option, cancel and postpone taking up the US option or keep the TSR-2 until after the strategic review was completed. Wilson then went round the table and asked each member to commit themselves to one of the options. At the end there was no clear majority, although about ten (the largest single group) favoured keeping the TSR-2 temporarily. Wilson summed up that the other two smaller groups together comprised a majority for cancellation immediately but that the choice of a replacement should be left for OPD to decide. Cancellation was announced in the Budget speech a few days later and within a few months OPD agreed to take up the option to purchase 110 F-111 at a cost of just over £300 million as Healey wanted.[18] After a complex series of negotiations he obtained a firm upper limit on the F-111 price and a credit-financing deal designed to spread the cost to the UK over fifteen years.[19] In addition, as Johnson confirmed in a personal message to Wilson, the United States agreed to buy just over £115 million worth of arms from Britain (some for use in Vietnam) and set a target of £140 million for extra British arms sales to other countries where the Americans would help to secure orders.[20]

The government had, therefore, for financial reasons and under strong pressure from Denis Healey, taken some tough decisions on cutting British projects and reducing the size of the aircraft industry. Having set a limit to defence spending, they did not have the money to keep the industry in the style to which it thought it was entitled. The only alternative was to buy American and in the process increase dependence on the United States. This policy had other hidden costs. Even though the Americans were persuaded to extend generous credit terms, the programme would take up over £700 million in foreign exchange at a time when the balance of payments was under severe pressure.

III. FUTURE STRATEGY

The fundamental question that the Labour government had to decide was the size of Britain's defence effort, what commitments should be retained and what forces were required to carry out those commitments. The last review of British defence policy in 1957 had abolished conscription, placed greater emphasis on nuclear weapons and reduced the size of the RAF and British forces in Germany. A major military presence was retained East of Suez, with key bases at Aden and Singapore and new bases developed in the Indian Ocean. But by the early 1960s it was becoming clear that the expected savings from the 1957 review were not materialising. The size of the RAF was beginning to increase again and expensive new aircraft projects had been started. There was also a major re-equipment programme under-way for the army in Germany. At the same time new problems were emerging East of Suez. Aden was increasingly difficult to defend against a growing rebel movement seeking independence and, more importantly, the threat fron Indonesia to newly inde-pendent Malaysia required the commitment of a major contingent of British forces during the period of 'confrontation'. Defence spending was rising steadily; it went up by 8% in real terms between 1957 and 1963. The underlying problem was that the forces available were not large enough to carry out all their existing responsibilities around the world. The Conservative government had responded, not by cutting responsibilities, but by trying to carry out the commitments at lower cost. But this policy could not be continued indefinitely without it becoming apparent that the resources available did not match the tasks they had to carry out. A fundamental reappraisal was required.

What assumptions did the key Ministers, particularly Wilson, bring to these problems? The most basic was that Britain was still a world power and should remain so. As Wilson told the Commons in December 1964:

> Whatever we may do in the field of cost effectiveness, value for money and a stringent review of expenditure, we cannot afford to relinquish our world role.[21]

The incompatible decisions to contain defence spending at £2 billion a year and maintain a worldwide presence raised acute problems of the relative priority to be accorded the commitments under NATO to station forces in Germany and the East of Suez role. There is no doubt that Wilson personally put greater weight on the Far East than Europe. As he told one journalist just after the 1964 election; 'Of course, I've always been an East of Suez man.'[22] Fred Mulley had the same message for the Americans earlier in the year when he was sounding out US views on the importance of BAOR compared with East of Suez:

> He [Mulley] made it clear that Mr Wilson and
> Mr Gordon-Walker were really committed to the latter.[23]

The Americans said they wanted Britain to maintain both roles but that, if forced to choose, East of Suez was more important. Wilson told McNamara a month later that

> Britain must at all costs ensure that both India and Malaysia were defended militarily and economically – the fall of either would mean the end of British influence in the area.[24]

Wilson seems to have regarded the defence of India (against China) as particularly important, even though India showed little sign of wanting British protection. He spoke of Britain's frontiers being on the Himalayas and in a private speech to the PLP in June 1966, which he does not quote in his memoirs, said:

> Does anyone think India wants us to leave her to become a cockpit, forced to choose between Russia and America to protect her from China? . . . Perhaps there are some members who would like to contract out and leave it to the Americans and the Chinese, eyeball to eyeball, to face this thing out . . . It is the surest prescription for a nuclear holocaust I could think of.[25]

The review of defence policy lasted from the spring of 1965 until February 1966. The Cabinet discussed the outcome only once, days before the White Paper was published. All the ministerial decisions were taken in OPD, which had ninteen meetings on the subject, including two weekend sessions at Chequers. The problem was clear. Having decided to put a ceiling of £2 billion a year on defence spending, some parts of the planned programme would have to be abandoned. There were two ways of achieving this objective. The first was to rethink Britain's commitments and withdraw from some areas. This would help to bring the limited forces available more into line with the responsibilities they had to carry out. The second course was not to reduce commitments but instead reduce the quantity and quality of the forces available. This was the policy adopted by previous governments, keeping up the façade of world power on an ever thinner shoestring.

The strong inclination of key ministers to maintain the East of Suez role meant that they had to look at the possibility of withdrawing forces from Germany. However, this proved to be too difficult because of Britain's obligations under both the Brussels and NATO treaties. Reluctantly they were forced to turn their attention to East of Suez. But here too there were problems. The first was operational: the continuing 'confrontation' with Indonesia in Borneo, although declining in intensity, still required a major commitment of troops. The second was political and economic, linked to the relationship with the United States. As we have seen in Chapter 3 the Americans were determined to keep British forces in the Far East, in particular at Singapore. And the deal that Wilson did with the Americans in September 1965 in return for support of the pound, by ruling out any cuts in the Far East, left no alternative but to adopt a piecemeal approach and take odd savings where they could be found in an attempt to maintain the existing defence policy but at less cost. The only commitment to go was Aden by 1968, where the sheer difficulty of maintaining a base against determined local opposition was too great. Elsewhere the Territorial Army was drastically reduced in size and the existing levels of British forces in Germany became a ceiling, although the major re-equipment programme went ahead. But these measures were not enough to bring planned defence spending within the agreed total and attention was concentrated on whether it was possible to keep the East of Suez commitment but carry it out much more cheaply.

OPD was forced to focus on the highly sensitive issue of the roles of the Royal Navy and the Royal Air Force in the Far East. This involved not just difficult strategic and tactical assessments but also fundamental questions about the future of the two services involved, which had long been engaged in bitter rivalry. The RAF case was for a force of F-111s operating from bases in the Indian Ocean to provide a long-range bombing and reconnaissance capability. The RN argued for a force of three aircraft carriers (only one could be East of Suez at any time) operating forty aircraft. From April 1965 until the autumn an extensive internal study was carried out within the Ministry of Defence on the relative merits of the two proposals. The results showed conclusively that land-based F-111s could carry out every role (except protection of an opposed invasion which wasn't envisaged anyway) more cost-effectively than aircraft carriers. The full buy of F-111s would amount to about £300 million whereas three carriers and their aircraft would cost about £1.4 billion – a sum which could not be found from within the defence budget limits. The other problem was that even if the carriers were bought, some F-111s were required as well. Fierce arguments raged within the Ministry of Defence but the RN, tactically maladroit as usual, refused any form of compromise and simply insisted that the government would have to increase the defence budget to accommodate their carriers. Healey recommended to his colleagues on OPD that the order for the new aircraft carriers should not go ahead. He refused to allow his navy minister, Christopher Mayhew, to put the navy's case to OPD as it had already been rejected by the rest of the Ministry of Defence. When the Cabinet agreed Healey's recommendations on 14 February 1966 there was no debate over the decision. Mayhew, who had been a junior minister under Attlee and resented working under Healey whom he regarded as his junior, resigned in protest at the decision. He was joined by the Chief of the Naval Staff. Their action had no impact.

Long before the Cabinet came to discuss the outcome of the defence review there were extensive consultations with the Americans, at the highest level. In the summer of 1965 Wilson had given a commitment to Johnson that nothing would be published before the Americans had had the opportunity to influence the decisions.[26] He gave the first outlines of the conclusions of the review to Johnson during his visit to Washington in December 1965. This was followed up by a trip to Washington by Healey and Stewart in January 1966 to discuss the review in detail. Although relatively relaxed about the pull-out from Aden, the Americans were worried about whether the review did not imply a cut-back in the East of Suez role once defence of Malaysia against Indonesia ended. Nevertheless, the Americans decided that they could live with the outcome of the review and that Wilson had not gone back on his pledges given in September 1965.

The White Paper published in February 1966 emphasised Britain's role as a world power and the importance of staying East of Suez (given the commitments made to the Americans, this is hardly surprising):

> It is in the Far East and Southern Asia that the greatest danger to peace may lie in the next decade, and some of our partners in the Commonwealth may be directly threatened. We believe that it is right that Britain should continue to maintain a military presence in this area.

The goal was summed up by Healey earlier in the month: 'We do intend to remain in a military sense a world power.'[27]

Although in the 1966 Defence Review the government had, like its predecessors, shied away from the difficulties of renegotiating the level of British forces in Germany they were determined to try and reduce the cost of keeping them there. In 1966 the cost in foreign exchange was about £95 million, half of which was met by Germany either by direct payments or through purchases of British military equipment. Britain decided to ask for American help in increasing the pressure on Germany to pay more. When the topic was discussed in January 1966 during consultations on the defence review, the American response was unhelpful:

> the Germans have made it clear that if we pressed them to buy more military equipment from the UK they would buy less from us. We should avoid agreeing to encourage a deliberate shift of German military procurement from the US to the UK.[28]

No further action was taken at that time because of the disruption to NATO caused by de Gaulle's decision to withdraw from the integrated military structure. However, after the July 1966 crisis the British made it clear to both the US and Germany that a new agreement on the costs of British forces in Germany was required by the end of the year. If the Germans refused to pay the full costs they threatened to withdraw troops until the costs matched what the Germans were prepared to pay.

This attitude caused considerable concern in Washington. The Americans were worried that any unilateral British action might start the unravelling of NATO commitments, particularly after the French action. They were also worried that withdrawals might call into question UK entry to the EEC, which they were keen to encourage. On 26 August Johnson sent Wilson a personal message asking him to take no action until the Americans had had time to set up talks between the countries involved.[29] Wilson agreed and by 6 October Johnson had secured German agreement too.[30] Johnson was determined to keep Britain in Germany and East of Suez. As he told Wilson in another personal message on 15 November:

> Your presence in Germany is as important to us as your presence in the East.[31]

When Brown visited Washington in the middle of October he stuck to the line that an agreement had to be reached by the end of November so that the British could decide what action to take by the end of the year.[32]

The three countries agreed to set up a series of ministerial talks, which began in November. The Americans decided to exploit the British demands to attain some of their own objectives. On 15 November Johnson offered Wilson a deal. In return for the US purchasing £12 million worth of British military equipment Britain was not to take any unilateral action in Germany until these tripartite talks ended and even then they were to consult further before making any decisions. It was also implied that the UK was to make no withdrawals from the Far East whilst the discussions continued.[33] As Rostow told Johnson, the whole package 'would further nail Wilson east of Suez'.[34] Wilson immediately queried whether the £12 million was additional to US purchases under the existing F-111 deal. Johnson confirmed that it was and sent Rostow to Britain to work out the details.[35] OPD accepted the deal and the American money on 2 December.[36]

Final agreement in the trilateral talks was reached in June 1967. It illustrated just how limited the room for manoeuvre was in making defence cuts in Europe. The UK would withdraw one army brigade and two RAF squadrons from Germany in 1968. In return German payments to the UK were increased (though not to the amount Britain wanted) and the Americans agreed to buy a further £7 million worth of military equipment in Britain. The Germans also gave the Americans a series of promises on international financial policy.[37] But a token withdrawal of forces and some additional compensation for keeping forces in Germany could only add to the pressure for more cuts in the Far East, despite the American objections.

The January 1966 White Paper on defence policy, which attempted to continue the existing policy of worldwide commitments with even less resources, could not form the basis for a coherent, long-term policy. What it had done was to provide the illusion of a review before the March 1966 election. However the secret commitments given to the Americans precluded any immediate public change of policy. Nevertheless the ministers involved recognised by the summer of 1966 that a further review was necessary and Healey obtained Wilson's agreement to carry out an internal Ministry of Defence assessment of the different options available.

Healey first presented his conclusions to an inner group of seven senior colleagues, not OPD, at Chequers on 22 October. He suggested continuing to cut costs in all areas but with no withdrawal from any commitments. He admitted that the more logical policy would be to withdraw from the Far East, but recognised that American opposition ruled out such a decision. George Brown was too drunk to make any serious contribution and Healey's proposals were generally endorsed. On 9 December OPD discussed a formal paper from Healey and Stewart embodying the conclusions of the Chequers meeting. It recommended cuts in all areas and a study of total withdrawal from the Middle East. It was only on the insistence of Callaghan and Crossman that a similar study on withdrawal from the Far East was also included. A group of officials, chaired by Burke Trend, was assigned the preliminary work.

The annual Defence White Paper which was published in February 1967 deliberately concealed the work going on within Whitehall and simply announced that forces in the Far East would be reduced by April 1968 to the level prevailing before the 'confrontation' with Indonesia with a saving of about £50 million. After rejecting the US proposal in early 1967 for a long-term multi-billion-dollar loan to ensure the future of the pound in return for the UK staying in the Far East, Wilson regarded himself as free from the commitments he had made in September 1965. His policy now shifted towards withdrawal from the Far East so as to reduce overseas expenditure and ease pressure on the balance of payments as another way of avoiding devaluation. The report produced by officials reflected this new approach. It suggested withdrawal from the mainland of South-East Asia (Malaysia and Singapore) but not until 1975. The withdrawal would save about £100 million a year in foreign exchange together with about 75,000 service personnel and 50,000 civilians. However the overall result of the review was an odd mixture of cuts and increases. The F-111s were to operate from bases in the Indian Ocean, a strategic reserve was to be maintained in the UK, a naval base developed in Australia and forces in the Gulf area doubled, operating from a base at Sharjah.

The Cabinet had a preliminary discussion on the report on 11 April 1967. Although half a dozen members were opposed to any withdrawal, a large number were worried that the proposals did not go far enough. They were unhappy about Brown's suggestion that he should go to the Far East for consultations but without putting forward any clear British policy proposals, no doubt fearing he would be too ready to listen to local objections. There were also complaints about the long period set for withdrawal, the amount of aid that was to be given after withdrawal and the minimal savings before 1970. Eventually Wilson had to concede that Brown was to do nothing that would prejudice the possibility of more radical decisions when the Cabinet discussed final options later in the year.

Brown met the expected opposition in the Far East, particularly from Lee Kuan Yew of Singapore, who spoke of a complete loss of confidence in the area. He ran into more trouble when he visited Washington for discussions with Dean Rusk, who told him that the United States

> would be seriously concerned if there were significant withdrawals of effective strength while the Viet-Nam war continued.[38]

Rusk asked for discussions with Australia and New Zealand because the US was not able to replace British forces. He also suggested that even if the decision was made there was no need to announce a date for final withdrawal at this stage.

The Cabinet discussed the situation on 30 May before Wilson's visit to Washington. Healey was strongly opposed to Brown's idea of developing a base in Australia, but it was agreed that Wilson would have to offer something to the Americans to try and sugar the pill of ultimate withdrawal. Although no decisions were taken the consensus was that some residual 'presence' would have to remain after 1975. This was the suggestion put by Wilson to Johnson during his visit at the beginning of June. He still received a stormy reception, as US documents reveal:

> President Johnson . . . took a very strong line against the impending British decision.[39]

But this time the Americans found that Wilson was not prepared to give in to pressure and they recognised that the decision was effectively taken.

Pressure on the British government not to announce the change of policy continued, however. Harold Holt, the Australian Prime Minister, visited Washington and London in June, and Lee Kuan Yew also visited London in early July. Before the final Cabinet meeting the Americans made one last effort to stop the withdrawal. Rusk wrote to Brown and Johnson sent a personal message to Wilson. They both expressed their 'deep concern' about any reductions and urged very strongly that 'this is not the time to rock the boat in any way'.[40] These representations had no effect and the Cabinet agreed on 6 July to a withdrawal by the mid-1970s. Only six members supported Crossman's plea for an early withdrawal by 1970.

In many ways the 1967 review, like its predecessors, tried to avoid any fundamental decisions about Britain's strategic role. The East of Suez role was still there, both in the Gulf and the Indian Ocean. The only commitment abandoned was the stationing of large-scale forces in the Far East and that not for another eight years. Nevertheless, despite the lack of clear decisions, an important milestone, principally psychological, had been passed. A date had been set for withdrawal from East of Suez. That this was a crucial departure was appreciated by the Americans, who had been unable to stop the change of policy. The deal that had been struck in September 1965 to stay in the Far East in return for support for the pound was ended. The government could not find the money to sustain the world role and US pressure could not overcome this fact. However, as late as December 1966 the inner group of ministers seems to have favoured thinning out all round and cutting back in the Middle East rather than the Far East, even though this made little strategic sense. The crucial event seems to have been the US offer, made early in 1967, for a multi-billion-dollar loan to support the pound in return for Britain staying in the Far East. This would have been a public arrangement, unlike the 1965 deal, and it was rejected by Wilson and Callaghan, almost certainly because it was unsaleable to the Cabinet and the Labour party. Once this deal had been rejected Wilson regarded himself as released from the 1965 agreement. If US assistance was only available on unacceptable terms then it was time to develop an alternative policy. Withdrawal from the Far East would help save foreign exchange and aid the balance of payments and therefore the pound. Wilson and Callaghan felt this might be enough to avoid devaluation and see the government through to the next election. Believing that they had identified a viable alternative the inner group of ministers felt they could now afford to resist American pressure and fall into line with the views of the majority of their colleagues in the Cabinet, who clearly favoured withdrawal. The July 1967 review was meant to be a long-term statement of strategic policy but it was to last only seven months before it had to be torn up in the post-devaluation crisis cuts of January 1968.

6
Economic Planning?

Labour's election manifesto featured economic planning as a cure for Britain's ailing economy. A new Department of Economic Affairs (DEA) would reduce what was seen as the negative role of the Treasury. A National Plan would provide the basis for increased growth, efficient use of Britain's resources and effective regional policies. These proposals were not revolutionary because the economic and political climate of the mid-1960s was favourable to the idea of 'planning'. The Labour party had always had an addiction to the concept as an economic solution; a belief that it must in some way be more efficient than laissez-faire capitalism. However, it had never expended much time or effort in working out schemes for implementing the idea. Indeed in 1945 the previous Labour administration had set about dismantling the impressive collection of wartime physical controls over the economy. One of the main advocates of what he described as a 'bonfire of controls' was the then President of the Board of Trade, Harold Wilson. The abolition process was completed under the Conservatives after 1951, although the government still accepted an obligation to manage the economy and maintain full employment. The methods employed in the next decade were essentially indirect. Instead of physical controls the government relied mainly on fiscal regulation: adjusting hire purchase terms or the level of investment allowances and influencing overall demand through changes in direct and indirect taxation. There was no industrial policy of the type found in Japan, no long-term planning as in France. Instead it was assumed that if the government achieved the right overall level of demand in the economy then industry would very largely be able to look after itself.

By the late 1950s doubts were beginning to arise about the effectiveness of this form of economic management. The British economy was under increasing pressure from abroad and its relative decline compared with the faster growing economies of Germany and France, and the rest of western Europe, was becoming more and more apparent. The vulnerability of sterling, particularly after it was made fully convertible in 1958, gave the government less room for manoeuvre; 'stop-go' economic policies tied not just to the defence of sterling but also to the political imperatives of the electoral cycle were clearly damaging the performance of key sectors of the economy. Industrial productivity was not rising as fast as that of Britain's competitors, raising further questions about the role of the trade unions, already under attack in a period of increasing real wages and growing inflation. Some form of wage and price control was, many argued, the appropriate response to these problems.

Britain was increasingly seen, to quote the title of a book popular at the time, as a 'Stagnant Society' falling behind its competitors but still capable, if a great effort was made, of recovering lost ground and regaining its place as a major industrial power. This mood increasingly permeated the political and administrative establishment. Opinion polls detected the same shift in public opinion. In 1956 only 15% thought that there should be more government planning and control of industry. By 1961 this had risen to 45% in favour and 'planning' had become not only fashionable but acceptable. It was typical of the inadequacies of the British political and administrative system that very little thought was given to the mechanisms by which planning would actually be achieved. There was much talk of 'indicative planning' on the French model of the 'Commissariat du Plan' but no attempt to develop a coherent and comprehensive system in Britain. Instead there emerged a series of *ad hoc* schemes never clearly worked out or integrated, and most relied in the end on little more than a mixture of exhortation and wishful thinking.

The key date in the move towards a greater emphasis on 'planning' came not with the advent of the Labour government in 1964 but two years earlier. The Conservative government had been moving towards a tripartite body comprising government, industry and the trade unions as a mechanism for discussing, and hopefully agreeing, a national economic assessment that might, in some nebulous way, help to improve economic performance and reduce wage and price rises. The National Economic Development Council (NEDC) had been set up in 1962 as a forum to bring together the three groups. Its exact functions were never clear except that it definitely had no power to implement anything. Whitehall was determined to keep total control over economic policy. What NEDC could do was first create committees at industry level, again with no powers (the 'little Neddies'), and second produce studies. In February 1963 it published 'Growth of the United Kingdom Economy 1961–6'. This first study exhibited all the weaknesses of later work in that it proceeded on the assumption that higher growth could best be achieved by 'talking up' expectations so that through some undefined process this sense of optimism filtered through to basic decisions about productivity and output. The report looked at the implications of a 4%-a-year growth rate in the economy, compared with the Treasury's assumption of 3% and experience over the previous five years of 2.7%. Similarly exports were assumed to grow at 5% a year compared with the 3% actually experienced. All of this required a growth in productivity of 3.2% a year, well above current rates. The report provoked a great deal of debate but no effective action. It proved of great significance for the Labour government as its targets were to form a baseline against which Labour proposals would be measured; the Labour government felt obliged, particularly in political terms, to go for an even more optimistic assessment.

The creation of the DEA had a respectable intellectual background. Many people, not only in the Labour party, had criticised the 'dead hand' of the Treasury over national economic policy. The Treasury, it was argued, put too great an emphasis on the balance of payments, the defence of sterling, maintenance of 'sound money' and restraint of public expenditure at the expense of the real economy where a more positive attitude was required. Harold Wilson had been in favour of removing economic planning from the Treasury as long ago as July 1952 and a year before gaining office he committed a new Labour government to the creation of a new ministry to undertake physical planning while the Treasury concentrated on financial and monetary policy. The other less respectable reason for setting up the DEA was, as we have seen, Wilson's own political problems of how to accommodate his two political rivals in the government, when he wouldn't give Brown the Foreign Office because he wanted it and Callaghan, as Shadow Chancellor, wouldn't give up his role. The DEA offered a neat solution to this particular difficulty.

However, reducing the role of the Treasury, the most powerful ministry, would not be easy and the mandarins in Whitehall, where both the head of the Civil Service and the Cabinet Secretary were Treasury men, could be expected to try and ensure that the traditional primacy of the Treasury in policy making was not radically diminished. In opposition Labour did not seriously prepare themselves to take on Whitehall, partly no doubt because it was only likely to spark a fierce battle between Callaghan and Brown over the exact division of their responsibilities. Wilson did have a pre-election dinner with the Head of the Civil Service, Sir Lawrence Helsby, to discuss the changes Labour would want to make in Whitehall organisation generally but no specifics were discussed and it was left to the Civil Service to draw up plans for the new DEA.

They decided that it would consist of the national economy group in the Treasury and parts of NEDC together with the regional policy divisions of the Board of Trade. George Brown was allowed to select his permanent secretary and chose Sir Eric Roll, the Treasury representative in Washington. The Civil Service nominated as his deputy Sir Douglas Allen from the Treasury and Brown's private secretary also came from the Chancellor of the Exchequer's office. Altogether, therefore, there was a very strong element of Treasury thinking in a ministry that was supposed to provide a whole new approach to economic policy making. The problems facing the DEA in establishing itself as a new venture in Whitehall were even apparent at the practical level. Its first few months were a nightmare of administrative chaos. At the beginning it had just one chair, used by George Brown, while the rest sat on the floor. There were no typewriters and no notepaper. Brown only received a copy of the economic brief for new ministers because his private secretary purloined a copy before he left the Chancellor of the Exchequer's office.

The division of responsibilities suggested by the Civil Service was that the Treasury should concentrate on short-term planning and DEA on the long term. This was discussed by Wilson, Brown and Callaghan on the Saturday morning after the election (it was the same meeting that ruled out devaluation). Adopting a different but equally vague formula, they decided that it was better to define the Treasury as dealing with monetary and fiscal policy and the DEA with real resources. For the next month attempts were made to draw up a 'concordat' that would spell out in specific terms the exact division of responsibilities between the two ministries. No agreement was ever reached: the DEA was left with its role loosely described as 'coordinating responsibility for industry and everything to do with the mobilisation of real resources for productivity and exports'.

To have 'coordinating responsibility' in Whitehall is to have no real power at all. The DEA lacked not only a clear purpose but powers of action. The established Whitehall ministries made sure that they kept all their key functions. The Treasury retained not just financial and monetary policy but also public expenditure – one area where the government has power to affect the real world.

The Board of Trade retained control over investment grants, a key part of regional policy, and the Ministry of Technology assumed control of the government's research and development spending. Similarly the Ministry of Housing and Local Government continued to operate the established system of physical planning controls. The DEA also failed in its bid to take over responsibility for providing economic statistics from the Cabinet Office because the Cabinet Secretary, Sir Burke Trend, argued that the Central Statistical Office had to retain its 'neutral' status within Whitehall.

The solitary area where DEA was in the lead was prices and incomes policy. It was largely through George Brown's personal efforts that he was able to construct the outlines of a voluntary agreement in the Joint Statement of Intent of April 1965. But these were fine words rather than concrete methods for controlling either prices or incomes and, as we have seen, the government was increasingly driven along the road to a statutory policy. In terms of Whitehall politics the venture was a welcome diversion. The Treasury was quite happy to see Brown and the DEA putting a great deal of their energies into this field, which supported their general strategy anyway, rather than devoting their time to criticising the Treasury's economic policy – one of the main aims behind the creation of the DEA.

These difficulties were exacerbated by the constant battles with the Treasury, the bad personal relations between Callaghan and Brown and Wilson's own interest in dividing the two main candidates to succeed him. Although in public the battles were portrayed as 'creative tension' that would somehow produce a better economic policy, in practice the outcome was usually more squalid and a great deal of time was spent on long and often fruitless rows between the two departments. Wilson watched the battle and made his own contribution, as the Head of the Treasury, Sir William Armstrong, described:

> Harold was unmerciful in his divide-and-rule. If he got some story about Jim from George, he would tax Jim with it. If he got some story about George he would say: 'We don't need to bother George yet. Perhaps you could ask him to look in after dinner.' It was meant to sound an innocent remark, but he knew that George would be incoherent by then.[1]

The July 1966 deflationary package finally confirmed that the Treasury's dominance over economic policy was to remain. The DEA went into decline when Brown left in August 1966 (despite

Wilson's brief period in charge) but continued as a separate ministry, concentrating mainly on prices and incomes policy. Even as late as November 1968 Wilson described it as 'a permanent, continuing and essential part of the machinery of modern government'. Less than a year later he abolished it. The high hopes of four years earlier had faded away. Why? The roots of the problem lie in two fundamental flaws in Wilson's method of seeking to loosen the Treasury's grip on economic policy. He never resolved the issue of the exact demarcation of functions between the Treasury and the DEA, nor did he face up to the question of whether the DEA had the necessary powers to carry out its grandiose theoretical remit. Given these problems it is not surprising that it failed.

The DEA did, however, produce the first and, so far, only National Plan, which proved a considerable presentational success for the government. It was sold in public relations terms as the keystone of Labour's new approach to the economy and when published in September 1965 it began with a fanfare:

The publication by the Government of the plan covering all aspects of the country's economic development for the next five years is a major advance in economic policy-making in the United Kingdom. Prepared in the fullest consultation with industry, the plan for the first time represents a statement of Government policy and a commitment to action by the Government.

The specific aims of the plan were equally grandiose:

The plan is designed to achieve a 25% increase in national output between 1964 and 1970. This objective has been chosen in the light of past trends in national output and output per head and a realistic view of the scope for improving upon these trends. It involves achieving a 4% annual growth of output well before 1970 and an annual average of 3.8% between 1964 and 1970.[2]

There was a so-called checklist of thirty-nine actions to achieve the aims. Some of these actions were defined closely (a ceiling on public expenditure growth of 4.25% a year); some were vague (more management training and education, and an industry by industry search for more exports); some required real action (cuts in overseas defence expenditure) whilst others were purely permissive (accelerate standardisation of output through the 'little Neddies'). The plan's targets were even more ambitious than the

1963 NEDC report. Labour force productivity was to rise by 3.4% a year and exports were now expected to increase in volume by 5.25% a year (nearly double the rate achieved in the past) at a time when UK competitiveness on world markets was falling because of the overvalued pound and when the government had ruled out devaluation.

The weakness of the plan lies to a large extent in the way in which it was compiled. In this case the idea came up against not the bureaucratic resistance of Whitehall but the overriding political imperative to have a plan in place before the next election. The struggling DEA had to have something to launch by the autumn of 1965 and, as the centrepiece of Labour's new approach to the economy, the document had to be not only optimistic but more so than the existing Conservative plans. Instead of working out what was possible for the economy the starting point was the assumption that 25% growth was possible by 1970 (no alternatives were considered) and then the DEA attempted to find some figures to support this conclusion. The consultations with industry were no more than a cursory check to ensure that the 25% assumption was at least plausible. There was no attempt to work out a detailed year-by-year path to the 1970 target and indeed the completely inadequate statistical base available to the government would have made any such effort impossible. The figure for growth in public expenditure at 4.25% represented the lowest acceptable point above the 4% featured in the plans inherited from the Conservatives. The Treasury refused to have any forecasts of prices included because they argued (as they have always argued inside Whitehall) such prophecies would become self-fulfilling.

The targets may have been hopelessly unrealistic but the crucial weakness in the whole document was the absence of any mechanism for implementation. As with the DEA there was a marked absence of advance planning, even for a National Plan. Like the earlier NEDC report it was no more than an attempt to talk up the growth rate without any clear idea as to how structural problems were to be overcome or indeed even how to ensure that every department in Whitehall gave overriding priority to the aims of the Plan. Yet the key to success was bound to lie in an effective method for ensuring follow-up action. Without this it would inevitably become no more than yet another report gathering dust in the filing cabinets of Whitehall. The checklist of actions that were supposed to help implement the plan were a peculiar mixture because they had been compiled from a trawl round Whitehall departments. As a senior figure in the Treasury, Sir Leo Pliatzky, confirmed, various Departments tabled statements of what they were doing and would in any case have been doing in their respective fields, which now became contributions to the National Plan.[3]

The plan's shortcomings were apparent when the Cabinet discussed the first four chapters early in August 1965. Barbara Castle rightly complained that as professional planning the document was hopeless and Tony Crosland pointed out that the plan still seemed to talk about a 4% increase in production when only a week before the government had introduced a deflationary package which would almost certainly ensure that this growth rate would never be achieved.[4] These gloomy prognostications were confirmed a month later, only ten days before the launch of the plan, by its author. George Brown told the Cabinet on 12 September that he could only foresee a 1% growth in production over the next year, unemployment would rise to 450,000 and that there was 'no evidence' of modernisation or investment in industry. But as always the political imperative was paramount. The National Plan was to be a fundamental part of the government's re-election strategy, as Brown told the Cabinet (although the irony of what he was saying may have escaped both him and his audience):

it was a national and not a party plan and we wanted to destroy the Tories by keeping it strictly national.[5]

It had taken a year to construct but it lasted as a theoretical planning document for only ten months. It was consigned to the dustbin after the July 1966 measures when overriding priority was given to defence of the pound and a deflationary package that made the targets unattainable. Afterwards there was little serious attempt to resurrect the concept. Although a committee of permanent secretaries was still working on a national economic assessment as late as August 1967, this was never published and that work, too, was lost in the aftermath of devaluation in November 1967.

Another aspect of 'planning' emphasised by the incoming government was the creation of regional plans. This in itself was nothing new, as plans for Scotland, the North-East and the South-East had been produced by the Conservatives before the election, and four of those published by Labour in 1965 had been started before the inception of the DEA. Labour's manifesto commitment, however, was to go further than this and to set up Regional Economic Planning Councils. Here again the crucial point was what powers were they to be given. According to the National Plan these new Councils were to produce 'firm regional plans for the consideration of ministers'. And this they duly did. Large studies were written full of facts about regional economies but containing very little about how the economies really worked or their linkages with the rest of the country. The basic weakness of these councils was that they had no power to do anything. As the wording of the National Plan implied, Whitehall refused to give up any form of control. The function of the Councils was purely advisory and most of their advice was ignored. As one of the Ministers involved commented, their powers were 'inadequate and meaningless'. Beneath the Councils were Regional Economic Planning Boards composed of representatives of central government departments working in the regions. But again they had no power to spend money and their role was strictly one of advice and coordination. In practice, therefore, the whole elaborate structure of 'regional planning' was little more than a public relations façade designed to divert attention from the fact that all effective decisions were still being taken in Whitehall in exactly the same way as before.

Although the supposed system of regional planning contributed very little, the Labour government did supplement it with other more practical initiatives. Again this in itself was nothing new. The first regional policies had been started in the 1930s and the Attlee government placed considerable emphasis on this area. Although the system fell into decline in the 1950s the recession at the end of the decade brought the question of how to ameliorate conditions in the less favoured regions back onto the political agenda. The 1960 and 1963 Local Employment Acts established the idea of Development Districts (defined as those where unemployment was over 4½%) where loans and grants from the Board of Trade were available together with tax concessions for investment. Factories were built in advance of specific demand and let at below market levels. In total about 15% of the workforce in 1964 was covered by the schemes. The Labour government was to build on this existing structure.

The 1966 Industrial Development Act thought up a new name for Development Districts – Development Areas – and increased the coverage to about 20% of the working population, though mainly in rural areas in Wales and Scotland. Tax allowances were replaced by grants on the theory that this would extend coverage to include firms which were not making a profit. In 1967 a Regional Employment Premium was introduced, aimed for the first time at increasing employment in depressed areas, whereas the existing schemes tended to favour capital-intensive projects. Set at £1.50 a man per week and guaranteed for seven years this subsidised all manufacturing industry (though not services) in Development Areas. The subsidy, worth about 7% of labour costs, probably reduced a firm's total costs by about 5%, so although useful it was hardly a massive subsidy. The Labour government also continued the scheme of Industrial Development Certificates designed to control the location of new industrial enterprises. Although the scheme did have an impact in the deferral and even abandonment of plans for new factories in already congested areas, it had little impact in moving projects into the development areas. Similarly the introduction of Office Development Permits in London in November 1964, extended to the west Midlands and the South-East by July 1966, reduced office developments in the pipeline by over 60% by 1970 but again had little or no impact in moving offices into the development areas. The government itself adopted a new policy in 1965 that any new government organisation should be established outside London and in 1967 decided to give preference to development areas. A few government departments were also moved out of London; the Royal Mint, for example, went to South Wales.

Although there were sound economic and social reasons for regional assistance, there were also strong political motives. Designation of constituencies as falling within development areas carried substantial political overtones, as was demonstrated in 1969 when the government considered the Hunt report. This examined how to help the so-called 'grey areas' – those that did not qualify for either development area status or the new Special Development Area status introduced in 1967 to provide even higher levels of assistance.

The Strategic Economic Policy Committee (SEP) considered the grey areas report in April 1969. The committee was chaired by Harold Wilson (whose constituency was Huyton, near Liverpool) and their first action was to reject a recommendation of the Hunt report that Merseyside should lose its development area status. Wilson made the purpose of the exercise clear: 'This was a highly political subject, elections were coming up and we must look at this with open political eyes.' Two members of the Committee, Dick Crossman and Dick Marsh, tried to argue that there should be more aid throughout the country, not on economic grounds but because there were many marginal constituencies outside the development areas. (They represented Coventry and Greenwich respectively, both outside development areas.) This idea found no favour at all, as Crossman reported:

> We were pushed aside because according to our colleagues so many promises have been made in Blackburn or Humberside, in Yorkshire, in Derbyshire and Plymouth that all kinds of expectations have been built up.

SEP then turned to the details:

> we got on with the pork barrel, sorting it out and sweating it round . . . Part of the solution was a decision to build the Humber bridge ten years earlier than the traffic requirements justify. This was something Barbara and I promised in order to win the Hull by-election in March 1966 and, ironically, the money was found by deducting it from the Development Areas.

So the areas in greatest need were to be deprived of money in order to try and buy votes elsewhere. This piece of sophisticated economic planning disintegrated when the subject came to full Cabinet for approval. Tony Crosland announced that the so-called 'redistribution' formula would not work in practice. By now it was too late and too difficult to start again, and so the Cabinet decided to go ahead anyway and think later where the money would be found. As Dick Crossman described:

> We were left with the appalling job of patching up a statement from Peter Shore so he could say that the whole cost of the new help to the grey areas would be financed out of the existing funds being spent on regional development but not exactly how.[6]

One other regional policy in the 1964 manifesto which was implemented was the creation of the Welsh Office. There had been growing parliamentary and public pressure for this since the 1930s, and when by the late 1950s seventeen Whitehall departments had separate administrative units in the principality the case for reform was strong and its political attractions in Wales obvious. The new department was established in October 1964. Yet Whitehall's resistance to change, particularly when it involves handing over responsibility, again made itself felt. By November it had been agreed that the Welsh Office would start by taking over responsibility for trunk roads and the functions of the Ministry of Housing and Local Government but would merely have oversight of the policies of other departments within Wales. The direct functions of the Welsh Office were only extended slowly and after long and difficult negotiations. Perhaps its main achievement in this period was the 1967 Welsh Language Act that granted 'equal validity' to the declining Welsh language and helped to start its slow revival.

How far was the government able to bring to fruition its ideas on planning? Although the National Plan was a feeble and ill-thought-out attempt at economic planning, it is worth examining how detached from reality its projections were and how far government economic policy diverged from the plan through its emphasis on the defence of sterling and creating a balance of payments surplus. The table below compares the forecasts in the plan with actual performance over the period 1964–70.

	National Plan	*Actual*
Economic Growth	+25%	+14%
Personal Consumption	+21%	+13%
Public Expenditure	+27%	+11%
Gross Investment	+38%	+20%

In addition the National Plan forecast an improvement in the balance of payments from a deficit of £721 million in 1964 to a surplus of £250 million in 1970 whereas a surplus of £622 million was actually achieved (all at 1964 prices). This shows the extent of the shift of resources made by the government into overcorrecting the external balance and, since at the same time unemployment over the period rose from 1.6% to 2.5%, these resources could have been diverted into improving the growth rate.

Despite the political manoeuvrings the government did have a moderately creditable record on regional assistance. Total assistance offered increased from £40 million in 1964/5 to £82 million in 1969/70 and over the period 1965–70 the number of factories completed was 50% higher than in 1960–4. This did have an effect on unemployment rates. In 1964 the unemployment rate in development areas was 2.21 times the national average and by 1970 this had fallen to 1.67. Although by the end of the decade national unemployment rates were higher than the early 1960s those in the development areas were actually lower and had not risen for three years. But many of the structural problems were untreated. Regional policy was not able to counter the huge problem of the decline of the old staple industries, where for example between

1964 and 1969 the Northern Region lost 45% of its mining jobs and 39% of its railway jobs.

The effective demise of the National Plan in July 1966 marked the end of the period when 'planning' was a fashionable concept in government. The plan had served its primary purpose in creating the impression that the government had a coherent economic policy for the future of the country at the 1966 election and after July it could be quietly forgotten. The emphasis then switched to the defence of sterling at the expense of other priorities. And from November 1967 until the election of 1970 the whole of the government's record seemed to depend on achieving a balance of payments surplus. The very word 'planning' was no longer mentioned.

7

A Better Society

One of the distinctive claims made by the Labour party was its belief in greater social justice; its desire to bring about a fairer and better society. Indeed perhaps the most influential post-war writer on the philosophy of socialism, Tony Crosland, in *The Future of Socialism*, had argued that the main task of socialism was to create a more equal society through the redistribution of wealth by taxation and public expenditure, and using the benefits of economic growth to improve public services, on which the poorest parts of society depended to a far greater extent than other groups. This spirit had been central to Labour's appeal at the election and was also to be a crucial factor in the acceptance of a voluntary incomes policy by the TUC. Labour's programme of reform went beyond the immediate benefits contained in the November 1964 Budget (abolition of prescription charges, a big increase in state benefits and abolition of the widow's earning rule) and embraced a much wider range of measures in housing, rents, land ownership, education and pensions. They were all areas where government action could have real and far-reaching impact on people's lives and prospects.

For over a decade before 1964 the politics of housing had consisted largely of a competitive auction between the two parties as to who could promise to build more houses. In 1951 the Conservative pledge to build 300,000 houses a year had been immensely popular and Harold Macmillan had launched his rise to No 10 on his success in achieving it. After 1955, and under his premiership, the government switched the main emphasis to the private sector: by 1959 house completions had fallen by 30% in the public sector together with a fall in standards. But by the early 1960s housing was back at the centre of the political stage, dominated by ideas of slum clearance and massive redevelopment projects. At the 1964 election both parties promised to build 400,000 houses a year and the Conservatives even undertook to clear all slums by 1973. Achievement was some way below this goal. In the early 1960s actual completions were consistently less than 300,000, although they had risen in election year to 336,000. A further 20% rise was possible but it would require a major programme from the building industry at a time when the economy was already working at nearly full stretch.

Wilson chose his close associate Dick Crossman, in his first ministerial job, to head Labour's housing drive. Two months after the election Crossman had lunch with Wilson and got his support for an expanded housing programme. Indeed Wilson was even more enthusiastic than Crossman, and keen to have a clear and popular policy that would win support. When Crossman asked for a target of 135,000 council houses for the next financial year Wilson immediately upped this to 150,000 which in total represented an increase of 30% over the existing rate. These proposals came to the Cabinet early in February 1965 but met total opposition from Jim Callaghan, who was resisting any increases in public expenditure. He told the Cabinet that he was under pressure from the bankers and justified his stance in his usual gloomy strain:

> It is no use my colleagues complaining that I am only allowing them to do as much as the Tories were going to do because the Tories never had any intention of carrying their programmes out . . . If you are going on like that we are sliding to catastrophe.[1]

But Callaghan met strong resistance from George Brown supported by seven other members of the Cabinet. They argued that there had to be expansion in the building industry as part of the drive to expand the real economy. In his summing up of the discussion Wilson edged his colleagues towards a larger housing programme. He asserted that they had to build more council houses than the last Labour government, thus implicitly endorsing the 150,000 target, but asked for more detailed work on how the new houses would help modernise the building industry. The idea of controlling private house development through licenses (recently introduced for offices) was also to be considered. It took another hour and a half in Cabinet a fortnight later before Callaghan could be forced to give in on this major piece of social policy.

Unfortunately the performance of the building industry did not meet the Cabinet's optimistic hopes. The number of council houses built did rise from 119,000 in 1964 to 133,000 in 1965 and to 142,000 in 1966 but meanwhile the number of private houses built fell from 217,000 in 1964 to 203,000 by 1966 so that the total number of completions was going up only slowly. Nevertheless Wilson and

Crossman were soon thinking in even more grandiose terms with an election approaching. At the end of May 1965 they agreed that other social programmes would have to take second place to a target of 500,000 houses a year by 1970. As Wilson told Crossman, 'We'll make housing the most popular single thing this Government does.' Callaghan was given his marching orders and Crossman announced the new target at the Labour party conference in the autumn. This new commitment formed a central part of the manifesto in 1966 when Wilson, speaking in Bradford during the campaign, gave an unequivocal commitment:

This is not a lightly given pledge. It is a promise. We shall achieve the 500,000 target, and we shall not allow any developments, any circumstances, however adverse, to deflect us from our aim.

Less than three months after they were re-elected Callaghan, now joined by Brown, was pressing for reneging on the target but Wilson and Crossman were able to beat off the challenge. The 500,000 target was to last another eighteen months until the post-devaluation cuts in January 1968 when it was unceremoniously reduced to 335,000. Wilson's promise that nothing, however adverse, would deflect the government was quietly forgotten without any protest in Cabinet.

It is highly unlikely that the 500,000 figure would ever have been reached; indeed it proved difficult even to get as high as 400,000. The peak of housing completions came in 1968 at 371,000 and under the impact of the post-devaluation cuts fell to 307,000 by 1970 (lower than when Labour came into office). Capacity constraints within the building industry made it very unlikely that an additional 130,000 dwellings a year above the 1968 total could have been completed. Much of the increase came in the private sector which reached a peak of 223,000 in 1968 and although council house building reached 159,000 in 1967 this was still well below the record annual figure of 203,000 set under the Conservatives in 1953. Nevertheless the Labour government's overall record on house building was creditable. During the five years from 1965–70 2.06 million dwellings were completed – a 45% increase on the total for the five years from 1960–4 under the Conservatives. Altogether the country's total housing stock (allowing for demolitions) rose by 1.3 million from 1965 to 1970 which can be seen as a significant achievement in the numbers game of housing policy.

So far we have only considered the housing programme in terms of quantity and not quality. Well before Labour came to power the ideas of large-scale slum clearance schemes through massive demolition, and mass rehabilitation of houses and high-rise development, had been growing in popularity, at least among those responsible for public-housing programmes. Increasingly during the 1950s public housing moved away from suburban estates towards high-rise blocks of flats. In 1953 just 3% of approvals for public housing had been for high-rise flats but this had risen to 26% by 1964. This trend had been encouraged by government subsidy from 1956. The early 1960s also saw the emergence of the 'industrialised building' concept run by the seven major national construction companies in alliance with the local councils and with the support of the Conservative government.

Certain features of this approach to building might conceivably have lessened its attractions for an incoming Labour government, however intent on quantity rather than quality. It reflected elitist concepts in architecture and town planning: the imposition of large schemes that delighted the bureaucrats but often enraged their clients, who had rarely been consulted about the schemes. High-rise costs were usually greater than building houses, often by as much as 50–150% and normally took 30% longer to complete. Much of the housing stock demolished was not unfit for habitation. Large-scale redevelopment often destroyed local communities along with their houses, frequently with no net gain in numbers. For example, between 1951 and 1966 Manchester destroyed 48,000 dwellings but only built 37,000 and in the GLC area between 1967–71 59% of the dwellings demolished were not unfit.

When Crossman came into office he was a quick convert to the idea of system building. After a visit to Oldham where he saw 750 houses being built by industrialised methods he developed a visionary scheme for clearing the whole inner area of the city, about 300 acres, and handing it over to the builders to show what they could do. His view of the standard of industrialised building was at least honest:

I see nothing to lose if we make the local authorities turn over to it since conventional architecture is so terrible it couldn't be worse.[2]

Luckily for him Crossman did not have to live on the estates that were being built by these methods and he continued to support massive redevelopment across the country, often against strong local opposition.

But already the climate was beginning to change. Approvals for high-rise flats fell rapidly after 1966 and after some difficulty the government was able to restructure the subsidy to local authorities so that it actively discriminated against high-rise construction. Slowly density limitations and cost controls were introduced. The real turning point came in 1968 after the dramatic collapse of Ronan Point, a large tower block in east London shattered by a gas explosion. The subsequent tribunal of enquiry was highly critical of procedures within the Ministry of Housing, its lack of expertise and inability to assess risks. So although the vogue for high-rise and industrialised construction was over by the end of the 1960s, the Labour government had only been following the trend rather than leading the way. There had been a major increase in construction but the quality of the work and the badly designed estates were to leave a sorry legacy for the decades ahead.

The sensitive issues of mortgages and rates had also featured in the 1964 manifesto, which included a pledge to introduce 100% mortgages and 'option mortgages'. The 100% mortgages were made available through local authorities but the idea of option mortgages involved long and difficult negotiations with the building societies. The aim was to try and broaden the group eligible for mortgages with a scheme whereby in return for guarantees from the government the building societies would lend to customers with lower incomes than they would normally consider and at a lower rate of interest. In return the borrower had to forgo tax relief on the mortgage. The scheme was postponed in the July 1965 cuts and finally introduced in 1968 but never proved very popular.

The other new scheme in the housing field was the introduction of rate rebates for those on low incomes. Crossman spent some time fiddling with the idea of reforming the whole rating system but like so many others found the area far too complex and difficult for a quick, easy solution. What proved more attractive was the idea of subsidising rates for the less well off. This had a redistributive function but ministers were quite clear that its main attraction was as a vote winner. When Crossman obtained Cabinet committee approval for the scheme in early August 1965 he wrote:

> The Committee knew perfectly well that rate rebates were something we had to give the electors if we wanted to survive the municipal elections.[3]

Two months later when the scheme was approved by the Cabinet electoral considerations were even more urgent; by then it was not the municipal elections in May 1966 that were influencing their thinking, it was the impending general election. After a fierce debate in Cabinet, with Callaghan strongly opposed to the scheme, Wilson summed up in favour of proceeding:

> if we were going to have a general election before the municipal elections it might be a good thing to have the rate rebates in operation.[4]

The Conservatives' Rent Act of 1957 had decontrolled rents and removed security of tenure for tenants, and the subsequent free market had led, not just to higher rents, but also to intimidation of tenants by unscrupulous landlords anxious to redevelop property at considerable profit. The activities of one of these landlords, Peter Rachman, in the Notting Hill area of London had become a byword for the social problems and injustice associated with rented property. The whole question of the private rented sector was an issue in the 1964 campaign and Labour was pledged to repeal the 1957 Act. However, Crossman found on taking office that no thinking had taken place in opposition on how to replace the existing legislation. The problem was that the 1957 Act could not simply be repealed; some new structure would have to be put in its place in order to regulate rents. He quickly accepted the advice of his civil servants to press ahead separately on security of tenure. Within three weeks of taking office a one-clause bill on protection from eviction had been agreed by ministers and it became law before Christmas.

There remained the much more difficult problem of devising a system for setting fair rents, indeed of actually defining what was meant by a 'fair rent'. Crossman was discontented with the official advice from the Ministry of Housing. He firmly rejected their attempt to exclude furnished accommodation from the new controls which, if it had been implemented, would have drastically reduced the scope of the Act and excluded the most vulnerable groups it was designed to protect. Instead he set up two groups involving Arnold Goodman, long-time unofficial legal adviser to the Labour party, Ashley Bramall, a Labour leader on the GLC, and Professor David Donnison from the London School of Economics to advise him on how to draft the bill. It was the outside advisers who recommended that the bill should not attempt to define a 'fair rent' but that it should be left for the Rent Tribunals to determine on a case by case basis. The bill was ready for introduction in the Commons by April 1965 and its provisions came into operation in December. The remaining problem was how to staff the Rent Tribunals. Here, with great reluctance, Crossman found himself accepting the advice of his civil servants and choosing safe, establishment figures. Despite his feeling that something different was needed he could find no other system for coming up with a list of possible candidates. The crucial appointment was that of Sydney Littlewood as head of the London Tribunal which was expected to set the ground rules for the operation of the Act. He was a safe, conservative lawyer who interpreted the Act in a cautious conservative way.

This episode demonstrated how difficult it could be to introduce really radical proposals when the politicians were themselves unclear about their policies and how to implement them. However, they did confront 'Rachmanism': conditions for tenants were improved and the worst abuses of the old system ended. If the idea of a 'fair rent' was less radical than many expected, it did have the merit, so far as the politicians were concerned, of removing these decisions to obscure local tribunals and defusing the problem as a national political issue.

Unexpectedly the issue of land prices, speculation and large profits had become a political issue in the early 1960s. The Labour party had protested that Conservative policy was bringing windfall gains for landowners whose land was granted planning permission for a change of use to house or office building. They argued that this was unjust and unacceptable in that these speculative gains were brought about by changes in public policy and not by the efforts of the private landowners. They also objected to the fact that speculation in land was driving up prices, including those paid by local authorities, and slowing up the supply of land for badly needed housing. The Labour party took the view that these speculative gains should in the main accrue to the public and that an element of public ownership in land should be introduced to reduce the scope for speculation.

In developing its own policies the Labour party had to take into account the special interests within its ranks, in particular Labour-controlled local authorities, who did not want a strong central body controlling land development and encroaching on their traditional preserve – housing programmes. The scheme eventually devised in opposition was an ingenious way of meeting the various problems. A Land Commission would be set up which would be able to buy all land for future development at its existing value (not its value with planning permission) plus a bonus of 30% to encourage sales. The Commission would then normally sell the land it acquired to local authorities or lease it to private developers. The new body would be funded by the government at the beginning but should become self-financing as its land sales progressed. This policy had a number of attractive features: land prices ought to be reduced, local authorities would get their land cheaper whilst retaining control of housing development and, moreover, partial national-isation of the land would gradually take place. To implement the policy they envisaged setting up a new Ministry of Land and Natural Resources, modelled on the old Ministry of Town and Country Planning from the 1940s, to control all land policy and take over the planning function from the Ministry of Housing and Local Government.

So when the Labour party came into office, they had identified a problem which not only cried out for action but which also had significant potential for shifting the focus from unfettered private exploitation towards a more equitable distribution of the benefits to be derived from development. And on this occasion they had even done some homework to prepare themselves to take action. In October 1964 Wilson appointed Fred Willey as head of the new Ministry of Land and Natural Resources and agreed with Dick Crossman that his ministry, Housing and Local Government, would pass their planning function to the new organisation. Within a week that plan was in ruins. On arrival at his new ministry Crossman explained to his permanent secretary, the formidable Dame Evelyn Sharp, what he had agreed with the Prime Minister. This triggered off an immediate explosion, followed by a vigorous rearguard action:

> The Dame explained to me that what I had unconsciously done was to demolish the whole basis of her Department, because in her view – which I now suspect is correct – it's quite impossible to give physical planning, the land policy, to a new Ministry without giving it all control of housing . . . As soon as she realised this Dame Evelyn got down to a Whitehall battle to save her Department from my stupidity and ignorance . . . I knew she had gone to the Head of the Civil Service, Helsby, and to Eric Roll, head of George Brown's new DEA. Regardless of anything Harold had said, she continued the war, capturing Fred Willey and putting him in a room by himself in our Ministry while she got hold of his new Permanent Secretary, Mr Bishop, and lectured him.[5]

Dame Evelyn won her Whitehall battle and the planning function remained with her ministry. Crossman had shifted his priorities from Labour policy to Whitehall politics and empire-building, and a weak minister (Willey) and weak permanent secretary (Bishop) had been defeated.

Wilson appears to have been too busy to notice what was going on whilst his instructions were disobeyed. In retrospect he says that he should have acted 'more firmly' but his inaction at the time virtually sealed the death warrant of the new ministry. Indeed by June 1965, as part of a complex series of moves at permanent secretary level, Crossman, Sharp and the Head of the Civil Service, Helsby, agreed that the Ministry of Land should be wound up altogether and merged with the Ministry of Housing a year later. Helsby fixed this arrangement with Wilson, who characteristically agreed only so long as Willey was not told about the impending demise of his ministry.

Creation of the Land Commission – the key to implementing the new policy – also ran into difficulties from the outset. The argument within the government about its exact powers and functions lasted almost a year until publication of a White Paper in September 1965. Undoubtedly there were serious technical problems to resolve, so much so that Crossman described it as 'a subject completely beyond comprehension' for most of his colleagues around the table at the Cabinet Committee on the Land Commission.[6] But many of the arguments reflected bitter internal Whitehall battles ranging the Treasury and Ministry of Housing against an isolated Ministry of Land. Labour had also, in opposition, completely overlooked two practical problems. How would it be able to recruit the large number of staff required and how would disruption to the housing market be avoided? If the housing programme was to be given priority, and it was clear that this was the government's intention, then the Land Commission would have to cope with about 100,000 transactions a year and there was no way they could recruit enough trained staff to deal with this volume of work.

These practical considerations were the core of the case against a Land Commission but, recognising that they might not be able to stop the Commission outright, the Ministry of Housing proposed an alternative scheme. The Commission would now only buy land required for redevelopment and large new schemes. This would inevitably create two markets in land – that operating through the Commission and that continuing under the existing rules. To avoid dual pricing a betterment levy, set at 50%, would act as a tax on all private land transactions. This would amount to an essentially fiscal approach with limited action from the Commission to ease some of the worst corners of the private land market. Not surprisingly it was strongly resisted by Fred Willey and the Ministry of Land. But they had to accept that for practical reasons a full Commission could not operate immediately. Gradually they were brought to accept the idea of a betterment levy though they wanted it set much higher at 70%. The Treasury rightly argued that if the main purpose of the Commission was to collect betterment levy then it wasn't needed at all since the levy could easily be collected through the normal taxation system. Indeed at one point Callaghan even suggested not having betterment levy at all and simply collecting the tax as Capital Gains Tax. By now some ministers were convinced that they ought to drop the whole scheme. As Lord Gardiner, the Lord Chancellor, commented wistfully, 'Is it really impossible for a Labour Government ever to drop an idea because it is found to be impracticable?' At various times the Land Commission was nearly dropped; the only factor that saved it was the pledge in the manifesto and so it had to be given some functions. By May 1965 a compromise was adopted. Initially the Commission would confine itself to collecting betterment levy, which was set at the low figure of 40%. Although the full powers envisaged for the Commission would be included in the bill, they would not come into operation for at least seven or eight years.

The new body finally began work in 1967 but its activities were severely circumscribed. It was only given £45 million by the Treasury to make purchases and was therefore unable to make much impact on the market. Although it could collect levy it was not allowed to retain it to buy land but had to give up all the receipts to the Treasury. The Civil Service had also ensured that its chairman was a safe establishment figure. This was Sir Henry Wells, a prominent chartered surveyor and estate agent who was already Chairman of the New Towns Commission. His view of the role of the Commission was clear: he was opposed to any form of nationalisation and the Commission would operate 'according to the laws of the market'. Sir Henry was as good as his word and in practice the Commission was to spend most of its time trying to obtain more land for commercial builders and putting pressure on local authorities to release more land for the private sector – the exact opposite of Labour's original intentions. During its brief existence the Commission purchased 2000 acres, sold 320 of them and collected levy worth £30 million. It operated at a loss of about

£2 million a year in buying and selling land. It was abolished by the Conservatives in 1970 on ideological grounds, since they objected to any interference (however limited in scope) with the free land market and the long-term threat of limited nationalisation.

The saga of the Land Commission is almost a paradigm of the difficulties of reform in the British political and administrative system. A good idea that could have worked in the long term was defeated by a combination of inadequately thought out policies in opposition, internecine warfare in Whitehall, ministerial indifference to the detail of policy and establishment conservatism. The best they managed to come up with was an emasculated Ministry of Land and Natural Resources and an impotent Land Commission – both ended in failure and the Labour party has not subsequently paid any great attention to the fundamental problems it might have helped to solve.

In both 1964 and 1966 Labour was pledged to an expansion of the education system and in particular to the abolition of the eleven-plus exam, the extension of the comprehensive system, the raising of the school-leaving age to sixteen and the continued growth of the higher education sector. The education policy of the new government was, throughout its six years in office, to be one of building on existing developments and following trends that were already apparent. Expenditure on education rose steadily at about 6–7% a year but it was not a radical policy except in one area of significant innovation – the Open University.

The main policy issue to be considered on taking office was the Labour party's commitment to comprehensive education in secondary schools. The move towards comprehensives was very much swimming with the tide and reflected a growing consensus outside Whitehall. In the 1950s there had been growing discontent about the existing tripartite structure of secondary schools and Local Education Authorities were already moving towards comprehensive schemes, particularly in rural areas (which were often Conservative controlled). Although by 1965 less than 10% of secondary-school pupils were in comprehensives, over half of the LEAs had either completed or were already working on comprehensive schemes and thirty of these schemes had been approved by Whitehall. In mid-January 1965 Michael Stewart, an ex-teacher and National Union of Teachers-sponsored MP, put a major policy paper to the Cabinet. His approach was essentially pragmatic,

130

encouraging existing trends, and realistic, recognising the need for a degree of coercion as a last resort. The paper pointed out some of the difficulties involved, such as inadequate buildings and the future of the direct grant schools. Whilst admitting that a complete transformation of secondary schooling would not be possible within five years, he anticipated that the move would probably have gone so far as to be irreversible. He sought approval for a circular requiring local authorities to submit plans on how they intended to introduce comprehensive education and also agreement that legislation should be introduced in the autumn of 1965 to deal with any recalcitrant authorities. This approach came up against pragmatism of a different kind. The Cabinet, led by Harold Wilson, wishing to avoid creating an issue for the Conservatives to exploit at the election, refused to agree to legislation. Only Fred Peart and Willie Ross, both ex-teachers, supported Stewart. So the whole policy of going comprehensive was left on a voluntary basis.

The circular (10/65) was issued by Stewart's successor, Tony Crosland (public school and Oxford educated); it requested local authorities to draw up comprehensive plans and submit them for approval. Issuing such a document helped marginally to speed up a process already underway. By 1970 32% of secondary pupils were in comprehensives and 129 schemes had been approved. As expected there were still recalcitrant authorities but not until 1970 was a bill introduced to compel LEAs to put forward comprehensive schemes. It had not been passed before the election and was immediately dropped by the new Conservative government.

Apart from presiding over a gradual drift towards comprehensive education, the government took no major initiatives of its own and showed little sign of tackling the roots of inequality in the system. In introducing the new Certificate of Secondary Education Whitehall was responding to ideas and pressure from within the educational establishment. In 1965 an Act setting up a new system for settling teachers' pay was passed but it was exactly as agreed and drafted by the Conservatives after long consultations with the Local Authorities and the teachers' unions. What the government did do was set up endless committees of enquiry under various members of the 'Great and Good', from Lady Plowden to Professor Donnison. One on the public schools had been promised in the 1964 manifesto. It was undertaken by Sir John Newsom but led to no changes. Spending per pupil in grammar schools remained 13% higher than on pupils at comprehensives and 31% higher than on secondary modern pupils. Spending on education rose steadily over the life of the government but the first signs of the controversial education cuts that were to be more apparent in the 1970s emerged in the post-devaluation public expenditure cuts of 1968. It was then that the Labour government abolished the requirement that LEAs should provide free milk at maintained secondary schools in order to save £4.5 million a year.

The biggest and most controversial cut of all in 1968 was the postponement of the raising of the school leaving age to sixteen. Planning for the introduction of the new leaving age had been proceeding on the assumption that it would be introduced in 1971, and a complex programme of new building and preparation was underway. The Treasury led by Jim Callaghan had been pressing for at least a two-year postponement since early 1967 but no formal decision had been taken because of the degree of opposition within the government to the idea. The Treasury seized its opportunity in the severe climate after devaluation and under the new Chancellor, Roy Jenkins, asked for a three-year postponement, no doubt expecting to 'compromise' on two years. Callaghan, now Home Secretary, did a quick volte-face and strongly opposed postponement but when Patrick Gordon-Walker, the Education Secretary, announced that he would rather spend the money on universities and ought to support the Chancellor, postponement became inevitable and a two-year term was agreed. Only Lord Longford resigned on the issue, disillusioned with a Cabinet that would not keep its promises, as he said:

> They lacked the inflexible spirit that prompted Beveridge whenever he was asked whether we could afford to abolish want. He invariably replied: 'Can we afford *not* to abolish it?'[7]

George Brown was even more bitter but chose not to resign, although later he was to write:

> I thought it was one of the greatest betrayals a Labour Government, so overwhelmingly composed of University graduates, could make of the less privileged people who, after all, had elected it.[8]

In the tertiary sector of education the main outlines of policy on the universities had been set by the previous Conservative government in 1963 when they agreed to implement the Robbins report. This meant doubling the number of places at universities by 1968 and creating several new ones. This expansion in higher education was rounded off in 1965 when Tony Crosland adopted the long-held Department of Education view on how the new polytechnics were to be established. They were not to be autonomous like universities but subject to both Department of Education and local authority control. They were to provide full- and part-time degree courses, and sandwich courses, which Crosland hoped would make them more responsive to social needs than the universities. They would also concentrate on teaching rather than research. By 1967 twenty-nine polytechnics had been named and were in the process of being established. But, as with schools, an elitist disparity in resource allocation persisted under Labour: and spending per student at universities in 1968 was 29% higher than on students at Colleges of Education. The one-policy initiative of which Crosland was particularly proud was the establishment of the Social Science Research Council to fund research in exactly the same way as the existing Science and Medical research councils.

The greatest innovation made by the government was the Open University (or University of the Air, as it was originally called). This had long been a pet project of Wilson's and in 1964 he asked Jennie Lee, Nye Bevan's widow, to take charge as part of her job as Minister for the Arts. Jennie Lee proved a tough fighter and was able to ensure that sufficient money was allocated to get the project established. This was partly because Tony Crosland was frightened of her and knew that if he tried to cut her budget she would immediately complain direct to Wilson. Wilson himself was not only deferential to Jennie Lee (perhaps his last gesture towards his Bevanite past) but also determined to establish the new university and he refused to allow any cuts. A White Paper on the project was published in February 1966, just before the election. It outlined how the new institution would work: there would be a combination of television and radio lectures together with a correspondence course with no specific entrance requirements. The university was to be responsible not to the University Grants Committee but direct to the Department of Education, a move designed to protect this unconventional institution from attack by more traditional centres of learning. But Jennie Lee's bold idea to set up a public corporation to run a fourth TV channel to fund the Open University and provide time for its programmes was rejected by the Cabinet. Instead programmes were relegated to unsocial hours on BBC 2. Before the Labour government had left office the Open University was operating successfully. It was perhaps one of the most revolutionary new policies implemented by the Labour government. It completely changed the view of what constituted a university and the type of person that attended. There can be little doubt that its social consequences were immense in enabling people, with a very high degree of personal motivation because of the effort involved, to make up for a lower level of education earlier in life or to embark on a new career. By 1981 45,000 students had received degrees and an annual rate of about 6000 had become the norm. The Open University may well turn out to be the most lasting monument to the work of this Labour government.

One immediate action of the Labour government on taking office in October 1964 was to announce an increase in pensions. However, this was a quick gesture to carry out an electorally popular manifesto pledge. The Labour party recognised that major policy initiatives were required to update the entire system of pensions and benefits, and had developed a clear blueprint in opposition of what they wanted to do. But in the autumn of 1964 ministers took a decision that was to prove of fundamental importance for their record on social policy. They decided to put on one side their plan for a major new national superannuation scheme and concentrate instead on modifications to existing short-term benefits. One of the main reasons behind this strategy was the need to be seen to be making progress before the next election. Although they did go on to bring in new benefits these were further piecemeal measures rather than part of any coherent plan for long-term restructuring of the system.

One new benefit to be introduced was a scheme to make redundancy payments available for all workers with more than two years service. This was introduced in 1965 and, although it did have egalitarian overtones and did establish the idea that the worker had some 'rights' in his job, it was mainly an attempt to reduce trade union opposition to redundancy and thus, it was hoped, help the modernisation of the economy. The same thinking lay behind the decision, announced before the 1966 election but not implemented until October 1966, to introduce earnings-related benefits for unemployment, sickness, industrial injuries and widows. The other change before the 1966 election was replacement of the existing National Assistance by Supplementary Benefit as the 'safety net' for those in the greatest social need. Even though most of the changes, like the new name, were largely cosmetic, it was still strongly opposed by Callaghan but he was overruled by the rest of the Cabinet keen to have the new scheme announced before the election.

The most controversial and difficult area with which the government had to deal in the benefit field was family allowances. An official report in 1966 showed that of the seven million families with children, 500,000 (with 1.25 million children) were living below the supplementary benefit level. In addition 160,000 low-income families (with 500,000) children could not be brought into supplementary benefit because, for example, the wage earner was badly paid. The government accepted that the only way these families could be helped was by increasing family allowances but, because this was a universal benefit available to all families, it would be prohibitively expensive to bring in the level of increase needed if the worst off families were to see any real improvement in their position. The government had to decide how to proceed and its debates show a fundamental difference in philosophy and approach by ministers.

In the latter half of 1966 Callaghan had been pressing in Cabinet for major cuts in the social services, including the end of free school milk and big increases in the charges for school meals. A large section of the Cabinet refused to agree to these proposals until improvements were made to the social security system. The crucial debate came on 23 February 1967 when the pensions minister, Peggy Herbison, put forward a major proposal to increase family allowances but at the same time 'clawback' part of the additional cost by increasing taxes for the better off to compensate, thus leaving only those on low incomes better off. The principle of a universal allowance was to be maintained, yet the scheme was affordable because the net cost to the government was contained through the extra tax revenue. Callaghan led the attack on this suggestion and made it clear that he wanted to end the whole concept of universal family allowances and introduce means testing instead. He was supported by Crosland, Jenkins, Healey, Marsh, Diamond, Hughes, Robinson and Gordon-Walker. Wilson, who had been strongly briefed by Burke Trend, the Cabinet Secretary, to support Callaghan, was not keen on the proposals. But the outright opposition came from Stewart, Gunter, Crossman, Castle, Silkin, Ross, Greenwood, Benn, and Lords Longford and Gardiner. They rightly pointed out that this was a major philosophical divide and that what Callaghan was suggesting was no different from what the Conservatives would have done. When it came to the vote the majority rejected Callaghan's alternatives. At this point he announced that he would not be dictated to and that since 'clawback' was taxation it was a budget-ary matter, and so could not be discussed in Cabinet, even adding for good measure that those who thought it should be were 'subverting the constitution'. Burke Trend tried to write up the minutes of the discussion so as not entirely to reject Callaghan's ideas and had to be overridden by Wilson.[9]

Three weeks later Callaghan raised the issue again at another Cabinet meeting. He was now prepared to accept the decision to increase family allowances but not 'clawback' and instead wanted to cut public expenditure by an additional £160 million to compen-sate. Some senior members of the Cabinet thought that Callaghan must have threatened to resign on the issue and that was why Wilson had allowed him to reopen the question. The Cabinet was again split exactly as before. Wilson's temporising counter-proposal, prompted by Trend, for a small increase worth £40 million (a quarter of the original proposal) with no decision on cuts or 'clawback' was not accepted either. Such a proposal would have solved none of the problems identified earlier because the money would have been spread so thinly. In the end a decision was postponed.[10]

The Cabinet returned to the issue on 19 July during the dis-cussions on public expenditure. Callaghan now argued for a straight 25p increase all round, whereas others wanted a 50p increase funded by 'clawback'. Wilson, showing more concern for the international than the domestic scene, was worried that if this latter proposal were agreed, international bankers would think that the government was 'going soft'. So he proposed what he described as a compromise of 35p across the board. This was the worst possible solution: it went to all families rather than just those in need and also put up the overall cost to the Treasury but Wilson was obviously trying to avoid both the means test and 'clawback'. In this he was supported by the civil servants, in particular Burke Trend, who were also trying to avoid the issue of principle and to keep the existing system going. At this point Peggy Herbison threatened to resign and eventually did so. She was replaced by Judith Hart, who had more influence with Wilson, and finally the 50p increase together with the introduction of 'claw-back' was agreed. It had been a long, hard fight and those in the Cabinet who favoured some form of greater social justice and who could remember the long opposition within the Labour party from the 1930s to the means testing of benefits had been able to triumph over the standard Treasury view, endorsed by Callaghan.

While all these discussions had been going on little or no progress had been made on the major reform of national superannuation to which the Labour party had been pledged at both the 1964 and 1966 elections. This was to prove a fatal mistake. The government should have realised that a long and complicated bill would take a considerable amount of time to draft; there would have to be a major series of consultations and the bill itself would take a year to pass through Parliament. Yet not until a year after the 1966 election was a Cabinet Committee established to consider how to proceed. Even then there was a lack of drive. By the end of 1967 progress had been minimal, partly because the Ministry of Pensions had only allocated four people to work full time on the most complex revision of state pensions since the 1940s. The Social Services Committee of the Cabinet did not approve the outline of a new structure until July 1968 and the Cabinet not until the end of October. A White Paper was published in January 1969 but the detailed consultations were not completed till the autumn when the Cabinet gave its final agreement. Almost four years after the election a bill was finally introduced in January 1970 but it was still in the Committee stage when the next election was called in June. The new Conservative government immediately consigned it to the wastepaper basket.

Even if the bill had become law it would have fallen far short of the fundamental and radical reform envisaged by the Labour party in opposition. The national superannuation scheme introduced in the 1940s and based on flat-rate contributions was what is known as a 'pay-as-you-go' scheme – contributions were made but the major part of the cost of benefits was met from taxation at the time they had to be paid out. The original scheme had two weaknesses – first, benefits could represent a major cut in income for the lower paid who were dependent entirely upon the state scheme, and second, there were doubts about the willingness of future governments to fund the benefits from taxation. In 1961 the Conservative government had introduced a graduated system of benefits and contributions but the scheme was correctly described as a 'swindle' by the opposition because its aim was simply to increase the level of contributions. Its basic fault was that benefits were strictly related to contributions in cash and therefore because of inflation people were bound to receive less than they paid in.

The alternative Labour party scheme had been developed by Dick Crossman, who had scored a major triumph at the party conference in 1957 when he had presented it. These proposals marked a fundamentally new approach. The 'pay-as-you-go' idea was to be replaced by a fully funded scheme where all the benefits were to be financed from contributions made earlier. The scheme would be redistributive in its effects. The level of contributions would rise steeply, particularly for the better off; the lowest paid would receive 60% of their pay as benefits, the average worker 50% and the higher paid less. Moreover, the new fund would effectively make private provision of pensions unlikely because of restrictions imposed on contracting out from the state scheme and the high level of state benefits. Under Crossman's scheme the state pension fund would accumulate vast assets and be allowed to buy shares on the Stock Exchange, thus effectively increasing the level of state ownership. This was a radical approach that could have transformed society through its redistributive effects, the inevitable decline of private pensions and the use made of the assets the state held.

The proposals worked out by Crossman when in office were to be only a pale shadow of his 1957 scheme. Most importantly, the concept of a fully funded scheme was dropped, and as so often the politicians found it easier to give out good news and to put the bill off to the distant future. Ministers were not prepared to spell out as clearly as the 1957 scheme would have required just how much extra people would have to pay as contributions. Instead the new scheme, like its predecessor, was to be 'pay-as-you-go' with benefits paid largely from future taxation. But ministers were still prepared to spell out that the benefits were to be kept at the high level envisaged in 1957 – 60% for the low paid and 50% for the average. As the Treasury rightly pointed out, this was equivalent to signing a massive promissory note against the future and only compounded doubts about whether the level of benefits under the existing scheme could be afforded from future taxation. Crossman no longer intended to make the private pension schemes redundant as in his 1957 proposals. Instead he entered into long negotiations with the pension companies that resulted in their position being permanently entrenched. Now people would be able to contract out from the state on relatively favourable terms. The whole idea of using pensions as a piece of social engineering and restructuring had disappeared. The last bow towards the 1957 proposals came in January 1970 when Crossman proposed to SEP that the Superannuation Fund should be allowed to make investments of up to £100 million a year although, as he admitted, it would be no more than a token gesture, since benefits would rely almost entirely on taxation. Jenkins (as Chancellor) and Wilson rejected the idea out of hand. Crossman seems to have been so ashamed of the end of his grand plan from 1957 that he omits all mention of the episode from his diaries.

The overall record of the government in the social field was hardly impressive. One major reform – pensions – never got off the ground and another – the Land Commission – ended in failure when judged against the hopes entertained in 1964. In education the government did little apart from following the existing trend of development and postponing the raising of the school-leaving age. In housing more houses were built but there were real doubts about the quality and social consequences of the new schemes. The target of 400,000 homes a year set in 1964 was not achieved and the even more grandiose, solemn promise to achieve 500,000, regardless of events, collapsed ignominiously. In one area – private rented housing – they met with some success. The worst scandals of the early 1960s were no more and if 'fair rents' turned out to be higher than many expected the new system did protect the rights of the tenants. The government also significantly improved benefits, particularly for the lower paid, which was very important as we shall see in the final section of the book when we consider the overall social and economic impact of the government.

8

The Shadow of the Past: Rhodesia

The most intractable problem that the new Labour government inherited was the future of the colony of Rhodesia. It was a problem whose roots lay deep in the past and one which raised strong emotions both at home and abroad. Faced by a controversial demand by the whites for independence in February 1964, the Conservative government had deliberately sidestepped the issue and left it over until after the election, when Labour found that the negotiations with the ruling minority under their intransigent leader, Ian Smith, were deadlocked.

The whites in Rhodesia (about 8% of the population) wanted independence on terms that would give them long-term and possibly permanent domination over the black majority. This could not be conceded by any British government given the state of world and indeed British public opinion. The negotiations conducted by both Conservative and Labour governments with the Rhodesian government were essentially aimed at finding a formula which would enable Britain to grant independence on the basis of white minority rule but with some form of guarantee that at some future date black majority rule would be achieved. But the whites were unwilling to provide any such guarantee and the threat of a unilateral declaration of independence (UDI) in order to preserve their position loomed large. Britain would be virtually powerless to stop such a declaration (or reverse it) short of the use of military force, since it had long ago conceded effective self-government to the white minority. The new government's room for manoeuvre was heavily constrained by the shadow of the past.

When Southern Rhodesia became a colony in 1923, its constitution gave extensive powers of self-government to the white population but reserved 'native' affairs for the Governor and therefore for the British government. Although in theory London had the power to intervene, in practice a large degree of autonomy was allowed and by 'convention' all legislative proposals were left to the Southern Rhodesian government including 'native' affairs. Nominally a colony, in effect Southern Rhodesia acted as a self-governing dominion. For forty years it had been virtually a one-party state with conservative governments drawn largely from wealthy farmers and plantation owners ruling in the interests of their fellow white settlers.

Largely left to its own devices Southern Rhodesia developed into a society similar to that of English-speaking South Africa. By 1960 223,000 whites coexisted with 2 million blacks within a highly segregated society. It was a prosperous country, at least for the white population. With high wages, low taxes and an average of two servants per household their standard of living was nearer to that of the United States than Britain's. It was based on the subordination of the blacks, whose wages were on average just 10% of those of the whites and for subsistence farmers about 1%. The 1931 Land Apportionment Act (approved by the then Labour government in Britain) ensured that the blacks were allowed to settle on twenty-eight million acres (only seven million acres outside the tribal reserves and none in the towns) and the whites then numbering 50,000 had forty-eight million acres reserved for them. Despite all the evidence of a racialist society arguments about standing by British 'kith and kin' had a strong emotional sway over parts of the British electorate and media.

The British government did intervene in the affairs of Southern Rhodesia in a way that was to be highly significant for the whole process of its transition to independence and the thinking of the whites. In 1953 it created the Central African Federation (CAF). The CAF was fundamentally flawed because it sought to combine a largely self-governing colony dominated by the whites (Southern Rhodesia) with a colony where an even smaller minority of whites wanted to secure power for themselves (Northern Rhodesia) with a backward colony with no form of self-government (Nyasaland). The Conservative government's long-term aim was clearly that the CAF should eventually become a self-governing dominion, run by the local whites with the blacks in a subordinate position. The blacks were opposed, fearing that they would be placed in a situation similar to that in South Africa. However, by 1960, the year that Macmillan made his famous 'Winds of Change' speech in Cape Town, the climate had changed significantly. Britain was moving rapidly towards granting independence to its African colonies. It no longer seemed possible to grant independence to a federation where 8% of the population in Southern Rhodesia, 3% of the population of Northern Rhodesia and 0.3% of that in Nyasaland would run the country, and where just 429 Africans could vote in Southern Rhodesia, ten in Northern Rhodesia and none in Nyasaland.

The British government went back on a previous pledge not to allow any country to secede and the CAF started to break up. In Nyasaland an African majority on the Legislative Council was conceded in 1960 and the black African leader, Hastings Banda, was committed to leaving the federation. By 1962 the same principle was applied in Northern Rhodesia. Six months later the British Cabinet agreed that Northern Rhodesia could leave the CAF. In 1963 Southern Rhodesia asked for independence when the CAF was dissolved but the British government refused unless constitutional changes were made to protect the position of the Africans. The federation was formally dissolved; the other two states achieving independence as Zambia and Malawi, leaving Southern Rhodesia still formally a British colony.

The Rhodesians were deeply aggrieved that the most 'advanced' of the three countries was denied what was being granted to their black-dominated neighbours. In the mid-1950s the relatively liberal but patronising Garfield Todd had been Prime Minister. His vague attempts at some amelioration of the position of the blacks led to resentment among the whites and his eventual overthrow in 1958. Increasing black nationalism led to a crackdown by the government under the 1960 Law and Order Maintenance Act that effectively turned Rhodesia into a police state.

As part of the complex negotiations for ending the CAF a new constitution for Southern Rhodesia was endorsed by the Conservative government in 1961. It was this document that was to be at the heart of the subsequent negotiations on the terms for independence. The Rhodesians believed that this constitution was an acceptable basis for independence but, whatever private informal understanding may have been made at the time, the British government maintained in public that major amendments would be required first. The 1961 constitution provided for a complicated voting system which ensured that fifty seats in the Parliament would be reserved for the Europeans and fifteen for the Africans. Britain only retained any control at all through the theoretical right to amend the constitution by Order-in-Council. These 1961 provisions would have preserved the position of the whites for decades, although there was the ultimate threat of majority rule if African educational standards slowly improved. The whites, though, could have controlled the pace of this change and put off any handover of power. However, unless either African representation were increased immediately or the Africans were given a minority blocking vote on retrogressive changes to the constitution, independence (which would remove the British constitutional veto) could lead to permanent minority rule. Hence the vital importance of the negotiations about the status and degree of control over the constitution to be given to the African group in Parliament.

Increasingly seeing itself isolated and surrounded by enemies, the white minority in Rhodesia turned away from the modern world and into its 'laager' as the South African whites had done. Fear for their privileged position and of the example of countries like the Congo, that had reverted to near anarchy on independence, drove them to reject any form of African advance. If Britain would not grant independence then perhaps Rhodesia should seize it anyway. In 1962 a new political force, the Rhodesian Front, emerged, led by Winston Field, with Ian Smith and 'Boss' Lilford as his henchmen. Field was the expendable, respectable front man for the hardliners behind him. They campaigned on a policy of no African advance and in the December 1962 election swept to power, winning thirty-five of the white seats. Just over a year later Field made it clear that he was opposed to UDI and in a party revolt he was replaced by Ian Smith as Prime Minister. Smith had always supported the most obdurate and intransigent elements in the party because they reflected his own parochial and extreme views, heavily influenced by his South African wife. He understood the Rhodesian whites but little else.

The period from the end of the CAF in 1963 until the British general election set the immediate framework that Labour inherited. The Conservative government implicitly conceded the principle that independence could be granted to the white minority but they also began to set out the minimum conditions that would make this possible. At the same time the Rhodesian government began to prepare its own position for UDI, should it be unable to persuade the British government to grant independence on terms acceptable to them. When Winston Field met the minister in charge of dissolving the CAF, Rab Butler, in 1963, he was told that the minimum conditions for independence would be a legislature of $\frac{1}{3} + 1$ Africans (to give a theoretical block on the whites amending the constitution after independence), widening of the African franchise and gradual repeal of the Land Apportionment Act. Field claims Butler offered him independence at the same time as the rest of the CAF but Butler denies this. In January 1964 Field came to London but although the government was sympathetic they claimed that Commonwealth opinion meant that constitutional changes were required before independence was possible. He also saw Wilson and the likely Commonwealth Secretary in any Labour government, Arthur Bottomley, who both accepted that there would have to be a slow evolution of power within Rhodesia. The formal demand for independence was tabled in February 1964 but the Rhodesian High Commissioner in London told his government that the Conservatives had said that they didn't want to do anything before the election:

> If they lose it will be on Labour's plate. If by some miracle they win, they would then do something knowing that there was a reasonable time ahead of them.[1]

In September 1964 Smith came to London but was told by Sir Alec Douglas-Home that there would be no independence on the 1961 constitution, though hints seem to have been dropped that if the 1961 constitution were acceptable to the whole population then independence might be possible. Smith wanted a referendum of the whites and consultation of the chiefs, who were placemen of the government, but the issue was not resolved before the general election. Meanwhile in Rhodesia the African opposition was banned, many leaders jailed and discreet preparations were started for possible UDI.

Labour therefore inherited an almost impossible position. The Rhodesian whites were in total control of the country except for the final legal declaration of independence. This would not be granted without some political and social concessions to the blacks that would enable Britain to present the deal as reasonable at the United Nations and to the British. At no time had Britain insisted on majority rule before independence and it had even conceded the principle of only amending the constitution with the agreement of the Rhodesian whites. Rather than accept the decades of domination promised under the status quo, the Rhodesian whites were transfixed with the idea that independence on their terms would give them perpetual domination over the blacks. Britain had virtually no cards in its hands against an intransigent, embittered and introverted government in Rhodesia, a government that, if it could not get what it wanted legally, looked set to seize it illegally in the near future.

The new government needed to balance a number of different

factors. The Labour party had a strong vein of idealism about colonial independence and the role of the United Nations, and granting independence to the Rhodesian whites on anything other than the strictest terms would be highly controversial. Wilson also wanted to avoid accusations of racialism from other members of the Commonwealth if Britain conceded too much to Ian Smith. But the overriding consideration in Wilson's mind was the political situation at home. With the narrow majority and the inevitability of an early election Wilson was determined that Rhodesia would not be an issue that the Conservatives could exploit. This ruled out military intervention, which could have been a difficult though not impossible operation, because of the risk that it might lead to whites being killed. It left negotiation as the only card in the British government's hand and Wilson was determined to play it so as to postpone UDI for as long as possible. If this failed then it was vital to ensure that UDI took place in such a way that there could be no accusations that the British government had not done everything possible to avoid the final breakdown. For Wilson the whole saga would also provide an admirable platform for personal diplomacy to enhance his own position as a national leader.

There was no discernable change in British policy with the advent of the Labour government. In October 1964 the fear in Whitehall was that Smith might declare UDI on the 26th when Northern Rhodesia (Zambia) became independent. A message from Wilson was cleared by OPD and the Cabinet on the 22nd. It asked for a clear assurance that UDI would not take place and spelt out what would happen if it did. All financial and economic links would be broken, there would be no recognition by the Commonwealth and Rhodesians would no longer be British citizens. The message was tough but the threats made were limited and did not imply any attempt to overthrow any illegal government. It is difficult to imagine that a Conservative government would have acted any differently. Smith made no immediate illegal moves but, acting on the hint dropped by Douglas-Home about the possible acceptability of the 1961 constitution, in a referendum of the whites he obtained a majority in favour which was repeated at a gathering of the 622 black chiefs (all appointed by the government). On this basis Smith was now to argue that the Rhodesian people supported independence on the 1961 constitution.

A series of attempts were made to initiate negotiations with Smith, who was showing no great enthusiasm for discussions. Arthur Bottomley, the new Commonwealth Secretary, was due to visit Zambia for the independence celebrations and proposed to go on to Rhodesia. But Bottomley demanded to be allowed to see the nationalist leaders Nkomo and Sithole, who were both in jail. Smith refused and the visit never took place. Wilson invited Smith to come to London but he refused because of the referendum. Wilson then suggested a visit by an all-party group of Privy Councillors which Smith also refused, as he did another invitation to London early in January 1965. The deadlock was broken at the funeral of Sir Winston Churchill at the end of that month. Smith attended the funeral but did not go to the subsequent lunch at Buckingham Palace even though he was invited. He was found eating at his hotel by a Palace equerry and taken to the Palace where Wilson persuaded him to go back with him to No 10. Here he was prevailed upon to accept a visit by Bottomley and the Lord Chancellor, Lord Gardiner.

The first formal contacts between the two sides were to prove inconclusive and unproductive with no solution to the underlying dilemma apparent. At his 'secret' and informal meeting with Wilson Smith had seemed to argue, no doubt realising that this was what Wilson wanted to hear, that the 1961 constitution would keep the whites in power for long enough to make UDI unnecessary. However, he was much less forthcoming when Bottomley and Gardiner went to Rhodesia at the end of February. He did tentatively put forward the idea that the Africans could be given a blocking vote of ¼ in Parliament rather than the ⅓ that Britain wanted, which Wilson did not reject. Nevertheless when Bottomley and Gardiner returned, their report to OPD was pessimistic, as Barbara Castle reported:

> They were very gloomy about the future. Smith . . . was bent on UDI at the slightest provocation and it looked as though he had taken defensive action against possible economic retaliation by us . . . Nobody seemed ready to make up their minds and it was left that Harold and Arthur would go on considering the various possibilities.[2]

At the Commonwealth Prime Ministers' Conference in June Wilson did not face any real problems. He was able to avoid any firm commitment to majority rule being the basis for independence, with only Tanzania objecting. There was, however, a demand that Britain should hold a constitutional conference (the normal prelude to a colony's independence). When the Cabinet met on 24 June they very reluctantly agreed to a proposal that if negotiations with Smith failed they would 'consider' such a conference. But this was only done on the clear understanding that they had no intention of actually agreeing to it and that this was only a diplomatic manoeuvre to have a non-controversial end to the Commonwealth Conference. Throughout the summer and early autumn of 1965 desultory negotiations with Smith continued. Cledwyn Hughes, the junior minister at the Commonwealth Office, visited Rhodesia and there was plenty of correspondence but no change in the fundamental views of either side.

Smith was meanwhile establishing his own position for UDI. On 7 May he held a general election with the specific aim of gaining enough seats to have a two-thirds majority in Parliament so that the entrenched clauses of the constitution could be amended. He claimed he was not seeking a mandate for UDI but nevertheless issued a White Paper about its implications. Smith won a resounding victory at the polls with his Rhodesian Front party, securing all fifty of the white seats and therefore over three-quarters of the total seats in Parliament. The decision to go for UDI was made after the May election. The government already controlled radio and TV, and control over the army was secured when the Chief of Staff (who opposed UDI) was retired and a Smith sympathiser put in his place. Likewise the High Commissioner in London, another opponent of UDI, was replaced. The Rhodesians were able to get a representative to Portugal so that discussions could start on the support that could be expected through the Portuguese colony of Mozambique.

The negotiations between Britain and Rhodesia now entered their final stage with a crucial letter on 21 September from Bottomley to Smith, which spelled out what became known as the 'Five Principles' that would be the precondition for independence. They were public and accepted by the Conservative opposition. Although they provided plenty of scope for interpretation, all possible settlements had to be judged against these minimum criteria. The principles were:

1. Unimpeded progress to majority rule would have to be maintained and guaranteed.
2. Guarantees would be required against retrogressive amendment of the constitution.
3. There would have to be an immediate improvement in the political status of the Africans.
4. There would have to be progress towards ending racial discrimination.
5. The British government had to be satisfied that any basis for independence was acceptable to the people of Rhodesia as a whole.

(The British added a sixth principle in February 1966 that there was to be no oppression of the minority by the majority and vice versa.)

There was never the slightest chance that Smith would accept these principles. Their function was therefore to define the essential framework for British acceptance of independence and to act as a useful statement of principles for both international and domestic consumption. The secondary result was that all governments (including later the Labour government) were constrained in their ability to settle with Smith by the need to ensure that the settlement in theory, if not in practice, conformed with the principles.

Smith had one last effort at trying to get the British government to agree to his terms. He came to London early in October and had two meetings with Wilson. He demanded immediate independence but refused to agree to any 'blocking' section of Africans to stop constitutional amendments, any referendum amongst the Africans to judge acceptability and any progress in African education which would increase their political strength. OPD met in the middle of the visit. Wilson reported that there had been total deadlock in the talks but did not appear downhearted. As Barbara Castle commented, 'He seemed almost to relish the fight – which was more than could be said for George or Jim.' The British High Commissioner in Rhodesia, who was in London for the visit, reinforced the gloomy message and

confirmed that there did not seem to be any basis for a settlement; he had asked Smith only recently whether he wanted European supremacy for ever, to which Smith had replied 'For the foreseeable future'.[3]

The talks broke up five days later when the communiqué stated:

Despite intensive discussion no means has been found of reconciling the opposing views. No further meeting has been arranged.

Wilson continued to try and avoid UDI, and soon came to the conclusion that his personal diplomacy could solve the problem. He suggested a mission by a group of Commonwealth Prime Ministers which Smith rejected. He also tried to find a new Governor for the colony: he wanted Lord Mountbatten on the grounds that as a member of the Royal Family he might make UDI more difficult for the Rhodesians but the Queen seems to have refused to agree. On 21 October Wilson announced to the Cabinet that he was thinking of flying to Rhodesia. What he did not tell them was that information from MI6 indicated UDI would take place on 25 October. The Cabinet was doubtful about the mission and the alternative of sending Bottomley, Sir Alec Douglas-Home and a third person was considered. Frank Cousins and Lord Gardiner supported the Wilson visit but it was strongly opposed by George Brown and others. Only then did Wilson reveal that he was not consulting the Cabinet but informing them since the arrangements for this last-ditch effort had already been made.

Wilson arrived in Rhodesia on the 25th and saw representatives of every group including Nkomo and Sithole. But within a day George Brown was reporting to the Cabinet in London that the situation was 'extremely bleak' and that Wilson was about to leave with nothing achieved. However, before he did he would play his 'last card', the idea of a Royal Commission to report on acceptable terms for independence. But this raised just as many problems as it solved because both sides were determined to ensure that it produced the result they wanted. Wilson proposed that it should be chaired by the Rhodesian Chief Justice together with a British member (he had in mind Rab Butler), a Rhodesian and an Australian. When Wilson left Rhodesia on 30 October he agreed to consult the Cabinet on the issue, and left behind Bottomley and the Attorney-General, Elwyn-Jones, to discuss details.

It was the details that were important. Did the Commission have to be unanimous or was a majority decision acceptable? Would it consider an amended constitution or Smith's proposal that it should simply say whether the 1961 constitution was acceptable? How was acceptability to be tested? The Cabinet discussed the proposals over two days on 1–2 November. Wilson outlined four possible options: to let the Royal Commission put Smith's proposals to the people; to do the same as the first option but with the UK dissociating itself from the proposals and to hope that the Commission would find them unacceptable; to put the UK and Smith proposals to the Commission, and test them both for acceptability; to reject the Smith draft and insist the Commission only consider the UK proposals.

Wilson argued that the time to stand firm had been reached. He judged that the first two options would put off UDI for a few months, though it was inevitable in the long run, whilst either of the last two options would ensure immediate UDI. Only Cousins and Castle argued against any compromise and in favour of the fourth option. All the rest of the Cabinet, no doubt thinking that a few months bought by the Commission might see them to the other side of the election, were in favour of compromise. Even Lord Gardiner, one of the most liberal members of the Cabinet, was for compromise on the purely pragmatic grounds that he believed that Smith would get away with UDI, that sanctions would fail and that the blacks would then be in an even worse position. Eventually the Cabinet agreed to support the second option, provided the report of the Royal Commission was unanimous and that there was also unanimous agreement among the members on how to consult the people. The Cabinet was clearly intent on buying time, but accepting option two virtually abandoned the first four principles and placed all the emphasis on the test of acceptability. The Rhodesian proposals would almost certainly have failed that test (as they did in the early 1970s with the Pearce Commission) but the government was placing great faith in the Royal Commission to ensure it never had to face giving Rhodesia independence on terms that breached their own principles. Wilson and the majority of the Cabinet clearly felt that Smith would not accept anyway, and therefore they would have shown how far they would go to try and stop UDI.

Smith indeed did not agree to these terms and on 5 November a state of emergency was declared in Rhodesia as an obvious prelude to UDI. Two days later OPD agreed that Wilson should offer to meet Smith in Malta to continue the negotiations but Smith rejected the proposal, telling Wilson that there were irreconcilable differences between the two sides. On 8 November the Rhodesian Chief Justice flew to London to try and save the Commission he was to chair. He asked the British government to commit itself to recommend independence on the 1961 constitution if the Royal Commission reported it as acceptable. The Cabinet met to consider the request on 9 November immediately after the State Opening of Parliament. Again the Cabinet was split. Crossman and Healey wanted to stall, whilst Jay and Peart favoured more concessions to Smith. Both Wilson and Bottomley were against any further concessions on a proposal that was an obvious dead duck. The next day the Cabinet cannily modified the proposals to indicate that they would accept only if Smith pledged himself to recommend to his Parliament any other proposal to emerge from the Royal Commission, and that, if the Commission found the 1961 constitution unacceptable, it would be able to go on to recommend a new constitution which Smith would also be committed to recommend to his Parliament. By now the British government was essentially shadow-boxing to establish their position after UDI.

Their aim was to show how hard they had tried to avoid it. But this was important politically because Wilson, who had carefully been keeping Heath in the picture, had obtained an undertaking that if he went to the absolute limit of concessions on the Royal Commission then the Conservatives would not support UDI.

The British knew from MI6 sources that Smith was about to go over the brink and that UDI would be declared on 11 November. Early that morning Wilson telephoned Smith to reformulate yet again British proposals on the Royal Commission, all of which Smith had so far rejected. Now Britain would recommend acceptance of independence on the 1961 constitution if the Commission reported it as acceptable, but if the Commission found against, then the Rhodesians would have to give up any claim to independence on that constitution, though they could continue under that constitution as long as they desired. Wilson had gone to the ultimate limit of concessions (with only a thin thread keeping them joined to the five principles), though he was fairly safe in assuming that Smith was not going to ask Britain to carry out this bargain. This final proposal was tacit acceptance of continued white rule in Rhodesia for decades and shows just how far Wilson was prepared to go to demonstrate that he had done everything possible to avoid UDI. But it made no difference, since UDI was declared at 11 am on 11 November 1965 with a ghastly pastiche of the American Declaration of Independence.

The government had always ruled out any attempt to overthrow an illegal Rhodesian regime by military force. Its options were therefore limited. The only course open was to introduce some form of sanctions in the hope of putting pressure on Smith. But was the pressure designed to bring Smith to the negotiating table or to bring down his government?

The government had begun to consider their response to UDI after the abortive Bottomley-Gardiner mission in March 1965. Work began almost immediately on compiling a list of actions that would need to be taken. This was ready by early October when it was considered by OPD. But there were already disagreements about what should be done. The Rhodesians had begun to remove government assets held in London but Callaghan didn't want to take any action until after UDI because it might unsettle other holders of sterling, and so the drain continued for the next month. Brown opposed any tobacco embargo because it might harm Britain more than Rhodesia and other countries might not follow suit. It was only when Arthur Bottomley pointed out that Britain had already bought the 1965 crop and had eighteen months stock that Douglas Jay was instructed to get the crop out of Rhodesia quickly.

With the final crisis imminent the government had to resolve the crucial question of what happened to the government of Rhodesia after UDI. The ensuing debate was to show the stark difference between rhetoric and reality. At OPD on 7 October Callaghan said he wasn't sure what the government's policy was after UDI. Was it to replace the Rhodesian government or put it beyond the pale? Wilson responded boldly, 'If there is a UDI there *is* no Government: we take over,' and he explained that the Governor would dismiss the Rhodesian ministers and impose direct rule from London, as he was to do after UDI. When Wilson was unwise enough to repeat the remark at Cabinet an hour later, he was taken apart by Dick Crossman in an episode described by Barbara Castle: 'Dick asked some penetrating questions about what we meant by taking over the Government ourselves.' According to Crossman himself, 'This was the first occasion on which I was a bit of a bastard and did the kind of Socratic cross-examination which people expect of me.'[4] The result of these exchanges made it clear to the Cabinet that whatever might happen legally, Smith would stay in effective control of Rhodesia and that without the use of military force there was nothing Britain could do directly to change the situation.

Wilson was totally opposed to any UK use of force in Rhodesia, even as part of a UN deployment, though others in the Cabinet, including Denis Healey, did not reject the UN option. Wilson also opposed Michael Stewart's suggestion that Smith should be told that the UK would not veto any UN resolution calling for the use of force. The reason was that he was deeply worried about reactions in Britain to the use of force, particularly in the run-up to an election; and in particular feared it would be ruthlessly exploited by Ted Heath.

The immediate response of the British government to UDI was legally correct – imposing direct rule – but all their actions were designed to limit upheaval. The day after UDI Wilson advised all civil servants in Rhodesia to stay at their posts but not to take an oath of loyalty to the new regime, something Smith was prudent enough not to impose. The Governor stayed in Rhodesia and in fact acted as a channel of communication with London. The remaining Rhodesian assets in London were taken under British control.

In Whitehall OPD continued to be the main Cabinet committee dealing with Rhodesia until the end of November when Wilson set up 'R' (later 'RX') to decide day-to-day policy. Its members were Wilson, Brown, Stewart, Callaghan, Bottomley, Healey, Gardiner, Jay and Bowden. The most important question they had to consider at the end of November was the position of Zambia. British industry was highly dependent on copper from Zambia, which in return relied on coal from Rhodesia and electricity from the Kariba Dam power station to keep the copper mines functioning. There was also the possibility that other African countries would become directly involved in the Rhodesian issue. As the only independent state with a common border with Rhodesia, Zambia would be the focus for any military action against the rebel regime that might be agreed upon by the Organisation of African Unity. At the end of November President Kaunda of Zambia asked Britain to provide aircraft to defend Zambia because he was worried that otherwise other African states would demand the right to do so. The Rhodesia committee worked on the proposal over the weekend of 27–28 November, and recommended that Britain should send nine Javelins to outclass the Rhodesian Canberras and Hunters together with part of the RAF regiment to guard the airfields. The Rhodesians were to be told beforehand that this was not a preparatory move for a British attack on Rhodesia. No ground troops would be sent and Zambia was to agree that nobody else could station forces in their country. The Cabinet met on the Monday morning and agreed to send the aircraft as requested but there was no clear idea of how this fitted in to any long-term strategy; it was an *ad hoc* response to an unexpected request. Wilson made the reason for the government's acquiescence in the proposal clear when he said that he personally

> didn't think Smith was going to attack Zambia, but it was a good excuse for giving us squatter's rights and keeping other people out.[5]

The next day the Cabinet discovered that Kaunda was not prepared to agree to keep others out unless Britain agreed to send in ground troops which would be deployed up to the Rhodesian border. The Zambians wanted the British troops to be ready to occupy the Kariba power station (on the Rhodesian side of the Zambesi) to ensure the continued flow of electricity. The Cabinet refused to allow British troops to go closer than 200 miles from the border and on this basis Kaunda refused to allow them in but accepted the aircraft, and also agreed to stop guerilla raids into Rhodesia. However, the Cabinet did agree, on the suggestion of Denis Healey, that the SAS should be ready to sabotage Kariba if

Smith cut off power to Zambia (though Healey, on security grounds, refused to mention the words SAS to his colleagues). This threat was quietly transmitted to Smith and it appears to have had the desired effect. No attempt was ever made to stop the flow of electricity. These moves and the cautious pre-emptive deployment in Zambia were the nearest the government came to any form of military intervention.

Even before UDI Wilson and the rest of the Cabinet were determined that the UN would play a central part in the reaction to any Rhodesian move, and agreed that the veto could only be used with specific Cabinet authority. At the UN Britain was under strong and immediate pressure to end the illegal regime as quickly as possible. On 18 November Stewart reported to the Cabinet that he had had to commit the UK to 'consider' oil sanctions and two days later the Security Council recommended sanctions against Rhodesia, including oil, but at this stage they were not to be mandatory. Oil was the obvious weak spot in the Rhodesian economy, since there were no internal supplies. Rhodesia had one refinery at Umtali linked by pipeline with the port of Beira in Mozambique. In the run up to UDI Rhodesia had been able to negotiate support from Portugal and stocks at Beira had been increased from twenty-seven days to three months by November. If the pipeline was closed Rhodesia would be dependent on the supply of refined products, which would have to be delivered either through Mozambique or from South Africa.

Although the legal and administrative procedures to make the Rhodesian regime illegal had been implemented, no plans had been devised on how to bring that regime to an end. Detailed planning had been rejected earlier in 1965 as 'too pessimistic' in accepting that UDI would happen. What emerged from the *ad hoc* series of decisions taken in the weeks after UDI was that the government had convinced itself that it was engaged on a 'quick kill' operation to bring down the Smith regime, in Wilson's phrase at the Commonwealth Prime Ministers' Conference in January 1966, 'in a matter of weeks not months'.

Six days after UDI OPD considered a paper from the Foreign Office and the Ministry of Power on possible oil sanctions. It was pessimistic, particularly about the possibility of effective enforcement and the likely scope for evasion. These doubts were shared by most of OPD but Wilson was optimistic. He rightly pointed out that it was not a question of whether there would be oil sanctions but when they would start, since the UN was bound to favour them and the UK would then have no choice but to support them. He was convinced that both South Africa and Portugal would go along with sanctions and that the international oil companies would do likewise. After the UN Security Council vote on 20 November OPD authorised discussions at official level with the United States on possible sanctions. On 29 November a meeting of ministers agreed that oil sanctions would only be introduced if the United States supported them.

US policy and opinions were, as on so many other issues, to be central to the government's thinking. US policy was stated at its clearest by Secretary of State Rusk when he told the British on 4 April 1966 that 'the United States could not hold the residual responsibility for the West, that [they] had a great load to bear and [they] simply could not take on another burden'.[6] The British were therefore in the lead but they took every possible opportunity to involve the United States in what they were doing. All the formal exchanges between Wilson and Smith were given verbatim to the Americans, and, for example, during Wilson's visit to Rhodesia at the end of October 1965 they were given special daily briefings on the details of the negotiations. One of the reasons for this was that the Government wanted American help on the balance of payments. In September 1965 the United States was told that the immediate costs of UDI would be £50 million through having to replace Rhodesian tobacco by purchases outside the sterling area. The United States agreed to supply some of their surplus tobacco at special rates if necessary. But they also made it clear that they could not undertake to make good any balance of payments losses and that political support for the UK did not imply open-ended economic support. This was particularly important over the question of Zambian copper which, if it were cut off, might have an adverse effect of up to £200 million on the UK's balance of payments. But the US also had problems of their own. Their demand for copper was high, partly because of the Vietnam war, and strong pressure was therefore put on the British not to provoke Smith into taking any action that might affect Zambian supplies, which made up 25% of the West's production.[7] This pressure helps to explain why Britain took such a cautious attitude over Zambian requests for assistance.

At the end of November a joint UK-US official group was set up to consider whether oil sanctions against Rhodesia should be introduced. Joint planning went ahead in great detail even down to whether to divert individual tankers.[8] The report from the joint group on oil sanctions was available early in December and its assessment was gloomy. Oil sanctions were unlikely to work because of the likely attitude of South Africa and Mozambique but the report recognised they would probably have to be introduced 'for whatever marginal effects it would have on the Rhodesian regime and as a diplomatic device with the Africans'.

Before oil sanctions could be introduced another problem had to be solved. Again it was landlocked Zambia that would be badly affected if, in response to sanctions, Rhodesia stopped transit of supplies. In the long term a new road and rail link was under construction but in the short term an airlift of supplies would be required, and because of the RAF's limited capacity US support would be needed. On 7 December Wilson told the Cabinet that he was not prepared to stop the flow of oil until a multilateral agreement was achieved and supplies to Zambia secured. But no long-term planning had taken place and no preparations had been made to supply Zambia. Over a month had now passed since UDI and Britain had still not taken any serious measures to weaken the position of the Smith regime; African sentiment at the UN was outraged at this inaction. Wilson flew to the United States to address the General Assembly and obtain US support. At the UN on 16 December representatives of 100 countries walked out when he started to speak but he faced just as many problems in Washington.

The day before Wilson saw Johnson, George Brown reported to the Cabinet that the US had finally agreed to an oil embargo but that problems still remained over the scope of the embargo, as the US wanted it to be more limited. At his meeting with Johnson, Wilson was able to obtain US support for the oil embargo and joint supplies to Zambia but this was hardly the 'complete turn-round in the American view' which he claimed it to be at the Cabinet meeting on 21 December. The US was determined to exact a price for their support. Although Wilson had already agreed to keep British forces in the Far East in return for US support for the pound, the Americans used oil sanctions as another weapon to reinforce this commitment. Wilson told the Cabinet he had reached an understanding with Johnson that 'if we stood firm on our present position in the Far East the Americans would back the oil sanctions'.[9]

UK oil sanctions against Rhodesia, finally implementing the UN resolution, were formally announced on 21 December, six weeks after UDI. Action was also taken to stop oil reaching Rhodesia from the coast. The company that owned the pipeline from Beira to Umtali in Rhodesia announced that it would be closed after existing stocks had been pumped through. In return the company was paid £540,000 compensation by Britain. After the Umtali refinery closed on 15 January, Rhodesia had to rely on imported refined petroleum products to keep going. In December 1965, after the imposition of the oil embargo, Wilson had scored what was to him an even more important political victory at home. When the Commons debated sanctions the Conservative party was in total disarray. Official policy was to abstain but thirty liberal Conservatives voted with the government and fifty hardline supporters of Smith voted against sanctions. Domestically the government was in a strong position despite the delays in formulating a policy: no blame was attached to it for UDI, there was international support for sanctions and the opposition was publicly divided.

The next problem for the government was the Commonwealth Prime Ministers' Conference in Nigeria in mid-January. There had been plenty of demands for Britain to use force to overthrow the illegal regime and a few governments had broken off diplomatic relations when Britain refused to do so. One of these was Tanzania and the immediate response from the Foreign Office was to propose cutting off all further aid in retaliation. The mood round the table at OPD was bitter. As Jim Callaghan put it, 'Why should we let these people push us around?' Wilson favoured keeping at least technical assistance going on the realpolitik grounds that it might stop 'communist infiltration'. Eventually it was agreed to put off discussion until after the Commonwealth Conference.[10] Later they agreed to stop all new aid to Tanzania. At the Conference Wilson was able to put off demands for firmer British action by claiming that sanctions were on the point of bringing Rhodesia to its knees ('in weeks rather than months'). It is clear that this was not some clever phrase thought up to avoid a difficult situation at the Conference but that Wilson genuinely believed Rhodesian collapse was imminent. No one else seems to have shared this belief. Certainly officials in the Commonwealth Office and the Ministry of Power took the opposite view, as did Michael Stewart and Arthur Bottomley. Just before Christmas Wilson had told Cecil King that he was 'confident' that Smith would be brought down and was talking about his plans for ten years of rule by Britain, with a multiracial Cabinet and African educational advance before independence.[11] Early in January he had told Barbara Castle that

> sanctions were really beginning to bite. Everyone was playing the game over oil and Smith was getting desperate . . . Kaunda was

157

anxious to cut off imports from Rhodesia but he had persuaded him to hold his hand till we were ready for the kill.'[12]

This optimistic assessment was to haunt Wilson for the rest of his period in office as the weeks turned into months and then into years.

Throughout these first months of UDI Wilson was determined to keep open the channels of communication just in case Smith felt like negotiating. Within a month of UDI Wilson had refused to rule out negotiations with Smith at the Cabinet meeting on 7 December and following his visit to the United States told the Cabinet that he wanted to keep open the links through the Governor, Sir Humphrey Gibbs. What he did not tell the Cabinet, although he did tell the Americans, was that he had, just six weeks after UDI, secretly sent a message to Smith saying that Britain could not put off more drastic action for much longer and suggesting talks. Smith hinted that he might be willing to negotiate on a return to legality. At the time of the Commonwealth Conference Wilson publicly offered a visit to Rhodesia by Arthur Bottomley for talks but Smith refused. Behind the scenes, though, talks were going ahead. In the month of the election a senior official of the Commonwealth Office was sent to Rhodesia to follow up Wilson's secret initiative and open talks on the mechanisms by which Rhodesia would return to legality. By the time of the March 1966 election the government seemed to be in a strong position on Rhodesia. Only as the weeks and months passed did it become clear that Rhodesia was a long way from collapse and that the government would have to decide how to react to this new situation.

UDI was almost certainly inevitable given the introverted culture and politics of Rhodesia and its rejection of the values of the rest of the world. But as a rational calculation UDI made little sense for the whites. Under the 1961 constitution they were guranteed a long period of continued domination which they could ensure would be very long by controlling the rate of African educational advance and hence their access to the franchise. UDI was only worthwhile on two calculations. First, if they feared a British government would, at some point, tear up the constitution and impose majority rule; or second, if the whites actually wanted to move backwards and not forwards. The first eventuality was highly unlikely and at no stage did the Labour government's conduct suggest it. The second explanation seems the most likely and it is borne out by what happened when the 1961 constitution was replaced in 1969. Then Smith introduced a constitution that was avowedly racialist and designed to ensure permanent white domination and eventual apartheid.

The Labour government came through the initial test on Rhodesia reasonably successfully. They inherited a difficult situation and their negotiations with an intransigent opponent, who held most of the cards, showed a degree of skill, and Wilson used the opportunity to enhance his own status and domestic position. They made numerous proposals for a settlement, some of which came very near to confirming the white minority in power for decades. But the government did ensure that when UDI came they did not incur the blame either domestically or internationally. The main doubt was whether the government should have used military force, either unilaterally or through the UN, to pre-empt UDI or overthrow the Smith regime afterwards. The operation would have been difficult, especially given the lack of nearby bases from which to mount it, but not impossible. Given the doubts about ultimate success and the possibility of white resistance, political considerations were paramount. Wilson, with some justification, was convinced that the Conservatives and a large section of the press would exploit any attack on what some regarded as British 'kith and kin'. With an election imminent there seemed no point in taking the risk, especially if an oil embargo would achieve the same result, though in slower time.

The response of the government to UDI had not been carefully thought through but before the end of 1965 a clear aim was established. The illegal regime was to be brought down as quickly as possible by means of economic sanctions, particularly those on oil. Lines of communication were kept open and preparations were made for a return to legality once sanctions really started to bite. What sanctions did not achieve was to bring Rhodesia to its knees in weeks rather than months. The fate of sanctions and the government's attempts to end the continuing deadlock are the subject of a later chapter.

9
Triumph:
The March 1966 Election

The month-long election campaign in March 1966 lacked the tension of the 1964 contest because of the consistent and substantial Labour lead in the polls. Subsequent polling reinforced the message of why Labour won. 42% blamed the Conservatives for Britain's economic difficulties and only 16% Labour. The attitudes established over the dismal period for the Conservative government of 1961–3 took a long time to fade. In 1966 a quarter of their own supporters thought they were not fit to return to government. The campaign was also a personal triumph for Harold Wilson; he outpolled Ted Heath on every characteristic. The Conservatives had a tough task under a new leader who had had little time to establish himself and in conditions where everyone expected them to lose. Their main aim was to contain the size of the defeat and establish the right long-term position. Although they had many policies to put across, their main message that the economy was built on sand was not accepted by the voters. Labour had a much easier task. Their message – 'You Know Labour Government Works' – and the argument that they should be given a fair chance to clear up the mess they had inherited struck a sympathetic cord in the electorate. The manifesto itself was little more than a compilation of the work of the government over the previous eighteen months with much the same promises as in 1964.

The difference in approach between the two parties could best be seen in their closing party political broadcasts. Ted Heath was slightly strident and spoke of the need for radical change, whereas Harold Wilson carefully cultivated his 'family doctor' image, and spoke in terms of patriotism and stability. Indeed in his two party-political broadcasts Wilson used the words 'Britain' forty-two times, 'government' thirty-nine times and 'Labour' not once.

The result itself was not in doubt after the first declaration at Cheltenham showed a 2.9% swing to Labour. The result was almost a mirror image of the Conservative victory in 1959. Labour won nearly 48% of the popular vote compared with 42% for the Conservatives and had 363 seats – a majority of 110 over the

Conservatives and ninety-eight over all other parties. It was their greatest triumph since 1945 and they even won some seats – Exeter, Oxford and Hampstead – that they had not won then. The main feature was the very uniform swing to Labour of 3.5% (they lost only one seat, Colne Valley, to the Liberals), though the highest swings were in the main cities, particularly Birmingham. But there was also a warning for the government in the figures. Turnout at the election at 75.8% was the lowest since the war and the opinion polls showed a level of enthusiasm for the government only marginally above that given to the Conservatives in 1964. The public mood seems to have been that the Labour government should be given a chance to see whether it could deliver the promises it had made.

Labour had therefore successfully achieved its primary aim since October 1964. It had survived with a slender, though not impossible, majority, and fought the election at a time of its own choosing and on the best possible ground. It was back in power for a full term. Much of this achievement must be credited to Harold Wilson's tactical skill as a politician. He had played most of his cards well and ruthlessly exploited the weaknesses of the opposition. The opposition rhetoric of bringing down the government was empty when they were behind in the polls under a lame-duck leader. When they had a lead in the polls and a new leader, Parliament went off on holiday and the opportunity was gone. By the autumn the Conservatives were behind in the polls and themselves split over Rhodesia. The economic difficulties of the government could be blamed on an appalling inheritance, and new government initiatives in the social field and the initial success of the National Plan made it very difficult for the Conservatives to construct a coherent alternative. Wilson had also been able to use the power of office to establish himself as a national Prime Minister of some standing. He had the additional advantage of a reasonably united government and party whose minds had been concentrated by the narrow majority.

The successes of the initial period of the government had been essentially tactical. To a large extent it had lived from hand to mouth and day to day. Through improvisation and by keeping its eye firmly fixed on the electoral imperative it had come through to a situation where it no longer had to worry about its existence. But the underlying problems, particularly in the economy, had not been solved. How the government now used its substantial new majority would determine its long-term fate.

PART THREE

THE ROAD TO DEVALUATION

MARCH 1966–JANUARY 1968

The Cabinet

(April 1966)

Prime Minister	Harold Wilson
First Secretary at DEA	George Brown
Lord President of the Council and Leader of the House of Commons	Herbert Bowden
Lord Chancellor	Lord Gardiner
Lord Privy Seal and Leader of the House of Lords	Lord Longford
Chancellor of the Exchequer	James Callaghan
Foreign Office	Michael Stewart
Home Office	Roy Jenkins
Agriculture, Fisheries and Food	Fred Peart
Colonial Office	Fred Lee
Commonwealth Relations Office	Arthur Bottomley
Defence	Denis Healey
Education and Science	Anthony Crosland
Housing and Local Government	Richard Crossman
Labour	Ray Gunter
Chancellor of the Duchy of Lancaster	George Thomson
Overseas Development	Anthony Greenwood
Power	Richard Marsh
Scottish Office	William Ross
Technology	Frank Cousins
Board of Trade	Douglas Jay
Transport	Barbara Castle
Welsh Office	Cledwyn Hughes
Minister without Portfolio	Douglas Houghton

Change on 4 July 1966

Technology	Tony Benn

Frank Cousins resigned.

Changes between 6–11 August 1966

First Secretary at DEA	Michael Stewart
Lord President of the Council and Leader of the House of Commons	Richard Crossman
Foreign Office	George Brown
Commonwealth Relations Office	Herbert Bowden

Housing and Local Government	Anthony Greenwood
Overseas Development	Arthur Bottomley

Change on 7 January 1967

Minister without Portfolio	Patrick Gordon-Walker

Douglas Houghton resigned.
Fred Lee and Arthur Bottomley left the Cabinet whilst retaining their ministerial posts.

Changes on 29 August 1967

Department of Economic Affairs	Peter Shore
Education and Science	Patrick Gordon-Walker
Board of Trade	Anthony Crosland
Commonwealth Relations Office	George Thomson

Douglas Jay and Herbert Bowden resigned. Michael Stewart remained First Secretary of State.

Changes on 30 November 1967

Chancellor of the Exchequer	Roy Jenkins
Home Secretary	James Callaghan

Change on 16 January 1968

Lord Privy Seal and Leader of the House of Lords	Lord Shackleton

Lord Longford resigned.

10

The Politics of Drift

After March 1966 the Labour government was securely installed in office for a full term. Only once before in 1945 had Labour achieved such a powerful position. The way was open for it to carry out the promises on which it had been elected and establish a record that could compare favourably with that of the Attlee government. With a majority of nearly 100 the day-to-day tactical problems of surviving with a small parliamentary majority could now be forgotten. Wilson's own position and status as a national leader had also been established. It was time to change gear and concentrate on their strategy for the next four or five years. By 1970 the government would no longer be able to blame problems on its inheritance from the Conservatives; it would have to stand on its own record.

It is perhaps the most remarkable feature in the life of the government that there was no rethinking of its position after the election triumph. Life continued much the same as before. The first decision taken by the Cabinet showed there were to be no radical new policies. The old legislative programme that had been started in the autumn of 1965, and largely lost because of the election, was simply reintroduced. The next crucial eighteen months were taken up in passing it into law. Little work was undertaken on the major bills promised in the manifesto for a new national pension scheme and reform of the House of Lords, both of which required considerable preliminary work and thought. There were no bold new policies on the economic front and no attempt was made to plan a coherent programme for the life of the government. There was no fresh start in the ministerial team. With the removal of the discipline imposed by the small majority, personality clashes within the Cabinet became more important. Wilson began to see plots everywhere (sometimes correctly) which heightened his deep sense of insecurity. The longer Wilson was in office, the more he slipped into the comfortable grip of the Civil Service and the establishment. At the same time the parliamentary party became more difficult to manage with the large majority. The eighteen months from the election until the forced devaluation of sterling in November 1967 was a historic missed opportunity.

Almost immediately after the general election the government's attention was concentrated on the seamen's strike, which they fought to try and maintain the prices and incomes policy. July was dominated by the ineptly handled economic and political crisis described in detail in the next chapter. The immediate consequence was a major deflationary package similar to all the earlier Conservative packages of the 'stop-go' cycle that Labour had condemned so vehemently when in opposition. The value of sterling was preserved but the National Plan lay in ruins and the DEA was decisively defeated by the Treasury. George Brown attempted to use the crisis to overthrow Wilson but failed and his public resignation was followed hours later by its humiliating withdrawal.

Although the government's performance proved far from spectacular, it kept its post-election lead in the opinion polls, albeit with a sharp drop after the July crisis. The government was to stay marginally ahead in the polls until the spring of 1967. The only by-election was at Carmarthen in July when the highly idiosyncratic constituency elected the first Plaid Cymru MP, Gwynfor Evans, who came from third place in the 1966 election to beat Labour. This was the start of the nationalist revival that affected both Wales and Scotland in the late 1960s, rather than the first sign of the disintegration of Labour's national position.

From the autumn of 1966 onwards the government's lack of direction became more and more obvious. Most of their time was taken up with long, drawn-out discussions on whether or not to apply for membership of the EEC, including a 'probe' of European opinion conducted by Wilson and Brown in the spring of 1967. Wilson was spending large amounts of his time on foreign affairs, notably on his abortive attempt to settle the Vietnam War in February 1967 and the equally unproductive discussions on a Rhodesian settlement with Ian Smith on board HMS *Tiger* in December 1966. The July measures had staved off the immediate economic pressures but the underlying causes of the weakness in the economy and the position of sterling remained uncured. Legislation passed slowly through Parliament but it had no strategic coherence.

The government began to run into real political trouble in the spring of 1967. The Conservatives went into the lead in the opinion polls and remained about 5–6% ahead until the autumn. There were few by-elections but they too showed the same picture: a

7½% swing to the Conservatives at Brierly Hill in March and a gain for the Conservatives at Glasgow Pollock after the intervention of the Scottish Nationalist split the Labour vote. But this was only a foretaste of what was to come later. The real disaster for Labour came in the local elections. In April they lost control of the GLC, winning only eighteen seats out of 100. At first Wilson remained calm, telling colleagues that this would only cause problems for the Conservatives in actually running local government and the large gains that they had made would have to be defended in 1970 when Labour was bound to recover, thus providing a good springboard for the general election. He soon changed his mind, telling Cross-man early in May, 'Well, the fact is we're not doing very well, are we?'[1] This realistic assessment was shown to be well founded when two days later the local elections outside London were held. Labour lost control of a whole string of authorities: Bradford, Bristol, Cardiff, Coventry (for the first time since 1945), Leeds (for the first time since 1953), Leicester, Liverpool, Manchester, Newcastle, Nottingham, Southampton and Wolverhampton (for the first time since 1952).

Through the summer and autumn of 1967 the Conservatives stayed ahead in the opinion polls. This was due less to the brilliance of the opposition's performance than to the inadequacies of the government's. The Conservatives' position was not easy. They supported defence of the value of sterling and the East of Suez role, and they favoured EEC entry. It was difficult to oppose the government on Rhodesia, where they were split, or on incomes policy, given the similar initiatives taken by the Macmillan government. Only on issues such as steel nationalisation, the Land Commission and transport policy was there a real opposition alternative. It was not until after devaluation that they had an opening for a concerted attack.

Before devaluation the government's position had begun to disintegrate in a series of by-elections. (The 1945 Labour government did not lose a single by-election during its six years in office and neither did the Conservatives in the five years after 1951. In their whole thirteen-year period in office the Conservatives lost just ten seats.) In the four years from 1966–70 Labour was to lose sixteen seats, roughly half of those that they defended, and often on large swings. Although such unpopularity in mid-term has since become much more common for governments, at the time it was unprecedented and further tarnished the government's reputation. On 21 September Labour lost Cambridge, a seat it had gained in 1966, on an 8.6% swing but more sensationally it lost Walthamstow West (Clement Attlee's old seat) on a 18.4% swing. Apathy and disenchantment seemed to be the main reasons. Turnout fell by 17% and one poll suggested that 35% of Labour voters in 1966 had abstained, 10% voted Liberal and 5% had made a straight switch to the Conservatives. On 2 November Labour held Manchester Gorton on a 9.4% swing against an unpopular Conservative candidate, Winston Churchill, but lost Leicester South-West (Bert Bowden's old seat) on a 16.5% swing. Even more sensationally it lost Hamilton where the SNP won 46% of the vote, even though they had not stood in the 1966 General Election. Three weeks later Labour finished third behind the Liberals in the Conservative seat of Derbyshire South-West. The Labour party were finding that party workers were heavily disillusioned with the government's record and unwilling to work at by-elections. This reflected the malaise amongst traditional Labour voters equally disenchanted with the government's performance.

After a General Election victory it is normal for a re-elected Prime Minister to reshuffle the government to give a new sense of purpose for the next four years. At the end of 1965 Wilson had explained to Barbara Castle that the small majority gave him little room for manoeuvre: 'I ought to make a political reshuffle and, if only our majority were even ten, blood would flow. If we win the election, it *will* flow.'[2] Now with a majority of 100 he made the smallest possible number of changes to the Cabinet. Frank Soskice finally resigned and was given a peerage, and Jim Griffiths, the elderly first Secretary of State for Wales, resigned, but it had always been agreed between him and Wilson that he would only serve for a short spell. Fred Lee was moved from the Ministry of Power to the Colonial Office to make room for the rapidly promoted Dick Marsh to take over responsibility for nationalising steel. George Thomson became Chancellor of the Duchy of Lancaster to take over day-to-day responsibility for the bid to enter the EEC. Outside the Cabinet Charles Pannell was sacked as Minister of Works for falling asleep in meetings and incompetence, a fact that Wilson had admitted since early 1965, and ten other junior ministers left. A new generation of younger MPs – Shirley Williams, Peter Shore, David Ennals, Merlyn Rees, Dick Taverne and Edmund Dell – were given their first chance of ministerial office. But the essential composition of the Cabinet remained unchanged.

At the beginning of July Frank Cousins finally carried out his threat to leave the government over the introduction of a statutory prices and incomes policy, and to help ensure Jack Jones succeeded him in the TGWU. His departure caused hardly a ripple but he left disillusioned with politics, government and Harold Wilson, whom he accused of not standing up to Callaghan and Brown. Before the 1966 election Wilson had asked his parliamentary private secretary, Ernest Fernyhough, to approach Michael Foot and sound him out as to whether he would be prepared to take over the Ministry of Technology when Cousins finally left. Foot refused on the grounds that he was a close friend of Cousins and agreed with his views. Instead of Foot, Wilson promoted Tony Benn from Postmaster-General.

After the withdrawal of his resignation at the height of the July crisis George Brown had obtained a promise from Wilson that he would be moved from what would be an increasingly irrelevant DEA. The only other job that was not an obvious demotion (which would be difficult after the degree of support shown for him among the backbenchers to stop him resigning) was the Foreign Office. Not that George Brown was keen, as he told a Cabinet colleague the next month: 'I hate it, I didn't want it. It was an order: this or I go.'[3] Nor was Michael Stewart pleased to be eased out of the Foreign Office to take over the DEA. As he wrote later:

> To console me, and I needed consoling, he [Wilson] added that I should become third, instead of sixth, in the official list of Cabinet Ministers . . . Jim Callaghan, who was fourth on the list, was understandably put out.[4]

The other important move was the promotion of Dick Crossman to Leader of the House of Commons, the first of Wilson's close associates to join the central core of the government. He became a member of three key committees – OPD, SEP and RX – and chairman of Home Policy. He was also charged with reforming procedure in the House of Commons. As Wilson said, 'I have had a non-political Leader of the House for too long; now I want a political one.' The 'non-political' Leader of the House, Bert Bowden, went to the Commonwealth Office, a move which delighted the Queen, and Arthur Bottomley moved from there to Overseas Development, where he replaced Tony Greenwood who took over Crossman's old job at Housing. Apart from solving the immediate problem of what to do with George Brown, for Wilson the reshuffle was part of a wider political plan. Callaghan had been briefing the press that he wanted to be Foreign Secretary and Wilson was determined that he should not be. As Crossman reported, Wilson 'made it clear that . . . one of his major preoccupations had been to fox Mr Callaghan' and Wilson went on:

> What I have done this time is to surround myself with friends and isolate Callaghan. When people see the result of what I have done they will realise he has been defeated. Only he doesn't realise it yet.[5]

After the attempted coup in July, Wilson was also determined to increase the number of his potential successors from just Brown and Callaghan. After August he reckoned there were six in the running: Brown, Callaghan, Stewart, Jenkins, Crossman and Healey.

Wilson conducted only two more limited reshuffles of the Cabinet before November 1967. In January 1967 its size was reduced from twenty-three to twenty-one when Fred Lee and Arthur Bottomley, both on the way down politically, lost their place in the Cabinet whilst retaining ministerial jobs. A month earlier Wilson had been doubtful about this move when Crossman had first suggested it to him:

> It's not so easy. I can't trust the rest of the Cabinet and those two provide me with two important votes.[6]

Gordon-Walker, who had a promise in writing from Wilson that he would be given a Cabinet post when he won the Leyton seat back at the general election, was put at the bottom of the list with no real job as Minister without Portfolio when Douglas Houghton retired.

In August 1967 Douglas Jay, who had been on the brink of resignation over the decision to apply for membership of the EEC, was sacked for his opposition to that decision. Wilson saw him at Plymouth railway station whilst they were both on holiday and told him that he was introducing a new, unwritten rule that Cabinet ministers would have to retire at sixty and that the decision had nothing to do with his opposition to EEC entry. Jay commented: 'This I no more believed that did anyone else.'[7] Tony Crosland took over at the Board of Trade and Gordon-Walker replaced him at Education. Wilson's original idea had been to ease out Stewart from DEA, where he had been a comparative failure, and replace him with Barbara Castle, with Peter Shore moving to the Board of Trade. At the last moment he decided to take over DEA himself with Peter Shore assisting him. Wilson still had hopes of turning DEA into a real planning department and taking control of the economy himself. His sense of euphoria lasted about three months until devaluation.

These reshuffles did not affect the basic power relationships within the government. Wilson retained a dominating personal position; he had the active political support of a solid third of the Cabinet and at least as many again were quite content to go along with whatever the Prime Minister decided. Wilson's opponents, apart from Brown in July 1966, were content to manoeuvre for long-term advantage – though Wilson found that threatening enough. George Brown, even after the resignation fiasco of July 1966, remained Deputy Prime Minister and No 2 in the government. He regularly attended the weekly meeting held on Friday mornings between Wilson, Burke Trend and the Leader of the House of Commons to plan the next week's business in Parliament, Cabinet and major committees. After August 1966 the old triumvirate on economic policy was broken up and in its place there developed a bilateral relationship between Callaghan and Wilson, with Stewart taking responsibility for prices and incomes policy. Bert Bowden dropped out of the inner circle after his move to the Commonwealth Office in August 1966. His place was taken by Dick Crossman, who played a key role as political and presentational adviser to Wilson. The inner group on foreign and defence policy consisted of Wilson, Brown, Callaghan and Healey, who took the critical decisions before discussion at OPD. Crossman was briefly invited to join, but his outspokenness and refusal to follow the consensus policy agreed between the other four meant that he was quickly excluded.

During 1966 it became clear that in many senses the government was not governing but simply administering. Instead of seeking to set the agenda for debate, seize the initiative and push through a clear programme it seemed content to tackle issues as and when they arose. Much of the blame for this state of affairs must be taken by Wilson. Hardly a radical in the past, the longer he was in office the more institutionally conservative he became. His experience as a wartime civil servant had left him with a strong regard for the well-oiled and superficially efficient Whitehall machine and he seemed increasingly content to operate the institutions of power as they were. He became absorbed into the Whitehall ethos: like the senior civil servants he too came to regard the efficient conduct of business within Whitehall as equivalent to successful government. As time went on he also became more introverted, concerned about what went on in the hermetically sealed world of Whitehall, forgetting that this was not the same as affecting the real world outside. Burke Trend as Cabinet Secretary, regarded by Wilson as the best civil servant he had ever known, became more and more influential in the inner counsels of the administration. Other ministers too settled down to the routines and rituals of Whitehall life, content to be in office. In addition Wilson's view of his own role and of politics in general was minimalist, the antithesis of an active government with a clear-cut strategy. It was a development of his idea of himself as 'the doctor' who quietly looks after the affairs of the nation, since the rest of the country were, in his words, 'not interested in politics and want to play tennis and clean their cars'.[8] All of these factors led to a loss of real political drive and a sense of drift.

Various members of the government became aware of a drifting sensation. As early as July 1966 Tony Benn, a long-time Wilson supporter, recognised reluctantly the root of their problem. After a discussion with Peter Shore he wrote that the latter

> retains a high regard and affection for Harold Wilson which is, in my case, fast evaporating. I do not think that Harold has a long-term vision of the sort of society we want to create and the short-term tactical dodging at which he is adept may have been perfect for the 1964–6 Parliament but has no place in the developing strategy for the next four years.[9]

By late September Dick Crossman was similarly gloomy about the government's long term aims:

> I don't feel I'm part of a Government pledged to fundamental change, with any idea of where it's going. When I'm in Cabinet I'm just sitting with a number of men who are running their Departments. And, strangely enough, just because we won an election, these men now feel that they can relax because they have five years ahead of them as Ministers.[10]

Ten weeks later Crossman found the same feeling in Roy Jenkins when they spoke on the steps of No 10 after a Cabinet meeting at which Wilson reported on the failure of the *Tiger* talks. Crossman began the conversation:

> 'Heavens,' I said to him, 'I wish we could have been given a clearer vision of his long-term policy in Rhodesia.' He replied, 'I'd give anything for evidence that we have a long-term plan for any part of this Government's policy, thank you very much, Dick.'[11]

By the end of 1966 Crossman was disillusioned with Wilson's performance and pessimistic about its implications for the government's future:

> I'm also more doubtful than ever whether he's going to lead us anywhere, whether he has any real vision of a future for this country which we in the Labour party can achieve.[12]

Part of the explanation for Wilson's negative behaviour lies in the fact that once the constraints and pressures imposed by a fragile majority were removed, the old rivalries, dislikes and disputes between ministers rose to the surface and proved a major inhibiting factor on the work of the government. Wilson had never been trusted by the right wing of the party and he was convinced that they were continually plotting to overthrow him. He felt isolated and surrounded by rivals for the party leadership. This was not paranoia on Wilson's part. There is no doubt that Brown still hoped to replace Wilson even after July 1966 and Callaghan too saw himself as a potential Prime Minister. And there were other longer-term rivals on the right such as Jenkins, Healey and Crosland (who acted as Callaghan's loyal lieutenant). Yet Wilson's real failing was that he spent too much time worrying needlessly about potential and sometimes imaginary threats. He underestimated his own power and neglected the fact that in Britain Prime Ministers are not normally overthrown in peacetime. And his own actions did much to create a vicious circle of growing suspicion. Almost every move by his colleagues tended to be interpreted as part of some immediate plot or long-term conspiracy. This was compounded by the willingness of all concerned to use the Lobby system to brief the press on the various machinations, thus stoking up the flames of rivalry and adding endless rows about 'leaks' to those already taking place.

Wilson also had problems with the Parliamentary Labour Party, which had been difficult to manage since the 1950s. The right wing of the party had always favoured stricter discipline and expulsions if necessary to stifle dissent. Nye Bevan was nearly expelled in 1955 and Michael Foot and three others were expelled in 1962. The narrow majority from 1964 to March 1966 left no room to tolerate dissent but Wilson's own preference was for a less strict disciplinary regime. In July 1966 John Silkin replaced Ted Short as Chief Whip and a month later Crossman took over from Bowden as Leader of the House. Both believed strongly in a more liberal disciplinary regime where the Whip would not be withdrawn simply for abstaining or even voting against the government. This new system was a combination of principle and expediency. The principle of greater tolerance of dissent was clear, but equally apparent was the difficulty of controlling the major influx of new MPs in 1966, most of whom would find themselves doing nothing constructive except endlessly trooping through the division lobbies, with very little chance of obtaining a junior post in the government. Many of the new intake were more radical than the government and could be expected to join forces with the older MPs on the left of the party. Opposition to aspects of government policy was inevitable and it was not practical politics to consider withdrawing the Whip from perhaps fifty or more MPs. The party and the government would have to learn to live with a greater level of dissent. Nevertheless there was plenty of opposition to the new regime within the party, particularly from the right, who wanted a return to the old system.

The simmering discontent came to the boil in March 1967 after sixty-two backbenchers abstained on the vote approving the 1967 Defence White Paper. Manny Shinwell, the Chairman of the PLP, asked for the Whip to be withdrawn from all sixty-two, but Silkin as Chief Whip refused. Four days after the vote the Cabinet met and, with civil servants excluded, debated what should be done. Wilson said that he would address the party 'and tell them some of the facts of political life'. In his subsequent speech to a meeting of the PLP, he referred to the fact that every dog was allowed one bite but that if it became a habit there might be doubts about renewing the licence. Crossman, who felt that this was an attack on his new regime, drafted a letter of resignation. Before sending it he discussed its contents with Silkin, who advised him not to send it. It was clear that Silkin did not want to be isolated and forced into a position where he too might have to resign. He therefore advised Crossman to redraft the letter to force Wilson's hand by making it into a clear choice between Crossman and Shinwell. Wilson did not want to have to make such a clear choice and sat on the letter for four days, sandwiched between the pressure from Crossman and George Wigg, Shinwell's long-time friend and PPS in the 1940s, who was backing him in this row and who had threatened to resign four or five times in as many days. When Crossman and Wilson eventually met they had a blazing row which ended with Wilson advising Crossman not to take any action and not to brief the press.

Over the weekend Shinwell made a major public attack on Crossman and the new liberal disciplinary regime. But he had over-reached himself; Wilson finally came off the fence and

THE POLITICS OF DRIFT

decided to support Crossman. He personally drafted a five-page code of conduct for the party which ignored Shinwell's views. The latter quickly resigned as chairman of the PLP. The new style of discipline had been established and the old guard defeated. For the rest of the life of the government there was continual dissent from the backbenchers. While there was no realistic alternative to tolerance, the spectacle of numerous parliamentary revolts did damage the government's standing among the wider public.

This episode demonstrated that George Wigg's influence over Wilson was beginning to decline as part of the shifting balance of forces within the 'Kitchen Cabinet'. Wigg, occupying the purely nominal post of Paymaster-General, had three major roles as confidant to Wilson. First he coordinated security across Whitehall, and acted as Wilson's link with MI5 and MI6 in an attempt to oversee their operations. Part of this job was also to keep an eye on the activities of government ministers with the hope of avoiding a Profumo-type scandal and Wigg certainly investigated the case of one member of the Cabinet who had a regular mistress. The second part of his job concerned Wilson's security: he was to keep in touch with what was going on among members of the Cabinet and warn Wilson of any impending threats to his own position.

The high point of these activities came in the July 1966 crisis when Wigg monitored the attempted coup with Wilson away in Moscow. Many Cabinet ministers feared Wigg, and were constantly worried that the slightest indiscretion would be reported back to Wilson and seen as evidence of unreliability. Wigg's third role was to act as general political adviser to Wilson. But increasingly Marcia Williams became the dominating influence, gradually pushing him to one side. Wigg deeply resented Marcia and her influence. Wilson did little to stop Wigg being pushed to the sidelines or to dissuade him from resigning finally in November 1967 to become chairman of the Horse Race Betting Levy Board.

Marcia Williams provoked strong feelings amongst those who worked with her. For example, Joe Haines, who became Wilson's press secretary, wrote that her influence with Wilson was

powerful – indeed, all pervasive ... No one who worked in his office ... for more than a few minutes could be unaware of it ... many went in dread of her; the fact of her power was like a baleful cloud hung permanently over their heads ... By her unpredictable

177

tempers she demoralised not only those who had to work with her, but Harold Wilson also.[13]

Yet to others such as Tony Benn, who admittedly did not have to work closely with her, the picture was different:

Marcia is infinitely the most able, loyal, radical and balanced member of Harold's personal team.[14]

Her influence over policy has been much exaggerated. Her technical job description inside No 10 was 'Personal and Political Secretary to the Prime Minister', yet she was accommodated in an old waiting room and placed bottom of the distribution list of documents so that she normally saw them only when it was too late to take effective action. Most highly classified information she never saw at all. She dealt with Wilson's constituency correspondence, and that with local Labour parties and the PLP. Not until 1966 was she able to get into the inner group where Wilson's speeches were drafted. She was more radical than Wilson on many issues, particularly in her opposition to United States policy in Vietnam, but she was unable to counter the overwhelming weight of official advice Wilson was receiving. Wilson valued her advice, particularly on party-political matters, where she was absolutely loyal, and her main influence came in the lunchtime and evening sessions which the 'Kitchen Cabinet' had with Wilson to gossip and consider tactics. Whatever the tensions Wilson would not countenance any attempt to downgrade her. When Derek Mitchell, whom Wilson had inherited as his principal private secretary, had a row with Marcia Williams in the autumn of 1965 and tried to remove her from No 10 to an office in the Commons, he lost his job.

Another member of the inner group, Tommy Balogh, was, like Wigg, beginning to lose influence over Wilson at this time. Balogh had long been antipathetic to the Civil Service and tried to get Wilson to sack its head, Sir Lawrence Helsby. Although Balogh had an office in the Cabinet Office he, like Marcia Williams, found it difficult to get himself on the circulation list for papers (an old but effective Civil Service device) and often was not invited to important meetings. Early in 1967 there was a major row between Burke Trend and Balogh: the former complained to Wilson that Balogh was 'snooping', rifling through the box of papers for the Prime Minister and putting in dissenting comments to advice given by

Trend. Wilson backed Trend and suggested to Balogh that it was time for him to return to academic life. He got Balogh's wife on his side, and agreed with her in January 1967 that Balogh should go and receive a peerage once back in Oxford. Balogh finally left when Oxford University demanded he either return or resign his Readership.

Those growing in influence in Downing Street during this period were Michael Halls and Gerald Kaufman. Halls had been Wilson's private secretary at the Board of Trade in the 1940s and in 1966 Wilson insisted that he should move to No 10 as the principal private secretary to replace the discredited Mitchell. He and Wilson got on well, and perhaps almost more importantly Halls was able to deal with the tempestuous moods of Marcia Williams. Kaufman had been a journalist with the *New Statesman* and was suggested by Tommy Balogh for a post at No 10 in 1965. Apart from acting as general factotum and dogsbody, his main role was to handle highly political aspects of managing the press, which the official press secretary, Trevor Lloyd-Hughes, did not relish. Often Wilson, Kaufman and Marcia Williams would be reading the early editions of the papers in the small hours of the morning at No 10, assessing the stories and trying to counter or even stop those they didn't like. This atmosphere of distrust of the press was to be at the centre of the most peculiar political episode of the whole government – the D-Notice affair.

In his generally anodyne account of his period as Prime Minister Wilson described the affair as 'self-inflicted, in personal terms one of my costliest mistakes of our near six years in office'.[15] And he also went on to describe his own handling as 'heavy-handed and over-hurried'.[16] Just what gave rise to this rare critical self-judgement?

The story began on 16 February 1967. An employee of the Western Union cable company told Chapman Pincher, a journalist specialising in national security stories on the *Daily Express*, that all outgoing commercial cables from Britain were collected every day by the government, read and then returned to the companies. Pincher checked the story with the Post Office, who confirmed it was true. He then spoke to Colonel Sammy Lohan, Secretary to the D-Notice Committee, who told him that no D-Notice was involved. (D-Notices are a voluntary system operated by the government and the media under which the media agree not to publish material falling into certain categories of information that the government believes would jeopardise national security.)

The next day Lohan mentioned the story to the Foreign Office and the government security machine swung into action. Lohan was told by MI5 to tell Pincher that security was involved and he must not print his story. In the Foreign Office, the head of the Permanent Secretary's Department (a euphemism for the section that controls MI6 and GCHQ) alerted ministers. The Foreign Office decided to deny the story. This they felt able to do on the basis that Pincher was saying that the cables went to the Ministry of Defence when in fact they went to GCHQ, which was technically part of the Foreign Office – a typical example of Whitehall being 'economical with the truth'. Lohan was then given a delicate briefing over the phone on why the story should be stopped. Despite the clear advice that Pincher's story did breach two D-Notices (those on the interception of communications and intelligence activities) Lohan decided over lunch with Pincher on 20 February to stick to his original advice that the story was not covered by any D-Notices. That afternoon the *Daily Express* decided to print the story. They knew that the *Daily Mail* also had the story and justified their decision on the grounds that the government's powers to intercept outgoing cables were public knowledge in the 1920 Official Secrets Act. In a series of garbled telephone calls that night the government thought they had got the agreement of Sir Max Aitken, the proprietor of the *Daily Express*, to stop publication, whereas Aitken thought he was free to publish as long as the story didn't breach D-Notices, which his staff assured him it didn't.

The next day in the House of Commons Wilson, reacting to the *Daily Express* story, stuck to the line taken by the Foreign Office and MI5, and attacked the newspaper:

> What I am concerned with today is a clear breach of two D-Notices despite the fact that the newspaper concerned was repeatedly warned that it would be contravening the notices.

Pincher replied to the charge in an article the next day saying that although Lohan had asked for the article not to be published, he had agreed that D-Notices did not apply. There was general Fleet Street support for the *Daily Express* and when the government tried to use the D-Notice Committee to investigate what had happened the media representatives refused to cooperate and one even resigned from the Committee. In this impasse, with the government's conduct and even its veracity under attack, Wilson was forced to agree to Ted Heath's suggestion that there should be a committee of Privy Councillors to investigate. Lord Radcliffe (the most distinguished of the 'Great and the Good', normally reserved for the most difficult enquiries) was appointed as chairman. The government was represented by Manny Shinwell and Heath nominated Selwyn Lloyd.

The committee took evidence from March to April and its report (after censorship for security reasons) was published early in June. The report's conclusions found against the government. With typical establishment litotes it stated that the Pincher article was 'not inaccurate' and 'it would not be right to say that the article amounted to a breach of the D-Notices'. And most telling of all 'we find no evidence to indicate that the decision to publish was taken with a deliberate intention of evading or defying the D-Notice procedure.' The government had lost the first round when it was forced to set up the Radcliffe Committee and it lost the second round when the report was published. It proceeded wilfully to lose the third round too. Having set up an independent prestigious committee to investigate, it now took the extraordinary step of rejecting its report. Wilson turned down the advice of Burke Trend to accept the Radcliffe report and his cleverly drafted form of words that would enable them to do so without too great a loss of face. Instead Wilson and Wigg prepared a White Paper stating that the effect of the Pincher article had been 'to cause damage, potentially grave, the consequences of which cannot even now be fully assessed' and going on to assert that the case was 'one which fell within the ambit of the D-Notices'. The White Paper was presented to the Cabinet in final form on the morning before it was due to be published in the afternoon. Moreover the agenda was rigged by Wilson so that they had a long discussion on Rhodesia and the Middle East, leaving only half an hour to discuss the White Paper. Even so Brown found time to argue against publishing and many of the rest of the Cabinet had similar doubts, but they were merely being presented with a *fait accompli*.

Not surprisingly the government White Paper met with almost universal hostility on publication. Its rejection of the Radcliffe report seemed like a vendetta against newspapers generally and against the *Daily Express*, Chapman Pincher and Colonel Lohan in particular. When the two reports were debated in the Commons on 22 June, the opposition attack was largely a personal one directed against the Prime Minister. Unusually Wilson did not open the debate but left it to Elwyn Jones, the Attorney-General, to do so. Wilson did wind up and therefore spoke last. Just before the conclusion of the debate he suddenly revealed to the House that

Lohan had not been positively vetted and that when he had been appointed in 1964 a decision had been taken 'to make specific enquiries, one of a number of questions being over-close association with journalists and especially with Mr Chapman Pincher'. Not surprisingly, after this glimpse of internal security matters and confidential reports on individuals who could not defend themselves, the debate ended in uproar. When the Lords came to debate the reports early in July, Radcliffe's contribution was described by one reporter as having 'taken apart the Government's case with the artistry of a surgeon, and at the end left it scattered about the operating theatre headless and limbless'.

Lohan had, meanwhile, resigned from the Civil Service but Heath argued successfully that he should be given the opportunity to clear his name. Wilson continued to control the government's response. A meeting with his close advisers, Crossman, Silkin and Marcia Williams, agreed that any enquiry would be private and undertaken by the Civil Service. As Crossman reported:

> Harold's main point was that he wanted to appoint Helsby, the ex-Head of the Civil Service, because he knew in advance what his report on Lohan would be.[17]

Wilson then set up what he chose to describe in public as the 'appropriate impartial procedure'. In addition to Helsby the members the government appointed to the enquiry were Sir James Dunnett (permanent secretary at Defence and therefore Lohan's boss) and Sir Harvey Druitt (Treasury Solicitor). Their report published early in August predictably said that the government accusations against Lohan were 'in accordance with the facts' and that Lohan had shown a 'lack of a proper sense of what is required of a responsible civil servant'.

The government had won a technical victory at the end of the affair but why did it act in such a self-defeating way? The true explanation is perhaps even more extraordinary than the affair itself and concerns the activities of Henry Kerby, Conservative MP for Arundel and ex-MI5 agent. For some time Kerby had been acting as a 'mole' within the Conservative party, passing on information to Wilson and Wigg. In 1969 he was to offer his party's election secrets to the Labour party in return for a peerage (later reduced to a knighthood). Before 1967 Kerby had already passed on to Wigg rumours about an affair between a Cabinet minister and a woman with communist leanings that had originated from Lohan and circulated among Conservative MPs. Early in 1967

Kerby had written to Wilson telling him that Lohan, who was fiercely anti-Labour, was giving Conservative MPs tips for parliamentary questions on defence. Wilson was keen to get rid of Lohan but sacking a civil servant was not easy. The D-Notice affair must have seemed a golden opportunity. Lohan had ignored all the advice from the intelligence agencies in letting Pincher print the story in what must have seemed to Wilson and Wigg a continuation of his campaign against the Labour government. The problem was that the evidence Wilson and Wigg had against Lohan could not be made public. In their determination to blame Lohan, Wilson and Wigg began to lose their sense of proportion. The rejection of the Radcliffe report was tactically unwise since it looked as though the government was conducting a vendetta against Lohan and the press. This, together with what looked like an attempt to smear Lohan, damaged the government's reputation, particularly in Fleet Street where they needed all the support they could get. This was one of the few occasions when Wilson's usually deft handling of day-to-day political affairs completely deserted him. Wilson seems to have told nobody else inside the government of the evidence against Lohan. As a result he became obsessed with his 'secret' information, forgot how the affair might appear to the average outsider and listened too much to the excessively security conscious George Wigg. In the aftermath Wigg's reputation and influence with Wilson declined rapidly. But by then the damage had been done.

By the autumn of 1967 the government had thrown away most of the advantages it had at the start of its second term. It had drifted for eighteen months without a coherent, long-term policy or goals that could be effectively communicated. The long-term economic problems had not been tackled and the deflationary package in July 1966 and the wage freeze had used up much of the goodwill within the trade union movement. Too much time had been spent on ephemeral issues that could not improve its political position, particularly in the area of foreign policy. It had also reached a position of almost unprecedented political unpopularity with the electorate. It was therefore in a weak position to deal with the aftermath of devaluation (which itself was a major blow to the government's prestige and economic record) and the series of disasters that rapidly followed.

11

July 1966: Economic Crisis and Political Plot

At the election, there will be only one choice – expansion, economic strength and full employment on the basis of planning: or, with the Conservatives, a prolonged plunge into deflation and unemployment.

Harold Wilson, 14 March 1966

From October 1964 the government had taken a risk in its handling of the economy in the run-up to the election in March 1966. It had adopted only moderate deflationary measures and avoided devaluation altogether. This approach had been vindicated politically by the election victory, but it left them in the spring of 1966 with a desperately unhealthy economic outlook. During the months after March there was no review of economic policy, no consideration of the options available and the implications for their social policies, no decisions on longer-term strategy and objectives. The ban on any collective discussion of devaluation remained in force. And their room for manoeuvre was limited as long as the deal made with the Americans in September 1965 remained in operation. It constrained their ability to make the fundamental choices that were required in the economic and strategic fields. As a result of all these influences the government's handling of a succession of problems, the Budget, the seaman's strike and the July crisis (when both the value of sterling and Harold Wilson's leadership were at stake) was uncertain and flawed.

The post-election Budget should, in theory, have given the government the opportunity to address the economic problems from a position of political strength. Yet there is no evidence of any fundamental reappraisal of economic strategy in the Budget. The government clearly hoped and believed that they could continue as they had for the previous eighteen months, and that a few more budgetary expedients combined with voluntary wage restraint would do the trick. The Chancellor had, as usual, to reconcile Treasury economic forecasts and political priorities. Immediately

184

after the election Callaghan's Treasury advisers were recommending increases in taxation. The latest internal forecasts for the balance of payments suggested a worse situation than in 1965 and the economy was operating at full stretch with little slack to provide more exports. Earnings in the first quarter of 1966 were 9½% up on the same period in 1965 and although this may have been good for Labour's re-election it showed that the voluntary incomes policy was not working. Uppermost in Callaghan's mind was the need to reconcile this with his own pre-election commitments. When the government had decided to go for a March election they were worried that the Conservatives might use the argument that a stiff Budget would follow any Labour victory. In order to defuse the problem Callaghan had made a statement in the Commons on 1 March in which he outlined the Budget he expected to introduce after the election. Betting and Gaming Tax would be introduced but the balance of payments was rapidly improving, short-term overseas debt was being repaid and he did 'not foresee the need for severe increases in taxation'.

Callaghan was in a nasty political dilemma. The way out was the introduction of Selective Employment Tax, a product of the fertile, if erratic, brain of his tax adviser, Nicky Kaldor. For its inventor it was a structural initiative designed eventually to reshape the ailing British economy. For Callaghan it was a useful deflationary measure to meet an urgent political need. He could present SET as merely a broadening of the tax base to help the economy and not a 'severe increase' in taxation. Kaldor took the view that the UK economy was becoming senile and that output could only be raised by stopping the drift of manpower into the service industries. This argument was based on his belief that the most thriving economies were produced by a flourishing manufacturing base although he never adduced any firm evidence for the linkage he sought to establish. Indeed it is just as likely that some economies had flourishing manufacturing sectors simply because the economy itself was healthy. SET was to be collected from all employers as part of their increased national insurance contributions at a rate of £1.25 per employee. Manufacturing industry would, however, receive a refund of this amount plus a premium of 37½p per employee. Services would get no refund, agriculture a refund but no premium. The net effect of SET (after the various payments, refunds and premiums were taken into account) was deflationary by about £315 million a year. It therefore met the requirement to take some of the heat out of the economy. However, its merits were less obvious to others and the hurried way in which it was introduced to achieve its deflationary effect did little to assist any assessment of its long-term impact. When asked what was the point of SET, the head of the Treasury, Sir William Armstrong, replied 'None at all'. The reaction of the Cabinet on Budget morning when they first heard of the proposal was bemused, as Crossman reported:

> When Callaghan started discussing this tax in Cabinet there was bewilderment and consternation. Nobody could quite follow what he was saying and he had the easiest time in the world.[1]

The problem with SET was that, despite its name, it was a blunt instrument for structural reform. It made no allowance for good or bad firms, their relative efficiencies or their location. Kaldor had also wanted the tax based on the numbers actually engaged in manufacturing within a plant, not the total workforce in a firm designated as 'manufacturing'. But the Department of Employment and the Treasury argued that it would be too complicated to do more than categorise firms and collect the tax on this broad basis. SET also required considerable administrative effort for very little revenue. As a measure for reducing demand it also had the drawback that for technical reasons the tax, and therefore its deflationary effect, could not be brought in before September. It remained to be seen whether this would be early enough to forestall an economic crisis.

In early May the government was faced with a potentially damaging industrial dispute between the shipowners and the National Union of Seamen, and a threatened strike that would badly affect Britain's trade. The NUS claim for a reduction in their working week from fifty-six to forty hours was equivalent to a wage rise of about 17%, compared with the 'norm' for the prices and incomes policy of 3½%. They were planning to strike from 16 May. Although not directly involved in the dispute the government had an interest on two fronts. The threat of disruption to trade meant they had to consider whether to take any action to maintain 'essential services' under the Emergency Powers Act. And they would have to try and ensure, through pressure on both sides, that the 'voluntary' incomes policy was not breached.

From the outset the government identified their aim: the NUS had to be brought to settle at or very near to the pay norm even at the expense of a prolonged strike. As Wilson told the Cabinet, '[they] had no choice: it was make or break for P and I'[2]. This reflected an earlier decision on their priorities. As early as January

1966 Ray Gunter and George Brown had told all ministers responsible for wage negotiations that the incomes policy was more important than conciliation. But on this occasion there was no consideration given as to whether the damage to the balance of trade from the strike would be greater than the damage to international confidence in sterling caused by a breach in the incomes policy.

In the days before the threatened strike the government tried to lean on the NUS. Ray Gunter, the Minister of Labour, twice saw the union and asked them to accept an enquiry but twice this proposal was rejected. Wilson saw the NUS to make one last appeal not to strike, but with no offer of extra money the appeal was rejected. Gunter told his Cabinet colleagues that the NUS had a good case but granted that acknowledging this would probably wreck the prices and incomes policy:

> Ray Gunter made it perfectly clear we could have a settlement at any time, since the owners were ready to put up the cash: it was the Government that was preventing the settlement because of the prices and incomes policy.[3]

The Cabinet agreed that this was not the battle they would have chosen, but felt that there was little option but to fight. The strike went ahead on 16 May.

Three days after the start of the strike the Cabinet met again and with only Dick Marsh dissenting decided to fight on. Four days later a State of Emergency was declared. The same day the Government announced the setting up of a court of enquiry under Lord Pearson, though the Cabinet had not discussed this at their meeting earlier in the day. The report of the enquiry, published on 7 June, recommended phasing in the reduction in the working week over a year – exactly half way between the employers' offer and the union's demands. The NUS rejected the report two days later. Having got into the fight the government was now becoming even more determined to win. At a bitter discussion in Cabinet on 14 June Wilson agreed to talk to the TUC, the NUS and the shipowners to try and settle the dispute within the incomes policy. But as one of his colleagues saw it his real aims were different: 'Harold is out to smash the seamen's union.'[4] Two days later after unsuccessful talks Wilson's views were changing. He reported to the Cabinet that his contacts with the shipowners had been an eye-opener: 'I begin to see what this strike is about,' he added.[5] He then suggested that there should be a radical examination of the structure and future of the industry.

But with the parties still deadlocked and a state of emergency declared the government had to decide what to do next. From the start of the strike an interdepartmental committee of ministers had been meeting daily under the chairmanship of the Home Secretary, Roy Jenkins, to consider how to respond. In practice the committee had little to do. Unlike many other industrial disputes the government did not have the option of moving in servicemen to keep supplies flowing – they could not start sailing ships round the world. Since the government could take no action, the declaration of a state of emergency was essentially a public relations exercise and a way of putting pressure on the NUS. Even after a month of the strike the government was able to cope without emergency powers. As Denis Healey reported to the Cabinet, 'Much as we should like a problem to solve, we haven't got one.'[6] Nevertheless ministers decided to set up regional emergency committees, 'even though there is no real need for them yet, in order to justify renewal of the Emergency Regulations'.[7]

Wilson now decided that more robust action was required. On 20 June he stated in the Commons that the executive of the NUS was dominated by Communists or near-Communists which he described as 'this tightly knit group of politically motivated men'. His information came from MI5 and was probably obtained through tapping NUS officials' phones – a common activity in industrial disputes. This put the NUS under more pressure and, with the TUC also backing a settlement, Wilson was soon reporting a deal was close. On 28 June the Cabinet agreed that Wilson should actually name the eight members of the NUS executive suspected of having Communist associations, which he did that afternoon in the Commons. The next day the strike was called off. After six weeks the NUS accepted terms very close to those recommended by the Pearson enquiry three weeks earlier. Even though they were disguised by elaborate formulae the terms clearly breached the government's pay 'norm'. Although it is not clear what finally persuaded the NUS to settle, it was probably a combination of a long dispute, TUC pressure, a clear stand by the government that they would not go beyond Pearson and the additional pressure from the allegations of Communist influence.

The government had fought a long and hard battle. Was it worthwhile? The dispute had an immediate short-term effect on the balance of payments. Exports were affected first, falling in June by £70 million (about 20%), and the monthly trade figures showed a deficit of £40 million, which was worse than the average for 1965. But this was bound to be a temporary phenomenon and the underlying situation was not so worrying; indeed the figures for the current account of the balance of payments for the second half of 1966 were to show a small surplus. Psychology, though, was just as important as reality and the international bankers had their pessimistic view of the future of sterling reinforced by the dispute. The gold and convertible currency reserves fell by £38 million in May, and further poor figures were published early in July. Another crisis for sterling and the British economy seemed to be rapidly approaching. Douglas Jay, the minister responsible for Britain's trade, thought the government's stance had not after all been worth it:

> It is perfectly possible that the balance of payments would have suffered either way. But, in retrospect, by a narrow margin, I am inclined to believe we were wrong.[8]

Wilson always argued that the government was 'blown off course' by the dispute and that it led almost inevitably to the July crisis.

At first the government did not believe that a crisis was imminent. On 1 July Wilson, Brown and Callaghan met to discuss the economic situation and concluded that there was no need for any special action as the outlook was reasonably optimistic. Meanwhile other members of the Cabinet were less sanguine, already convinced that the May Budget had failed, and that a stark choice between devaluation and massive deflation was looming. But there was no general discussion of the situation outside the inner group of ministers and no attempt at contingency planning. Early in July a further round of speculation against sterling was underway on the foreign exchanges and the atmosphere was not improved by remarks made by the French Prime Minister, Georges Pompidou, during his visit to London on 7–8 July. At a press conference he urged Wilson to straighten out the British economy, spoke about the success of the major French devaluation of the franc in 1958 and hinted that Britain would have to do the same before entering the EEC. Suddenly devaluation became an issue, even a practical possibility, which added to the existing speculative atmosphere.

By 9 July the government was faced with the need for decisions. On that day the new Governor of the Bank of England, Sir Leslie O'Brien, met Wilson and Callaghan at No 10. O'Brien reported that speculation on the foreign exchanges was causing a major drain on Britain's gold and currency reserves, and advised that action had to be taken to cut back domestic demand in order to raise the confidence of overseas bankers and preserve the level of sterling. He specifically asked for a 1% increase in Bank Rate as a signal of determination and also argued in favour of a major deflationary package, and a stiff prices and incomes policy. It was the standard response to an old problem. This put the economic crisis firmly on the Whitehall agenda where it was quickly linked with the discussion of public expenditure plans already scheduled for the middle of July.

On 12 July the Cabinet discussed a major paper from Callaghan on public expenditure. He admitted that the May Budget had failed: he had hoped to hold back consumption until SET took effect in September but now public expenditure cuts were required to do the job. Bids for future expenditure from individual departments were in excess of the total that could be afforded and he wanted an overall cut of £500 million, about three times the level of the crisis cuts made in July 1965. Predictably there was strong opposition to Callaghan's proposals. He wanted £100 million cut from overseas expenditure (which would have the advantage of a direct effect on the balance of payments), but Brown and Stewart argued strongly against. Others, in particular Crossman and Crosland, spoke out against any cuts in public expenditure. This forced Callaghan into another of his gloomy warnings, as Crossman later reported:

> At this point the Chancellor woke up and said that he must tell Cabinet frankly that he didn't know how we were going to get out of the mess. We had totally failed to reach our objectives, we were drifting into devaluation in the worst possible conditions and he didn't know how he could retain his position as Chancellor.[9]

The day after that Cabinet meeting Callaghan came to a firm conclusion. At the Treasury he informed Nicky Kaldor and his private secretary, Ian Bancroft, that 'I've decided we'll have to devalue'. Worried by the likely strength of the opposition in the Cabinet and the reaction of Labour backbenchers to a massive deflationary package, he gave instructions to start contingency planning for devaluation on 31 July. He then went to see Wilson to tell him of his conversion to a new economic policy. This was to be the crucial meeting of the whole crisis. What options were available to the two men?

The government had to choose between three possible courses. The first was to act directly on the balance of payments by imposing import controls and making major cuts in overseas expenditure, both civil and military. Import controls had been vaguely considered as an option as early as October 1964 and rejected. They were to remain a theoretical possibility for the next three years but were never seriously contemplated. The problem with import controls was that they could only be a temporary solution that would buy time to put right the underlying imbalances. Major cuts in overseas expenditure also posed problems. A majority of the Cabinet would have had no compunction about slashing the aid budget but cuts in overseas defence expenditure would seriously have affected British commitments in the Far East, the Gulf and Germany. The second option was devaluation of the pound combined with a deflationary package designed to offset the inflationary effects of higher import prices by reducing domestic demand and shifting resources into exports. The third option was yet another bout of deflation in the tradition of the 'stop-go' policies that had failed to provide a long-term solution in the past.

Callaghan must have known that his advocacy of devaluation would place Wilson in a difficult position. In 1964–5 it had been ruled out for many reasons. Although the electoral imperative had now receded, other considerations still weighed heavily with the Prime Minister. His status and position, indeed even the success of the government, had become linked to maintaining the value of the pound. His view was that the government had to do everything in its power to try and avoid devaluation. As he was to write in his memoirs:

> If in the end we lost, then the world would know we had done everything to avoid it, and would know that we had not chosen devaluation as an easy way out.[10]

But there was also another reason not acknowledged in the memoirs behind Wilson's thinking: the deal made with the Americans in September 1965 to defend the pound. In return for this support Britain had had to promise not to devalue, to restrain internal demand, toughen the prices and incomes policy, and agree to maintain its forces in the Far East. The United States did not see this as a short-term bargain and by July 1966 the American administration was again worried about the British economic situation and the failure of the support operation to bring about a substantial improvement in Britain's economic situation. At the beginning of the crisis Johnson and his senior advisers considered what message to send to the British. The result was a blunt warning and demand for action:

191

The United Kingdom performance since the announcement last September of the support operation . . . has been disappointing. It shows no sign of the major improvement that is needed for confidence in sterling, the early restoration of balance, the prevention of the dissipation of the reserves that have been accumulated as a result of aid by others. In our view, if the United Kingdom is to avoid devaluation, maintain the pound as a reserve currency, restore its position and avoid the risk of a dangerous dislocation of international financial affairs, much stronger stabilization measures than those presently invoked are required. The details of these measures cover some compression of demand, the prompt inauguration of an effective incomes policy, and some effective substitute for the import surcharge which is scheduled to expire. All seem indicated. It is only fair to state our view that absent [sic] such a program the existing financial cushion provided by our support and that of others will be dissipated. It is also our impression that no further financial support beyond that already committed could be marshalled on a multilateral basis.[11]

The other part of the September 1965 deal was also still in place as John Stevens, the Treasury representative in Washington, confirmed when he returned to London in the middle of the crisis to brief Wilson for his forthcoming visit to the United States. He dined with one of the directors of the Bank of England and told him that

Johnson had made it clear to Wilson that the pound was not to be devalued and no drastic action east of Suez was to be undertaken until after the American elections in November. In return the pound would be supported by the Americans to any extent necessary.[12]

Wilson also had to take into account the views of George Brown who was now violently pro-devaluation. He had always been sceptical about continual deflationary packages and the July 1965 measures were the end of the road for him. Afterwards he put work in hand within the DEA on the effects of devaluation, which provided an intellectual justification for a change of policy. There were also two other factors. Brown was strongly in favour of entry into the EEC and he saw devaluation as a necessary first step. Even more important, if the Treasury won the battle for yet another deflationary package, then the DEA's National Plan would no longer be worth the paper it was written on and Brown's work at the DEA would be largely worthless. But there was also a strong element of political calculation. He had never been reconciled to Wilson as leader of the party and still wanted the leadership himself. But Wilson had just won a major electoral triumph and if he stayed in office until at least 1970 then Brown would be too old to succeed him. For Brown to replace him it had to be done as an internal coup – an almost impossible task against a sitting Prime Minister. Nevertheless he tried hard over the next six days, using devaluation as the issue and making much of Wilson's dependence on President Johnson, to split the Cabinet and isolate Wilson.

Wilson lost no time in stopping any moves towards devaluation. If Callaghan were to join Brown in advocating devaluation then he would find himself isolated in the inner economic policy-making group and other members of the Cabinet might also begin to waver. His first task was, therefore, to win over Callaghan, and ensure that Brown and not himself was isolated. In a long session Wilson eventually persuaded Callaghan to change his mind. In return for his agreement to support a deflationary package and reject devaluation, Callaghan obtained concessions. Whereas in July 1965 Callaghan had been forced by the Cabinet to announce the cuts, now Wilson agreed that he would do so. In this way Callaghan hoped to ensure that he would not take the blame for the harsh measures and that Wilson's own reputation would be put on the line. Did Wilson offer more than this? Callaghan was keen to leave the Treasury and Wilson may have hinted at the possibility of the Foreign Office. Certainly Callaghan later briefed the press that he wanted to be Foreign Secretary after the crisis was over. If there was an informal understanding it was never implemented and in the August 1966 reshuffle Wilson was to boast of how he had been able to 'outfox' Callaghan.

With the Chancellor back in line, Wilson felt able to make clear the government's position. By taking a public stand he deliberately cut off the line of retreat and made the issue of devaluation into one of confidence in his leadership. Speaking at the Guildhall that evening he attacked the 'defeatist cries, moaning minnies and wet editorials' of the 'sell-Britain-short brigade' and added:

> I give an assurance that the value of sterling will be maintained. We shall not shrink from any further measures, however severe or unpopular, that may be necessary.

On the morning of 14 July the Cabinet had their first discussion on the crisis. Wilson opened by describing the pressure on the pound and said that he and the inner group of ministers had decided that Bank Rate would be going up by 1% that day. He also explained that the inner group favoured a mixture of domestic and overseas cuts but that no details had been settled except that the overseas cuts would amount to £100 million. He stressed that the group were agreed on 'avoiding conventional deflationary methods' (whatever that meant), though he himself favoured stiffer hire purchase terms. Other items the inner group were discussing included import controls from the end of 1966, when the surcharge imposed in 1964 finally ran out, and a wage and price freeze together with higher taxes for the better paid. He argued that the mood of the country favoured a tough package. The timescale he suggested for announcements was relaxed. He would be away over the weekend in Russia and then had to go to Washington so that the package should be agreed by early in August. It was Barbara Castle, unaware of the secret deal, who suggested that a statement before the visit to Washington might be presentationally better so that it didn't look as though it had been done under American pressure(!). The rest of the Cabinet agreed and the date for the package was brought forward to the end of July.

The main debate in Cabinet was over the cuts in overseas expenditure. Not unexpectedly Michael Stewart as Foreign Secretary was strongly opposed, arguing that they would mean a massive reduction in British influence and a cut in troop levels in either the Far East or Germany. Others in the Cabinet were keen to retain the references in the preliminary statement that Wilson was to make that afternoon in the Commons so as to try and ensure that some defence cuts were made. Eventually a compromise was reached – overseas cuts would be referred to but no specific figure would be quoted. Jenkins argued for a firm commitment to a wage and price freeze but others felt that it should be left to the main package. That afternoon Wilson spoke in the Commons in a relaxed vein: he confirmed that the government was reviewing the situation and that in the near future some deflationary measures could be expected.

Wilson was, however, still worried about his political position and the role of Brown and Callaghan. In his memoirs he denied any threat to his leadership:

There was no plot, no conspiracy, no cabal, no organisation.[13]

That was not how he felt at the time according to Barbara Castle's contemporary record:

In the tea room ran into Harold on the prowl. He told me there was a great plot on by George and Jim to get rid of him. 'You know what the game is: devalue and get into Europe. We've got to scotch it.'[14]

On Saturday 16 July Wilson flew to Moscow for a three-day visit. At home these three days saw a ferment of activity among his political colleagues. He was kept constantly in touch with developments on all fronts. Private secretaries from No 10 flew out with preliminary drafts of the package and George Wigg kept him informed of the political manoeuvrings. That day George Brown was at the Durham miners' gala in a highly emotional and confused state. He first told Tony Benn that he was going to resign that night but after a phonecall with Wilson before the latter left for Moscow he was slightly more relaxed and was now going to resign later in the week. Brown also spoke on the phone to Roy Jenkins, who described him as 'hysterical', and to Sir Leslie O'Brien, trying to increase the group favouring devaluation.

The next day was one of intense political activity as Cabinet ministers sounded each other out about their views. They were divided over policy and confused about how to handle the situation. Six members favoured devaluation – Brown, Crosland, Jenkins, Crossman, Benn and Castle – but only Brown was prepared to push his views to the point of threatening resignation. Crossman wanted devaluation but hoped to use the issue to achieve his long-desired aim of setting up a small group to direct economic strategy (with him on it) and at no time was he prepared to overthrow Wilson. Benn was opposed to a severe package but remained optimistic that the Cabinet would not endorse one. As he told Barbara Castle:

> We should draw up the package needed to put the economy in order and then let the pound float. Otherwise we should deflate and still have to devalue later.[15]

Benn did not believe that Brown would resign but if he did nobody should follow, as he wrote in his diary: 'Political unity at this moment is more important than anything else.'[16] Others, including Peter Shore and Douglas Jay, were worried about the severity of the package but did not favour devaluation, whilst Fred Lee wanted major defence cuts. Some, like Dick Marsh, were more masochistic. He wanted really savage cuts which he thought, in some way he never clearly articulated, would enable the government to start again. The less important members of the Cabinet were likely to follow the Prime Minister, the Chancellor and the majority of their colleagues. There was not a united front among the government's economic advisers. Both Kaldor and Neild favoured floating the pound but Tommy Balogh, although in favour, out of loyalty to Wilson tried to convince doubting members of the Cabinet not to devalue at this stage. These confused views and aims were to be one of Wilson's strengths in the next forty-eight hours.

Wilson was still out of the country, although he had decided that because of the increasing tension in Whitehall and Westminster he would resolve the issue quickly by announcing the package the day after his return. Virtually the whole of 18 July was spent by ministers in lobbying, seeking out support and agreeing who would say what at the Cabinet the next day. The main organiser of the anti-devaluation group was Douglas Jay, who was busy rounding up support and arranging for Douglas Houghton to speak in the Cabinet debate. Crossman was determined to try and organise a group in favour of floating the pound, and arranged to see Jenkins, Castle and Crosland that evening in the Commons. Both Jenkins and Crosland favoured floating in order to give the government some room for manoeuvre in its economic policy. Castle took the same line and both were agreed that the government had to have a clear strategy. As Crossman put it:

> The first thing we must do tomorrow is ask what the package is *for* . . . We mustn't get drawn into discussion of details on the package before we have this out first.[17]

The one thing that the pro-devaluation group could agree on was that the issue of entry into Europe should not be raised so as not to alienate the anti-EEC members of the Cabinet.

But the key figure was still George Brown. He was in an emotional, though not alcoholic, mood, convinced that Britain should be less dependent on the US, pull out of the Far East and not accept American money to save the pound. But this, he told a few colleagues, was impossible because Wilson was 'bound personally and irrevocably to President Johnson and had ceased to be a free agent', and he warned them that when Wilson flew to Washington he would yet again 'cook up some screwy little deal' with Johnson.[18] But Brown could not bring the other pro-devaluationists to turn against Wilson. Those on the right wing of the party, such as Jenkins and Crosland, were not prepared to resign with him. For those on the left the thought of Brown as

196

leader was enough to make them stick with Wilson even if they disagreed with him strongly over policy. This was made very clear in a long discussion between Brown, Benn and Castle that evening in the Commons. Benn described the scene with Brown in an excited mood:

> He repeated definitely that he was going. He said he had warned Harold a year ago that he was not prepared to put up with another episode of this kind and that Roy and Tony agreed with him. Barbara said she thought there would be a majority in the Cabinet in favour of his view but George said that it was impossible that this could carry the day as Harold was so heavily committed publicly to maintaining the value of the pound. Barbara said she thought Harold would accept the majority view and George said, 'No, this involves his leadership. Do you want me as leader, Barbara?' Barbara replied firmly, 'No.' 'Then Harold will win,' said George.[19]

Exactly the same happened when Brown saw Crossman:

> 'Look, would you support me if Harold had to resign?' I said, 'Certainly not.' And he said, 'Well, Barbara said the same thing to me. Of course, you two are bound to Harold, that's why you can't do any good.'[20]

Already that evening Wilson was starting to put the pressure on any wavering members of the Cabinet. George Wigg made it apparent that he knew what was going on, that loyalty to Wilson would be the primary test. There was, he warned, a clear choice between accepting the package or resigning.

Wilson returned from Moscow at lunchtime on 19 July and the Cabinet met from 5 pm until nearly 10 pm. During that long session there was no discussion of the contents of the package, only of the case for and against devaluation. Wilson opened by making the surprising admission that the cuts might not work but that the government could afford to let unemployment double to 700,000 and concluded that 'my view is that we have not yet reached the point where it is clear that devaluation is the best course'.[21] He felt that the best time to float (which he preferred to devaluation) would be in the spring of 1967 and that the aim should be to pick a time when the pound would float upwards. Crossman spoke next in favour of floating, arguing that the package was no different from 1965, just more severe, and that there was no guarantee it would work. He wanted a carefully worked-out strategy linked to floating. In this he was supported by Jenkins, Crosland, Benn and Castle.

Then the anti-devaluation group spoke. They were led by Douglas Jay, who argued that devaluation had solved nothing in 1949. He was supported by Douglas Houghton, who spoke of the betrayal of obligations and stressed that devaluation should only take place under severe pressure. All the ministers with overseas responsibilities (Stewart, Healey, Greenwood and Bottomley) spoke against devaluation, as did Fred Peart and Willie Ross, together with Lords Gardiner and Longford, and Cledwyn Hughes who argued for major cuts in the social services. Callaghan joined this group but indicated he would not be opposed to a carefully worked-out strategy for devaluation in 1967. Brown only said that he was thinking of resigning.

Wilson, with about two-thirds of the Cabinet on his side, had ensured that his view would prevail. Nevertheless after all the machinations he felt it prudent to make a few tactical concessions. He accepted the need for a long-term strategy and agreed that if unemployment rose above 480,000 he would consider devaluation, and that the methods and timing for any devaluation would be discussed by a Cabinet committee. (None of these ideas was ever properly implemented.) The meeting broke up with Wilson explaining that if the decision had gone in favour of floating the pound he would have considered resigning.

The Cabinet began to consider the contents of the package at 9 am on the 20th when an announcement was due that afternoon, and the CBI and TUC were to be told beforehand at 2.30. As Douglas Jay explained:

> The Treasury papers before us, making precise proposals and not offering alternatives, had only been in ministers' hands for about thirty hours. This was a mockery of sensible government, and I had never seen anything like it in the eleven years which by that time I had worked in the government machine . . . I no longer expected or hoped for the right decision, but merely sought to prevent disastrous blunders.[22]

Crossman had the same reaction:

> Cabinet was a desultory affair. Nothing had been adequately prepared. Nothing had been thought out properly. We were fixing things, once again, horribly inefficiently, at the last moment.[23]

Discussion of the £100 million cut in overseas expenditure rapidly degenerated into farce. Instead of any change in policy (which was ruled out by the secret commitments given to the United States) ministers decided to assume that somehow they would receive more money from Hong Kong, Libya and Germany as a contribution towards keeping British troops stationed there. The one real cut they could agree on was to reduce overseas aid by 10% (£20 million). There was a long discussion about import controls, which Wilson agreed had to come, though later. Callaghan, backed by Castle, suggested cutting ministerial salaries but this was rejected as a gimmick and instead a 10% surcharge on surtax payers was imposed. A foreign exchange allowance of £50 for overseas holidays was agreed after Callaghan read through a handful of travel brochures. Brown was quiet and withdrawn, and only became animated when he insisted that he personally should tell the CBI and TUC about the wage and price freeze.

The package announced by Wilson that afternoon was the usual collection of Treasury measures introduced after each crisis in the previous ten years, though this time much stiffer. Severe restrictions were imposed on hire purchase together with a 10% increase in purchase tax, petrol and excise duties (apart from tobacco). The £100 million 'cut' in overseas expenditure was matched by a £150 million cut in public investment. The size of the squeeze on the economy was about £350 million in 1966–67 and over £500 million in a full year. Most drastic of all there was to be a complete wage and price freeze for six months followed by six months of 'severe restraint'.

20 July was to be yet another day of fluctuating moods for George Brown. Suddenly at 1.45 he told Wilson that he was resigning and a formal letter was sent across to No 10. Wilson was worried by this threat. If Brown resigned then the Cabinet would be seen as disunited with Brown, deputy leader of the party, publicly advocating what many would see as a much more attractive policy option – devaluation. This might not bring Wilson down immediately but could seriously damage his long-term position, particularly if deflation did not work. He asked Brown to think again but Brown was not in the Commons for Wilson's statement that afternoon. Wilson sent Wigg round to argue with Brown and later he was joined by Bert Bowden. Their discussions went on throughout the evening. At the same time Bill Rodgers, a junior minister at the DEA and strongly right wing, was in the Commons collecting about 100 signatures for a petition to ask Brown to stay. Eventually at 10.30 Brown and Wilson met. Brown was asked not to make the position of sterling worse in any resignation speech he made. This effectively neutered anything that he could say and

Wilson, together with the various appeals for loyalty from Wigg and Bowden, gradually wore him down until eventually the resignation was withdrawn in the full glare of the TV lights and cameras in Downing Street. The coup had collapsed ignominiously – Brown, left isolated, could not bring himself to resign at a moment of crisis for the government and party he had worked for all his life. But the real gainer from his sense of loyalty was Wilson.

The July crisis was the crucial turning point in the life of the government; the moment when the wrong direction was taken. By the early summer of 1966 it was (or should have been) clear that the moment of reckoning on economic policy was fast approaching. Faced with a range of options from import controls and defence cuts through devaluation to deflation, they chose to implement the standard Treasury deflationary package that had been used in every economic crisis for the previous ten years – except this time it was more drastic because the situation was worse. Such packages had not worked in the past and there was no evidence to suggest that it would work now. The major cut in domestic demand would produce an improvement in the balance of payments simply by lowering the demand for imports and slightly improving the attractiveness of exports because of the shrinking home market. But this was no long-term policy to correct the underlying problems causing the existing deficit. Deflation in itself did nothing to shift resources into correcting the external balance. The root of the problems lay in the increasingly uncompetitive nature of British industry. The July package tried to deal with this problem by the old policy of reducing wages so as to increase competitiveness rather than increasing productivity. But the wage freeze was only short term and showed no signs of causing any fundamental shift in Britain's economic performance, and no effort was made to increase investment (in fact it was cut) so as to raise productivity.

Deflation in 1966 only made sense if it was a long-term solution which it clearly was not. Instead it had serious consequences for the future of the government. The wage freeze, which was accepted by the TUC, used up valuable political capital which would have been better preserved for a devaluation package. Deflation marked the end of the National Plan with its optimistic aim of a 25% increase in national wealth by 1970 and the end of Labour's pretensions to be planning rationally the future development of the economy. In addition the package lost valuable time. As a result of July 1966 the government was driven to devaluation in the worst possible circumstances in November 1967. Eighteen months were lost to pointless deflation. By then the government's stock had fallen to an all-time low and the time available to reap the benefits of devaluation was very short. July 1966 ensured that devaluation seemed even more of a political defeat than it need have been.

After mishandling the Budget and the seamen's strike ministers became swept up in the atmosphere of crisis and allowed themselves to take decisions in the worst possible way. They never had a clear set of objectives, no alternative packages were properly considered and the timescale for discussion had a ludicrously short self-imposed deadline. Not surprisingly the whole package lacked any coherent thought or strategy; it was yet another hastily compiled set of measures that showed the inability of the Whitehall system to produce well-planned and organised policy making.

The blame for the way the crisis was handled and its outcome must rest squarely on the shoulders of Harold Wilson. It was Wilson who ensured that devaluation did not take place in July 1966. If he had backed his Chancellor at the crucial meeting on 13 July and agreed to devalue instead of forcing him to change his mind, there can be little doubt that the triumvirate of Wilson, Callaghan and Brown would have carried the rest of the Cabinet. Throughout the crisis Wilson was determined that there should be deflation, not devaluation, and that the Cabinet should be forced to accept that line. Apart from his own personal views Wilson was still bound by the secret deal he had made with the Americans in September 1965. Their support for the pound required British action beyond simply avoiding devaluation. In September 1965 a statutory prices and incomes policy had been introduced, and the economy had not been reflated. Now the real price had to be paid. Not only did the government not have freedom to pull out from the Far East but it had to deflate and introduce a wage freeze to keep the confidence of the Americans and the other central banks.

Ironically Wilson was able to get his way relatively easily because of the attempted Cabinet revolt and not despite it. Open dissent from about a third of his colleagues, including some powerful figures, did not develop into a coherent policy debate largely through the activities of George Brown. He failed to put forward a clear and cogent case to his Cabinet colleagues why devaluation was the right economic course to take. His legitimate reasons for wanting devaluation were eclipsed by his manoeuvrings in the interests of his own political future. This was his last chance to overthrow Wilson and secure the leadership but it was a botched and incompetent effort. In the end key ministers such as Crossman, Castle and Benn put loyalty to Wilson before what they saw as the right economic policy. Wilson exploited their dilemma to keep wavering members of the Cabinet in line by making the issue one of confidence in his leadership. Brown was left isolated and his abortive attempt to resign on the day the cuts were announced left in tatters the remaining pieces of his political reputation. The position of Callaghan was, as so often, enigmatic. Although involved in negotiating elements of the deal with the United States, unlike Wilson he clearly didn't feel bound to continue to rule out devaluation. He secured an improved long-term position by watching Brown destroy his chance whilst leaving Wilson the disagreeable task of announcing the cuts and committing his reputation to the new policy. Similar factors probably dissuaded Jenkins from resigning since he had his own long-term ambition to replace Wilson and saw no need to help Brown. Crosland, the other important devaluationist, had long been loyal to Callaghan.

After ten days of hectic, unplanned and chaotic activity the government finished up imposing the most severe example of the 'stop-go' policies that had dominated British economic policy since the mid-1950s – a policy they had consistently derided in opposition. They had been trapped in the same policy failure as previous Conservative governments. They also introduced a wage and price freeze which they had rejected only months earlier during the election. Then Wilson had said:

> a wage freeze, if by that you mean a law to hold back wage increases, that would be unthinkable.[24]

And on another occasion:

> As to the idea of freezing all wage claims, salary claims . . . I think this would be monstrously unfair . . . I do not think you can ever legislate for wage increases and no party is setting out to do that.[25]

In September 1965 Brown had told the Cabinet that he only agreed to the introduction of a statutory policy on the strict understanding that it was not the first step to a freeze. Now he was the strongest advocate of the freeze.

The outcome of the crisis demonstrated a lack of political will, as Tony Benn had recognised before the crucial decisions were taken:

> This is really a political crisis and when we have to choose what to cut it will be a test of our own political faith. The economists can't help us at this stage, beyond giving us a general indication of the lines on which we should go.[26]

But the ability of the politicians to use words to disguise policy failure still remained. Good old deflation now became, in Wilson's words,

> a shake-out which will release the nation's manpower, skilled and unskilled, and lead to a more purposive use of labour for the sake of increasing exports and giving effect to other national priorities.

By the time of the Labour party conference in the autumn the view had become even rosier:

> The July measures must now provide us with a once-for-all opportunity to break the whole miserable cycle we inherited. So far from being a rejection of expansion they create an opportunity to continued expansion.

The final irony was that little changed apart from the rhetoric. There was no long-term planning and devaluation remained a forbidden subject within Whitehall. The July measures avoided dealing with the real problems and simply postponed the inevitable decisions until a much less favourable climate politically and economically. The next eighteen months were spent travelling up a dead end.

12
Europe:
The Cold Ante-Chamber

Britain watched the creation of the European Economic Community in the mid-1950s from a distance. Only when the new organisation had succeeded did Britain help establish and join an alternative – the European Free Trade Association – and that was only a trading bloc with no supranational or integrationist tendencies. Yet by the early 1960s possible entry into the EEC was at the centre of the political and economic debate for two reasons. First, there was growing concern over the relative failure of British economic performance compared with that of other West European countries, and second, there were doubts about Britain's strategic role following the withdrawal from Empire. There was also a strong political motivation behind the British application to join the EEC which was made in 1961 and vetoed by General de Gaulle in 1963. The Conservatives needed a new issue as the centrepiece of their programme at the next election after thirteen years in power. As one senior Conservative party official put it:

> Europe was to be our *deus ex machina*; it was to create a new, contemporary political argument with insular Socialism; dish the Liberals by stealing their clothes; give us something *new* after 12–13 years, act as the catalyst of modernisation; give us a new place in the international sun. It was Macmillan's ace, and de Gaulle trumped it. The Conservatives never really recovered.[1]

Hugh Gaitskell as Labour party leader had been strongly opposed to EEC entry, speaking of the end of 'a thousand years' of British history. Opposition to entry on any terms that were likely to be negotiable was Labour party policy. It was combined with the important strain of pro-Commonwealth opinion, which had always existed within the Labour party, to create a general disenchantment with what was seen as an inward-looking and protectionist Europe. Before taking office in 1964 the Labour party was divided into three camps. There was a small, strongly pro-entry group led by Brown and Jenkins on the right of the party. There was a larger group opposed to entry consisting of some left-wingers such as Castle but also those on the right such as Jay, and most important of all Gaitskell. The majority, including Wilson, were agnostic; content simply to attack the Conservative efforts to join. However, the issue virtually disappeared from British politics after de Gaulle's veto and Wilson showed no interest in reviving it before the 1964 election.

Once in office this lack of a strong view within the party left the government open to the pressures both within Whitehall and the establishment generally. It was the received wisdom in both quarters that Britain should join; not for the economic benefits, which were dubious, but to preserve Britain's position as an important international power, and keep it involved in the inner circle of diplomatic and strategic affairs. There was also significant pressure from the United States government in the same direction. Since the early 1960s it had been US policy that Britain should enter Europe and find the role which it had lost in the world with the decline of the Empire.

In office the Labour government began steadily and perceptibly to shift its position towards a pro-EEC stance. In the first few months some small initiatives were taken to increase trade within the Commonwealth but Wilson became disillusioned with its role and future, particularly after India and Pakistan accepted Russian assistance to end their border conflict in 1965. In the early part of 1965, during a visit to Rome, at a Socialist Conference at Chequers and at EFTA Conferences in Vienna and Copenhagen, Wilson raised the possibility of some form of association between EFTA and the EEC. This would have involved industrial free trade between the two groups but with EFTA keeping its own agricultural policies and political independence. EFTA formally invited the EEC to discuss these issues but, since the benefits from the proposed arrangement would have been almost entirely in favour of EFTA, the EEC never responded.

Opinion within Whitehall was changing. The Department of Economic Affairs was starting to reflect the strongly pro-EEC views of George Brown and the Foreign Office, which had originally been somewhat sceptical about the EEC, was rapidly becoming a vigorous proponent of entry. In June 1965 Douglas Jay and Fred Peart (two strong opponents of entry) responded to Wilson's request, and produced a paper on the trade and agricultural implications of entry that came to gloomy conclusions. The Foreign Office made its own position clear when, in December 1965, Michael Stewart advised Wilson to make an immediate application to join the Community. Wilson refused to allow any papers to be circulated to the Cabinet.

His refusal to discuss the issue was because of the forthcoming election. He knew that part of the Cabinet was opposed to entry and he also wished to pose as a sceptic during the campaign in contrast to the much more enthusiastic Heath. Those who spoke to Wilson before the election gained the strong impression that he favoured joining and during the campaign he was careful to say that 'we shall go in if the conditions are right'. However, he then went on to spell out conditions on free access to cheap food and raw material markets in the Commonwealth, and rejection of supranational control of foreign policy, which were impossible to reconcile with EEC membership.

Immediately after the election the climate changed. On 19 April Wilson told Cecil King that Britain ought to be in the EEC within two or three years. Inside Whitehall he set up a European Committee of the Cabinet chaired by himself and composed of Stewart, Brown, Callaghan, Healey, Peart, Thomson, Bowden and Jay. Of these only Brown was strongly in favour of the EEC whilst Healey, Peart and Jay were opposed and the others unclear in their views. The most significant omission was Jenkins, whom Wilson had deliberately kept off the group. At the first meeting on 9 May the paper by officials concluded that 'We believe we should refrain from taking any initiatives ourselves for the time being, even in the form of informal probes.' This caution did not restrain Brown's enthusiasm, as one participant put it:

> It was staggering to hear George Brown taking the bit between his teeth and announcing our collective determination to go into Europe.[2]

At a Labour party NEC meeting three weeks later Brown was much more circumspect in front of a more hostile audience. Then he explained Britain probably wouldn't get into the EEC whilst de Gaulle remained in power and devaluation would also be essential before entry in order to get the economy right.

It was the move of George Brown to the Foreign Office in August 1966, where he worked with the fanatically pro-EEC official Con O'Neill, that was to increase further the pressure within the government to make an initiative of some sort. An all-day conference of the Cabinet was held at Chequers on 22 October 1966. The morning session was attended by senior civil servants as well as Cabinet ministers. The proceedings were odd in that nobody knew whether the civil servants were there to give advice to their ministers, answer detailed questions or give their own views. The official papers before the meeting were based on British entry by 1968. Sir William Armstrong, the head of the Treasury, immediately torpedoed this by saying that the British economy would be too weak for at least two years for an application to be made (and possibly two years after that). He also told them that devaluation would almost certainly be needed and abolition of exchange controls would produce major problems. Most of the officials, apart from those from the Foreign Office, were against entry. Nevertheless the discussion went on as though an application would be made, and with the media fully briefed about the meeting and expecting results there was considerable pressure on the Cabinet to agree to something.

In the afternoon, with officials absent, ministers revealed their own views. Brown and Stewart were unequivocal: Britain had to join not for economic reasons but to keep up its international status and its place 'at the top table'. They wanted a 'declaration of intent' to join. The Cabinet was divided; nine spoke in favour of EEC entry – Brown, Jenkins, Crosland, Gardiner, Longford, Houghton, Gordon-Walker, Hughes and Benn – while eight expressed opposition – Healey, Peart, Bowden, Marsh, Ross, Castle, Jay and Greenwood. Callaghan was uncommitted and Crossman's attitude was that, although opposed, he would go along with an attempt to enter because 'the General will save us from our own folly'.[3] Many others opposed to entry privately took the same view that it was not worth fighting over the issue when it was obvious that de Gaulle would use the veto again. As Denis Healey put it, 'We talked absolute tripe about a change in the French attitude. There was no change.'[4] Wilson carefully did not state his own position and left many ministers genuinely mystified about his real views. Was he sceptical and trying to hold Brown back or was he a secret advocate of entry? Wilson tried hard to create the image that he was more sceptical than Brown and proposed that they should make a joint 'probe' of EEC attitudes to a British application. The implication was that Wilson would act as a brake on Brown's enthusiasm but it is difficult to imagine that Wilson would have allowed Brown to make solo visits and claim the credit for any progress. A number of the Cabinet were opposed to the idea but it was clear that Wilson had made up his mind and, having agreed the suggestion with Brown beforehand, would not be talked out of the proposal.

The Cabinet resumed discussion on 3 November when Brown, Callaghan and Stewart all suggested a declaration of intent to join rather than a 'probe'. Wilson, however, would not be moved and it was finally agreed to follow his suggested plan of action. This consisted of a conference of EFTA leaders, followed by a declaration of intent to join and then a series of high-level visits whilst consultations with the Commonwealth were underway. A study of fall-back options in the event of failure was included, largely as a sop to those opposed to entry. A few days later Crossman and Silkin, as Leader of the House of Commons and Chief Whip, advised Wilson that there was no major opposition within the parliamentary party. Crossman recommended that if the application was to be made it should be wholehearted and enthusiastic, even if in the end it failed. When Wilson made the announcement on 10 November he had clearly accepted Crossman's advice:

> The Government are approaching the discussions I have foreshadowed with the clear intention and determination to enter the EEC, if, as we hope, our essential British and Commonwealth interests can be safeguarded. We mean business.

Shortly after the failure of the first attempt to enter the EEC Wilson had boldly declared:

> Never again must a British minister be put in a position of sitting outside in a cold ante-chamber while six European nations decide the fate of his country.[5]

That is exactly the position he now put himself in. The 'probe' of EEC views lasted from January until March 1967; virtually nothing was learnt that was not known before, despite the glowing account of these visits that Wilson gives in his memoirs. After Rome came the crucial visit to Paris. In George Brown's words there was 'no shaking de Gaulle's opposition to having Britain in the Common Market'.[6] The French President made it clear that there were strong objections to the reserve role of sterling, British dependence on the United States and the changes that would be necessary within the EEC to accommodate Britain. He suggested instead some form of association for Britain, an idea he consistently favoured until his resignation in 1969. Wilson was particularly opposed to this idea because he believed the French would use it as a pretext to keep Britain out. Despite the hostile reception in Paris, Wilson remained convinced that he had made an impression on de Gaulle and that if it came to the crunch he could get a deal, even though others had failed. It was yet another example of his unshakeable belief in the potency of his personal brand of diplomacy. He told one colleague:

> Perhaps in the last resort I shall have to see General de Gaulle alone and spell out to him the real alternatives. Either we come right in, I must say, or we are hostile members of an American bloc.[7]

Not the sort of argument likely to impress de Gaulle.

The rest of the visits were equally negative. After the trip to Brussels both Wilson and Brown reported to the Cabinet that 'The discussion with Ministers had been even more discouraging than those in Italy.'[8] Before the visit to Bonn the Ambassador reported that if faced with a choice between the EEC and the alternative suggested by de Gaulle of an association including Britain then the Germans would chose the EEC. The visit itself confirmed this assessment when the Germans made it clear that they would not put pressure on the French to get Britain in.

After the 'probe' a sixty-page briefing document was circulated to the Cabinet and discussed on 21 March. Wilson admitted that de Gaulle didn't want enlargement and that the other five were not prepared to take him on. Once again he kept the discussion well away from the principle of whether or not to enter and concentrated on particular problems. Brown argued that Britain had to be in the EEC by 1969 in order to abolish the worst features of the Common Agricultural Policy in the renegotiation that would take place then (not stopping to think that the Six might prefer to keep Britain out until then so that the CAP could continue). After two and a half hours' discussion the Cabinet found that they had gone so far along the road that they could not draw back without loss of face. They therefore agreed to discuss a series of papers on detailed aspects of membership.

Referring to the next phase of the Cabinet discussions – consideration of whether to apply for membership – Wilson wrote in his memoirs:

> I was anxious that no colleague should feel that the decision was in any way rushed . . . I told my colleagues that the fullest time would be available for so important a matter.[9]

In fact he told his colleagues at their first discussion on 6 April that a final decision must be reached by 10 May, although no explanation was given as to why this deadline was set. The secret reason was that the United States had asked, at the beginning of March, for the application to be made after the conclusion of the 'Kennedy

Round' of negotiations on liberalising world trade which would be concluded at the end of April.[10] For the next five weeks the Cabinet met at least once a week to discuss papers on different aspects of membership. Wilson kept up the pressure on his colleagues by announcing to the parliamentary party on 27 April that a decision on whether to enter would be made soon. At every meeting Wilson consistently knocked down arguments against entry and showed himself as a convinced pro-EEC figure. As Barbara Castle wrote:

> After this we can only decide against entry by repudiating him. The whole long-drawn out nonsense has been ruthlessly stage-managed, under cover of the soothing phrase: 'It is of course for Cabinet to decide.'[11]

The Foreign Office under George Brown was also trying to ensure that the Cabinet reached the 'right' decision. Ambassadors were instructed not to issue their normal assessments of the position in their respective capitals, which would have been circulated to the Cabinet. Instead they were to send their reports privately to the Foreign Office which would digest them and then circulate a version to the Cabinet. The Foreign Office also tried to suppress a letter from Sir Frank Roberts, the Ambassador in Bonn, advising that the application be postponed until at least the autumn. The letter was sent at the beginning of March, but the Foreign Office denied its existence until the end of the month when they were finally forced to circulate it. Walter Hallstein, the President of the EEC Commission, also advised delay.

The difficulties encountered by Douglas Jay (the strongest opponent of entry) in getting his own papers discussed also illustrates the extent to which the terms of debate were being fixed in favour of entry. He tried to circulate a general paper on the sensitive issue of the economic and balance of payments consequences of entry on 19 March, but the Cabinet Secretary advised him to leave it till later in the month. When Jay saw Wilson on 30 March the latter refused to allow the paper onto the Cabinet agenda until ministers considered what papers they wanted. This was disingenuous because Wilson was masterminding the production of papers within the Cabinet Office. Clearly he was not going to have alternative and more gloomy assessments than the bland official documents circulated. On 9 April Wilson refused to circulate Jay's contribution until all the official papers had been discussed and by then it was too late.

The Cabinet had five meetings plus a weekend conference to consider about a dozen official papers, all of which pointed in favour of entry. The first paper was on regional policy and capital movements. Opponents of entry pointed out that membership would destroy regional policy but Wilson remained optimistic. After entry, he asserted, UK industrial investment would go up 20–30% so that any effects on the regions would be minimal. A week later they addressed immigration policy (which would give precedence to Europeans), and legal and constitutional problems, none of which according to Wilson would cause any insuperable difficulties. A paper on the future of sterling argued that it too would no longer be a problem since the Six had been reassured that no assistance would be required in any future crisis. Five days later it was the turn of agriculture. Here there were undeniably major problems in applying the CAP, which would, as Wilson put it, result in Britain paying 'an outrageously big proportion' of the levies. It was agreed that transitional arrangements would not be enough; Britian would have to obtain a long-term change of policy. On 20 April the Cabinet discussed alternatives to the EEC. Two possibilities – either a 'go-it-alone' policy or a North Atlantic area – were set out in separate papers by Burke Trend; the fact that both options were rejected revealed the establishment wisdom that there was no alternative for Britain outside the EEC. The Cabinet accepted these conclusions but not the Trend view that, if the application failed, Britain should stand on the threshold and wait. (When the application failed this was exactly the policy that was adopted.) At the end of April the most gloomy official paper, arguing that membership would affect the balance of payments adversely by between £400 and £920 million a year – enough to cause major balance of payments problems every year – was discussed. By now the pro-EEC group was too committed to draw back and there was little discussion of the implications.

Opponents of entry were not making much impact on the debate, although in the margins Douglas Jay did try to organise a group to resign on the issue. The one who came closest to joining him was Fred Peart. On several occasions he almost committed himself but none of the other opponents would go that far. Jay saw Castle on 25 April but she was, as in July 1966, too close to Wilson to resign and anyway she couldn't stand Jay. As she wrote in her diary, 'I'm not having my breaking-point dictated by someone like Douglas with whom I have so little sympathy politically.'[12] In the end even Jay could not bring himself to resign, although in retrospect he thought he should have gone. It made little difference

211

because Wilson sacked him four months later in the next reshuffle. Bert Bowden was also unhappy at the outcome but told Wilson privately that he would like to resign quietly later, which he did at the end of August.

Before the decision to apply was announced on 2 May the Cabinet had to go through another all-weekend session on 29–30 April. By now most of them were bored and just going through the motions of debating. The first day was spent at No 10 and officials were present in the morning. This time there was to be no repetition of Sir William Armstrong's negative intervention at the previous conference. Officials had to sit behind their minister and only speak at his invitation. Most of this first day was spent on the economic case for entry, which the papers made clear was marginal at best. The case for entry rested on the need to maintain Britain's perceived role as a major power. At Chequers the next day the main paper for discussion was one from Wilson and Brown setting out the alternatives, and coming down strongly for entry. Brown was euphoric about the political benefits of entry. Looking ahead to the next election he saw Britain already benefitting from all the favourable transitional arrangements that would be negotiated. The disadvantages of membership would only be apparent after the election.

When the Cabinet met on 2 May for a final discussion (a week ahead of the deadline) Wilson put on the table a draft statement he was to make that afternoon in the Commons announcing the decision to apply. Again there was no consideration of principles. The two hours allowed for discussion were devoted entirely to details of drafting. There was a sort of vote at the end. Only Castle and Marsh were definitely against applying for entry, with Jay and Peart saying weakly that it all depended on the conditions obtained in the negotiations. The best that opponents of entry could manage was to insert a passage about the safeguards necessary to maintain Britain's 'essential interests'. These remained carefully undefined. Wilson had swept the Cabinet along with him and he had little problem in obtaining parliamentary approval. Both parties had three-line whips to vote in favour operating and the decision to apply was endorsed by the Commons by 488 votes to sixty-two, with thirty-six Labour MPs voting against and fifty-one abstaining.

Scarcely had a new Cabinet committee, chaired by George Brown, started work on the terms of entry when de Gaulle made it clear, at a press conference on 16 May, that he intended to veto the application. He was adamant that Britain had not made enough of the changes necessary to enter the EEC. A month later Wilson tried out some of his personal diplomacy again. His meeting with de Gaulle changed nothing, but he claimed to the Cabinet on 22 June that the chances of entry had improved. In early October de Gaulle spelled out the French position for the British Ambassador, Sir Patrick Reilly. He claimed to have no objection in principle to Britain joining the EEC but felt the country was not yet ready for membership: the economic situation was not right, there was too great a dependence on imported food and British membership would disrupt the community. In the circumstances he argued it was better not to have any negotiations and once again suggested some form of 'association'. The economic objections made by de Gaulle were those identified by the Treasury mandarins at the start of the internal debate over membership. And de Gaulle had not wavered from his 'unshakeable' opposition to British entry identified during the 'probe'. The formal veto was announced on 27 November 1967.

After this failure British policy was to remain eager to start negotiations on entry while waiting for something to turn up. Two years later something did. British chances of at least opening negotiations on EEC entry were much improved when de Gaulle resigned as President to be replaced by Pompidou in 1969. By this stage, however, domestic preoccupations meant that the government was unwilling to press for an early start to negotiations so soon before an election. They preferred to campaign in 1970 on a general willingness to enter if the terms were right, thus avoiding any immediate split in the party. It was clear that Wilson's new-found enthusiasm, the humiliating rebuff from de Gaulle and two years of waiting 'in a cold ante-chamber' did not increase the level of support for joining the EEC within the Labour party. Years of bitter wrangling between the pro- and anti-entry wings of the party were to follow in the 1970s.

Wilson's own position on the issue reveals him apparently moving from criticism of Macmillan's bid through electoral scepticism to masterminding a rush to apply. His motives for this shift are more difficult to pin down and his personal views difficult to judge. Indeed his Cabinet colleagues were never able to decide what they were. Nevertheless Wilson's whole method of handling the issue suggests that he genuinely wanted to obtain a decision to apply. It was a measure of his political skills that he was able to obtain it without a single resignation from the Cabinet. He did this by never addressing the simple issue of principle. Instead the question was always presented in terms of practicalities; the problem was divided up into discrete areas and Wilson only ever asked for small steps along the way – the decision to probe possible attitudes or to find out terms – which were difficult to make into resignation issues. Once underway the process developed its own momentum that swept the government from one stage to the next. He was also helped by the fact that most of the opponents were convinced that de Gaulle would veto any British applicaton and that therefore there was no point in making it a resignation issue. Wilson must have been aware that de Gaulle would use the veto, although at times he seems to have thought that by exercising his own diplomatic skills he would be able to overcome this formidable barrier. In the circumstances why did Wilson press so strongly for negotiations and entry? It can to some extent be seen as another example of his preference for working with the grain of Whitehall and United States opinion (a powerful combination) rather than against it and he also found it easier to work with rather than against George Brown as Foreign Secretary on the issue. In addition the actual process of negotiation gave Wilson plenty of opportunities to indulge in personal diplomacy with its attendant publicity.

The main reason, though, for this ultimately unsuccessful saga was political. Wilson believed he had nothing to lose and much to gain from making the application to join the EEC. To some extent, like the Conservatives earlier in the decade, he too needed a policy that might provide a new opportunity to break out from successive failures of economic policy culminating in the July 1966 measures. He also knew that Heath was fanatically pro-EEC and would want to make it a major issue in the 1970 election. Wilson's tactics, as with many other issues from 1966–70, such as Rhodesia and trade union reform, were to defuse potential issues that the Conservatives might exploit. If the negotiations succeeded, the Labour government would obtain what Wilson, and many others, felt would be the credit of bringing Britain into the EEC. If they were unsuccessful, he would have demonstrated the difficulties so that the Conservatives could not accuse him of failing to try. Although the negotiations did fail, he achieved his object of making the EEC a largely bipartisan issue and not a matter of controversy in 1970. The danger for Wilson was that this sort of approach, when applied in a number of areas, meant that the government seemed to be adopting increasingly conservative policies, out of line with the views of their supporters in the country and increasingly within the parliamentary party. So in addition to the politics of drift Wilson was indulging in the politics of consensus that might well undermine any distinctive appeal that the Labour party could make.

13

Peace and War

British foreign policy since 1945 had been, by tradition, bi-partisan. Labour had helped devise many of the organisations that formed the structure of the western world after the war and the leadership had repulsed attempts from within the party to produce a radically different policy. Throughout its life the Wilson government had to devise policies on a number of issues that raised questions, in different degrees, about the importance to be given to the Anglo-American alliance, the room for independent British action and the weight to be given to humanitarian considerations in a world of power politics. Its actions demonstrate a determination to remain in the traditional mould. This chapter concentrates on six of those issues: overseas aid, Vietnam, the Arab-Israeli Six-Day War, the Nigerian civil war, the invasion of Anguilla and the building of the large military complex on the Indian Ocean island of Diego Garcia.

I. OVERSEAS AID

By the early 1960s the question of aid to the newly independent countries of the Third World was firmly on the political agenda. The Labour party, which had long campaigned for colonial independence, was in a strong position to take a lead in advocating a generous policy towards the developing countries. There was also a degree of personal commitment among senior Labour politicians. For example, in the 1950s Harold Wilson had been a strong proponent of aid; he had written a book, *The War on World Poverty*, and helped to found the charity, War on Want. The 1964 manifesto promised a range of measures to help Third World trade and to create a new Ministry of Overseas Development (ODM). The idea of an ODM was not original. In the autumn of 1963 senior officials in Whitehall were already discussing the future of the small Department of Technical Cooperation (DTC) and by the summer of 1964 ministers in the Conservative government were considering the idea of a separate ministry responsible for overseas aid but no final decisions were taken before the election. It was therefore relatively easy for the new ODM to be set up in October 1964 under Barbara Castle.

The new ministry faced enormous difficulties from the start and neither it nor the proposed new policy on aid were to live up to expectations. The first problem – as always – was to define the role and responsibilities of the new department, which provoked a major internal Whitehall battle. The end result was that the new department did not have responsibility for overseas development. For example trade policy, and particularly policy on Third World imports into the UK, remained with the Board of Trade and ODM made little impact on foreign, defence or immigration policies. It was to be simply a ministry for allocating aid. It was therefore vital to establish the priorities to be followed in that allocation. Was priority to be given to the neediest countries or was aid to be used to assist foreign and defence policies? There was an ambivalence – a clear desire to have it both ways (as in all governments' aid policies) – reflected in the first White Paper on aid published in August 1965 (the date was chosen by the Cabinet to try and 'balance' the simultaneous publication of their highly restrictive proposals on immigration). The White Paper[1] bore all the signs of Whitehall compromise in its careful combination of contradictory cliches: 'The basis of the aid programme is a moral one' but 'the provision of aid is to our own long-term economic advantage'; 'aid is not a means of winning the friendship of individual countries' but 'we are glad to offer aid to our friends'. There was also continual hostility within Whitehall over both the status of ODM and its demands for resources. Although Castle was a strong minister, she moved on after only a year and altogether ODM was to have four ministers in its first three years. The real blow though came in January 1967 when the minister, Arthur Bottomley, lost his Cabinet seat – confirmation that ODM was to remain an unimportant ministry on the fringes of Whitehall.

In practice the requirements of foreign and defence policies dominated the aid programme. There was a slight drop in the proportion of aid going to the 'strategic' countries round the edge of the Communist world and a slight rise in the share going to the poorest countries. But some of these poorer countries could be badly treated when British strategic interests were at stake. As we have seen new aid to Tanzania was cut off because of a row over Rhodesian policy. By contrast in April 1965 OPD decided to give £1.2 million of aid to Malta on purely political grounds in order to try and secure the re-election of the incompetent but right-wing Borg Olivier against the more radical Dom Mintoff, who

Hugh Gaitskell looks suspiciously at his main rival for the leadership, Harold Wilson. George Brown still hopes to be leader too. (Labour Party Conference, Brighton 1962)

Past and future Labour Prime Ministers: Harold Wilson and Clement Attlee. Two deputy leaders – George Brown and Jim Griffiths – look on. (Royal Albert Hall, April 1964)

'Fire in their bellies and humanity in their hearts': Wilson rallying the people for a better future with Labour. (Royal Albert Hall, April 1964)

16 October, 1964: the threshold of power. Harold and Mary Wilson leave Transport House for Buckingham Palace, George Brown centre stage but in reality only deputy leader.

The dynamic new Labour government: official Cabinet photograph, July 1965. *Back row* (left to right): Fred Lee, Frank Cousins, Douglas Houghton, Anthony Crosland, Douglas Jay, Barbara Castle, Anthony Greenwood, Lord Longford, Richard Crossman, Ray Gunter, Fred Peart, Tom Fraser, Sir Burke Trend. *Front row* (left to right): William Ross, Sir Frank Soskice, Michael Stewart, Lord Gardiner, George Brown, Harold Wilson, Herbert Bowden, James Callaghan, Denis Healey, Arthur Bottomley, James Griffiths.

Chancellor of the Exchequer Jim Callaghan smiling grimly through another crisis Budget, spring 1966. In private he was far more pessimistic.

(Above) The special relationship (1): Harold Wilson admires President Johnson. (White House, March 1964)

(Left) The special relationship (2): Dean Rusk (US Secretary of State) talks down to Michael Stewart, Foreign Secretary. (NATO summit, Lancaster House, May 1965)

(Right) The special relationship (3): Harold Wilson in pseudo-Medieval academic dress faces anti-Vietnam War demonstrators. (Sussex University, July 1966)

(Below) The special relationship (4): Harold Wilson is still dogged by those opposed to British support for the United States in Vietnam. (Hampstead Festival Fair, June 1967)

(Left) George Brown: architect of the failed National Plan and Prices and Incomes Policy. His controversial and difficult personality dominated the inner circle of the government for three years.

(Below) Foreign Secretary Patrick Gordon-Walker sets off for a humiliating defeat and resignation. (Leyton by-election, January 1965)

(above) Three men in overcoats
at Liverpool Street Station:
Michael Stewart, Tony Crosland
and Frank Cousins.

(right) Douglas Jay (President of
the Board of Trade): on the
changes of the Cabinet inner
group on economic policy he fell
out with Wilson over EEC entry
and was sacked.

(Above) The 'Kitchen Cabinet': Marcia Williams admires the view inside No. 10. (Photo taken in 1974)

(Left) From 'Kitchen Cabinet' to House of Lords. George Wigg, Harold Wilson's *eminence grise*, becomes Lord Wigg.

International diplomacy (1): President de Gaulle is not amused by Wilson and Brown's attempts to join the EEC. (European 'Probe', Paris, January 1967)

International diplomacy (2): a grim Wilson and Soviet Premier Kosygin in Moscow. A similar mood characterised Wilson's abortive attempt to end the Vietnam War.

International diplomacy (3): Harold Wilson and rebel Prime Minister Ian Smith as far apart as ever over the future of Rhodesia. (HMS *Fearless*, October 1968)

Denis Healey: Defence Secretary for the life of the government. (Cyprus, May 1968)

Barbara Castle points the way to disaster over 'In Place of Strife'. (Shopworkers conference, April 1968)

Dick Crossman: an intellectual in politics and confidant of Harold Wilson, he saw his role as unofficial chronicler of the life of the Labour government before writing a book on British government.

Chancellor of the Exchequer Roy Jenkins: he hoped 'sound finance' was the route to electoral success. (Budget, spring 1969)

threatened to upset Britain's defence arrangements. As some compensation for these policies the greatest success of the new ministry under Barbara Castle was to introduce interest-free loans to the poorest countries.

Within the Cabinet there was considerable hostility to the idea of aid, stemming from a combination of factors. Against the background of a generally unsympathetic attitude towards Third World problems, the emphasis placed on restoring the balance of payments and therefore on reducing overseas expenditure meant that aid was seen as a tempting, and easy, target for cuts. This was not how Labour politicians had seen it in their opposition days. In 1957 both the NEC and the party conference had agreed that the level of Britain's aid budget should reach 1% of GNP within five years of taking office. The 1964 manifesto contained no target figure, but it did commit the Labour party to increasing the share of national wealth going on aid. The aid programme was about £150 million a year in the early 1960s and rose to £207 million in 1966, entirely on outstanding commitments from the Conservative government. The government's commitment to increase spending on aid lasted as long as its first review of public expenditure in June 1965. Then there was a concerted attack on the programme led by Brown and Callaghan, supported by Cousins. Brown talked of cutting the aid programme in order to get industry to look for 'real exports' and Callaghan refused to accept that aid could be a special case. The National Plan, so ambitious in other areas, was the first to cast public doubt on Labour's 1964 commitment when it said that 'aid . . . will be restrained and the effectiveness of each pound of aid increased'. There was no commitment to any increase in funding in the 1966 manifesto. In July 1966, as part of the major cuts in public expenditure, the programme was cut by 10% (the largest proportionate cut) and there was little recovery later. The net result was that far from increasing the share of national wealth going on aid the Labour government made a major cut. The percentage of GNP spent on aid fell from 0.53% in 1964 to 0.37% in 1970. This was not inevitable but a simple question of priorities and power. Few ministers cared very much about aid, it was easy to cut and it didn't have a powerful lobby behind it like the defence budget. In March 1968 OPD rejected the new UN target for countries to achieve 1% of GNP by 1980 because, as Roy Jenkins admitted to his colleagues, they had absolutely no intention of meeting such a commitment. Only in the run-up to the 1970 election, when they wanted to project a more caring image, did the manifesto suddenly incorporate the idea of reaching the 1% target by the mid-1970s.

217

However, no detailed plans for achieving it were laid and judging by their poor track record it must be doubtful whether, given another opportunity, they would have done any better than in the past.

II. THE VIETNAM WAR

When the Labour government took office the Vietnam conflict was reaching a crucial turning point. The Geneva conference in 1954 had divided the country, a division the Communist North had never accepted. A US-backed dictatorial regime in the South became increasingly corrupt and unpopular, and a growing revolt, well exploited by the Communist-dominated Vietcong, had, by the early 1960s, begun to take control of key provinces from the government. The United States, under President Kennedy, stepped up the programme of military assistance to include military 'advisers' and massive logistical support, and the more aid the United States gave the further it was sucked into the conflict. Increasingly the American government saw South Vietnam as the last bulwark against Communist advance in Asia. An almost certainly mythical 'attack' by North Vietnam on US destroyers in the Gulf of Tonkin in the summer of 1964 started a programme of retaliatory bombing of the North. With the situation in the South continuing to disintegrate and the North sending regular army units across the border the deployment of US ground forces on a large scale seemed only a matter of time. Britain had steered clear of the military conflicts that marked the end of French rule in Indochina and in 1954 had co-chaired the Geneva conference with the Russians. Inevitably as a close ally of the United States Britain was under pressure to provide moral support and military assistance. On the other hand Vietnam raised powerful emotional reactions against US intervention and bombing. The most vociferous protest came from outside Parliament but a significant minority within the Labour party was strongly opposed to US actions.

The situation in Vietnam was not high on the agenda in the first months of the new government, nor at Wilson's first meeting with President Johnson in December 1964. US deployment of army combat forces was still six months away and although Johnson asked Wilson for British support in Vietnam he was not greatly surprised when Wilson refused. Instead Wilson offered facilities for jungle training and advice on counter-insurgency warfare. It was not until February 1965 that Wilson made his first attempt to intervene, only to come up against the limits of his influence with Johnson. After a series of attacks by the Vietcong on US servicemen in the South, he spoke to Johnson on the 'hot line' to urge restraint. He suggested, rather like Attlee had done when the US contemplated using atomic weapons in Korea, that he should fly to Washington and give his advice at first hand. Johnson, in a few choice phrases, told him that his visit wasn't required and neither was his advice unless Britain was prepared to offer concrete assistance in Vietnam. After a pause for thought the US administration, realising they might have offended a useful ally, took immediate steps to placate Wilson. The US Ambassador in London, David Bruce, saw Wilson to explain in detail US thinking on how their Vietnam policy was developing. He obtained what the US wanted when Wilson said he would 'solidly support' US policy, although he did emphasise the importance of the US balancing military action with a willingness to negotiate.[2] Six weeks later Wilson told the Commons, 'We have made absolutely plain our support for the American stand against Communist infiltration into South Vietnam.'[3]

But how far would that support for the US go? Wilson never had any intention of meeting American demands for British forces in Vietnam for two reasons. The first was practical. UK forces were already heavily overstretched and there were simply not enough available to take on a major new commitment. The second reason was political. The government was already under attack from a sizeable proportion of its backbenchers for even expressing support for the US position. Any attempt to deploy British forces to fight alongside the Americans in Vietnam would have split the Labour party at a time when they had a parliamentary majority of three. And even outside the Labour party, whilst there might be more understanding of the US decision to fight in Vietnam, there was no strong feeling that this was a conflict that involved UK interests directly.

In the spring of 1965 the US and British governments came to an understanding about the limits of UK support. It was formulated in outline during Michael Stewart's visit to Washington in March and finalised when Wilson met Johnson in the middle of April. The UK was to continue its general support of US policy in Vietnam and in return the US promised advance information (but not consultation) about any decision to bomb the North or commit ground forces in the South. Johnson reluctantly accepted that the UK would not provide troops and that the best way for the UK to help the US would be in the diplomatic field. In its capacity as co-chairman of the 1954 Geneva conference Britain was in a position to explore various peace offers and be useful to the US in this field. It was understood that any UK initiatives in this area would support the US position and any proposals would be cleared with the US in advance. This understanding was to remain valid for the rest of the life of the government. Johnson occasionally asked for support in Vietnam but understood the limits of how far Wilson could go and never made it a condition of US support for the pound. There were occasions when the UK chose to dissociate itself – in suitably cautious phraseology – from specific US actions, such as the bombing of Hanoi and Haiphong in June 1966, and the invasion of Cambodia in 1970, but diplomatic support for the US remained virtually absolute. Despite continual dissent from that policy on the part of a sizeable minority of the PLP, a large proportion of the party outside Parliament and a considerable section of public opinion, the government never even considered abandoning its support for United States policy.

The fact that the UK was not providing troops did not mean that there was no direct support for the US in Vietnam. The UK provided a small team of counter-insurgency advisers, led by an expert from the Malayan emergency in the 1950s, to help the US programme. There was also a small police team training the South Vietnamese police. There were also other areas where Britain was able to assist, in particular over the use of North Vietnamese ports by British registered shipping. The US put strong pressure on the government to stop British ships sailing to North Vietnam. In the early 1960s the Conservative government had rejected similar pressure to stop ships supplying Cuba but the Labour government decided to agree to this American request. However, they did not want to take any public measures in order not to provoke opposition, particularly within the Labour party. Instead pressure was put on the shipowners informally. By July 1966 the trade was virtually at an end.[4]

More important, however, was the question of arms sales. In the House of Commons on 17 May 1966 Wilson said, 'We are not supplying arms directly or indirectly for the fighting in Vietnam.'[5] That statement was incorrect. A year before the US had asked for both naval and airborne weapons. The latter had not been supplied (only because none were available) but naval weapons had been provided. The only aspect that worried the British was that the story might become public. As the British Ambassador, Sir Patrick Dean, told Dean Rusk, the Secretary of State, on June 22 1965:

the UK had received a request through Navy channels for certain bombs to be used in Vietnam. The UK was naturally only too happy to sell the bombs but preferred in future it not be said that they were to be used in Vietnam.[6]

Indeed at the time Wilson was speaking in May 1966 the government had just produced a long list of lethal weapons for possible purchase by the US as part of the deal to meet the costs of the purchase by the UK of the F-111.[7] Under pressure from Labour backbenchers in the Commons on 23 June Healey went even further than Wilson and said, 'We do not propose to supply arms directly or indirectly for the fighting in Vietnam.'[8] This statement caused real concern in Washington and considerable pressure was put on the UK to put right what Walt Rostow described to Johnson as Healey's 'serious error'. Wilson made one attempt to fudge the situation; he took the line that the UK made no intentional supply of arms for use in Vietnam but would not ask for guarantees from the Americans on how they used any weapons supplied.[9] But this did not go far enough to satisfy Washington and under further American pressure Wilson replied to a pre-arranged question in the Commons in mid-July by stating that the UK put no restrictions on arms sales to the US. This reply was judged to be so important that it was sent to Washington and seen personally by President Johnson.[10]

The British were involved in a number of peace initiatives between 1965 and 1967. Not only were these peace efforts made with prior US approval, all of them were based on American rather than British ideas. Wilson was keen to exploit Britain's role as co-chairman of the Geneva conference to open up channels of communication with Moscow in the hope that the Russians could exert pressure on North Vietnam. But early in 1965 the Russians made it clear that they did not favour any initiative within the Geneva framework, almost certainly because this would in turn involve the Chinese.

After this initial rebuff Wilson decided to use the Commonwealth Prime Ministers' Conference in June 1965 as the start of a new effort. The idea was that three or four Prime Ministers (led by Wilson) would tour the capitals of all countries involved to try and find a peace formula. Wilson, though, had no ideas as to what this formula for peace might be. He secured Australian support and together the two Ambassadors in Washington saw Dean Rusk two days before the Conference opened. As they explained, 'The aim of the British and Australian governments was to be helpful to the

US.' They hoped that an initiative now might defuse demands for more radical action at the forthcoming conference of non-aligned countries at Algiers.[11] US approval was given and the conference also agreed after Wilson had already leaked the proposal to the press. Wilson obviously saw this as another opportunity for personal diplomacy but also knew how far he could push the Americans. When Barbara Castle asked him why one of the Afro-Asian premiers was not leading the delegation he replied, 'Washington would never have stood for it.'[12] But it is doubtful whether Wilson ever expected the mission to get further than creating good publicity for himself. Just after the conference, with the mission waiting to see whether it was acceptable to all concerned, Wilson told one colleague, 'I think we have got most of the value we can out of it already.'[13] The mission never got off the ground because none of the Communist countries involved agreed to see them. Not discouraged, Wilson made another effort, this time using Harold Davies, his old colleague from Bevanite days and one-time PPS. Davies had contacts with some North Vietnamese and with Wilson's authority he suggested to them that he might go to Hanoi. Wilson consulted Johnson who agreed that Davies could go. The mission ended in failure after its existence was leaked in London. The North Vietnamese refused to allow the official accompanying Davies to enter North Vietnam and Davies himself finished up seeing only low-level officials.

The next British attempt at mediation was the so-called Brown initiative at the end of 1966. Brown was due to visit Moscow in November and was desperately anxious to make some peace initiative during his talks with the Russians. He discussed the possibilities with two US officials in early November and after their return to Washington badgered them to produce some proposals he could take with him. Eventually the Americans decided that he could be allowed to produce a plan, known as 'Phase A-Phase B', as if it were his own. The idea was that there would be a secret understanding between the US and North Vietnam on how they would act. The US would halt the bombing of the North, apparently unconditionally (Phase A). This would be followed within a week by a previously agreed decision by North Vietnam to stop infiltration of men and supplies to the South, and by an eventual halt in US reinforcements (Phase B). In this atmosphere it was then hoped to move on to more constructive negotiations. In public, and with the Russians, Brown presented this plan as his own idea. The Russians, however, took little interest in it and the discussions produced no result.

What the Americans had not told Brown was that the Phase A-Phase B idea had already been tried and had failed. The first attempt had taken place in June 1966 through a Polish diplomat who worked for the moribund International Control Commission on Vietnam set up in 1954. His position on the commission gave him access to Hanoi and he had floated the US idea with the North Vietnamese but without success. In January 1967, when the Poles leaked information about the talks and the US plan, Wilson and Brown suddenly realised they had been duped. The US had not told them about their use of the Poles as intermediaries and Brown had been left to present as his own idea a US plan already rejected by Hanoi, one almost certainly known to the Russians from their North Vietnamese and Polish allies. Chet Cooper (the former CIA station chief in London and now a senior US official on the National Security Council) was sent to London to try and appease the offended pair. Brown and Wilson demanded an assurance of full consultation over any American diplomatic moves on Vietnam. The US gave some general assurances but no absolute commitment. Cooper's intention to visit Paris also caused offence. Brown and Wilson were worried that the French might attempt to mediate, a role they persisted in regarding as their own preserve.

Wilson was not discouraged by the failure of Brown's effort, nor by evidence that he did not have the full confidence of the Americans. He resolved to try again during the visit to Britain by the Soviet Prime Minister Kosygin at the beginning of February. The time was auspicious, in that the visit coincided with the traditional truce during the Vietnamese New Year (Tet) celebrations, and there might therefore be an opportunity to turn the pause into a longer ceasefire and start negotiations. Indeed the US had agreed to maintain the Tet bombing pause until Kosygin left London. In his memoirs Wilson gives a twenty-page account of how, in the words he used privately to the Cabinet immediately after the visit, he was 'twice on the edge of peace'[14]. However, previously highly classified US documents show that the true picture is very different from Wilson's account of his venture into international diplomacy between the superpowers.[15]

Wilson began as usual by getting US approval for his peace effort. He later claimed that Johnson 'set great store' by his involvement with the Russians. In fact the President was highly sceptical and thought that if the Russians had anything important to say they would say it direct rather than through an intermediary. However, he reluctantly went along with the initiative. Cooper was sent to London to brief Wilson and at the latter's request stayed for the duration of the Kosygin visit. At the first meeting between Wilson and Kosygin on 6 February the Russians advocated a North Vietnamese proposal for an unconditional cessation of the US bombing of the North as a precondition for talks. Wilson responded by suggesting a reconvening of the Geneva conference (rejected by the Russians for the previous two years) or the old Phase A-Phase B proposal. He reported this initial exchange to Cooper who, after consulting Washington, advised him that the North Vietnamese proposal was unacceptable (which was pretty obvious from the start) and that he should concentrate on Phase A-Phase B.

The second meeting with Kosygin on Vietnam took place on 9 February. The Soviet Prime Minister again pressed the North Vietnamese formula and Wilson urged the reconvening of the Geneva conference. Neither met with any response. Wilson then repeated the Phase A-Phase B proposal, and surprisingly Kosygin showed great interest and asked for it to be put down in writing. Cooper and the US Ambassador (Bruce) were called in, and together with Foreign Office officials drafted the proposals. (These proposals were virtually identical with those which had already been sent to the North Vietnamese twice and twice rejected.) The text was then sent to Washington for clearance. It took until late in the evening of the next day to receive a reply. Meanwhile, tired of waiting, Wilson had given Kosygin a copy of the unofficial text before the Russian party left to catch the overnight sleeper for a brief visit to Scotland.

The reply from Washington instantly demolished Wilson's efforts. Even before Wilson started his discussions with Kosygin the US administration had decided on a new, tougher policy which was to be conveyed directly in a letter from Johnson to the North Vietnamese leader, Ho Chi Minh. The new American position was a complete reversal of the Phase A-Phase B proposal: there would now be no cessation of the bombing until North Vietnam had stopped infiltration of troops and supplies to the South. This change of policy reflected the growing US conviction that they were winning the war and did not need to make any concessions. So Wilson was instructed to give a message to Kosygin setting out the new terms. This was done just as Kosygin's train was leaving Euston station.

After the telegram from Washington the mood in London was vicious. Cooper, furious at being misled by his own administration, had a row with Walt Rostow over the telephone and was told curtly, 'Well, we don't give a goddamn about you and we don't give a goddamn about Wilson.'[16] The atmosphere at No 10 was equally pungent. Cooper recalled the mutual recrimination session:

> Wilson and Brown just went at each other, it was just terrible. Brown accused Wilson of being too premature; and that time and time again during these discussions Wilson didn't inform Brown as to what was going on; Brown on at least three occasions resigned as Foreign Minister.[17]

Wilson sent a stinging message to Johnson about the 'hell of a situation' he was now in with Kosygin. It made no impact in Washington. The next day the mood was still bad: both Brown and Wilson were talking of 'betrayal' by the Americans. Eventually Wilson, Brown, Bruce and Cooper decided they would have one last effort with Kosygin during the final discussion session at Chequers. Cooper was to be installed in an attic room in continuous contact with Washington in case anything happened.

Kosygin did not raise the topic of the US volte-face two days earlier (there is no evidence that either of the proposals was ever sent to Moscow for transmission to Hanoi). The two sides were working on the terms of the official communiqué when Cooper came up with a new idea which he tried out on Wilson. With the truce still in effect he suggested that it should be continued, and that there should be no more troop movements to the South and no bombing of the North for a specified period whilst attempts at negotiation continued. Wilson agreed to put forward this proposal and Cooper talked to Washington. No reply was received before Kosygin left Chequers to return to his suite at Claridges. When Wilson returned to No 10 the US reaction was available: they would agree to the proposal provided North Vietnam agreed within twelve hours. Within this ludicrously short deadline it was clearly impossible for Kosygin to talk to Moscow, for a message to get to Hanoi, for the proposal to be considered and for a reply to return along the same route. Wilson tried to talk to Johnson but got no further than Walt Rostow. He then went round to Claridges and found Kosygin completely unimpressed, although he did send a message to Moscow on this occasion. Wilson and Cooper managed to secure an extra six hours from a Washington that was plainly not interested in the efforts being made in London. By the time Wilson was telling the Commons about his talks with Kosygin US bombers were already in action over North Vietnam.

Wilson was to claim that during this week 'A historic opportunity had been missed.'[18] On the evidence available, especially on

US attitudes, this claim must be dismissed as hopelessly exaggerated. Wilson put forward an old idea that had twice produced no result and there is no evidence that Kosygin ever took the proposal very seriously. The Americans regarded the negotiations as so marginal that they did not bother to tell Wilson that the proposal he was putting forward was already moribund and superseded by a new, harder line policy (unacceptable to the North Vietnamese) that had already been transmitted direct without Wilson's help. When an attempt was made at the last moment to salvage something from the fiasco it was Cooper, not Wilson, who made the suggestion. But Washington never took that idea seriously either or gave it any scope to succeed. Cooper himself reflected on Wilson's claim about what he had nearly achieved: 'Wilson is wrong. He didn't have peace within his grasp, he was always overly optimistic about it.'[19] This was the last time that Wilson tried to mediate in the Vietnam War and the Americans were left to extricate themselves. The February 1967 episode is a sad comment on Wilson's belief in his personal diplomacy, his own relationship with President Johnson and the idea that Britain had a useful role to play between the superpowers. Wilson had religiously stuck to his side of the bargain and cleared all his proposals in advance with the Americans. The US administration regarded Wilson at best as marginal, at worst as a nuisance, and did not bother to keep him informed of their own thinking, even when he thought he was negotiating on their behalf.

III. THE ARAB-ISRAELI WAR

Three months after the abortive Vietnam peace negotiations the government was to be embroiled in trying to avert war in the Middle East – an attempt that at one stage led to a Cabinet revolt against Wilson and Brown and their proposals to deal with the crisis. During May 1967 there was growing tension in the region over Palestinian raids into Israel and Israeli reprisal raids on Syria. On 19 May the UN Secretary-General, U Thant, agreed to remove the UN peacekeeping force from Sinai, followed three days later by President Nasser's announcement that the Straits of Tiran, at the entrance to the Gulf of Aqaba, would be closed to all Israeli shipping. This was the main route for crucial Israeli supplies, including 90% of their oil. They could not afford to see this route blocked, and war between the Israelis and the Arabs seemed inevitable.

A top secret US National Security Council history provides striking new evidence about Britain's role in the crisis.[20] On 22 May, immediately after Nasser's announcement, Walt Rostow of the State Department spoke to the UK Ambassador and asked for the UK to 'stand with the US' during the crisis. What this meant was explained by President Johnson at a National Security Council meeting when he said that he wanted to exhaust action at the UN first but then, 'I want to see Wilson and de Gaulle out there with their ships lined up too.'[21] News of the US request reached London the next morning and at a hastily convened meeting Wilson, Brown and Healey decided that the UK should go further than the US suggested. They wanted an immediate declaration by the US and UK of the right of innocent passage through the Straits of Tiran but no consultation of the UN. This declaration was to be enforced by a joint US-UK naval task force which would, if necessary, fight its way through the straits. Other maritime powers were to be invited to join the declaration and the force at some stage but this was to be primarily a US-UK operation. The Cabinet was summoned to an emergency meeting to ratify the decision just taken.

When the Cabinet heard the proposal there was what one member described as 'utter dismay'.[22] Callaghan made clear his total opposition, forecasting that if the idea went ahead then the economy would be drastically affected, given the likely total hostility of the Arabs. The real problems for Brown and Wilson arose when Healey spoke. Over lunch he had, for the first time, consulted the Chiefs of Staff. They were appalled at the whole idea and pointed out the obvious operational problems. The ships required were in the Mediterranean and would need to pass through the Suez Canal to reach the Gulf of Aqaba. Moreover they advised that it would be essential to launch a pre-emptive strike on Egyptian airfields to remove the threat of air attack on the ships. Healey now came down against the idea. Jay, Castle and Peart registered their opposition too, reminded uneasily of the parallels with Suez just eleven years before. Castle even had the temerity to mention the dreaded word 'collusion'. The strongly pro-Israeli ministers – Brown, Gunter and Bowden – continued to press for action. So did Wilson, who said that the US would intervene on the side of Israel and that if Britain did not act the US would 'write us off'. At one point Callaghan said, 'Some of us won't have this policy', to which Wilson snarled back, 'Some of us won't have this constant obstruction.'[23] Eventually Healey's practical objections and the weight of Cabinet opposition wore Wilson and Brown down and they had to accept that there would be no task force.

The Cabinet agreed that George Thomson should go to Washington for discussions but should not commit the UK to anything. There was to be no US-UK operation. The idea could only go ahead if other countries joined in and diplomatic activity was to be centered on the UN. It was a defeat for Wilson and Brown.

That evening in Washington Rostow was already making it clear to the British Ambassador that the US did not want to take any initiative or be 'out in front', since they were confident they had been able to restrain the Israelis for the moment. Unlike Wilson and Brown they wanted no US-UK action unless all possible routes through the UN had failed. It was left that Britain was to approach other maritime powers to see if they wanted to make a joint declaration. The next day (24 May) Thomson was given a cool reception in Washington; the US would go no further than saying that the UK idea of a declaration was 'encouraging'. The proposal was soon bogged down in complex UN diplomacy and competition with a French suggestion of a four-power (US, UK, France and Russia) initiative. The UK sounded out a wide range of nations but although there was sympathy for a declaration of the rights of innocent passage, they found no enthusiasm for the idea of using force. By early June the idea was effectively dead with only five countries firmly prepared to support even a declaration.[24] The US had agreed to low-level contingency planning with UK military staffs. They recognised that only forces already East of Suez could be used and there would have to be 'full-scale airstrikes against all [Egyptian] military targets'. The UK would provide one aircraft carrier (*Hermes*) and four destroyers for the operation.[25]

Among the politicians the desire for military intervention was fading rapidly. As the Americans told the British on 2 June during Wilson's long-planned visit to Washington, 'It would have been disastrous if we had been caught in military planning last week.'[26] It was during this visit that the British began to express concern about their financial position if the Arabs and Israelis went to war, with the possible closure of the Suez Canal and interruption in oil supplies leading to a run on the pound and the limited sterling reserves. The US administration said that it was not prepared to take any action before war started but that if it did they would then give any help that was necessary. War broke out on 5 June and when the Cabinet met the next day all were agreed that given the parlous economic situation they simply could not afford to alienate the Arabs and would stay strictly neutral. (This view makes it clear that a fortnight earlier neither Wilson nor Brown had thought through the implications of taking action that would have inevitably alienated the Arabs.) The swift Israeli victory in the war did lead to closure of the Suez Canal and a temporary stoppage of oil supplies. However, the damage to the British economy was not great, although Wilson was later to claim that closure of the canal was one of the main causes of devaluation in November 1967.

Wilson, Brown and, initially, Healey had badly miscalculated in May. After an ambiguous message from the Americans they were obviously keen to demonstrate that they could act as the United States' main ally in policing the world. (This desire may have been heightened by the fact that they were just about to act contrary to US demands by announcing a date for withdrawal from the Far East.) Only the common sense of their military advisers and the determination of the rest of the Cabinet stopped what would have been a disastrous plan. It was also the rest of the Cabinet that insisted that the UN should be at the centre of the government's efforts – a policy the Labour party had always advocated in public.

IV. THE NIGERIAN CIVIL WAR

The outbreak of the Nigerian civil war in May 1967, when the Eastern Region declared itself independent as Biafra, was to create almost more moral anguish in Britain than the Vietnam War. The conflict dragged on for nearly three years as the Federal forces waged a long campaign to defeat a landlocked and isolated Biafra. Through a well-organised press campaign the plight of the starving population of Biafra evoked strong sympathy. Their predicament was made worse by the Biafran refusal to open a land corridor for relief supplies because they wanted to use night flights of food from other countries as a cover for arms deliveries. The Federal authorities regarded these flights as legitimate military targets. Whatever the humanitarian aspects of the conflict, in which about one million Biafrans were to die, the Labour government gave greatest weight to Britain's economic interests in Nigeria where the UK had massive investments, especially in the oilfields which supplied 10% of the UK's requirements (particularly important after the Middle East war). Nigeria was Britain's largest market in Africa, outside South Africa, and there were over 15,000 British nationals working in the country. The UK had, therefore, a strong interest in maintaining the unity of Nigeria and this was to form the basis for all policy between 1967 and 1970.

The story of those three years is too complex to examine in detail but there is an overall pattern. After initial successes by the Biafrans the war settled down to a long grind of attrition by the Federal forces. The longer they took to subdue Biafra the greater the domestic pressure on the Labour government to take some action either to halt the war or help the starving of Biafra. This pressure came from the humanitarian-aid agencies, and a group of both Labour and Conservative backbenchers. Throughout the three years about 100–130 MPs were prepared to sign motions backing a ceasefire, an arms embargo and a massive relief operation. The Conservative front bench was quietly sympathetic to the government's policy and did little to press the issue. Within the Labour party about a quarter of the backbenchers were opposed to the government's policy. The Labour party conference in both 1968 and 1969 called for a ban on arms supplies but was ignored. There was a series of parliamentary debates but none where the government seemed likely to be defeated. At any time when opposition was beginning to become serious the government would decide to take an initiative to try and defuse the situation. This usually consisted of sending a minister to Nigeria for discussions (in March 1969 Wilson even went himself). These discussions produced no change of policy and were not intended to do so. Their immediate purpose was achieved once the appearance of movement was given.

British policy remained firmly in the hands of Wilson and the Foreign Office. There were few discussions in Cabinet and only token dissent from a few members – Callaghan, Castle, Crossman and Gardiner – on two occasions (December 1968 and November 1969), when they argued for greater emphasis to be placed on getting relief supplies into Biafra. The only occasion when Wilson considered a shift in the government's public-relations position was in December 1969. On 8 December fifty-seven backbenchers revolted over government policy on Vietnam and Wilson feared the government might be defeated after a debate on Nigeria the next day. If it was, he proposed to announce that the government would then support an arms embargo at the UN. He did this safe in the knowledge that the Secretary-General, U Thant, was opposed to an embargo and that there was no majority in favour in the General Assembly, and that the government would therefore be able to go on supplying arms. In the event the government did not lose the vote, and less than a month later Biafra finally collapsed and the war was over.

The basic aim of the government was to ensure that the Federal government won. This meant it was willing to supply them with

arms on a major scale and this was the issue at the heart of the disputes over British policy. As the main supplier of arms to Nigeria
after independence, the government wanted to retain its position.
It also wanted to keep out as far as possible Russian influence
following their supply of elderly Mig-15s and Ilyushin bombers
(mainly piloted by Egyptians). The US imposed an arms embargo
but only after it was reassured that Britain would continue supplies.
The Americans were determined that Britain should take the
lead in maintaining Western influence in Nigeria because, as Dean
Rusk said in July 1967, 'We regard Nigeria as part of Britain's
sphere of influence.' However, the Labour government did not
have the courage to advocate in public a policy of supplying as many
arms as were needed in order to allow the Federal government to
finish off the rebellion as quickly as possible. Instead it preferred
to adopt a more hypocritical position, arguing in various contorted
ways that it was doing little more than before the outbreak of the war.

The essence of the government's position on arms supplies
rested on two propositions. The first came from Michael Stewart in
July 1969 when he said,

> the arms we have supplied to the Nigerian government have been
> broadly both in quantity and quality what we were supplying before
> the war began.[27]

The second was that the amount of equipment supplied by Britain
remained 'about fifteen per cent of the total value of Nigeria's
arms'.[28] (It was important to stress value and not quantity because
of the Russian supply of a small number of expensive aircraft.)
These two explanations were hardly consistent in themselves given
the increase in the Nigerian army from 8,000 in 1966 to 120,000 by
the end of the war but the government maintained that one or
other, or occasionally both, were correct.

The reality was very different. Official Nigerian figures and a
leaked confidential report by the British Army adviser in Nigeria
(for which three people and the *Sunday Telegraph* were prosecuted
by the government under the Official Secrets Act and acquitted)
both show the UK arms exports to Nigeria were worth about
£70,000 a year before the war but increased to over £10 million by
1969. In that year the Russians supplied about £3 million-worth,
giving the UK about 70% of the Nigerian arms imports. Indeed in
1969 alone the UK supplied forty million rounds of small arms
ammunition and six ships for the Nigerian navy, with two more
under construction.

The government's policy of supporting the Federal side could have been admitted and defended as being in Britain's short- and long-term economic interests, and as preventing a member of the Commonwealth from disintegration. In private it followed this policy to its logical conclusion – the large-scale supply of arms. But it tried to conceal the true situation behind the flimsy barricades of Foreign Office drafting. It ended up trying to justify a policy of 'no change' from the pre-war situation, as though this was somehow a morally defensible position and the other was not.

V. THE INVASION OF ANGUILLA

The invasion of the tiny West Indian island of Anguilla in March 1969 was the comic-opera episode in the life of the government. As the last parts of the Empire were liquidated, Whitehall realised that many of the remaining small colonies would not be viable as independent states. A system of associated states was established that gave autonomy to the colonies but left Britain with responsibility for foreign and security policy. As part of this arrangement the government decided to federate a number of the smaller islands in the Caribbean, and Anguilla (population 6000) was linked with the islands of St Kitts and Nevis to form an associated state in February 1967.

The root of the later problems was that the Anguillans regarded the federation as a takeover by St Kitts and they strongly resented outside rule by their neighbours. The force of this argument was not appreciated in London. Within three months of the federation's inauguration the aggrieved Anguillans ejected the police from St Kitts and effectively ruled themselves whilst remaining nominally a member of the federation. Over the next two years there was a series of discussions involving Anguilla, the federation government and Britain about future arrangements but no solution was found in the face of continuing Anguillan hostility to the federation which Britain consistently supported. In January 1969, after the final breakdown of talks, Anguilla unilaterally declared independence and the British representative on the island was withdrawn.

The Foreign Office was in a panic over the possible consequences of Anguillan UDI, as the Foreign Secretary, Michael Stewart, later admitted:

> I was told that the island might be seized by desperadoes who would turn it into a centre for tax-dodgers, drug-pushers, even gun-runners.[29]

The British government refused to recognise that the Anguillan leader, Ronald Webster, whom it saw as a petty dictator, might genuinely represent the views of his fellow islanders. In March a junior minister at the Foreign Office, William Whitlock, was sent to the West Indies. After discussions with the federation government he attempted to land on Anguilla. The Anguillans, who with some justification regarded Britain as a supporter of the federation, hustled him back on to the boat and refused to talk.

This insult to one of Her Majesty's ministers and the implied threat to Britain's authority was not taken lightly in Whitehall. An emergency meeting of OPD was called for 14 March where, as one member described, they had the benefit of

> Mr Whitlock, very bronzed, giving us as a result of his half-hour on the island his assessment of the situation.[30]

After a solemn speech by Stewart on the need to intervene, the discussion turned to the military planning required. Healey was worried about the lack of intelligence on the forces that might resist an invasion and wanted time to gather the necessary information. There was also the problem of the UN and whether Britain could be declared guilty of aggression. But the crisis brought out the bulldog spirit in at least one member, Jim Callaghan, who told the meeting:

> Whatever you may say, Defence Secretary, we've got to go in. We can't have our nose twisted. I'll give you twenty policemen to keep peace on the island once you have restored law and order.[31]

OPD agreed that a rapid military invasion should be mounted. After the meeting all the ministers present were warned by No 10 that the discussion had been classified 'top secret'. A 'War Cabinet' of Wilson, Healey and Stewart was established to control the operation. It rejected Crossman's idea, based on his wartime experience, for a full-scale psychological warfare plan and decided on a policy of maximum force. There was to be an all-out assault on the island rather than any attempt to re-establish control by putting a commissioner on the island with a small armed guard. The 'desperadoes' on the island were in for a nasty surprise.

The Anguillans were certainly startled to wake up on 18 March to find a wave of British paratroopers assaulting the island. It was then that the truly farcical nature of these bizarre proceedings emerged. A small group of peaceful islanders was confronted by a

233

British occupying force. There were no arms on the island (only one old rifle was found and that was handed in voluntarily) and the whole idea of a mafia takeover turned out to be no more than a series of unsubstantiated rumours. The troops were withdrawn to be replaced by London policemen and British administration was re-established. It was this administration that finally had to come to terms with the real feelings of the islanders. (There was a happy ending – by the mid-1970s Britain finally did allow Anguilla to become an independent associated state separate from its hated neighbours.) The media and the British public, quite rightly, treated the invasion as a huge joke and the episode was soon forgotten. It can be regarded as merely a harmless sideshow in the process of decolonisation but the sight of ministers working themselves up into a chauvinistic mood for gunboat diplomacy, in the light of admittedly poor intelligence, is worrying. And the willingness to use force on this occasion rather than negotiate with the Anguillan leader was in marked contrast to the government's attitude over the illegal declaration of independence in Rhodesia.

VI. DIEGO GARCIA

The Labour government also presided over the fate of another group of small islands, another part of Britain's colonial legacy, this time in the Indian Ocean. Decisions were taken in great secrecy because these particular islands happened to be of interest to the United States for military purposes. In 1962 the Pentagon had recommended to the State Department 'making arrangements with the British that would assure the availability of selected islands in the Indian Ocean'. This work began in 1963 when a joint US-UK survey of the area identified a number of possible sites for development, the prime candidate for use as a base being Diego Garcia. In the spring of 1964 the US decided that it should develop what it described as 'austere facilities' for communications and storage, that the US would bear the costs of construction and would share the facilities with the UK. But this position had not been transmitted to the British before Labour gained power.[32] All the key decisions were, therefore, taken by the new Labour government.

The Foreign Secretary, Gordon-Walker, visited Washington almost immediately after taking office in October 1964 and some of the principal decisions were taken then, for by the spring of 1965 a plan of action had been agreed between the Foreign Office, the

Colonial Office and the Ministry of Defence[33] on how to set about turning these islands into military bases. They formed part of the colony of Mauritius and so had to be treated differently when Mauritius came to be granted independence. The US had been pressing for the islands to become directly administered from London and in April 1965 the Colonial Secretary, Tony Greenwood, told Mauritian leaders that before independence was granted the whole group of islands, known as the Chagos Islands, 1200 miles to the north-east of Mauritius, would be detached and become a separate colony. Mauritius was to be paid £3 million as compensation for this dismemberment of their territory. OPD considered policy on the islands at the end of August 1965. It is clear from the discussion that everybody was well aware that the islands were to be transferred to the Americans. Doubts were expressed about forcibly removing the islands from Mauritius by compulsory purchase and queries raised about the legal right to take such action. This did not worry either Wilson or Stewart:

> Harold and Michael blandly maintained we had every right: anyway the islands were a long way from their owners![34]

Later in 1965 the government created a completely new colony – the British Indian Ocean Territory (BIOT). Although nominally a colony, it was in practice ruled directly by the Colonial Office in London. The first step towards establishing the bases had been taken.

The next step was to negotiate an agreement on the use of the islands. This was complicated by the fact that at this stage the eventual role of the islands was far from clear.[35] Although the British considered setting up an oil storage depot, they decided there was no real requirement. The only military use would, therefore, be American but the Americans too had doubts about the use of the islands. The original idea of a communications facility disappeared because of the increasing use of satellites. A final agreement was signed and made public as an international treaty in December 1966. Under the terms of the treaty the British colony of BIOT was leased to the United States for a minimum of fifty years with an option on another twenty. (The British had wanted only thirty years but the US had insisted on the longer period.) The US was given a free hand to establish whatever bases it liked on the islands and by 1966 the US navy had plans for a base facility. The first US units arrived on Diego Garcia in 1971 and constructed for the US fleet in the Indian Ocean a major naval base capable of docking nuclear-powered aircraft carriers. In the mid-1970s more work was done to provide a major air base from which nuclear-armed B-52s regularly operated.

The US-UK Treaty of 1966 was never debated in Parliament and the truth about Diego Garcia was concealed for years. US documents show, however, that there was a secret annexe to the 1966 Treaty (it was secret at the request of the UK government). This annexe provided for the US and UK to share the cost of the removal of the population. The government always pretended in public that only a handful of migrant workers were involved but the islands were inhabited by a long-established and settled population of just over 2000 (much the same size as that of the Falkland Islands) engaged in fishing, subsistence farming and harvesting copra. A French journalist who visited the islands in the early 1960s described them as moderately prosperous and as having

> the look of a French coastal village, miraculously transformed whole . . . roots have been struck and a society peculiarly suited to the islands developed.[36]

However, the local population and their society were inconvenient for the Americans who wanted uninhabited islands for the base development. This had been recognised as a problem from the start of the talks about the islands in 1963 and the Americans always insisted that the British should be responsible for removing the inhabitants. The Labour government was happy to oblige. The tactics adopted ranged from a process of attrition to deportation. The government realised that if the removal of the islanders against their will became public knowledge it could jeopardise the whole plan. Apart from alerting the islanders to their fate it also ran the risk of starting an outcry about human rights. The removal was in direct contradiction of the UN Declaration of Human Rights, which provides that 'no one should be subject to arbitrary exile' (Article 9) and 'everybody has the right to return to his country' (Article 13). The whole process had to be handled quietly, aided by the remoteness of the islands.

After BIOT was set up in 1965 any islanders who travelled to Mauritius, as they often did, were simply denied permission to return home. In 1967 the government bought out the sole employer on the island for just over £1 million and closed down the copra-gathering operation. Food ships were stopped from calling at the island and the inhabitants left to survive on whatever food they could grow. Between 1965 and 1970 about half the population of

Diego Garcia was removed from the island (the remainder went by 1973). The people who were removed were left in destitution on Mauritius, which was paid the princely sum of £650,000 for relief work. A decade after they were ejected over 80% of the islanders still wanted to return home. Eventually, after a long campaign against the British government, they were given a total of £4 million by way of compensation in 1982 but only on condition that they gave up all claims to return to their homes.

As the government had agreed secretly to share the costs with the Americans special arrangements had to be made to cover up the sums involved and stop any awkward questions being asked in Parliament. The UK finished up paying a total of over £15 million to set up the BIOT and remove the inhabitants. Some of this was disguised as aid to Mauritius. The US contributed only £5 million but that could not be paid directly or it would have become public in the published accounts of the Ministry of Defence. Instead, to keep the deal secret, the US agreed not to charge Britain for that part of the bill for the purchase of Polaris which related to research and development.

The fate of the remote island of Diego Garcia shows up the relative priorities that the Labour government gave to the demands of the American government and strategic considerations on the one hand and the rights of the native people affected by that policy on the other. Humanitarian considerations played no part in policy making. This lack of emphasis on the humanitarian aspects of foreign and strategic policy was repeated in the low priority given to overseas aid. A similar pro-American stance was also taken over Vietnam where there was no discussion of a more detached policy. On the sale of arms to the Americans for use in Vietnam, the supply of arms to the Nigerian federal government to defeat Biafra and the consequences of constructing a major military base on Diego Garcia, the government was not prepared to admit what it was doing. Its actions could have been acknowledged openly and robustly defended as simply those of realpolitik. All governments have to take a view on where they believe the 'national interest' to lie and often that means taking unpopular decisions. However, the Labour government did not want to defend its actions in public on these grounds. Instead it preferred to cover up many of its actions – actions that were in the mainstream of traditional British foreign policy as practised by all post-war governments.

14
Negotiations and Sanctions: Rhodesia 1966–70

Quite apart from the repugnance, which I hope we all share, about
negotiating with the illegal regime, the very idea it would be
successful . . . is the product of the most woolly-minded thinking I
have come across.

Harold Wilson, House of Commons, 21 December 1965

After the illegal declaration of independence in November 1965
and in the run-up to the election, the government had mounted a
successful holding operation on Rhodesia. Commonwealth countries had reluctantly accepted voluntary economic sanctions as an
alternative to British military intervention. The UN call for sanctions had been generally accepted by the international community
apart from South Africa and Portugal. Rhodesia was isolated
politically and economically, and Britain had, with the United
States, taken steps to cut off oil supplies to Rhodesia. The overland
pipeline was closed and British oil companies were prohibited by
law from supplying Rhodesia. Rhodesian stocks of oil, built up to
about three months before UDI, were, barring supplies from
South Africa or elsewhere, expected to be exhausted fairly rapidly.
At the beginning of April 1966 the Cabinet decided to go to the UN
to obtain authority to stop the flow of crude oil through the
Mozambique port of Beira. This was obtained on 9 April when the
Security Council declared Rhodesia a 'threat to peace' (the first
time this had been done since the Korean War) and authorised
Britain to intercept shipping on the high seas. Within days
the Royal Navy had diverted oil tankers away from Beira and
established a blockade.

Despite public optimism ministers were doubtful whether Ian
Smith could be forced to return to legality by sanctions. At the end
of April the Cabinet discussed what to do next. After UDI the
British government had kept open the lines of communication with
Smith via the Governor, Sir Humphrey Gibbs, and even as he was
ridiculing negotiations in public, Wilson was sending secret mess-

ages to Smith. In March 1966 an official had gone out to Salisbury to discuss ways of ending the rebellion. Overcoming any repugnance it may have felt, the Cabinet accepted the opening of discussions with the Smith regime, partly because the Governor was threatening to resign unless they started. Between May and August 1966 there were three rounds of talks: they started in London in May, continued in Rhodesia in June and concluded at the end of August. In late June Wilson informed the Cabinet the talks had made no progress and nobody expected any positive results. Before the August round Judith Hart, one of the ministers in charge of the negotiations, told a colleague what was envisaged:

> the proposals we were going to put at the resumed talks were quite unacceptable to Smith but would put him in the wrong. It was largely a presentational exercise.[1]

Smith's only interest was in seeing whether Britain would legitimise his regime on terms acceptable to him and his right-wing supporters. So long as sanctions were largely ineffective he had every incentive to maintain the status quo and no reason to negotiate seriously, let alone surrender. The talks, not surprisingly, were abortive.

Britain's other option was to try and reinforce sanctions. Ministers first considered this possibility in May and Judith Hart was sent out to Zambia to see if she could persuade President Kaunda to cut off all trade with neighbouring Rhodesia. Only months before Zambia had actually wanted to impose sanctions but had been held back by Britain. Now it was unwilling to act because it thought sanctions were going to fail and saw no reason to disrupt its own economy. It asked for £8 million of assistance from Britain, which was reluctantly agreed by the Cabinet in early August, with many dissenting on grounds similar to those of President Kaunda – that sanctions were going to fail. The deal finally collapsed when Kaunda asked for a commitment to no independence for Rhodesia before majority rule. This, ministers, and particularly Wilson, were not prepared to give, since it would rule out any negotiations with Smith who would never accept the idea.

By the summer of 1966 it was obvious, from the simple fact that the Rhodesian economy continued to function, that substantial oil supplies were getting through via South Africa or Mozambique (or both). Sanctions against South Africa were ruled out but at a meeting of RX (the Rhodesia Committee) at the end of August

Wilson raised the possibility of sanctions against Portugal to stop the flow of oil through Mozambique. He was defeated by the outright opposition of Brown, Healey and Bowden who thought they would be ineffective (supplies would still get through via South Africa) and too difficult to enforce, since the Ministry of Defence estimated that it would take seventeen ships to enforce a blockade of Lourenço Marques (Beira took five).

When RX and Cabinet then considered future policy at the end of August the situation was difficult and their room for manoeuvre limited. Britain had no effective power in Rhodesia and with sanctions not working Smith had no reason to give in. As the government was not prepared to go for all-out sanctions against South Africa, they decided that they had little choice but to maintain sanctions against Rhodesia and continue negotiations with Smith in the hope that something might emerge. Yet in these negotiations Britain was tied to principles that Smith would not accept. The Cabinet decided not to break off the current talks (Gibbs was still threatening to resign if they were ended) but felt there was no realistic prospect of success.

Within a week ministers had a more robust policy forced on them as a result of the Commonwealth Prime Ministers' meeting in London, later described by Wilson as 'a nightmare conference'.[2] The Afro-Asian delegates were tired of British policy over Rhodesia. At the previous conference in Lagos in January Wilson had promised sanctions would bring an end to the Smith regime. Given their obvious failure to do so, there were overwhelming demands for an effective policy. After sitting through three days of hostile speeches, Wilson summoned an emergency meeting of the Cabinet on the Saturday morning. Bowden opened the proceedings by saying that concessions were required to prevent a major walkout. Wilson was keen to keep talking to Smith and also wanted to limit any sanctions so as to exclude South Africa. The key intervention came from George Brown. He threw away his departmental brief from the Foreign Office, which argued strongly against sanctions, describing its advice as 'moral nonsense'. He swung the meeting over to accepting the principle of no independence before majority rule (NIBMAR), which ministers had rejected only weeks before when it was requested by Zambia. After further sessions of the Commonwealth Conference a new policy was agreed. Britain set a deadline of 30 November for Smith to come to an agreement. If he failed to do so, a policy of NIBMAR would be adopted (effectively ruling out any future agreement, or even negotiations, with Smith) and Britain would go to the UN to ask for selective mandatory sanctions.

Wilson was determined to take advantage of the two months breathing space he had won from the Commonwealth Conference to try and reach an agreement with Smith. He kept in close touch with Gibbs in Salisbury, refusing to circulate the telegrams to members of the Cabinet, even though the Americans were given verbatim accounts of the exchanges he had with Smith during this period. At the end of September Bowden and Elwyn Jones had long discussions with Gibbs and fruitless ones with Smith. On their return they told the Cabinet that Smith was only prepared to return to legality once the constitutional arrangements for independence were agreed. He would not agree to any action to ease racial discrimination or introduce a fairer apportionment of the land. The scope for a possible compromise agreement was clearly very limited but the Cabinet agreed to draw up their own terms for a settlement.

When RX considered a draft in the middle of October, ministers were uncertain whether the terms were for public-relations purposes after the talks broke down or whether they were a genuine attempt at a settlement. No clear decision was reached. The terms were built around the famous 'Five Principles' but also included other miscellaneous possibilities, such as a mission of Commonwealth legal experts, or a visit by Commonwealth Prime Ministers or even, most extraordinary of all, an act of union between Britain and Rhodesia.

The British terms were sent to Rhodesia on 15 October and within ten days it was clear that Smith would not accept them. The formal rejection came early in November, although Smith invited Bowden to visit Rhodesia. When RX met on 8 November, one member detected a mood of widespread resignation:

> nearly all the committee [are] now convinced that there is no point in negotiating further with Smith, [but] Harold [is] still trying to find ways of keeping the dialogue going.[3]

Time was running out fast and with the deadline only days away RX discussed on 21 November tactics for winding up the negotiations at the end of the month, proclaiming NIBMAR and going to the UN for mandatory sanctions. But Gibbs was yet again threatening to resign unless Bowden accepted Smith's invitation. The problem was that Bowden was also threatening to resign if he was forced to go. Eventually fear of the consequences of the Governor quitting over the government's failure to keep negotiations going proved stronger and on 24 November the Cabinet agreed that Bowden should go to Rhodesia. Two days later in Salisbury Smith seemed to hint to both Bowden and Gibbs that he was prepared to return to legality on the basis of the 1961 constitution – if so it was virtually the equivalent of unconditional surrender and ought to have been treated with considerable suspicion. But with both sides eager to avoid the public odium of responsibility for a total breakdown, RX agreed to negotiations, even though they recognised they were clutching at straws. Wilson told his main Cabinet dissident on Rhodesia, Barbara Castle, that Smith had 'met us on all constitutional points. The only trouble is that I don't trust him.' When Castle surreptitiously read the telegrams from Rhodesia through the courtesy of her friend Judith Hart she saw a different picture:

> Our boys there realised that Smith's proposals were very clever presentationally and would be difficult to make a breaking point but that they provided no real answer and were impossible to sell to the African Commonwealth and the rest of the world.[4]

On Bowden's return RX agreed a negotiating brief for talks between Wilson and Smith on board HMS *Tiger* off Gibraltar. When the Cabinet met there was no attempt to address the fundamental points on which Britain could not make concessions. Instead George Brown suggested they simply gave the Prime Minister their best wishes.

What was Wilson hoping to achieve from the talks? Undoubtedly he still hoped to obtain the credit of finally settling the Rhodesian problem through his personal diplomacy. Even if he failed in that, he believed he would successfully defuse the issue in domestic politics by showing he had tried every possible course before embarking on a stricter policy towards Rhodesia. As he told a colleague just before he left for the talks:

> This is the game of musical box . . . and the person who's holding it when the record stops loses. I shall have handed the box back to Smith and shaken off the blame on myself. I can't lose.[5]

The problem was that Smith thought he was in the same position. He was in *de facto* control of Rhodesia and if no agreement were reached would remain so. He had nothing to lose by finding out how far Britain would go to end the rebellion.

The talks on HMS *Tiger* lasted three days (2–4 December).

Wilson believed that he had obtained a prior agreement from Smith that the latter could make a settlement without reference to his colleagues in Salisbury. If he had given such a promise Smith did not stick to it. At the end of the first day Smith said he had to consult his Cabinet by telegram. Then the next morning he said he would have to fly back for consultations. He left the next day having done no more than initial a record of the discussions. Wilson had not been able to force Smith into genuine negotiations. His tactics throughout the discussions rested on the illusion that Smith was a 'moderate' who would break with his supposedly more extreme colleagues. Wilson therefore tried to tempt him to sack part of his Cabinet, accept five new ministers, including two non-nationalist Africans, and remain as Prime Minister of a new, 'broadly based' administration that would rule in conjunction with Britain during the transition to legal independence. Smith would not give Wilson such a commitment.

The terms for independence discussed on HMS *Tiger* excluded any idea of NIBMAR and centered on complex amendments to the 1961 constitution, in particular the creation of a mechanism to enable the Africans to prevent retrogressive amendments to the constitution and preserve their eventual right to majority rule. The *Tiger* terms produced a worse deal for the Africans than independence on the 1961 constitution or any of the deals offered by the Labour government in 1965 to avert UDI. Although their number of reserved seats was to increase immediately, it would in practice be more difficult to obtain majority rule. This could only be done through the so-called 'A-roll' seats, where there was an educational and property qualification. Under the 1961 constitution the Africans would have an overall majority in Parliament once they won 36% of these seats. Under the *Tiger* terms they would have needed to win 51½%. In 1966 only 5000 Africans out of one and a half million were qualified to vote on the 'A-roll' and the *Tiger* terms contained no proposals to lower these qualifications and no commitment to a programme for African education. The acceptability of the deal to the Rhodesian people (the crucial fifth principle) was to be tested by a Royal Commission, not a referendum. Another Royal Commission was to investigate racial discrimination and police powers (the fourth principle). But Smith would have been able to veto all appointments to the commission and independence would have been possible before any progress had been made on ending discrimination.

The Cabinet met on Wilson's return on 4 December. He thought he had obtained an agreement from Smith and was hopeful about

Rhodesian acceptance. He recognised the concessions he had had to make:

> This is a British Government which has failed to achieve its objectives painfully accepting the best agreed terms they could get for the voluntary winding-up of the rebellion by the rebels themselves and since that is the case we can't quite expect the terms we would have imposed if we'd won.[6]

Wilson asked for, and obtained, the Cabinet's acceptance of the terms agreed on HMS *Tiger* with only Castle dissenting. Wilson then prepared a statement to the Commons to announce a settlement with Salisbury. Other ministers were examining their consciences. One member of the Cabinet, Barbara Castle, was ready to resign and she would have been joined by three junior ministers, Judith Hart, David Ennals and Shirley Williams. Lord Caradon, the minister at the UN, had already told Wilson that he too would go if power was handed over to a minority white regime.

Attention then focused on Salisbury. After an all-day discussion, the Rhodesian Cabinet rejected the terms, ostensibly because they disliked the idea of a broadly based government during the transition to independence. The underlying reason, though, was that on balance they felt that, despite the threat of mandatory sanctions, and with oil still getting through, it was better to continue as they were rather than accept the deal and the possibility, however remote, that there might be African rule. So confident was Wilson of success that no alternative Parliamentary statement had been prepared. After news of the failure was received his speech had to be altered hurriedly whilst on his way to the Commons.

The major compensation for Wilson in the failure was that it avoided considerable political embarrassment. The *Tiger* terms would have been approved by Parliament – with the Conservatives in favour – but some ministers would have resigned and there would have been a revolt among some Labour MPs. The effect on the Commonwealth is more difficult to judge. The Afro-Asian countries thought they had at last brought Britain to accept NIBMAR in the September conference. Now Wilson had not only ignored NIBMAR, which he was theoretically entitled to do under the September agreement, but had stretched the Five Principles to breaking point to try and get an agreement. Some countries would almost certainly have left the Commonwealth if Rhodesia had accepted the *Tiger* terms. As it was Wilson still had some credit for his personal diplomacy and for making the effort with Smith. The parcel had been handed back to the Rhodesians and Wilson had largely escaped the blame for failure.

After the unsuccessful *Tiger* talks mandatory sanctions were imposed by the UN and just before Christmas Wilson announced that British policy would now be NIBMAR. Before the announcement the Cabinet had discussed future policy. They agreed Bowden's firm paper saying that there should be no negotiations, although Wilson was still keen to try and keep open some sort of dialogue by sending a commission to Rhodesia to spell out the sort of constitution that would operate under majority rule. The rest of the Cabinet simply refused to agree. For the next six months there were no developments.

In June 1967 Bowden told the Cabinet about a 'private' trip by Lord Alport, an ex-Conservative junior minister and former High Commissioner to the Central African Federation. He would be going to see the Governor but would be 'available' to see Smith. A month later Bowden reported that the Alport visit had got nowhere and that there was no sign of any shift in Smith's position. Nevertheless Wilson proposed to try and resurrect the whole *Tiger* package by sending a Royal Commission to Rhodesia to investigate whether the settlement was acceptable to the people as a whole. The only conditions he wanted to impose on Smith were the lifting of censorship and some concessions on civil rights. Again he met unanimous opposition from the rest of RX and had to drop the idea.

The next major review of policy came three months later. During the summer there had been an abortive attempt to get South Africa to persuade Smith to settle in return for Britain agreeing to sell the South Africans a large package of arms. On 18 October OPD had a long discussion on where to go next. Debate centered around two options. One was simply to soldier on as before and try to make sanctions more effective. The alternative, suggested by Brown and Thomson, was to examine the possibility of giving up altogether and handing the whole problem over to the UN to resolve. This was the policy adopted in the 1940s over Palestine but that had been a UN-mandated territory, not a Crown colony. The idea generated no great enthusiasm but neither did Wilson's repeated suggested of sending out a Royal Commission. With no solution in sight, they ended up by sending Thomson to Rhodesia in the vain hope that Smith might have shifted his position. A month later he reported that Smith had indeed shifted his position but only to go back on some of the agreements reached during the *Tiger* talks. In this position of total sterility a new committee, chaired by Lord Gardiner, was set up to examine in detail the idea of handing the whole problem over to the UN.

By the time the committee's work was completed in March the atmosphere had suddenly changed. On 6 March 1968 the Smith regime executed three Africans, even though the Queen had exercised the prerogative of mercy. This act of defiance caused a short-lived hardening in the Cabinet's attitudes. Wilson said, 'It is absolutely impossible to negotiate now or to reach a settlement.' But there was greater caution over what action to take and no decision was reached, apart from trying to score a tactical victory over the Conservatives by putting down a motion in the Commons condemning Smith, hoping they might support it.[7] The next day OPD agreed to enhance British sanctions by cutting off TV programmes and jamming radio broadcasts. In addition the UN was to be asked for comprehensive mandatory sanctions against Rhodesia. But OPD insisted that South Africa be consulted before the UK tabled the resolution to ensure that they were not worried about a possible extension of the resolution to include themselves. That resolution was accepted by the UN but Rhodesia continued to survive, oil continued to flow and there seemed to be no way out of the impasse.

In June 1968 Wilson launched a new initiative and this time he tried a rather different approach. He still wanted to settle the Rhodesian question by getting an agreement with Smith but he knew that Smith would never agree to NIBMAR. Wilson himself admits that at the *Tiger* talks he told Smith:

> Once the principle of 'no independence before majority rule' was formally adopted, there could be no going back and no more concessions of the kind the British Government had been ready to make in order to promote this last meeting and to give [him] and his colleagues a final chance.[8]

After *Tiger* Wilson had committed the government not to put forward any proposals for a settlement that were inconsistent with NIBMAR. Within months he was already complaining to one colleague, 'But if we stick by NIBMAR there will never be a solution of Rhodesia.'[9] By June 1968 he was to start negotiations and abandon the principle of NIBMAR.

In June 1968 Wilson handed over to his solicitor, Sir Arnold Goodman, and Sir Max Aitken (son of Lord Beaverbrook) outline proposals for a settlement that they were to take on a 'private visit' to Rhodesia for discussion with Smith. The proposed terms were essentially those agreed on *Tiger* with new ideas about the mechanism for the return to legality. No mention was made of the idea of NIBMAR. Goodman and Aitken returned in August and indicated that a settlement on this basis seemed possible. Wilson then discussed the terms with a small, informal group of ministers at the end of the month. There was considerable opposition to the idea of further negotiations, little optimism about the outcome and a general belief that it was not worthwhile simply to suffer another rebuff. But Wilson was determined to have another opportunity for personal diplomacy and sanguine about his chances of ultimately clinching an agreement with Smith. He also had another motive – one that had underlain so much of his tactics from the start. He wanted to suppress Rhodesia as a political issue either by reaching agreement or showing one was impossible:

> If no honourable settlement could be reached, the Rhodesian question would be buried as a matter of inter-party controversy for the remainder of the Parliament and over the period of an election.[10]

At the Labour party conference in September Wilson consulted those members of the Cabinet he already knew favoured his flying to meet Smith. Then the day before he was due to leave the Cabinet was summoned and he went round the table asking whether he should go until he drew this response from Callaghan:

> I get a bit sick of being asked for my view when the TV cameras are outside and everybody knows you're going. I will wish you good luck and say no more.

A large proportion of the Cabinet were sceptical about the wisdom of meeting Smith and dubious about the prospects for success. The background papers before the Cabinet confirmed, as one member recorded,

> that the result of the Goodman–Aitken probes on the one side and the probe by Bottomley [an official in the Commonwealth Office] on the other was to extract not a single concession from Smith.[11]

The Cabinet refused to allow Wilson to make any concessions beyond those made in the *Tiger* talks but there was no mention of the abandonment of the NIBMAR pledge. The liberals in the Cabinet were worried. Castle was on the point of resignation again (as was Reg Prentice) and when she saw Lord Gardiner she learnt that he had refused to accompany Wilson to the talks. Having been consulted about the negotiations, he was convinced that Wilson would settle for worse terms than *Tiger*:

> Gerald sighed heavily and said how disappointed he had been in a Labour government: Vietnam, Biafra and now this.[12]

The talks on board HMS *Fearless* off Gibraltar lasted five days (9–13 October). This time there was no attempt to reach an immediate settlement and both sides returned home to consider the outcome. The terms were little different from *Tiger*, although a crash programme of African education was now envisaged. As before the Rhodesians identified an unacceptable element – on this occasion it was not the idea of a broadly based government during the transition to independence but the mechanism for appeals to the Privy Council as a guarantee of unimpeded progress to majority rule. Most of the Cabinet realised that Smith was just using this as an excuse not to settle. At the end of October Smith asked for Thomson to visit Rhodesia but gave no idea which parts of the agreement he accepted. After a fortnight in Rhodesia in early November Thomson reported that he had made no progress and that there were at least eight major areas of disagreement between the two sides. There were no more negotiations.

The *Fearless* talks ended in failure in much the same way as *Tiger* and for much the same reason. Smith and his government preferred to go on as they were rather than accept the concessions the British had made because of the ultimate threat of majority rule. Wilson had been, as usual, over-optimistic about his ability to negotiate a settlement, an illusion shared by few other members of the Cabinet. But he had achieved his other objective in showing that a settlement with Smith was impossible and Rhodesia disappeared as a party-political issue. However, that aim had been achieved at a price to Britain's reputation. Britain had gone back on its pledge not to negotiate except on terms including majority rule before independence. In January 1969 Malcolm Macdonald, the government's roving High Commissioner in Africa, reported that a settlement on the *Fearless* terms would have led to a mass exodus from the Commonwealth (only Malawi would have stayed) and concluded:

> the British Government's word is no longer trusted in Africa.[13]

After the collapse of the *Fearless* talks the Rhodesian regime showed itself in its true colours. In June 1969 a new, unashamedly racist constitution was inaugurated. According to its provisions after about 100 years the Africans might achieve parity with the whites in Parliament but they could never achieve a majority. In March 1970 Rhodesia became a republic and the Governor left the colony.

On 17 December 1965 an Order-in-Council had made it a criminal offence for any British company to supply oil to Rhodesia or to anybody else if they knew, or could reasonably be expected to know, that the eventual destination was Rhodesia. Oil was the weak link in the Rhodesian economy. With supplies of crude oil cut off by the Beira patrol and the closure of the Umtali pipeline Rhodesia had to have secure supplies of refined petroleum products. There were only two possible sources of supply. The first was South Africa where the government and the local oil companies were sympathetic to Rhodesia. However, it was difficult to move large quantities of oil straight to Rhodesia from South Africa because there was no direct rail link. The obvious supply route was, therefore, the port of Lourenço Marques in the Portuguese colony of Mozambique that did have a direct rail link with Rhodesia. Large quantities of oil were already shipped through the port not just to Mozambique but also to South Africa.

The situation was made more complex by the internal arrangements of the oil companies. Shell and BP, Rhodesia's main suppliers (together with the French firm Total), had a complicated joint marketing arrangement involving two subsidiary companies in South Africa and Mozambique. The Shell-BP South African subsidiary was a South African company and therefore not subject to British law. In January 1966 the South African government instructed the oil companies in South Africa to continue to supply Rhodesia, as before UDI, with its 'traditional' supplies, which were mainly lubricants and aviation fuel. Shell and BP were, however, warned by the British government on 28 January that to continue to supply their South African subsidiary knowing that some of that oil would go on to Rhodesia would be an offence under British law. Their Mozambique company was registered in London with a board largely composed of British citizens and was, therefore, on both counts subject to UK sanctions legislation. It was a criminal offence for it to supply oil either directly or indirectly to Rhodesia.

By the summer of 1966 it was obvious that large-scale evasion of sanctions must be taking place. How did the British government react to this situation? South Africa was the obvious loophole, so the first question was what, if anything, to do about their refusal to take any notice of the UN sanctions. The government's policy was to avoid the imposition of sanctions against South Africa at all costs, indeed their aim was to increase trade with South Africa. This effectively ruled out taking any action against the oil companies for supplying their South African subsidiaries with oil that was eventually destined for Rhodesia.

However, the government soon realised that South Africa was not the main source of supply. At the end of August 1966 a Top Secret Joint Intelligence Committee report identified Lourenço Marques as the only possible route for the large-scale supplies Rhodesia was clearly receiving. There followed a series of moves to try and limit supplies through Mozambique. The government's approach was discreetly to negotiate some sort of scheme with the oil companies that would reduce the amount of oil going through Lourenço Marques in the hope that this might limit supplies reaching Rhodesia. During 1967 it was to try four different schemes on the oil companies, none of which were successful. In January George Brown proposed a rationing of supplies through Mozambique, a suggestion followed up only half-heartedly by the Ministry of Power. It was soon apparent that there was a division of views within Whitehall. The Ministry of Power, close to the oil companies and sympathetic to their problems, did not press them on what it saw as a Foreign Office problem. The rationing idea never got off the ground. On 19 January officials at the Ministry of Power were told informally that the leakage to Rhodesia did not come from the refinery at Lourenço Marques and that some of the BP-Shell imports might be finishing up in Rhodesia through various secondary companies. Ministers were not told about this information and instead were left to think up another idea. In March George Thomson suggested that Shell and BP should buy all the output of the refinery at Lourenço Marques which was surplus to Mozambique's requirements. (This idea was based, of course, on the mistaken assumption that Rhodesian supplies were coming from the refinery rather than direct shipment of refined oil.) When the companies asked the government to pay the additional costs of £1 million a year the Treasury refused and that idea also collapsed. In October the Ministry of Power suggested that supplies for parts of South Africa currently being shipped via Lourenço Marques should in future go via Durban to keep supplies at the former port to a minimum. The oil companies refused on the grounds that it would increase their costs. In December Thomson put to Shell and BP a slight variant of the previous scheme, in which they would only sell to their bulk customers in South Africa from stocks in South Africa rather then through Lourenço Marques. That request too was rejected.

At this stage ministers were convinced that the French company Total was the main culprit in supplying Rhodesia. Official talks with the French took place in early 1967 and Wilson raised the subject with de Gaulle during his visit to Paris in June 1967 but no action was taken by the French to put any pressure on the company. Other governments had different ideas as to which companies were supplying Rhodesia. On three occasions in 1966 and 1967 the Portuguese government told the British Ambassador in Lisbon that it was Shell and BP who were the main culprits. A minimal amount of investigation took place, and the government accepted the word of the Shell and BP head offices that they were not involved. In June 1967 Thomson wrote to a backbench Labour MP in categorical terms;

> We are absolutely satisfied that British oil companies are not involved in the supply.[14]

Then in February 1968 President Kaunda of Zambia published detailed figures on the supply of oil through Mozambique. These showed that the amount shipped had risen from 19,500 tons in April 1966 to an average of about 43,000 tons a month and in some months was over 50,000 tons. The figures also gave a detailed breakdown of the ships involved (a large proportion were British registered) and the companies shipping the oil (Shell and BP were major operators). Kaunda publicly accused British firms of supplying oil to Rhodesia.

Six days after Kaunda's speech two senior directors from Shell and BP had a meeting with George Thomson, the Commonwealth Secretary, called at their request. They told him that their Mozambique subsidiary had been supplying roughly half Rhodesia's total requirements for the past two years. Did this news come as a surprise to the government? They had known for eighteen months that Lourenço Marques was the supply route, and that both Shell and BP were major operators in Mozambique. They had their own diplomatic and intelligence sources. If the Zambian government could provide detailed information on movements it is surprising that the British government remained so long in ignorance. After the indications earlier in the year that Shell and BP were involved, the Ministry of Power also received regular reports after October 1967 from Mozambique of Shell and BP rail tankers travelling to Rhodesia. They merely passed these on to the companies and took no further action. Indeed before then it is difficult to imagine that British representatives on the spot and other agents can have been entirely unaware of the vast increase in traffic through the port and its destination. What is clear is that there was a marked reluctance in all quarters (including the headquarters of the oil companies) to ask any embarrassing questions during the year-long negotiations over Mozambiquean supplies. There is no doubt that it was easier to blame other countries such as France for breaking sanctions.

Whatever had taken place before February 1968 the position was now clear. Shell and BP had admitted that their Mozambique subsidiary, which was subject to UK law, had been supplying Rhodesia. How did Thomson react to this *prima facie* evidence of a criminal offence? At no time was there any suggestion of a prosecution. Indeed throughout the meeting it was assumed that the government and Shell and BP were on the same side, and had the same interest in getting out of an awkward situation. Thomson was mainly worried by the presentational problem. Britain had been attacking others for breaking sanctions and now had overwhelming evidence that they were themselves a major culprit, and that Portugal and Zambia had been right in the past. No minister would relish telling the public what had really been going on.

Thomson was offered a way out of the dilemma by Shell and BP who, before the meeting, had arranged a new system of supply for Rhodesia with the French company Total. In order to safeguard their share of the Rhodesian market whilst not technically breaching UK law they agreed their outlets in Rhodesia would order from Shell and BP but would be supplied by Total. Total would be compensated by Shell and BP providing an equivalent amount of oil in South Africa. Although this 'swap agreement' broke the spirit if not the letter of sanctions law, it did provide a way out for Thomson. Although doubt has been cast upon whether the implications of the swap were fully understood at this meeting, the minutes of the meeting make it plain that the officials present did appreciate the significance of what they had been told. What concerned them was the need to devise a public formula that would disguise what had happened whilst still saying Britain was not supplying oil. The idea that Parliament should be told about the activities of BP and Shell was never raised. The crucial part of the minutes reads:

in any statements in the the House of Commons or elsewhere, Ministers would be stating the position *with complete accuracy* [my italics] if they used a formula along the lines 'No British company is supplying POL [oil] to Rhodesia.'[15]

By using the present tense, that is just about an accurate statement but it is certainly an excellent example of Whitehall being very parsimonious with the truth.

After this meeting the government knew that British companies had probably been breaking UK law for two years but no evidence was ever sent to the Attorney-General to consider what action to take. It is all the more extraordinary, therefore, that five weeks after the meeting Thomson could tell the House of Commons:

> no other country does more in the field of sanctions than the United Kingdom. I do not claim any special virtue for this. It is Britain's duty to do it . . . If the general membership of the United Nations were to apply sanctions and supervise the activities of some of their business firms as well as Britain does, the impact of sanctions would be substantially and significantly increased.[16]

As Thomson told Shell and BP, 'a great deal of politics normally is a problem of presentation'.

Three months after the meeting with Thomson, officials in the Ministry of Power were given detailed information by the oil companies on how the swap agreement was operating. They sent this on to officials in the Commonwealth Office. Shortly afterwards the Portuguese gave a report to the French, who passed it on to London, showing that Shell and BP had supplied 40% of Rhodesia's requirements in 1967. Because the swap agreement was now operating, the report was merely noted and no action taken. In January 1969 the Portuguese published more figures on the oil supplied by Shell and BP, and as a result there was a further meeting between the oil companies and Thomson in February 1969. At that meeting neither side seems to have been under any illusions about the significance of the 'swap'. Thomson asked how the swap agreement was working. The oil companies referred to the swap as only a 'cosmetic' arrangement. Thomson himself expressed relief that no news about the swap had leaked, as the official minutes of the meeting record:

> One would have expected that if they [the Portuguese] had got wind of the exchange arrangements between Shell-BP and Total (South Africa) they would have regarded this as a sufficiently damaging discovery in itself.[17]

The 'damaging discovery' about connivance at the evasion of sanctions was not to become public for another ten years.

Apart from George Thomson, who else in the government knew that Shell and BP had been breaking sanctions, and that the government now connived at continued evasion? When the saga was exposed George Brown, Foreign Secretary at the time of the initial revelations in 1968, said that 'None of us then in office could claim ignorance on the position.'[18] His successor, Michael Stewart, knew about the details of the swap agreement in February 1969 and raised no objections. The minutes of both meetings between Shell-BP and Thomson were, in accordance with normal Whitehall practice, copied by Thomson's private secretary to the secretary at No 10, Michael Palliser, who dealt with foreign affairs. Were these papers seen by Wilson? It is important at this stage to distinguish between knowledge of the illegal supply and knowledge of the swap agreement. In a Commons debate in 1978 Wilson said, after having consulted the archives, about the note of the second meeting between Thomson and the oil companies in 1969: 'There is no record of my seeing it.' This contained unequivocal evidence of the 'swap' and Wilson denies he knew about the existence of such an arrangement until 1978. He put all the blame for agreeing the 'swap' onto Thomson, saying:

I certainly do not believe that when my noble Friend heard what was said he realised the implications.[19]

However, Wilson did not categorically deny that he had seen the 1968 minute about illegal supply, and the assumption must be that all the senior ministers involved were aware of the activities of Shell and BP before 1968.

On 28 March, a month after the first meeting between the oil companies and Thomson, OPD discussed a forty-page report by the Foreign Office on the flow of oil through Mozambique. Thomson subsequently explained:

when it was discovered that British oil was being diverted into Rhodesia at Lourenço Marques, this fact was reported by the Foreign and Commonwealth Secretary to [OPD].[20]

Whether the full details of the swap were set out is more doubtful, because Wilson spent a long time trying to convince his colleagues that they should put pressure on Total to try and stop the flow of oil. None of the other members of OPD had any enthusiasm for trying to block this route, arguing that even if they were successful oil would still reach Rhodesia through South Africa. Since the government opposed sanctions against South Africa there was little they could do.

Oil sanctions, mandatory under UN resolutions, were continued even though the government had connived at a scheme that rendered them useless. Not surprisingly the Smith regime continued to prosper until the collapse of the Portuguese empire in 1974. Then with a hostile Mozambique it had to rely on South African supplies and face increasing guerilla activity from surrounding territory. By 1979 the pressure was too great, and Smith finally had to accept a transfer of power and 'no independence before majority rule'.

The illegal regime in Rhodesia survived because Britain could not put on enough pressure to end the rebellion. Negotiation was a fruitless exercise since Smith and his colleagues preferred to continue as they were rather than accept an agreement that posed even a remote threat of majority rule. Yet Wilson devoted much effort and time to this course – obsessed by the possibility of success and the impact this would have on his reputation. The *Tiger* talks demonstrated how far he would go in bending the Five Principles but even this was not enough for the Rhodesians. Wilson was only saved from a major row over *Tiger* because of Rhodesian intransigence and rejection of the terms. What he hoped to gain, after this lesson, by tearing up the NIBMAR pledge for the sake of another hopeless session with Smith it is difficult to imagine. The only alternative to negotiation was sanctions and of these the crucial one was oil, without which the Rhodesian economy would rapidly collapse. When sanctions were imposed at the end of 1965, and after the closure of the pipeline to Rhodesia and the blockade of supplies at Beira, only Wilson was optimistic that the end would not be long postponed.

Rhodesia survived because of the help of friendly countries – South Africa and Portugal through the colony of Mozambique. The British government never contemplated taking any measures that would involve pressure on South Africa. Indeed one of their greatest fears was that they might have to impose sanctions against that country. Their stance on sanctions against Rhodesia was ambivalent: on the one hand, an expensive naval blockade off Beira, and on the other, no tough measures to restrict supplies through Lourenço Marques. Early on ministers decided that there was little they could do to make sanctions fully effective, given the scope for easy supply and the willingness of many countries, and their oil companies, to secure a place in the Rhodesian market, regardless of UN sanctions. And some parts of the British government sympathised with the desire of Shell and BP to retain their market shares in Rhodesia.

When the government was told that UK firms were supplying Rhodesia these problems came to a head. They took the line that since sanctions weren't going to work, illegal activity by British companies didn't matter and that it was in the national interest to protect their commercial position by tacitly accepting the swap agreement. It is not unusual for a government to have to strike a balance between moral and economic pressures. In this case the Labour government chose to adopt the morality of the oil companies. It now became an utterly cynical exercise in realpolitik. Britain's responsibility for all the people of Rhodesia took second place to a policy of expediency, compounded by hypocrisy. Their response was to grasp at any straw that would stop the true facts becoming public and enable them to maintain their public position that British firms were not engaged in the supply. It was also a short-sighted policy on purely practical grounds. Having allowed the 'swap' with Total to go ahead, a fact that was well known to the French government, they were in an impossible position to complain about other countries that continued to flout sanctions. Seen from the inside, the story of Rhodesian sanctions is one of the shabbiest episodes in the life of the Labour government.

15

A Modern and Civilised Society

Labour came into power stressing the need to modernise Britain's institutions. After thirteen years of Conservative rule it presented itself as the party of long overdue social change and reform. Its aims were grandiose. As the 1964 manifesto put it, 'Labour has resolved to humanise the whole administration of the state.' Its methods were left unspecified. Only in three areas did it signal firm intentions: introduction of an Ombudsman, a programme of law reform and the giving of parliamentary time for a bill to abolish capital punishment.

The time was ripe for change. Labour's attitude reflected a growing mood in the country that had been evident from the start of the decade. British customs, institutions and methods of government were increasingly seen as out of date and irrelevant to the needs of a modern, industrialised nation. Indeed if Britain was to make the sort of economic and technological progress that was thought necessary, then modernisation of whole areas of government would be a prerequisite. In the early sixties political satire was popular and iconoclastic television programmes such as 'That Was The Week That Was' and magazines such as *Private Eye* were part of this new, critical, questioning approach.

The incoming government had first to decide what it wanted to do and then find ways of working with existing institutions whilst at the same time reforming them. Their efforts were largely concentrated on the Civil Service, the legal system and House of Lords (the latter is considered separately in Chapter 21). Their degree of commitment to social change in other areas was also tested by the need to respond to several private members' bills. At first there was little progress under Frank Soskice as Home Secretary and it was not until the arrival of Roy Jenkins at the Home Office that reform became a serious possibility, encouraged by the other great proponent of reform in the Cabinet, the Lord Chancellor, Lord Gardiner.

In 1964 Labour proposed to institute an Ombudsman who would, in the words of the manifesto, have 'the right and the duty

257

to investigate and expose any misuse of government power as it affects the citizen'. The Ombudsman idea was new only in Britain. Sweden, which had invented the concept, had had one for 150 years and other Scandinavian countries had followed suit early in the twentieth century. The idea was simple. The individual citizen had the right to ask the Ombudsman to act on his behalf and the Ombudsman had the power to investigate, report and demand remedies and even compensation when he judged that any organ of the state had acted improperly or oppressively. Work on the idea had started in Britain in 1961. A report by 'Justice' (part of the International Commission of Jurists), which had among its members future ministers in the Labour government such as Gerald Gardiner and Elwyn Jones, recommended the establishment of an Ombudsman. The Macmillan government rejected the concept but the Labour party was more sympathetic and in July 1964 Wilson promised that a Labour government would implement the idea.

Immediately after the October election work started in Whitehall. What emerged was a pale shadow of the Scandinavian model. In the first place even before the election the Labour party had agreed that the public would not have direct access to the Ombudsman: only an MP would be able to refer a case for investigation and whether or not to refer would be entirely at the MP's discretion. Then, instead of a wide-ranging power to investigate the activities of the state, the Ombudsman would only have the right to investigate 'maladministration'. This was a difficult concept that was carefully not defined, but ministers were clear that the purpose was to cut down the number of investigations. Indeed the chairman of the Cabinet Committee drafting the proposals, Douglas Houghton, an ex-Inland Revenue tax inspector, was so convinced of the perfection of the Civil Service that he did not think 'maladministration' could exist in the British system! A further limitation on the Ombudsman's powers compared with Scandinavia was in the areas he could investigate. Local Government and the National Health Service were excluded, as were all police activities, Civil Service personnel matters and the armed forces.

These proposals, eventually put before Parliament after the 1966 election, were a far cry from the bold declaration of intent in the 1964 manifesto. Yet even this tame version nearly proved too much for some of the would-be humanisers of the administrative system. After the bill had started on its passage through the Commons some ministers began to get cold feet about its implications now that they were ministers. At the Ministerial Committee in December 1966 there was a near revolt, led by Roy Jenkins, at the prospect that the Ombudsman should investigate 'their' ministries. One participant recalled that: 'As the discussion went on they began to wonder whether this Bill should be allowed to become law.'[1] But it was too late to draw back and the Ombudsman started work in April 1967. The Civil Service ensured that no radical was appointed to the post. The first incumbent was an ex-Permanent Secretary, Sir Edmund Compton, who was chosen because of the requirements of a complex series of moves at that level in Whitehall. Not until the next election neared did the government see the attractiveness of the Ombudsman again. In July 1969 the Cabinet agreed to extend his activities to local government. As one participant recorded:

He [Wilson] is now moving into the stage where he sees everything in terms of elections and popularization and he wanted to make a Statement saying we were going to extend the Ombudsman's jurisdiction.[2]

Introduction of the Ombudsman into the hermetic system of British government was at least a move in the right direction. He did have his successes: investigations did uncover instances of 'maladministration' in British government and he did obtain remedies in a number of cases. But it could not and did not 'humanise the whole administration of the state'.

In 1963 Lord Gardiner had published a pamphlet, 'Law Reform Now', which strongly appealed to Wilson. It set out a blueprint for the reform of English law under a law commission to be chaired by a minister. This would be the first coherent attempt to modernise and rationalise the archaic and obscure aspects of both criminal and civil law. In October 1964 Wilson appointed Eric Fletcher as Minister without Portfolio to look after the process in the Commons whilst Lord Gardiner, as Lord Chancellor, masterminded the reform programme. Almost immediately the idea ran into trouble. At the Cabinet Home Policy Committee on 13 November there was strong opposition to Gardiner's proposals led by the Home Office and Frank Soskice. They disliked any idea that the criminal law, a Home Office responsibility within

Whitehall, should be subject to the commission and other departments took the same possessive view of areas of law for which they took responsibility.

After a great deal more argument an emasculated law commission was set up in 1965. The chairman would no longer be a minister but a judge; the first was Sir Leslie Scarman. It was an advisory rather than an executive body, charged with reviewing the law, reducing the number of separate enactments, eliminating anomalies and repealing obsolete statutes. While this was a useful tidying-up exercise it hardly amounted to a fundamental reform of the law. Some good work was done – on divorce law reform and unfair conditions of contract – but because the reports were only advisory, final decisions were left to the usual Whitehall machinery and even when agreed there was often insufficient parliamentary time to pass legislation.

Some other useful reforms were passed on the joint initiative of Jenkins and Gardiner. In 1966 the system of appeal in criminal cases was drastically revised and the grounds on which an appeal could be made were extended. The 1967 Criminal Justice Act produced the usual balancing act of, on the one hand, giving the police greater powers and introducing majority jury verdicts in an attempt to obtain more convictions, whilst on the other abolishing corporal punishment in prisons and restricting the power of magistrates to refuse bail. Lord Beeching was also tasked to review the administration of justice, and recommended a radical restructuring of the court system with the abolition of the old assizes and the introduction of Crown Courts, which was implemented in the early 1970s. In 1966 Roy Jenkins for the first time allowed individuals the right to appeal to the European Court of Human Rights in Strasbourg. This little-noticed measure was to have a major long-term impact, bringing major changes in British law and practices in a number of areas from prisoners' rights to corporal punishment in schools. By the 1980s Britain had lost more cases at the Court than any other country.

Although the Labour party had not made any specific proposals for reform of the Civil Service in 1964, there was a strand in its thinking that was antagonistic to the upper echelons in Whitehall. For example, in a Fabian Society pamphlet, Tommy Balogh had attacked the 'dilettantes of the administrative class' with their 'jejeune amateurism'. Reform of Whitehall also fitted in well with

Labour's wish to be identified with the idea of 'modernisation'. It was in this mood that Wilson appointed an old crony from his days as a wartime civil servant – Lord Fulton – to head a committee of enquiry into the Civil Service.

The work of the committee was hamstrung from the start by its restricted terms of reference (drafted by the Civil Service). As Wilson made clear when he announced the enquiry:

> The Government's willingness to consider changes in the Civil Service does not imply any intention on its part to alter the basic relationship between Ministers and Civil Servants.

The report when published in 1968 was paradoxical. Its first chapter was a major attack on the state of the Civil Service which, according to Fulton, required 'fundamental change' because 'the Service is still essentially based on the philosophy of the amateur' and 'the present system of classes in the Service seriously impedes its work'. The rest of the report was much more conservative and the actual recommendations were strictly limited. Wilson saw Fulton before the Cabinet discussed the report and accepted the idea of setting up a Civil Service College, something Whitehall favoured anyway, and a new Civil Service Department. But Roy Jenkins, as Chancellor of the Exchequer, responsible for the Civil Service, was not consulted and at the Cabinet meeting on 20 June 1968 there was strong opposition to the report from him, Healey, Stewart and Crossman. As Crossman recorded:

> All the support Harold got was from Wedgy Benn and Peter Shore, his two hirelings. He was so upset that at this point he stopped the meeting.[3]

Five days later the Cabinet resumed discussion. This time there was little interest in the report and no opposition. The case for a presentational success to boost the 'modernising' image was generally accepted as Crossman again noted:

> Harold started on the Fulton report, where we gave him a very easy time. It's a second-rate report written in a very poor style . . . However, it's been a success with the press and the public. Harold needed a success for himself and Cabinet consented to his getting it with a Statement tomorrow.[4]

Accepting the report was very different from implementing it. In practice only those bits of the Fulton report that the administrative elite in Whitehall liked were ever implemented. The crucial recommendation was the abolition of classes within the Civil Service. If this had been implemented then the generalist administrators (the public school-Oxbridge-educated arts graduates) would lose their key role as amateur advisers to ministers to professionally qualified accountants, economists and statisticians. The reason that recommendation was not implemented was that much of the process, and all the key work, was left in the hands of the administrators and they were not prepared to commit suicide. Cosmetic changes were introduced but the underlying structure remained and the amateur administrative elite was left in control. For example, Fulton recommended the abolition of all classes within the Civil Service: when he reported there were forty-seven service-wide classes and 1400 just in single departments. Ten years later the figure was still thirty-eight and 500 respectively. In every area the picture was the same. A small amount of progress whilst the issue was at the top of the agenda was followed by inaction and, after an interval, reversal of the changes that had been introduced.

The government did nothing to implement the Fulton report's recommendation for greater openness in the way Whitehall operated. But it did take one small step by opening government records to the public after thirty years instead of fifty. The Cabinet discussed the idea in August 1965 and although both Michael Stewart and Jim Callaghan were opposed on the grounds that the reputation of civil servants might be damaged whilst they were still alive, Wilson forced it through on the basis that it would be good for the government's 'liberal image'. Even so, when the bill came up for approval in April 1967, the Foreign Office had tried to put so many restrictions on what could be released at the thirty-year point that the whole exercise would have been rendered nugatory. It took an intervention from Wilson to stop this sabotage effort.

The control of honours is very largely in the hands of the Prime Minister and Wilson had the opportunity to make changes. On the surface he took this opportunity. In 1964 he announced that there would be no more hereditary titles (a policy that lasted until the second Thatcher government); in 1967 the automatic honours for the Civil Service were reduced by half compared with the level a decade before and there was also a drastic reduction in the number of political knighthoods for backbench MPs. In addition, after a considerable battle within Whitehall, a new, more populist element in the award of honours was introduced. In the New Year's Honours in 1965 Stanley Matthews was given a knighthood and later there were awards for other sportsmen such as Alf Ramsey, Bobby Moore, Tony Jacklin and Don Revie. There was also a greater emphasis on popular entertainment, from MBEs for the Beatles to OBEs for David Frost and Violet Carson (Ena Sharples of 'Coronation Street').

But underneath not much had changed, and Wilson continued to use the system to reward friends and those with influence. Fleet Street did well under Wilson (twice as many peerages as under any other modern Prime Minister) and so did many people associated with him in various ways. In 1969 there was a CBE for John Meyer, the main director of Montagu Meyer, a firm of timber merchants which had employed Wilson as a consultant for eight years in the 1950s. In 1966 there was a knighthood for Frank Schon, another old friend who had employed Wilson as a consultant in the 1950s. In 1965 he gave a knighthood to George Eadie, the secretary and agent of the Blackburn Labour party and leader of the Labour group on the Council, even though the Civil Service advice was that Blackburn was not big enough to justify such an award on the accepted establishment scale. As Barbara Castle (MP for Blackburn) loyally commented when Wilson discussed it with her:

> He was prepared to sweep aside nonsense like that to help his friends. His reformism consists not of altering the conventions like Honours, but in using them in unorthodox ways.[5]

The 1970 resignation honours contained many of the same names that were to cause so much controversy in Wilson's 1976 resignation honours. George Weidenfeld, the publisher of Wilson's books, received a knighthood, as did Joseph Kagan, whose Gannex raincoats Wilson often wore, Joseph Stone, his doctor, and Rudy Sternberg, who was later to help finance Wilson's private office in opposition. (All four received peerages in 1976.) John Brayley, the owner of the Canning Town Glass Works, who donated a large part of the shares in the company to the Labour party, received a knighthood. He became a minister in the 1974 government but resigned when the Fraud Squad started investigating the company.

In October 1966 Wilson announced that there were to be no more political honours. The reality was very different at a meeting at No 10 late in September when Wilson and a few close advisers discussed the idea. Here too his 'reformism' turned out to be of a dubious kind. As Crossman recorded:

I realised that excluding political honours really meant excluding Party agents and regional organisers and virtually no one else. When Harold heard this he replied, 'We'll include them all under public honours.' But of course once you do this your announcement is merely a gimmick.[6]

When it came into office the Labour government had no plans to transform the law in the moral and personal sphere but it did help pass backbench legislation which did so. This was due less to the moral climate in the Cabinet – the attitude of the government to these measures was often ambiguous – than to the political and social climate in Parliament and the country. There was strong Parliamentary support for these reforms for a number of reasons. First many of the new Labour MPs elected in 1966 felt that this was the one area where they could make a real contribution to radical change. Parliament was also reflecting the results of often long, drawn-out campaigns from pressure groups advocating particular reforms. And public opinion was also going through one of its rare phases of support for reform as part of the creation of a more modern and humane society.

The one area where Labour had already promised support in 1964 was in providing government time to pass a bill abolishing capital punishment. The Commons first voted in favour of abolition in 1948 when it was rejected by the Lords and the same sequence occurred in 1956. On both occasions the government had been opposed to abolition but in 1957 as a response to the 1956 vote it passed the Homicide Act which attempted to classify murder into categories, only some of which carried the death penalty. Not surprisingly this produced anomalies which only strengthened the argument for total abolition. Although only 23% of the public supported abolition, the vote in the Commons in December 1964 was 355–170 in favour. When the Conservatives tried to block progress by voting to take all stages on the floor of the Commons and not in Committee, the government managed to defeat the motion by eight votes. The bill was only approved by the Lords with an amendment restricting its operation to five years. In December 1969 the Cabinet decided to go for total abolition as soon as practicable and before the general election. The Conservatives fought hard to put off a decision until 1973 but the bill was passed by 336–185 in the Commons and 220–174 in the Lords.

This pattern of tacit government support for backbench legislation, largely through the provision of time in the Commons, was to be repeated in a number of other areas. The first was a measure to legalise homosexual acts between consenting adults in private. This had been recommended by the official report of the Wolfenden Committee in 1957. The first motion for reform was defeated in the Commons in 1960 but was supported by many who were later to be members of the Labour government, in particular Roy Jenkins, Douglas Jay, Tony Greenwood, Eirene White and Kenneth Robinson. In October 1965 a reform bill had been approved by the Lords and a similar measure, sponsored by the Conservative member Humphrey Berkeley, was given a second reading in the Commons but did not make any further progress because of the election. In June 1966 the bill again passed the Lords and the backbench Labour MP, Leo Abse, introduced a similar ten-minute rule bill in the Commons which was approved by 244 votes to 100. The ballot for private members' bills had already taken place and without a place here Abse's bill was bound not to make any further progress despite the large amount of support for it.

At the end of October Jenkins, as Home Secretary, asked the Cabinet to provide government time to pass the Bill. George Brown was very strongly opposed to reform, let alone providing government time, and both Callaghan and Wilson thought the government should remain neutral. Crossman, as Leader of the Commons, pointed out that it would be very difficult for the government to stay neutral because of the amount of support in both Houses for the bill. He continued, as he describes in his diary:

> In that case it was clearly better to let the House of Commons debate the matter freely now and to provide time for this rather than let the subject drag on until nearer the election. With this highly tactical argument we persuaded the PM to drag the rest of his colleagues with him.[7]

The second reading of the bill was agreed in December without a vote, mainly because the main opponent was too drunk to stand up and object at the right moment. The government then ensured passage of the legislation by arranging for the bill to be considered by a new standing committee to avoid any hold-up and also provided time for the report stage and an all-night sitting in July 1967. The bill finally passed both Houses later that month.

Similar assistance was given to the bill to liberalise the law on abortion. When the Liberal MP David Steel won third place in the private members' ballot in 1966, he consulted Jenkins about what bill to introduce. Jenkins suggested a measure on homosexual law reform but Steel thought this would be too controversial with his constituents and decided on abortion law reform instead. Since 1953 there had been six unsuccessful attempts to change the law but there was a strong pressure group backing reform and in 1965 the Lords had passed a reform bill by a large majority. Public opinion was also behind the measure – an opinion poll in 1965 showed that 72% favoured reform. Steel also had the advantage of a long session in which to get the bill through. The second reading was passed with a majority of almost 200 in July 1966 but almost a year later the bill was still stuck in the committee stage. The government now had to decide what their attitude would be.

Wilson and Brown originally wanted to leave the bill uncompleted and recess Parliament as planned at the end of July 1967. (Wilson was worried by the number of Catholics in his constituency of Huyton.) Crossman and the Chief Whip, John Silkin, however, were making fairly public contingency plans to extend the session by a week, which they knew was a good threat to hold over the Conservative members who wanted to go on holiday. The Cabinet met on 6 July to decide tactics. The bill was strongly supported by Jenkins, Crosland, Castle, Benn and Gardiner, and only opposed by Willie Ross and Lord Longford. Wilson remained dubious but the clinching argument was that the back-benchers wanted the bill. On this basis it was agreed to provide whatever time was necessary. Once it was clear that the government would ensure the bill was passed the opposition in the Commons quickly collapsed. After some opposition in the Lords it became law in October.

Divorce law reform was to prove to be a more complicated process. In January 1964, after consultations with the Conservative government, the Archbishop of Canterbury had set up a study group which reported in July 1966. The group recommended that the concept of the 'breakdown of marriage' should replace the existing idea of a 'matrimonial offence' and that any court proceedings should be in the nature of an inquest to ensure that the marriage had broken down rather than the naming of a 'guilty party'. Lord Gardiner referred the report to the Law Commission for advice and they quickly drew up a practical scheme based on the report. On 12 October the Cabinet approved a bill drafted by Lord Gardiner, with only Lord Longford and Ray Gunter dissenting, and agreed that it should be given to a backbencher and that government time would be provided to ensure its passage if necessary. The first attempt to pass the bill in the 1967 session failed through lack of time. The reason the government did not provide extra time was because it had already refused to do so for the much more controversial law to amend Sunday trading (which failed to pass the Commons in both 1967 and 1969). The Divorce Law Reform Bill was reintroduced in the autumn of 1968 but not completed until June 1969 after the government had provided time both for the second reading and at the report stage.

The issue that caused the greatest controversy within the government was the future of theatre censorship. Censorship by the Lord Chamberlain in the Royal Household dated back to 1737 – one of the more obvious candidates for modernisation. Increasingly in the twentieth century he created storms of controversy by banning plays such as Wilde's *Salome* and Shaw's *Mrs Warren's Profession* or even Gilbert and Sullivan's *Mikado* during a visit by the Japanese Crown Prince. In 1957 Beckett's *Endgame* was accepted in French but banned in English and the play *US* by the Royal Shakespeare Company under Peter Brook banned because of its anti-American sentiments. A Theatre Censorship Reform Committee set up in 1958 had Roy Jenkins as a member and when he became Home Secretary he suggested to another member, Lord Annan, that he should call for a joint committee of both Houses of Parliament to investigate. This move was accepted without any dissent after the 1966 election. The report from the committee, which included the current Lord Chamberlain, unanimously recommended reform.

In July 1967 the government considered how to respond. At the Home Policy Committee Jenkins asked for approval to bring in an immediate bill. The committee accepted the aim of the bill, but argued there was no space in the programme of legislation. Wilson then intervened to ensure that the issue went to the Cabinet on 27 July. His concern was not that the abolition of censorship might lead to nudity on stage but that it might allow 'character assassination' of prominent figures (no doubt prompted by the forthcoming play, *Mrs Wilson's Diary*, based on the successful *Private Eye* column). When Jenkins argued that it was difficult to ban satire on the stage when it was possible on TV, Wilson revealed that Lord Hill, Chairman of the BBC Governors, had reassured him that he would take steps to stop it on the BBC too. Wilson saw the bill as 'a terrible mistake' and went on to disclose that the Palace had made representations to him to try and stop the bill. Jenkins was instructed to go away and find a method of protecting members of the establishment from such attacks. As the official Cabinet minutes record, in a tone of Civil Service moderation disguising illiberal attitudes:

> In neither medium would ordinary political satire be forbidden but there should be safeguards against the theatre being used deliberately to discredit or create political hostility towards public political figures.

After the parliamentary recess Jenkins decided to stand firm against the pressure he was under. As he told Dick Crossman on 7 September:

> I'm not prepared as a radical and liberal Home Secretary to have my image ruined by being ordered to impose worse conditions on the live theatre than they are getting now under the Lord Chamberlain.[8]

Jenkins made it clear to Wilson that he was prepared to resign on the issue. At the end of November at the Home Policy Committee he simply reported that there was no way to meet the objections of the Palace. The Cabinet accepted this view just before Christmas with Wilson absent on an overseas visit. Crossman made one last effort to stop reform in February 1968 but to no avail. The Home Office drafted the bill and George Strauss, who had chaired the joint committee, was able to steer it through, even though he only had tenth place in the private members' ballot. Indeed the issue was so uncontroversial in the Commons, as opposed to the Cabinet, that there was not even a division on the second reading.

The Labour government came into office with vague and ill-defined notions about reforming Britain's institutions. Its one specific proposal, albeit diluted – the Ombudsman – was implemented. Its scope was narrow but within its limitations it did establish the principle that the citizen needed to be protected from abuses of power by those in authority. Apart from some adjustments to the legal system, it achieved little else of significance. The government's main contribution was an indirect one: it assisted the passage of private members' bills on a range of issues that were to transform large areas of social behaviour. The government's motives, as they emerged in the privacy of the Cabinet Room, were not always those of zealous radicals, despite the liberal image they clearly enjoyed presenting to the country. They mainly wanted to remove contentious items from the political agenda before the next election. The greatest impetus to genuine reform came from Roy Jenkins as Home Secretary; without his help and advocacy the bills would have foundered amidst the doubts of his colleagues and in the morass of Parliamentary procedure. Just how limited the government's commitment to modernisation could be was demonstrated in the case of theatre censorship. Virtually nobody could be found to defend the archaic and inconsistent censorship exercised by the Lord Chamberlain, but the Palace, Wilson and other members of the Cabinet felt personally threatened by its removal, and so made a major effort to replace it by another form of censorship to protect their own position and that of other members of the establishment. Nevertheless a wide-ranging reform programme from abolition of capital punishment to divorce law reform, easier abortion, legalisation of adult male homosexuality and abolition of theatre censorship was enacted. This legacy has proved to be one of the lasting monuments, if not to the work of the government, at least to its period in office.

16

The 'White Heat' of Revolution

One of the major themes of Harold Wilson's first year as Labour leader had been the emphasis placed on the modernisation of Britain, and Labour's willingness to harness technology and the ideas of scientists excluded by the old-fashioned values of the Conservative government. Wilson called for a major effort to make use of British inventiveness and adaptation to what he called the 'white heat' of the 'technological revolution', together with a policy of direct government intervention and support for industry. Only in this way, he argued, could Britain successfully compete with its rivals, and attain greater prosperity and growth. Weaving these various threads together into a coherent policy that could be implemented once in power was a difficult task and not one the Labour party had attempted before October 1964.

The one specific proposal in the 1964 manifesto was the establishment of a Ministry of Technology (Mintech) which would 'guide and stimulate a major national effort' to bring modern technology into industry. If the creation of the Department of Economic Affairs had not been thought out and its exact powers never defined, compared with the creation of Mintech it was a model of clear-sighted planning. There was no consultation with the Civil Service before the election on how to establish the new ministry and no idea of what its powers were to be. Wilson then compounded these difficulties by an extraordinary series of decisions in the early days of the new administration. First, he chose the completely inexperienced Frank Cousins to head the new organisation. The problem was that he did not have a seat in the Commons until the Nuneaton by-election in January 1965 and therefore could not speak in the House. Even then he never adapted to the peculiar rituals of the Commons and remained ineffective in that forum. Then Wilson chose C. P. Snow as the junior minister. This he saw as a bold and imaginative appointment of the man who had originated the idea of the 'Two Cultures'. In practice Snow was to be even more of a disappointment than Cousins and after an unhappy year he left the government. It was not until the summer of 1966 and the appointment of Tony Benn as Minister that the new department really took off. The ministry itself started in one room in Whitehall, and recruitment of staff was slow and not always suitable for what was supposed to be a dynamic new ministry. As so often, civil servants transferred to the new organisation tended to be those their old departments had been wanting to get rid of for years.

The most significant weakness was that Mintech's role and powers were never clearly defined. It started by being made 'responsible' for the computer industry, machine tools, telecommunications, the National Research and Development Corporation (NRDC) and the Atomic Energy Authority, and other parts of the government's Research and Development effort. Over the next five years it grew into one of the largest ministries in Whitehall but only by taking over existing bits of Whitehall activity mostly to do with industry rather than with technology as such. Much activity by officials amounted to little more than vague 'oversight' – monitoring of statistics, liaising with employers and trade unions, and arranging ministerial visits. In June 1966 it took over 'responsibility' for weights and measures, engineering standards and 'sponsorship' of the electrical and mechanical engineering sectors. In February 1967 it added the aviation and shipbuilding industries, and in October 1969 it took over the old Ministry of Power, the Board of Trade's responsibilities for the chemical and textile industries, and the remaining functions of the DEA on the distribution of industry and industrial planning. But simply amalgamating existing areas of activity did not in itself produce a coherent new policy. Mintech remained an odd collection of various Whitehall activities operating within the existing bureaucratic framework. There was never any attempt to forge a new relationship between Whitehall and industrial and technological development, nor even to work out in detail what responsibility for and sponsorship of an industry actually meant in practice. And the powers available to revolutionise British industry remained an odd mixture of limited and often parochial measures.

Throughout its life the Labour government's industrial policies had two inconsistent aims – an attack on monopolies and encouragement of mergers. The attack on monopolies and unfair prices formed part of the 1964 manifesto. This commitment was theoretically met by passing the Monopolies and Mergers Act of 1965. Closer inspection would have revealed, however, that the act bore a very strong resemblance to proposals outlined in a White Paper issued by the Conservative government in 1964. The act

271

gave the Monopolies and Mergers Commission a new remit to investigate services as well as manufacturing industry but the Commission had few powers of its own. The greatest increase in power was given to Whitehall and the Board of Trade to refer mergers to the Commission, delay mergers and even dissolve them if necessary. In practice the work of the Board of Trade was perfunctory, reflecting Whitehall's traditional blend of amateurism and caution. Each merger was considered for no more than two or three weeks and of the 350 mergers that fell within the scope of the act between 1965 and 1969, only ten were referred to the Commission (and two of these concerned newspapers, an obsession of Wilson's). Of these referrals four were found to be against the public interest. In the same period there were another seventeen references involving existing monopolies and half of these were found to have some aspects that operated against the public interest. But the Board of Trade usually implemented only parts, often very small parts, of these reports by the Commission.

The received economic wisdom in the 1960s was 'large is beautiful' – only by amalgamating into massive units could British industry benefit from the economies of large-scale operation and compete effectively in world markets with the giant industrial corporations of countries such as the United States. Mergers were therefore to be encouraged and the government's contribution was the Industrial Reorganisation Corporation (IRC) set up in January 1966. It had the grandiose aim of 'promoting industrial efficiency and profitability and assisting the economy of the United Kingdom'. All of this was to be done on a total budget of £150 million. In practice the IRC was able to use some of its money to encourage several mergers. In particular it backed the creation of the GEC empire, first through the takeover of Associated Electrical Industries by GEC, and then the subsequent merger of GEC and English Electric. The IRC also put up a loan of £25 million to encourage the merger of Leyland and the British Motor Corporation (BMC), and in May 1969 achieved the merger of the three existing British firms in the ball-bearing industry to try and meet competition from the Swedish firm, SKF.

The effect of this policy was, not surprisingly, to help increase the percentage of manufacturing output from the country's 100 largest manufacturers from 37% of the total in 1965 to 45% in 1970. But there is no evidence to suggest that these mergers did anything to increase the competitiveness of British industry or cure other underlying problems. All the policy did was to encourage firms to grow by acquisition rather than by investing in modern plant and finding new markets. Since it increased their monopolistic power and their ability to lobby governments it was the opposite of an attack on monopoly powers. The one area where merger was clearly successful in protecting British industry was computers. The first task given to Frank Cousins by Wilson was to save the British computer industry, which was suffering badly from American competition and lack of government support. The rescue job was not completed until 1968 when the three British computer companies were merged to form ICL. The government provided loans and capital investment, but their attempt to make Whitehall departments buy British computers was only partially successful. Nevertheless the share of the UK market held by British companies did rise from 25% to 40% over the lifetime of the government.

Despite its traditional importance in Labour circles, nationalisation played only a very small part in the government's industrial policy. Steel was finally nationalised in 1967 but the minister in charge, Dick Marsh, saw it as an essentially pragmatic move. It was a way of rationalising a fragmented, out-of-date industry under threat from more efficient foreign producers. In practice much of the reorganisation was designed to stop any subsequent denationalisation. The problem was that the people put in charge of the new industry were the usual collection of the 'Great and the Good', plus some necessary political appointments. After a long search Marsh could only find Lord Melchett, a conservative Old Etonian who had never worked in industry before, to be the new chairman. Others on the board lacked qualifications and included a working trade unionist, described by Marsh as 'quite frankly a political gesture'.[1]

Ministers showed little enthusiasm for extending nationalisation. In the car industry, Rootes, which was 49% owned by the American firm Chrysler (a move Labour in opposition had bitterly opposed), remained in serious financial trouble. In 1966 Tony Benn tried to persuade Leyland and BMC to take it over but despite a government offer to pay 90% of the cost the British companies refused. The Cabinet rejected nationalisation and Benn was left to put up IRC money to allow Chrysler to take over complete control. In the aircraft industry Benn was trying to implement the policy, started by the Conservative government in the early 1960s, of producing a single company by getting BAC and Hawker Siddeley to merge. When negotiations broke down ministers again rejected nationalisation as an alternative. Only in the docks, which were suffering from substantial decline and persistent labour problems, was there a move towards nationalisation. After a report by Lord Devlin on 'decasualising' the workforce, Barbara Castle as Minister of Transport proposed to nationalise all docks. But her successor Dick Marsh ripped up her scheme and took so long to devise an alternative that the bill implementing the scheme had not been passed before the 1970 election. In an uncontroversial move the Post Office was converted from a Whitehall department into a nationalised industry.

Policy towards existing nationalised industries showed little departure from traditional Whitehall practice, apart from some small moves to allow them to expand their activities into new fields. The Labour government inherited a system for controlling the nationalised industries based on the conflicting notions that they should set prices equal to their long-run marginal costs (though these were often impossible to identify), that their investment should be judged against a test rate of return and that they should be set a financial target (although this was often incompatible with the first two requirements). This system remained unchanged and so did the practice of using the prices of nationalised industries as hidden taxation. In the ten years from 1959 to 1969 their gross trading surplus as a percentage of sales revenue rose from 12½% to 20% (way above that for the private sector). Between 1965 and 1969 this surplus amounted to about £400 million or the equivalent of the tax increases in the highly deflationary 1968 Budget.

On transport policy it was equally difficult to see how the government's approach was in any sense 'socialist'. In theory the government was committed to that chimera – 'an integrated transport policy'. But this was impossible to define, let alone create, and in practice it amounted to little more than a vague hope that some freight traffic could be transferred from road to rail. In fact the share of both freight and passenger traffic carried by rail continued to fall throughout the 1960s. In addition the highly controversial cuts in the rail network accepted by the Conservative government after the Beeching report were largely carried through, although subsidies were introduced for a few lines where opposition to closure was particularly vocal or where a number of marginal seats were at stake.

Their general laissez-faire attitude to the nationalised industries and the inability of Whitehall to plan a coherent policy was captured by Dick Crossman at a meeting of SEP on 18 October 1967 which had just taken a total of twenty minutes to agree the White Paper on future policy:

As I got up from the table I said to Callaghan, 'This is a very poor paper.' 'What does it matter?' he said. 'It's only read by a few dons and experts . . . personally as Chancellor I couldn't care less. I take no responsibility and I took no part in composing it.'[2]

The difficulties involved in grappling with the problems of British industry are well illustrated by the cases of the automobile and shipbuilding industries. In the mid-1960s the car industry was a superficially successful operation. It controlled over 90% of the British market and the output of cars was still rising. Yet underneath the problems that were to be so devastating by the mid-1970s were already becoming apparent. The output of commercial and agricultural vehicles started to fall after 1966, and the car sector was badly hit by the endless changes in purchase tax and hire purchase terms every government introduced as part of the stop-go cycle. Output of vehicles per employee started to go down after 1965, even though it was only half that of the US industry and below that of France, West Germany and Italy. Japan came from a rate below Britain in 1965 to an output double the British level by 1970. The first signs of severe erosion in the British market were also apparent as import penetration rose from 5% in 1965 to 14% in 1970. (It was to reach nearly 60% by 1980.) Despite these ominous signs the government developed no policies to deal with the basic problems. Its one initiative was, as we have seen, to merge Leyland and BMC but this produced no rationalisation in plant and facilities, and the old problem of inadequate investment remained. There was no sign of the government having any idea of how to bring modern technology into the industry.

Shipbuilding, on the other hand, was an industry well into terminal decline by the 1960s. Its share of world output had fallen from almost 40% in 1950 to under 10% and it was bedevilled by appalling labour relations, inadequate management and chronically low investment. Indeed investment in the mid-1950s had been only £4 million a year when the replacement cost of existing equipment alone was put at £6 million a year. The government appointed the Geddes Committee to examine the industry in 1965 and accepted its report that the industry should be reorganised by merging yards. In 1967 the Shipbuilding Industry Board was set up to supervise the reorganisation but it was questionable whether the top management had the right experience – the chairman came from the motor industry and his deputy from women's fashions. They soon found that merging already declining yards was not a solution to the industry's problems. They also found it difficult to change inherited practices and the rivalries between existing yards. The long-standing problem of lack of investment was not tackled and only a third of the money from the Board went into capital investment. The first crisis came at Upper Clyde Shipbuilders (UCS) in 1969. A crash programme of 3500 redundancies, new management and nearly £10 million of public money did not remove the threat of imminent bankruptcy. By the end of the year the Board was convinced that UCS was not viable but with an election coming up the government was not prepared to let the yards close and a further loan of £7 million was made, which staved off the collapse until 1971. The government had staggered on from one expedient to another but with no long-term solution. These two studies illustrate the difficulties in identifying and dealing with either the problems facing a superficially prosperous industry about to go into decline or reversing the decline of a battered industry. In this failure the Labour government was no different from either its predecessors or its successors.

All governments seem to be irresistibly attracted to the glamour of high-risk, high-cost, high-technology projects. The Labour government, with its commitment to the 'technological revolution', was more vulnerable than most but it was to find that these projects were not an easy solution to national and industrial problems, and they often brought immense problems of their own. They inherited the most difficult of all – Concorde – and started their own – the Advanced Gas Cooled Reactor.

Concorde had begun in the early 1960s based on highly optimistic assessments of both costs and sales. Distrust of French intentions had led the Conservative government to insist on a binding international treaty to stop their partners from quitting the project. Although in public the Labour government remained attached to this symbol of British technology, in private its views were different. In the middle of November 1964 the Economic Development Committee (EDC) considered a paper by Roy Jenkins, Minister of Aviation, on the future of Concorde. He suggested five possible options, varying from cancellation to trying to establish a tripartite project with the Americans. Both Brown and Callaghan were strongly for cancellation, and were joined, perhaps surprisingly, by Frank Cousins, who argued that the plane took up too much scarce technological and scientific effort. Opposition to cancellation came from the Foreign Secretary, Patrick Gordon-Walker, and the Attorney-General. It was the latter who raised the legal argument that was to dominate discussions for the next six years. As costs rose steadily, sales forecasts fell but the French consistently refused to consider ending the project. Each time the government was desperate enough to consider unilateral withdrawal the legal advice was that the cancellation charges the French could insist on under the terms of the treaty would be greater than any savings. The compromise agreed in 1964 was that Jenkins was to go to Paris and try and negotiate a way out of the project. He found the French did not even want to discuss the future, let alone negotiate, and the whole attempt collapsed ignominiously.

Eighteen months later, with costs rising rapidly, another attempt was made to get out of the project. Wilson raised the possibility of cancellation with Pompidou during his visit to Britain in July 1966 but got no response. A year later, when the British contribution to the project had tripled since the last attempt to cancel, the Cabinet Committee on Science and Technology reviewed the situation. This time the Attorney-General thought that it might be possible to get out because the costs had escalated so much, and it was agreed to try and put the onus on the French for cancellation. This ploy also failed, as did two attempts early in 1968 to cancel as part of the post-devaluation cuts. In August 1968 the Cabinet finally decided that enough was enough. It agreed a set of criteria on costs, specification and likely sales that would have to be met for the project to continue. They also decided that if the French did not accept these criteria then Britain would cancel. At the end of October Tony Benn reported that the French would not agree to the British criteria and would not cancel the project whilst there was any chance of orders being placed. Despite its earlier firmness the Cabinet now backed down in the face of French intransigence and let Concorde continue. Late in 1969 once again ministers almost steeled themselves to do something when their private estimates of the scale of the economic disaster reached crisis proportions. Now, though, there was an election looming, as Barbara Castle explained:

Most of us agreed that it was politically not on to cancel before the election, though the aim should be to cancel immediately after.[3]

All the government could do was to pass the problem on to its successor, and try and claim what credit it could. The state-owned airlines – British Airways and Air France – had their arms twisted to fly the aircraft, though they had to be heavily subsidised both to buy it and to operate it. No other airline bought any and only sixteen were ever produced. In retrospect it would have saved money not to have produced the aircraft after having developed it and never to have flown it even after producing it, and unilateral cancellation would have been cheaper than continuation at any stage. The Labour government had inherited a difficult situation but this was one area where it did not want to blame its predecessor, and it remained attracted to the glamour of high technology and the effect this might have on its image. As Barbara Castle noted in 1969:

> Harold has refused to do what I suggested a long time ago and tell the House plainly that we had been landed in a mess by the Tories' appallingly mismanaged treaty. His reason: Concorde might be a success and then we would want to claim the credit.[4]

Other projects on the frontiers of technology were to prove equally enticing but just as risky, as Rolls-Royce was to find out. In April 1968 the company signed a fixed-price contract with Lockheed to develop the RB-211 engine for the Tri-Star aircraft. On the basis of some flimsy information from Rolls-Royce, Tony Benn provided £47 million from the government as aid for the project. Within three years the escalating cost of the project was to bankrupt Rolls-Royce and force the Conservative government to nationalise it.

Ever since the mid-1950s the government had been committed to a large-scale programme of nuclear power station construction, despite the evidence that such stations produced more expensive electricity than conventional ones. The Labour government was to adopt an equally pro-high-technology line in its fuel policy. In 1964 the Conservative government had postponed until after the election a choice between the British-designed Advanced Gas Cooled Reactor (AGR) and the American Pressurised Water Reactor (favoured by the Central Electricity Generating Board). It was not surprising that the new government, given its public commitment to British high technology, chose the AGR in 1965. When he announced the decision, Fred Lee, the Minister of Power, was euphoric about the prospects for Britain's technological future and for cheap energy. He described the AGR as 'the greatest breakthrough of all time' and also increased the ordering programme for nuclear power stations by 60%. Ironically he was to bequeath a disaster worse than Concorde to future governments. The first AGR at Dungeness took twenty years before it generated any power for the national grid and cost twice the original estimate. The oft-repeated promise of cheap electricity remained unfulfilled.

The AGR itself turned out to be a technological dead end when the Conservative government in the 1980s chose the PWR for the next generation of nuclear stations.

The 1967 White Paper on fuel policy was still strongly committed to a nuclear stance, promising that by 1980 nuclear power would be the principal fuel for new generating capacity. This policy meant that the already declining coal industry was to be the main victim, despite Labour assurances before 1964 that the industry would be maintained. The number of mines and employment in the industry had fallen by half since 1951, and even before 1967 the Ministry of Power had been keen to cut back the industry still further. In June 1965 Fred Lee suggested ending all subsidies to pits in both Scotland and South Wales, with consequent large-scale closures, only to be overruled by the Cabinet for political reasons. But the 1967 White Paper policy was to have much the same effect. Employment in the coal industry was to fall from 419,000 in 1967 to 65,000 by 1980 and output was to drop by 31%. The most symbolic decision was that taken in 1968 to build an AGR at Seaton Carew right by the Durham coalfield. (That too turned out to be a disaster and did not produce electricity before 1985.) The planned massive contraction in the coal industry had to be put rapidly into reverse after the quintupling of the oil price by OPEC in 1973.

One of the reasons for Britain's poor economic performance was low investment. The government did take some measures to try and remedy this state of affairs. Its approach to the problem had two prongs. The first was Corporation Tax, introduced in the 1965 Budget, which radically changed the basis of company taxation. Its effect was to encourage the retention of profits rather than their distribution as dividends and thus it was hoped, as a secondary effect, to increase investment. Overseas investment was also discouraged by removing its existing exemption from profits tax. The second prong was the replacement of investment allowances by investment grants which, it was hoped, would have a greater take-up. This change had been strongly opposed by Callaghan and the Treasury in 1965 on the grounds that it would cost over £200 million a year more. Overall this policy did have some effect, since capital investment in Britain reached its highest ever level in 1970, even though it was still below European levels and only half that of Japan.

279

Another aspect of the problem of inadequate or misdirected investment was the high proportion of Research and Development devoted to military projects. The government was responsible for spending nearly 60% of all of Britain's expenditure, and nearly two-thirds of this went on military projects. Labour had the opportunity to alter this situation but little effort was devoted to the problem. Lord Zuckerman, the government's Chief Scientific Adviser, did produce a report on how to divert some of the military effort into the civil field in 1969. Its fate could stand as a memorial to the faded hopes of the technological revolution. In May 1969 Wilson threw the report out of the window, telling colleagues:

I am afraid there is no political capital in this because nothing we decide will have any effect until years after the next Parliament gets going.[5]

After just over five years in office the government had little to show for its efforts. Transformation of British industry through the 'white heat' of technological revolution had not occurred. Perhaps some of these problems were beyond the capacity of any government to solve. But what was certain was that a few slogans about technology, a new ministry operating in the same way as its predecessors, together with some ill-thought-out proposals for change that lacked any coherent plan, were not enough even to tackle the problems, let alone solve them.

17
Downhill to Devaluation

At the height of the July 1966 crisis Harold Wilson admitted to his Cabinet colleagues, in a rare moment of candour, that the massive deflationary package might not work. Similar packages introduced over the previous decade had not succeeded in correcting the underlying weaknesses and imbalances in the British economy. The government had perhaps gained eighteen months' breathing space before the next crisis. The question was whether it could use this limited opportunity either to strengthen the economy or its own ability to cope with the next crisis. The National Plan was now dead and the government's industrial policy showed no signs of tackling the fundamental impediments to Britain's economic performance. Productivity was not improving and the government was left with the policy of trying to keep wage levels down instead – hence the incomes policy and wage freeze. But it was doubtful whether this could be sustained for long.

Although the government had announced a six-month wage and price freeze on July 20 it had no idea how the policy was to be implemented. Indeed in June the main architect of the freeze, George Brown, told the Cabinet that he had rejected the idea as 'unworkable'. A week after the July measures were announced the Cabinet had to decide how it would work. A Prices and Incomes Bill (giving new statutory powers to refer increases to the Prices and Incomes Board, and to delay their implementation) was already going through the Commons. Brown proposed to add a new Part IV which would give statutory backing to the freeze. The powers he wanted were sweeping: the government would be able to freeze prices and compel an employer not to pay a wage increase, and also provide employers with a legal indemnity against any contract that would be broken by the failure to pay. His most controversial proposal involved major constraints on the trade unions: it would be an offence for any trade union to put pressure on an employer (through a strike, work-to-rule or any other action) to pay an increase. An offending trade union could be fined and failure to pay a fine would inevitably lead to imprisonment.

Brown's proposals on the trade unions, which were backed by

the Attorney-General, caused a Cabinet revolt led by Crosland, Crossman and Castle. Their case was simple. As Barbara Castle put it: 'A Labour Government couldn't survive giving itself statutory strike-breaking powers.'[1] Most other members of the Cabinet agreed and the idea had to be dropped. Crosland and the others then went on to argue that a simple price freeze would be enough, since it would put pressure on employers not to pay wage increases. A vote was taken but only eight members of the Cabinet supported this suggestion. The main opposition came from Callaghan who was worried that it would create a bad impression with foreign bankers. The Cabinet was prepared to accept the new Part IV (minus the controversial trade union powers) but it was agreed that its statutory provisions could only come into effect by affirmative order in Parliament and Cabinet approval would be needed first. In effect the government had decided to see whether a voluntary freeze would work and only if it failed to consider implementing statutory powers.

When the Commons voted on Part IV in August 1966 there were twenty-seven Labour rebels opposed to the statutory powers but the Cabinet agreed that there should be no harsh disciplinary measures. As one member pointed out, both Wilson and Brown had rejected a freeze before the election and

> Part IV is unprecedented and has no kind of support in the Party manifesto or in any previous statement of Party policy.[2]

The Cabinet agreed that for tactical reasons they would try to avoid giving statutory backing to Part IV before either the TUC or Labour party conferences in September and early October. But they only just succeeded.

At the end of September the moment of truth finally arrived. A union won a court case to force an employer to pay a wage increase that was due under their contract (since there was no statutory freeze the decision was inevitable). The government was saved from having to act in this case when the Newspaper Proprietors Association voluntarily decided to pay an increase. The blame for the breakdown of the voluntary policy could therefore be put on the employers. A hastily convened meeting of ministers at the Labour party conference agreed to go ahead with statutory powers which came into effect just after the conference ended.

At the end of November the government announced that the six-month freeze would be followed by six months of 'severe restraint' with in effect a 'zero norm'. This would last, with statutory backing, until July 1967. The problem was what would replace these provisions when the legal powers in Part IV expired in July 1967. Ministers started to consider the problem in January 1967. Michael Stewart (in charge of DEA) wanted some form of statutory policy to try and stem the flood of increases building up in the pipeline for the end of the freeze. From the start it was clear that a number of ministers had changed sides. George Brown now supported a voluntary system on the grounds that he had given 'pledges' in the summer of 1966 that the statutory system would only last for a year, (not something he had told the Cabinet at the time). He was backed by Ray Gunter (Minister of Labour). The two main opponents of the August measures, Castle and Crossman, were now hawkish advocates of a statutory policy. Callaghan, who since 1965 had been vehemently arguing for wage controls and a freeze, was now arguing that the state of the economy was so good that they could manage without a statutory policy and that 'An incomes policy in a free society won't work.'

The first decision the Cabinet took was to drop Part IV when it expired. Stewart then had a series of discussions with the TUC and CBI that revealed, as expected, that both wanted a voluntary policy. The Cabinet instructed Stewart to try and get the TUC to agree to the government taking some reserve powers whilst a voluntary policy was tried out. After a major revolt at the NEC and opposition from the trade union group of Labour MPs the Cabinet began to waver. By the end of March Wilson realised that there was little support for a statutory policy (other than powers on notification and postponement) in the CBI, TUC, the Cabinet or the Labour party. Depressed by the failure to establish any credible, long-term prices and incomes policy he even talked in his lowest moments of a Labour party separate from the unions. He consoled himself with the thought that without union agreement to compulsory powers:

> What we should have to do is to cut public expenditure. If they take too much in real wages we shall have to cut their schools, their hospitals and housing.[3]

The government had been forced to accept that the freeze would be followed by the same policy that had failed up to July 1966. The freeze had been a one-off, short-term measure that had done no more than hold back wages rather than provide any new departure. More importantly, it had used up the government's credit with the unions. Brown had given pledges in the summer of 1966 that it would only last for a year and the trade unions made sure that the government stuck to the pledges. One of the main planks of the government's economic policy had disintegrated within a year. How well thought out and sustainable was the rest of that policy?

During the July crisis Wilson had reluctantly given in to his critics within the Cabinet and conceded a committee to oversee economic policy. Wilson didn't like the idea and didn't expect anything from the Strategic Economic Policy Committee (SEP). As he told one member:

> Don't lay too much hope on this strategic committee. You've insisted on it and I can promise you that you are going to get it. But don't have too high hopes of it.[4]

The committee was set up in August but met only once before the end of October. It consisted of Wilson, Stewart, Callaghan, Brown, Gunter, Jay, Healey and Crossman. The first discussion was about import quotas where, as usual, decisions were postponed. By November the committee was meeting regularly to discuss the worsening economic situation described by one member as 'blacker than ever'. The latest figures showed that the July measures were having their expected impact with unemployment at 541,000 (over 2%) and production only 1% above the 1965 level. Callaghan wanted unemployment up to 2½% so as to act as a brake on inflation and production lower in both 1967 and 1968. Others were doubtful. Jay and Crossman wanted expansion through a relaxation of hire purchase, Wilson was content for the depression not to get worse and hoped to be able to reflate in 1967.

The oversight role of SEP came to an end after the meeting on 21 November. At that meeting Wilson was reminded that he had agreed in July that if unemployment rose above 480,000 he would consider devaluation. Jay, Stewart, Healey and Crossman all wanted the option examined. Wilson said he wasn't opposed but that no paper could be written because officials could not be trusted. The real reason was, as Stewart remarked, that all their economic advisers still favoured devaluation but Wilson and Callaghan were opposed. The mere mention of the sensitive topic of devaluation sealed the fate of SEP. Moves by Wilson to diminish the importance of its agenda and increase its membership soon ensured that it did not develop into a mechanism for directing economic policy. By January SEP was relegated to examining the briefs for Wilson and Brown's 'probe' of European opinions. It met only intermittently throughout 1967 with, at one stage, twenty-one out of the twenty-three members of the Cabinet as members.

The July cuts had not resolved any of the underlying problems the government faced in matching their spending plans with the money the Chancellor was prepared to find. Early in August 1966 Callaghan told the Cabinet that spending plans until 1970 needed to be cut by about 5%. Wilson set out his list of priorities. First came measures for industrial productivity, then spending on housing, education and hospitals, followed by social security and finally private consumption, and he added:

> If we'd thought of it . . . we would never have abolished prescription charges, but in those days we were young and inexperienced. Instead, we would have to cut back school meals.[5]

Detailed discussion on this was postponed till the autumn. Then Callaghan proposed at the first meeting of the Public Expenditure Survey Committee at the end of October that the cost of school meals should be doubled, patients should be charged for visits to the doctor and the linking of pension increases to wage rises should be postponed. There was little attempt to balance these cuts in social programmes. Cuts in defence spending were not considered possible in the short term and the old Conservative plans for a 43% rise in the transport budget, mainly for building more roads, were still retained.

The Cabinet met in the middle of November to take final decisions. Callaghan now also wanted major cuts in housing including the end of the 500,000 homes a year target of which Wilson was so proud. On this occasion the Prime Minister was able to ward off the attack as Barbara Castle reported:

> Harold urged that we should at least be able to say we had kept one pledge.[6]

The Cabinet agreed cuts, including rises in school meals charges and reducing free school milk balanced by rises in family benefits. (This decision was to lead to the acrimonious exchanges over benefits and the 'clawback' scheme described in Chapter 7.)

The cuts agreed in the autumn of 1966 did nothing to settle any long-term expenditure problems. By January 1967 Callaghan was back at the Cabinet warning of the need for further cuts of £500 million a year which he favoured finding by reducing housing and health expenditure, together with a lower rate of increase in the state pension than that achieved by the Conservatives before 1964. At the end of June 1967 the Cabinet discussed the results of that year's survey of future spending. Callaghan still wanted cuts of £500 million a year. He was strongly opposed by Crosland, who pointed out that Callaghan's plans allowed for private consumption rising at a faster rate than that achieved by the Conservatives in the first part of the decade. Wilson backed the Chancellor and Crosland was defeated. Callaghan remained gloomy about rising public expenditure and the inability to fund it without income tax at 45p in the pound. Both he and Wilson wanted the raising of the school leaving age to sixteen to be postponed for two or three years. Wilson also gave the Cabinet a long philosophical monologue about public expenditure. It had been increasing under both parties but he wondered whether it had now gone too far, and he doubted whether the electorate wanted more expenditure and higher taxation in place of more private consumption. But the Cabinet reached no decisions before the whole question of cuts was swept up in the post-devaluation crisis.

The July 1966 package had a short-term beneficial effect on the economy. Because of lower demand the level of imports fell rapidly so that in the last quarter of 1966 there was a surplus on the balance of trade of £86 million. This improvement produced a small surplus on the current account of the balance of payments for the whole of 1966 (£83 million compared with the deficit of £52 million in 1965). The same pattern had occurred in every previous 'stop' phase in the management of the economy over the past decade and had always proved shortlived. The prospects for a sustained improvement were considered to be poor according to official estimates. In August 1966 the Bank of England was privately forecasting a balance of payments deficit of £237 million for 1967. By March 1967 the Treasury, which had earlier been more optimistic than the Bank of England, reduced its estimated surplus for the year to just £23 million. In August the Treasury was estimating a deficit of £380 million, with the picture for 1968 even worse. (The eventual deficit for 1967 was £298 million.)

In public ministers remained optimistic about prospects. Introducing the April 1967 Budget Callaghan forecast 3% growth over the year, a balance of payments surplus in 1967 and an even bigger one in 1968. The Budget was neither deflationary nor inflationary and introduced no significant changes in taxation. The aim was to keep unemployment at about 2% and hope that by running the economy below capacity a small balance of payments surplus would result. In his memoirs Wilson writes that Callaghan accepted Treasury advice for a no-change Budget and Callaghan had kept him 'fully informed about his assessment and proposals'.[7] At the time his view of Callaghan's behaviour and motives was very different, as Dick Crossman described:

> He [Wilson] said that the budget lacked imagination and that Callaghan had never shown him any draft or asked for any advice until it was too late. He was particularly angry because he was convinced that it was Callaghan who was responsible for the articles in the weekend press about himself as the crown prince . . . Apparently he thought his great Budget would make him even more of a crown prince but he'd come unstuck and Harold was being quite cheerful about it.[8]

In June Callaghan felt able to say in public that 'The period of standstill is finished . . . we are now beginning on a period of controlled growth and expansion.' Wilson too was optimistic. In a speech at Newport in September he said:

> Overseas payments have reached a position of basic balance and growing strength . . . We now face a turning point . . . Production can now increase without plunging us into the overheating, wasteful use and indeed famine of labour which, in the past, have plunged us into crises.

He had exactly the same message for the Labour party conference at the beginning of October, speaking of rising production, productivity and employment.

In private ministers, despite the official predictions of disaster ahead, were looking towards reflation. At the end of July Wilson was a keen advocate of such a package to counter what he saw as Callaghan's too restrictive approach. He wanted a relaxation of hire purchase controls, bulk buying of machine tools by the government and selective import controls (including newsprint rationing). He was supported by Douglas Jay and other ministers but Callaghan was totally opposed to any package before the autumn and Wilson was forced to give way. At the end of August Wilson took over direct control of the DEA in an attempt to get greater control over economic policy. He told Crossman that the prospects for economic success had risen from 50% to 130% since he had taken over the DEA and went on:

If I can't run the economy well through DEA I'm no good. I was trained for this job and I've taken the powers to run the economy.[9]

Wilson was always to claim that the Six-Day War in the Middle East and the subsequent closure of the Suez Canal, together with the dock strikes in Liverpool and London during September and October, were the causes of devaluation. Most estimates put the balance of payments cost of the closure of the Suez Canal at no more than £20 million a month and the dock strikes had a smaller impact. If these were the causes of devaluation then they only demonstrate the brittle nature of the economic recovery allegedly sustained since July 1966. In fact the reasons for devaluation and the process which brought the government to the final decision were much more complex.

In February 1967 the United States proposed to put the September 1965 deal over economic policy and commitments in the Far East on to a permanent basis. The US now wanted a long-term agreement to create a joint sterling-dollar area that would protect both currencies and the position of gold. A twenty-five-year multi-billion-dollar loan would fund all sterling debts to provide stability for sterling at its present exchange level. In return the US wanted the UK to maintain a major strategic role in the Far East. This proposal was rejected for two reasons. It would have made entry into the EEC impossible on both political grounds (French opposition) and economic grounds (the UK would have been too closely tied to the US). Moreover this new deal, unlike that in 1965, would have been public and Wilson realised that domestically within the Cabinet and the Labour party he could not find support for such a long-term, pro-American policy, particularly when it involved maintaining indefinitely an expensive defence presence in the Far East.

In early 1967 the Treasury had, in great secrecy, examined the case for devaluation, and again Wilson and Callaghan had rejected the option. The Wilson-Callaghan alternative strategy (if it can really be called a strategy) was to keep the economy running under full capacity with unemployment at about 500,000 and, by keeping demand down, hope to have a small balance of payments surplus in 1967 and 1968. Then they hoped that the cuts in overseas expenditure flowing from the rundown of forces East of Suez – which were now possible after rejecting the US proposals – would give enough room to manoeuvre until 1970 and the election. It was the old policy that had been run since October 1964 of making no fundamental adjustments in the economy and hoping to muddle through with a series of short-term expedients to avoid the politically damaging admission of failure represented by devaluation.

Wilson now regarded himself as free from the 1965 deal and his own views were slowly starting to change. He was beginning to realise that the next crisis for sterling might well involve terms for support from the US and the central banks that would be politically unacceptable. There were also electoral considerations. By the autumn of 1967 the run-up to the next election was only eighteen months away and another bout of massive deflation might finish off Labour's chances, given their already rapidly sinking popularity. At the end of July he held a special meeting at Chequers with his close political allies and friends; Crossman, Silkin, Shore, Benn, Castle, Hart, Balogh and Marcia Williams. Towards the end of the meeting Wilson himself suddenly raised the subject of devaluation to the amazement of the other participants. Tommy Balogh responded by pointing out that it wasn't a solution in itself and that other measures would have to be taken in conjunction with it. Wilson, pleased with this response, offered his own analysis, although carefully shading his views to appeal to his audience. He said that he was not opposed to devaluation but that it had to be done at the right time and for the right reasons, which were political not economic. Then, he added, showing how far his views had changed since 1965, if the US got tough, that would be the time to move:

> This must be a political issue when it comes: we devalue to defend our independence.[10]

When the crisis came at the end of October it was sickeningly familiar – poor trade figures, a run on the pound and insufficient resources to support it. The first indication was the publication of the September trade figures showing a deficit of £52 million, which meant a huge deficit for 1967 was inevitable. By early November the government also knew that the October figure would show a record deficit of £107 million. The foreign exchange position was also weak. The reserves were £150 million lower than in the autumn of 1966, short-term credits taken up were worth £750 million with only another £220 million available before recourse had to be made to the IMF. The UK was already negotiating with other central banks for a further credit of £107 million simply to enable it to repay outstanding debt to the IMF in December. Despite all the loans and support operations, combined with substantial deflation, the underlying position was as bad as it had been when Labour took office in October 1964. After Callaghan had spoken to Henry Fowler, the US Secretary of the Treasury, and gained his approval, Bank Rate was raised ½% on 19 October. This caused alarm bells to ring in Washington and Fowler obtained Johnson's approval to increase US resources for the support of sterling by 30%. This was all part of what the US administration described as 'the last ditch British effort to hold the sterling rate'.[11]

The government was faced with an acute dilemma. Unemployment had risen to 2.4%, the highest October level for twenty-five years. If there was another deflationary package to defend the pound how far would unemployment rise and could the government then expect to win the election? To many observers at the time it had seemed obvious that the July measures only led to a dead end. Now it was staring the government in the face.

On 2 November Sir Alec Cairncross (the head of the government's Economic Service) saw Callaghan and told him that devaluation was necessary. Callaghan was unsure and, like Wilson, was still hoping they might be able to get through the winter and then in the spring a boom in the economy would improve the situation. Cairncross told him that the government would not get through the winter without devaluation. Callaghan asked, 'Is it my duty?' and Cairncross replied, 'Yes, it is your duty.' On 4 November Callaghan brought Wilson details of the mounting crisis: speculation against the pound was growing, the reserves were falling and rumours of devaluation were rife. The next day Wilson told Callaghan that there was no veto on devaluation, and they agreed to sound out both the EEC and the US on their attitude. Despite the fine words Wilson had used in the past, this was not devaluation from strength or devaluation for political reasons: their economic policy had failed and they had at last run out of options.

On 8 November at a meeting of SEP, discussing yet another paper by Tony Crosland on import controls, Wilson started a discussion on devaluation. Crosland, Crossman and Stewart were all in favour of devaluation but Callaghan was still not reconciled to the inevitable, arguing that Britain could not freely decide to devalue, and that:

we must soldier on . . . we must not underestimate the catastrophe of devaluation. It would be a political catastrophe as well as an economic one.[12]

By the evening Callaghan was finally convinced. He admitted to Wilson that although the short-term position had improved slightly, the long-term outlook was bad. The Treasury was now forecasting a worsening of the balance of payments in the first part of 1968 with no improvement for at least a year. He recommended devaluation in ten days' time, accompanied by a deflationary package of extra taxation and public expenditure cuts. The crucial point had been passed. Although no final decision had been taken, both Wilson and Callaghan were working on the assumption of devaluation. The next day they told Brown of their view but he was now less keen on devaluation than in July 1966 and suggested consulting the Americans before any final decisions were taken. On 10 November Callaghan wrote to Fowler admitting that the game was virtually up:

> I think we are getting to the end of the period when we can afford to carry on a hand-to-mouth basis month by month. It is not a good posture . . . if we carry on too long . . . we shall not have sufficient reserves to defend attacks on any new parity . . . I think the time for long-term decisions one way or the other is very close at hand.[13]

A Treasury official was sent to Washington for discussions.

Over the weekend that followed it looked as though the Americans and the central bankers meeting in Basle, both strongly opposed to devaluation, would put together another package to preserve the value of the pound. The question was whether their terms for this support would be acceptable. In Downing Street the crucial decisions were taken on Monday 13 November. Early in the day Callaghan was in his usual masochistic mood, grimly relishing the prospect of either the terms available to save the pound or the deflation that would accompany devaluation. As he told one colleague:

> Well, we are for it . . . unless we get the right answers this morning. This time the bankers' terms will be unacceptable . . . The only point of devaluing would be the package we could lay down . . . it'll be a chance to teach the people of this country what a fools' paradise they've been living in.[14]

That evening the Governor of the Bank of England, Sir Leslie O'Brien, reported to Wilson on the outcome of the talks in Basle. The central bankers were agreed that any support for the pound would have to be a major long-term operation involving an IMF stand-by credit of $3 billion which would only be available on stringent conditions. There would have to be strict credit control, a statutory prices and incomes policy, deflation and an agreement not to float the pound, accompanied by strict IMF monitoring of the UK economy. On this basis, and knowing Wilson and Callaghan's views, O'Brien advised devaluation. Late in the night of 13 November Wilson and Callaghan, together with Sir William Armstrong and Burke Trend, decided to reject the bankers' package and devalue. The Treasury was instructed to start secret planning.

The morning after that decision was taken the Cabinet met. Roy Jenkins asked for a discussion about the economic situation. Wilson was not prepared to take the Cabinet into his confidence and said, 'We'll have a full discussion in about two or three weeks' time.'[15] Instead Wilson set up a special committee consisting of himself, Callaghan, Brown, Thomson, Healey, Crosland and Stewart. When they met that afternoon there was general support for the decision taken the previous evening with the exception of Brown and Thomson, who preferred to accept the IMF package and consider devaluation in the spring of 1968. From then on planning went steadily ahead with the final decision to go for a new fixed rate of $2.40 (a devaluation of 14%) taken the next day, even though the United States was still trying to get together a support package.

The Cabinet met again on the morning of 16 November. After a brief introduction from Wilson, Callaghan broke the news to his colleagues and gave details of the accompanying deflationary package consisting of a rise in Bank Rate to 8%, tighter hire purchase controls, the virtual ending of SET repayments (so that it became just a tax rather than a mechanism for structural reform of the economy), increased corporation tax and a £100 million cut in defence expenditure. Callaghan concluded sombrely:

> This is the most agonising reappraisal I have ever had to do and I will not pretend that it is anything but a failure of our policies.

However, Wilson was, as usual, more sanguine about the impact of devaluation:

> It would be a relief to our people . . . they will feel that at last we have broken free.[16]

The package of cuts was generally accepted, except that a proposal to postpone the raising of the school leaving age was left out after strong objections from Roy Jenkins.

The key to a succesful operation was to keep the decision secret for the next two days. Just as the Cabinet was finishing its discussion news arrived that a Labour backbencher, Robert Sheldon, had put down a private notice question for answer that afternoon about a possible IMF loan. The Cabinet considered asking him to withdraw it but decided that it was too dangerous a course to take now that the question was public. Instead John Silkin, as Chief Whip, was sent over to see the Speaker to ask him to disallow the question. The Speaker refused and the Cabinet decided they had no alternative but to leave Callaghan to deny the rumours of an IMF loan even though negotiations were taking place on stand-by credits to support a devalued pound. That afternoon in the Commons Callaghan did not deny the rumours but used instead a much weaker formula: 'I did not start the rumours and I do not propose to comment on them.' The day after devaluation Callaghan admitted to a colleague that he had not denied the rumours because he could not face another row with the back-benchers over allegations of misleading them. His actions only increased speculation about devaluation and probably cost the foreign exchange reserves about £200 million in a day.

Devaluation was announced late in the evening of Saturday 18 November. The next day Wilson broadcast to the nation, adopting the line suggested by Dick Crossman that this was a new start, that the country was suddenly free of the old restraints. It was the best line that could be devised but it was hardly convincing after the three-year fight Wilson and the government had put up to avoid devaluation.

On 18 November Callaghan, who had already hinted to Wilson that he would quit, handed in a letter resigning as Chancellor but he carefully did not resign from the Cabinet. As we have seen Wilson had long wanted to get rid of Callaghan but now he had doubts. Callaghan had wanted to leave the Treasury for some time but now fought hard for his political future. His speech defending devaluation in the Commons on 22 October was judged a success. The next day Peter Jay (Callaghan's son-in-law) had an article in *The Times* purporting to describe all the occasions that Callaghan and the Treasury had argued for devaluation, only to be overruled by Wilson. On 24 November Callaghan also saw Brown and told him that he did not want the Foreign Office, thus ensuring his support. On 27 November Wilson discussed Callaghan's future with Crossman and Silkin, who favoured a straight swap between Callaghan and Jenkins (Callaghan wanted Crosland to succeed him). The next day Wilson agreed to offer Callaghan the Home

Office and if he refused then Crossman would take it on whilst remaining Leader of the House. Callaghan accepted and Jenkins became Chancellor. In political terms Callaghan had emerged relatively unscathed and preserved his long-term position. Although Wilson had had little choice but to promote one of his main rivals, he and Jenkins were now inseparably locked together. Both desperately needed a successful economic policy.

For three years the Labour government had fought to avoid devaluation. They had rejected it as an option in October 1964 and introduced two deflationary packages in July 1965 and July 1966 to try and preserve the value of sterling. A large amount of political, and in Wilson's case personal, capital was invested in the defence of the pound. Whatever words were used in November 1967 to try and disguise the fact, it was, as Callaghan frankly admitted inside the Cabinet, a major policy failure. Successive governments had seen the value of sterling as a prestige symbol and taken severe economic measures to preserve it. The act of devaluation was therefore bound to be seen, both at home and abroad, as evidence of Britain's economic decline and symbolic of her decline as a great power. Wilson accepted this analysis when, in July 1961, he told the Commons:

A second devaluation would be regarded all over the world as an acknowledgement of defeat, a recognition that we were not on a springboard but on a slide.

The crucial question is, therefore, why devaluation in the autumn of 1967?

In both 1965 and 1966 it had been possible to put together packages to defend sterling and the government could present themselves as defenders of British national interests, even though the measures were the result of the secret deal made with the Americans. By the autumn of 1967 the position was different. The price of American and international support was far higher now, and the strings attached would have been only too public. The prospects of a joint dollar-sterling area, and twenty-five-year financial and defence commitments, were unthinkable. And the idea of the IMF effectively dictating and monitoring Britain's economic policy was unacceptable. Wilson took a political decision that acceptance of such a package would inevitably mean the loss of the next election. The July 1966 measures had already produced the highest level of unemployment since the war and there was no chance of the trade unions agreeing to another freeze. Indeed it is doubtful whether Wilson could have carried the Cabinet, let alone the parliamentary party, for such an international rescue package. Nor was he prepared for the loss of face involved in the IMF openly dictating terms.

Only in these circumstances did devaluation look a more attractive alternative. Whatever the short-term drawbacks, at least it offered the chance of economic recovery before the next election. Wilson and the other senior ministers and officials involved were also convinced that they could get away with introducing measures far less draconian than those in the international rescue package. The measures actually introduced in November 1967 reflect this belief. There were cuts, but they were limited and there was little attempt to reduce consumer spending. It was only in the weeks after devaluation that ministers gradually realised that their initial judgement was unfounded and began to consider further measures. In the end the measures taken after devaluation (described in the next chapter) were at least as severe as those that would have been required to defend the pound. But their political judgement was right in one respect: at least the government could claim that they were carrying this out as their own policy, and not at the behest of the Americans or the central bankers and the IMF. Nevertheless the effect on the government's standing and electoral prospects was disastrous, and not just in the short term.

Devaluation in November 1967 was an admission that the government had bungled its economic policy. The most damning criticism is that when the crisis came the underlying situation was as bad as in October 1964. All the intervening measures, the stiff budgets, the packages of July 1965 and July 1966, a prices and incomes freeze, the deal with the Americans in the summer of 1965 and the international support, had all made no long-term difference. The same dilemma had to be faced and resolved – but in much more difficult circumstances. Now the burden of debt to be paid off after devaluation was much bigger and the economic difficulties in making devaluation work were much greater. And time had been wasted. The government had not freely chosen the right moment to devalue. It was dangerously close to the next election and the room for manoeuvre that much more limited. It now faced an uphill battle against mounting unpopularity and the time needed for the drastic measures belatedly taken after devaluation to work. To compound these difficulties, almost immediately after devaluation it plunged into the worst of all its many internal disputes.

18
Conflict, Crisis and Cuts

In December 1967, within a fortnight of devaluation, the government was plunged into a crisis over the sale of arms to South Africa, which Wilson later described as 'more serious than any other in our six years of Government'.[1] When this had been resolved another long argument followed over a new round of public expenditure cuts to try and make devaluation work. The January 1968 package involved abandoning major areas of domestic policy and the final withdrawal of forces from East of Suez. By the end of January 1968, after these semi-public rows, instead of 'breaking free' after devaluation, as Wilson had hoped, the government was battered, deeply divided and sinking to an unprecedented level of unpopularity. Behind all of these conflicts lay a bitter dispute about Wilson's leadership and the direction of government policy.

The Labour party's long-standing opposition to apartheid in South Africa had been heightened by events in the early 1960s, in particular the Sharpeville massacre by the security forces. The government entered office pledged to end the sale of arms to South Africa and within days of taking office Wilson issued a personal letter from No 10 to all departments with instructions that the trade was to stop. Burke Trend moved quickly to halt action on Wilson's minute and convinced him to first hold a meeting of OPD to discuss the implications for the Simonstown agreement, which might be abrogated by South Africa in retaliation for an embargo. This agreement provided facilities for the Royal Navy in South Africa, and also covered the exchange of intelligence information between South Africa and Britain.

At issue was a South African order for sixteen Buccaneer aircraft and associated spares for their navy which had been negotiated by the Conservative government. In October 1963 Barbara Castle, speaking for the National Executive, had told the party conference that

> a Labour Government would cancel that order and substitute a better one . . . for example defending the frontiers of India against aggression.

After an OPD meeting in November 1964 Wilson announced a significantly modified approach. Existing contracts would be fulfilled but new ones would not be made. The Buccaneer order could therefore go ahead. Within six months the interpretation of their 'no new arms sales' policy was pushed to its limits when Vauxhall was given permission to export its four-wheel drive chassis intended for South African-produced armoured cars. In opposition Wilson had taken a different view of the use to which the vehicles would be put. At an anti-apartheid rally in 1963 he had attacked

> the role played by British-made Saracen armoured cars in the brutality we condemn today.

From the start the government did not place any other restrictions or sanctions on South Africa. On the contrary they did all they could to encourage trade. In February 1966 a special South African section of the British National Exports Council was established. Earlier in March 1965 it seemed possible that the Afro-Asian countries at the UN might introduce a resolution calling for sanctions against South Africa. A special Cabinet committee was set up to study the problem and Lord Caradon, the Ambassador at the UN, summoned back to London. He was instructed that if necessary the UK would use its veto in the Security Council to block any call for sanctions. The debate in the UN fizzled out and the Labour government never had to make public just how far it was prepared to go to stop sanctions. But the threat of sanctions continued to worry Wilson. In October 1967 he told the Cabinet that sanctions against Rhodesia were not fully effective but no action could be taken through the UN 'for fear that it would lead to a demand for similar action against South Africa'.[2]

By the middle of 1966 British attitudes towards South Africa were causing concern in Washington. Britain had failed to back the Americans' strong line over South African occupation of Namibia and had told them that it proposed to relax further the arms embargo to permit the export of the Beagle unarmed aircraft for the South African air force, even though the United States had refused to allow the sale of a similar American aircraft. The State Department was worried that

> if we dilute our policy towards South African to harmonize with the UK, we risk becoming identified as a protector of the white redoubt.[3]

In June 1967 the South Africans requested further arms worth about £100 million made up of more Buccaneers, together with frigates and other naval items. The initial decision was not, as the 1964 policy implied, to immediately rule out the order but rather to see if anything could be gained in return. Wilson agreed with Brown that the South Africans should be told that no decision would be taken before the end of the year and OPD agreed that Brown should talk to the South African Foreign Minister 'to see whether a *quid pro quo* could be obtained for the arms deal in the form of help to secure a settlement in Rhodesia'.[4]

The three ministers most closely concerned with the negotiations wanted to go further. In a joint paper to OPD in September Brown, Healey and Thomson, emphasising the UK requirement for the Simonstown base, argued for a major change of policy formally to end the 1964 ban by accepting the current South African order. Wilson's views in June are not clear but there is no doubt that he allowed Brown to go a long way with the South Africans in holding out the hope of a change of policy. Now he came out against the sale, arguing that six members of the government would resign on the issue and the effect on the parliamentary party would be even worse. He was supported by Michael Stewart, who wouldn't accept what he described as the 'policies of pure expediency and opportunism'. Crosland was neutral and Crossman argued that it looked odd to sell arms to South Africa whilst standing out on Rhodesia. (Privately he was prepared to sell out on both.) OPD agreed to postpone a decision but Brown was irate about Wilson's volte-face, as he told him the next day:

> You know, Prime Minister, I have come to all kinds of personal understandings about this change of policy, as you agreed I should do some months ago. It will be pretty awkward to go back on those personal understandings just now.[5]

The crisis started with a heated discussion in OPD on December 8. The proposal put to the committee in September to accept the South African arms order was submitted again. Wilson made clear his opposition but found himself outnumbered. To try and help him Crossman suggested leaving the issue till after the forthcoming review of expenditure but that had little support. Wilson, knowing he would be defeated, refused to take a vote in OPD and insisted that the issue went to Cabinet. Three days later Callaghan, who had not been at OPD, indicated in an after-dinner speech that he favoured arm sales to South Africa. His remarks sparked off a fierce debate within the Labour party.

The issue of arms to South Africa was bound to be sensitive within the party. But it had had to accept unpalatable policies in the past three years and was to do so again before 1970. The reason that there was such a bitter row over this issue lies in the internal political situation. Between September and December the climate had changed. After devaluation Wilson's personal prestige was low and many in the government felt that because of devaluation export orders had to be accepted regardless of their destination. A group of right-wing ministers also sensed an opportunity to remove Wilson as leader. They seem to have thought that, if Wilson were forced to accept a change of policy on arms for South Africa, he would be even more discredited and demands for his removal would be overwhelming. The lengths that Wilson went to in order to avert the change demonstrate how acutely aware he was of the threat to his position. Callaghan's intervention, far from being an off-the-cuff comment, has the hallmark of a coordinated strategy by a group of Wilson's opponents – led by Brown, Callaghan, Healey, Crosland and Thomson. But they underestimated Wilson's ability to fight back. After the majority against him in OPD and the prospect of defeat in Cabinet he embarked on a campaign to neutralise those opposed to him by stirring up the parliamentary party where the backbenchers would be strongly opposed to any sell-out.

The day after Callaghan's speech an Early Day Motion was put down in the Commons (eventually signed by 136 MPs), expressing continued support for the government's embargo on arms sales. This motion was the work of the Chief Whip, John Silkin, as Dick Crossman, Leader of the House, commented:

> the Chief was busy getting *his* motion on South Africa around the House and ensuring that a really large number of back-benchers signed it [my italics].[6]

On 13 December, after getting Silkin to mobilise the back-benchers, Wilson stepped up his campaign by enlisting the efforts of Barbara Castle, a life-long opponent of South Africa. He told her:

> Now I wouldn't mind it being known that George and Denis are behind this move. Let the Party be mobilized. And I wouldn't mind getting a letter from junior Ministers saying they won't stand for a change of policy. But remember, none of this must be traced back to me.[7]

Castle went off to round up support and arranged for an emergency question to be tabled for Wilson to answer the next day. Determined to exploit the media to stoke up the debate, Wilson told Crossman that he was giving the whole story to the *Guardian* and that:

> I'm taking on briefing the press myself. This time I'm damn well going to get the result I want.[8]

The Cabinet was due to discuss the issue on 14 December but George Brown was fog-bound in Brussels and Wilson postponed the subject after a series of sulphurous exchanges. In the Commons Wilson took the opportunity of responding to the questions he had helped generate by stating that no change of policy had been agreed (which was correct) and that discussion had been postponed until Brown returned. The latter point, whilst technically correct, indirectly confirmed the press speculation that Brown was the main advocate of selling arms to South Africa.

The Cabinet meeting of Friday 15 December was perhaps the bitterest of the whole administration. The atmosphere was described by Barbara Castle as 'nastier than I have ever known in Cabinet'. It started according to Dick Crossman with 'an hour and a half of mutual abuse'. Brown began by protesting that he was being singled out for attack when he had only been carrying out the policy agreed at OPD:

> Far from being isolated, he maintained, he had been strongly backed and some, like the Lord President [Crossman], who were now trying to stir up feeling against him, had been advocating a change of policy just as much as he had.

This reference to Crossman's activities may help explain why his diary entries for the previous week are missing. The editor suggests that he accidentally erased the tape on the dictating machine. If so it was the only time he did it in six years. It is possible that it was done deliberately to cover his rapid change of view; after all he had been known as 'Dick Double-Crossman' for years.

Wilson responded to Brown's speech by complaining about the attempts at 'character assassination' on him but accepted that he had been prepared to explore the issue if South Africa would help on Rhodesia (something he omits from his memoirs) but now that no help was likely he believed 'to sell out on this issue, for nothing in return, was intolerable'. He went on to attack Brown and

Callaghan for stirring things up, and remarked that the parliamentary party had 'risen up' of its own accord (conveniently forgetting his own activities thirty-six hours before). This was followed by a carefully coordinated and concentrated attack from Brown, Healey and Crosland. Brown argued that Britain's economic position was so bad that the order had to be accepted and that if Britain didn't somebody else would. Healey was even more blunt:

Why were we being such hypocrites? We had not been applying the argument for some time: we had sold [South Africa] ammunition, Wasp helicopters and replacement aeroplanes since 1964.

After this furious exchange the Cabinet was split right down the middle. Eight favoured selling arms (Brown, Healey, Callaghan, Crosland, Ross, Gunter, Gordon-Walker and Thomson); eight were opposed (Wilson, Shore, Gardiner, Benn, Greenwood, Stewart, Castle and Hughes) and five (Jenkins, Crossman, Peart, Marsh and Longford) favoured postponing a decision till the major package of cuts was announced in January. Wilson tried to sum up that the Cabinet was eleven to seven against making a change of policy, only for Brown to respond: 'Some of us can count and we don't make it out that way.' Wilson now had to backtrack. He agreed to postpone a decision but stressed that no change of policy had been agreed. He intended to make a Commons statement after the weekend on these lines and meanwhile all members of the Cabinet were instructed not to brief the press.[9]

Saturday's papers were full of stories of how Wilson had stabbed Brown in the back and mobilised the Whips to stir up the party against him, all clearly planted by Brown. This is exactly what Wilson had expected. He told Castle:

It is all going very well. This time George had over-reached himself. I am just ringing to say: no counter-briefing. George and his friends must have no alibi.[10]

Some of Wilson's other supporters were less relaxed. Benn for example argued that 'we must force these buggers to eat dirt, make them accept unconditional surrender'. On the Sunday evening Crossman found Wilson working on two statements. The first confirmed the Cabinet decision that no change of policy had yet been agreed. The second was to be agreed by Cabinet the next day and would repudiate all the press stories planted by Brown. Brown, by breaking the agreement not to brief the press, had given

301

Wilson the issue he needed to bring the Cabinet back into line.
Wilson, though, was clear on one thing, saying that he

> would never work with George Brown after such an act of deliber-
> ate treachery . . . this was the final bloody limit.[11]

The Cabinet met on the Monday morning. Wilson was in
determined mood as Castle noted:

> I have never seen him so grim and white, whether from fear or
> deliberate anger it was difficult to tell.

He started by laying into Brown as Crossman described:

> I've never heard anybody publicly scourged as George Brown was
> scourged by Harold this morning.

Wilson demanded a statement from the Cabinet repudiating the
stories about him stabbing Brown in the back. Wilson's opponents
had no evidence to support these claims because he had covered his
tracks efficiently. With the parliamentary party supporting the
Prime Minister Wilson's opponents had little choice but to back
down. It was Callaghan who was first to break with his allies, saying
that it was now impossible not to back the Prime Minister, that a
holding statement on arms sales couldn't possibly be made and that
the arms embargo would have to be maintained. Gordon-Walker
agreed and although Brown, Healey and Crosland tried to argue
for postponement, most other members had by now had enough of
Brown and the way in which they thought he had used the issue
against Wilson. The Cabinet insisted that Wilson include a passage
in his statement to the Commons saying that there was to be no
change in policy. It was, as Crossman put it, 'a complete and total
victory', and much greater than Wilson could have expected three
days before.

Once again Brown was outmanoeuvred by a more tactically
adroit Wilson. There is no doubt that part of Brown's complaint
that he was only carrying out government policy is correct. For
some time the government had been edging towards a more
accommodating attitude to South Africa and in June 1967 had
agreed to consider the possibility of renewed arms sales in return
for South African assistance on a Rhodesian settlement. Perhaps
Brown went a little too far with the South African Ambassador in
leading him to expect a new arms sales policy. Certainly it should
have been clear to him by September that other Ministers had real

doubts and that the parliamentary party was unlikely to be enthusiastic. Wilson's opponents underestimated his ability to fight back. After losing the initial round in OPD, Wilson used the Whips, his friends, backbenchers and the press to mount a campaign against his Cabinet colleagues. Not surprisingly Brown retaliated in kind but was not clever enough to cover his tracks as Wilson had done. Brown had handed to Wilson an unassailable position of upholding Cabinet decisions and the proprieties of government procedure. Wilson was therefore able rapidly to rescue a difficult position in Cabinet and turn it into an easy victory.

The net result of all the plotting was to strengthen Wilson's position. He could now claim to stand behind party policy in opposition to his colleagues who seemed ready to sell out on a matter of principle. The campaign by the right had badly misfired. In retrospect it is difficult to see why they thought this was a winning issue. Perhaps they felt that Wilson's morale was so low that he wouldn't fight. But what of Wilson's own explanation of events? The account of the crisis Wilson gives in his memoirs is highly misleading. He asserts that the crisis began accidentally through Callaghan's after-dinner remarks and that when, on 8 December, OPD considered the matter, 'it was the first time that any suggestion that our ban on South African arms shipments should be rescinded had been put to any Cabinet committee.' That claim is obviously wrong, as the OPD discussions in June and September 1967 demonstrate, but it helps to disguise Wilson's own part in the earlier moves to come to an accommodation with South Africa. Wilson also claims that both he and the Chief Whip acted entirely correctly and neutrally throughout. The actions of both of them after the OPD meeting on 8 December show that such a claim is also wrong. Perhaps the last scene of the crisis should be No 10 on the evening after Wilson had secured his victory, when he entertained the Lobby correspondents to Christmas drinks. After the furious attack on Brown that morning for leaks to the press, Crossman was fascinated to overhear Wilson talking to a group of correspondents:

'On my best calculation there were sixteen members of the Cabinet who explicitly wanted me to make the Statement I made this afternoon.' Then he told them it was a lie that there was ever any majority in favour of selling arms . . . After this he went on to describe what had happened in Cabinet this morning . . . he really and sincerely believes that . . . he only briefs the press and never leaks.[12]

At the height of the row over South African arms Wilson circulated a top secret paper to the Cabinet on the economic situation. He admitted that devaluation had failed to work, the pound still had to be supported on the foreign exchanges and money was flowing out of London because of fears of another devaluation. All in all the economic situation was 'menacing'. On 20 December the Cabinet met to decide how to try and stop the rot. Jenkins told them that they had to achieve a balance of payments surplus of £500 million in 1968 (a massive turnround of £800 million compared with 1967). This required public expenditure cuts of £800–850 million (twice the level of the agonising July 1966 cuts) and increased taxation in the Budget – a total deflationary impact of over £1 billion.

There was little dissent from this analysis, yet just before he became Chancellor Jenkins had told a colleague devaluation was necessary but if there was to be another deflationary package then a group of ministers ought to say, 'This is too much, and be ready to go.'[13] A month in the Treasury completely changed his view. Only once was the need for deflation on this scale challenged in Cabinet. Tony Crosland submitted alternative proposals for only £800 million of deflation and of that only £400 million from public expenditure (half Jenkins' figure) with the rest coming from taxation. This was very much in line with his philosophy of the 1950s of using public expenditure as a good tool to redistribute wealth. But with both Jenkins and Wilson opposed he stood no chance of winning.

The basic balance of the package was determined by ministers on political grounds. From late in December Wilson and Jenkins (though not the Cabinet) were agreed that the reintroduction of prescription charges and postponement of the raising of the school-leaving age were necessary to appease the bankers (even though devaluation had been intended to cut Britain free from these influences over economic policy). To balance the package and make it saleable to the parliamentary party two major symbols of defence policy – the East of Suez role and the F-111 purchase – were to go too. The Cabinet had only agreed so far that cuts in the civil and defence programmes would be equal (which meant a higher proportionate burden on defence).

After the New Year ministers settled down to an intensive series of meetings to settle the details. Fairly rapid agreement was reached on a number of items, many of which the Treasury had been trying to cut for years. Wilson's promise of 500,000 homes a year was finally abandoned, Civil Defence was put on a care and maintenance basis and free school milk in secondary schools was abolished. A more controversial item was reimposition of prescription charges. Wilson had resigned from the Attlee government in 1951 on this very issue and one of the first actions of the new government in October 1964 had been to abolish charges. However, Wilson was now strongly in favour of reintroducing charges and the argument was mainly about whether there should be exemptions. In an abortive attempt to stop all charges Kenneth Robinson, the Health Minister, tried to argue that they were administratively too difficult. When it became clear that this tactic would fail a workable scheme was devised by his department. But the real battle was to come over three items – postponement of the raising of the school-leaving age to sixteen, the timetable for withdrawal from East of Suez and cancellation of the order for the American F-111 aircraft.

The raising of the school-leaving age to sixteen had featured in both the 1964 and 1966 manifestos, and had been envisaged as far back as the 1944 Education Act as a crucial part of the drive to create a more equal education system. Jenkins' proposal (which he had strongly opposed before becoming Chancellor) was to postpone the change for three years. The crucial discussion took place on 5 January when the Cabinet was split largely on class lines. The opposition was led by the working-class ministers who had not been to university, in particular George Brown and Callaghan (who had argued vigorously in favour of postponement for over a year as Chancellor). They were joined by the ex-teachers, Thomson and Stewart, and just two graduates, Crosland and Benn. It was Tony Crosland who got to the heart of the matter when he said:

> Only 400,000 children. But they're not our children. It's always other people's children. None of us in this room would dream of letting our children leave school at fifteen.

But the crunch came when the Education Minister, Patrick Gordon-Walker, refused to fight and instead backed Jenkins as long as the postponement was only for two years. This led to the following pointed exchange between Brown and Gordon-Walker:

> *Brown*: I want a straight answer to a straight question. If you had to choose between these 400,000 fifteen year olds and university students, which would you help?
> *Gordon-Walker*: If I had to make such a choice I suppose I'd help university students.
> *Brown*: May God forgive you.[14]

A vote was taken and postponement for two years was agreed by eleven votes to ten.

Although George Brown thought of resigning, only one minister, Lord Longford, did so. He had long been an isolated and ineffectual figure in the government and he knew that he would shortly be replaced as Leader of the House of Lords by his deputy, Lord Shackleton. He therefore took the opportunity to go on an issue of principle. As he said afterwards: 'I felt it was time to go. I felt if I swallowed this, there was nothing I wouldn't swallow.'[15] His resignation passed largely unnoticed.

The most contentious item in Jenkins' list of cuts was the proposal to withdraw from all defence commitments East of Suez by March 1971. In July 1967 the government had issued a White Paper setting a date of the mid-1970s for completing the withdrawal from the Far East. This White Paper was supposed to set the shape of defence policy for the next eight to ten years. Now just five months later the Cabinet was being asked to tear it up.

On 4 January 1968 the Cabinet had its first discussion on the new proposal to withdraw all British forces by March 1971. Jenkins and his supporters argued that the move was necessary psychologically, not just for the Labour party but also for the country as a whole, to demonstrate that they were entering a new era after devaluation. Instead of opposing the move outright, Brown, Healey, Stewart and Callaghan argued that the earliest possible date was March 1972; any withdrawal before this date would, they alleged, lead to major instability. (Six months earlier they had argued that withdrawal before the mid-1970s would have the same destabilising effect.) The real, unspoken reason for advocating a difference of only one year was the effect it might have on the final outcome. All of these ministers were under strong departmental pressure to delay the process for as long as possible. Acceptance of the 1972 date would mean that if the Conservatives won the election in 1970 they would have time to reverse the policy. If they only had a few months it would be too late to re-establish all the facilities. Perhaps they also hoped that Labour policy might change if they were re-elected in 1970.

After two and a half hours' discussion Wilson's summing up concluded that the Cabinet was narrowly in favour of withdrawal by March 1971. Brown then demanded that the decision not be publicly announced, which Wilson rightly rejected as impossible. Instead it was agreed that Brown and Thomson should visit Washington, the Gulf and Commonwealth countries in the Far

East, and in discussion stick to the 1971 date. If this provoked a violent reaction in any area the Cabinet might think again.

The Cabinet immediately moved on to discuss the future of the F-111 fighter-bomber which Britain was buying from the United States. They were originally bought for the East of Suez role and were never intended to be based in Europe but, according to Healey and the defence chiefs, they were now essential for the defence of Europe. Healey also argued that the savings from cancelling the order would be small, perhaps only £350 million over ten years. Again the opposition argued that the planes had to go for psychological and political reasons. After two hours of debate Wilson summed up that the Cabinet was narrowly in favour of cancellation (there was one vote in it) but they would look at the subject again.

The discussion was resumed a week later after the Foreign Secretary had returned, jetlagged and only semi-coherent from a round-the-world tour. Brown said bluntly he had come from 'a bloody unpleasant meeting in Washington this morning with Rusk' (Secretary of State). In Rusk's view Britain was 'opting out', it was the 'end of an era'. He had also complained of 'the acrid aroma of *fait accompli*'. Brown reported that the United States was worried not by the Far East, where they thought they were winning in Vietnam (this was a month before the devastating Tet offensive that demonstrated the fragility of the American position after years of effort), but by the Gulf, where they wanted no announcement made. Callaghan intervened and spoke of his worries for the future if the United States was giving up on Britain. This prompted Jenkins to remark:

> The Home Secretary and I have a fundamentally different approach. He wants us to continue as we have done for the past three years. I don't believe we can afford to do so.

Then Wilson made a significant intervention. Surprisingly he swept aside American objections, pointing out that the United States didn't consult Britain before taking action; they looked after their own interests and Britain must do the same. A final decision was postponed till the next day when Thomson was due to return from the Gulf.

Again the discussion moved on to the F-111. This time Healey was confident of victory by one vote, having earlier persuaded Longford to change sides. There were no new arguments but there was increasing recognition of the need to balance the package.

Cledwyn Hughes changed sides to support cancellation and Gordon-Walker announced that after the education decisions he too favoured cancellation. Healey lost by eleven votes to nine without Wilson voting (he too favoured cancellation).[16]

On 15 January the last of six Cabinet meetings in ten days heard another plea from Thomson, after his trip to the Gulf, to postpone the withdrawal by a year to 1972. This started another two-hour discussion. Some ministers were beginning to waver under prolonged pressure from Brown, Callaghan, Healey and Thomson, when Wilson again intervened to rally support for early withdrawal. He took the unusual step of circulating two telegrams he had received from President Johnson threatening retaliation for cancelling the F-111. Wilson said he wasn't worried and that Britain should look after its own interests. The Cabinet reacted against this overt American pressure and when Wilson suggested a compromise date of the end of 1971 the battle was essentially over. Brown and Healey said they would have to consider resigning but nobody believed they were serious. A few desultory attempts were made to reopen decisions that had already been taken but ministers were scared that if one change was made the whole package would come unstuck, so they agreed to stop any further discussion.

Wilson announced the complete package of expenditure cuts on 16 January. Originally he had been content for Jenkins to do so but he became so alarmed at the favourable publicity Jenkins was getting in the papers that he took on the task himself. The cuts amounted to £716 million and were a fundamental reappraisal of government policy. In the social field central commitments, such as 500,000 homes a year and the raising of the school-leaving age, were abandoned and initiatives from the early days of power, such as the abolition of prescription charges, reversed. The withdrawal from East of Suez, the withdrawal of all aircraft carriers from the Royal Navy and the cancellation of the F-111 were equally important in the strategic field, and marked the end of the slow retreat from Empire.

Although the Cabinet had managed to construct a package that balanced cuts in social expenditure and defence spending, it was hardly a well-managed exercise. Once again the amount of time for decisions was short because of self-imposed deadlines. There was virtually no discussion of alternative strategies or options for spending cuts. At the end of the process the package was almost identical to the one first presented by Jenkins. The most important feature of the Cabinet's discussions was Wilson's change of attitude. For three years he had worked closely with the right-wing ministers who held all the key posts in the field of defence and foreign policy, and had gone along with American policy. Now he broke with them, and supported withdrawal from East of Suez and the F-111 cancellation, even in the face of opposition from Washington. The explanation for his turn-round lies in domestic political considerations. After devaluation he had to show that the government was not in a dead end but that a new departure in policy was possible. He also knew that his own position was under threat. He turned away from his old allies on policy, Brown, Healey, Callaghan and Thomson, who were his opponents personally. He built a new alliance with Jenkins, thus splitting his right-wing opponents, and moved towards some of his old friends on the left. After the row over South African arms he was even less willing to side with the right-wing group which had tried to defeat him.

The last scene of the post-devaluation drama was played out in March 1968 when Jenkins introduced the most deflationary Budget ever in peacetime. During the public expenditure discussions in January some ministers had urged Jenkins to introduce a stiff budget immediately so as to have the maximum public impact but he pleaded lack of time. By increasing taxation by over £900 million the Budget was intended to stop the expected 2% rise in private expenditure in 1968 and 1969, and turn it into a 1% fall in living standards. Selective Employment Tax was increased by 50% and betting tax doubled. Duties on petrol, wines, spirits and tobacco all went up as did purchase tax. There was also a special direct levy for one year on all incomes above £3000 in addition to income and surtax. There was no dissent in Cabinet or among Labour MPs to the drastic measures proposed by Jenkins. Like the January package, the March Budget demonstrated the seriousness of the economic crisis, and how determined and ruthless the government was prepared to be in order somehow to get back on the road to recovery.

PART
FOUR

DISASTERS
AND
RECOVERY

JANUARY 1968–JUNE 1970

The Cabinet

(January 1968)

Prime Minister	Harold Wilson
First Secretary	Michael Stewart
Lord President of the Council and Leader of the House of Commons	Richard Crossman
Lord Chancellor	Lord Gardiner
Lord Privy Seal and Leader of the House of Lords	Lord Shackleton
Chancellor of the Exchequer	Roy Jenkins
Foreign Secretary	George Brown
Home Secretary	James Callaghan
Agriculture, Fisheries and Food	Fred Peart
Commonwealth Relations Office	George Thomson
Defence	Denis Healey
Education and Science	Patrick Gordon-Walker
Housing and Local Government	Anthony Greenwood
Labour	Ray Gunter
Power	Richard Marsh
Scottish Office	William Ross
Department of Economic Affairs	Peter Shore
Technology	Tony Benn
Board of Trade	Anthony Crosland
Transport	Barbara Castle
Welsh Office	Cledwyn Hughes

Change on 16 March 1968

First Secretary of State at the Foreign Office	Michael Stewart

George Brown resigned.

Changes on 6 April 1968

First Secretary of State at Department of Employment and Productivity	Barbara Castle
Agriculture, Fisheries and Food	Cledwyn Hughes
Power	Ray Gunter
Transport	Richard Marsh
Welsh Office	George Thomas

Education and Science   Edward Short
Lord Privy Seal
and Leader of the House of Commons   Fred Peart
Paymaster General
and Leader of the House of Lords   Lord Shackleton
Patrick Gordon-Walker resigned.

Change on 1 July 1968

Power   Roy Mason
Ray Gunter resigned.

Changes on 17–18 October and 1 November 1968

Secretary of State for Social
Services   Richard Crossman
Minister without Portfolio   George Thomson
Lord President of the Council
and Leader of the House of Commons   Fred Peart
Lord Privy Seal
and Leader of the House of Lords   Lord Shackleton
Chief Secretary to the Treasury   John Diamond
Paymaster-General   Judith Hart

Changes on 6 October 1969

Chancellor of the Duchy of Lancaster   George Thomson
Minister without Portfolio   Peter Shore
Secretary of State for
Local Government and Regional
Planning   Anthony Crosland
Board of Trade   Roy Mason
Anthony Greenwood and Judith Hart left the Cabinet whilst
retaining ministerial posts. Richard Marsh resigned.

19
The Politics
of Disaster and Recovery

By the autumn of 1967, eighteen months into its second term, the Labour government was already in deep political trouble. The Conservatives were well ahead in the opinion polls and Labour was losing by-elections on swings of 18%. The government was therefore in a weak position to withstand the disasters still to come in the next eighteen months. Despite Wilson's rhetoric that devaluation marked a new departure, the general mood of the electorate was one of disillusion. But the government still had at least three years before an election and with its majority of 100 it was not going to lose power, however many by-elections were lost. The mood within the party was one of grim determination after the sacrifice of so many cherished goals. The only course was to slog on and hope for economic recovery, and with it better political fortune.

Devaluation and its aftermath also affected Wilson's personal prestige both in the country and among his colleagues. The level of satisfaction with his performance as registered in the opinion polls plunged from 69% in May 1966 to 33% in January 1968 (only Eden at the time of Suez had been lower) and ministers were speculating about his successor. Wilson was convinced at the end of 1967 that a right-wing group led by Callaghan and Healey was plotting to remove him. They were, he believed, intriguing with the City and members of the establishment (led by Lord Mountbatten) who wanted to see a National Government, formed from all parties and a number of 'non-political' individuals. The *Daily Mirror*, under the egocentric rule of Cecil King, was running a strong anti-Wilson campaign. Even Wilson's old friend Crossman was losing faith in him and trying to get closer to Jenkins, the man he regarded as his likely replacement, but over dinner at the end of May 1968 Jenkins suggested that Crossman should become the new leader as the compromise between left and right. Not surprisingly all this activity only reinforced Wilson's paranoia. He was deeply suspicious of most of the Cabinet as he told Castle in February: 'Do you really think there is anyone of them I can trust?'[1]

There were also major changes in the power structure within the

Cabinet, particularly in the inner circle of ministers. Until devaluation the three strongest members in the government had been Wilson, Callaghan and Brown. July 1966 had marked the end of their dominance of economic policy making, to be replaced by a bilateral relationship between Callaghan and Wilson, although Brown as Foreign Secretary had remained a key member of the inner group. After devaluation Callaghan moved out of the inner circle, and at the Home Office was to spend much of his time improving his relations with the parliamentary party and the trade unions. The key relationship on economic policy was now between Wilson and Jenkins. Although Jenkins was a long-term rival to Wilson, in the short term they both had a vested interest in a successful economic policy. Brown's resignation in March 1968 marked the end of the old power structure that had lasted since 1964.

The period between devaluation and the 1970 election falls into three phases. The first lasted till the autumn of 1968 when the government appeared to be recovering from the worst effects of devaluation. The second phase, which began with the economic crisis measures in November 1968, marked the worst period for the government. Their popularity declined sharply again and they plunged into a series of disastrous internal arguments over legislation on industrial relations. With the Cabinet and the PLP badly divided, and the TUC hostile, Wilson's leadership was at stake. Only a humiliating climbdown, the institution of a collective leadership and an 'inner Cabinet' preserved his position. The last phase began in the late summer of 1969 and saw a steady recovery in the government's standing and the decision to hold an early election in June 1970 in an attempt to benefit from a sudden lead in the opinion polls.

I. DISILLUSION: JANUARY 1968–OCTOBER 1968

Devaluation was an obvious signal of the failure of the government's economic policy for the previous three years. Labour support in the opinion polls fell to an all-time low of about 21% in May 1968 (compared with 48% at the 1966 election). On 28 March they lost three seats at by-elections. Overall the swing to the Conservatives was about 18% but the most devastating result was at Dudley, George Wigg's old seat, which he had held since 1945. It was lost on a swing of 21% and even more worrying for Labour this was caused not just by abstentions from their supporters but by a substantial increase in the Conservative vote since March 1966. At the beginning of May came the local election results, which demonstrated the scale of disenchantment throughout the country. Labour lost control of Sheffield and Sunderland for the first time since 1945, and even lost overall control of Glasgow. In London they were left controlling just four boroughs out of thirty-two. They lost control of the Inner London Education Authority and the Conservatives even won such Labour strongholds as Islington and Hackney. Altogether Labour lost about 600 seats, leaving them in their worst position since 1945.

As we have seen, George Brown resigned countless times from the government, often two or three times in the course of a single meeting, but only once – in July 1966 – had this been serious. Then he had been talked out of going by appeals to his loyalty to the party. Relations between him and Wilson, always bad, reached their lowest point at the end of 1967 over arms sales to South Africa. The final breakthrough came not on some great issue of principle but over the way in which decisions were taken in the government.

After devaluation pressure on the American dollar had increased. On 14 March the United States asked Britain to close the London Gold Pool on the next day while a weekend conference of central bankers worked out a new scheme for funding the international monetary system. The first indications that the London Gold Pool might have to be closed did not come until 6 pm London time and the American request was finally received at 10.40 pm. Meanwhile the Treasury and the Bank of England had decided that they wanted to close the foreign exchanges as well, so as to reduce any pressure on the pound. This required a Bank Holiday to be declared, which itself required an Order-in-Council, which could only be authorised by a meeting of the Privy Council. Wilson started to get together an *ad hoc* group of ministers at No 10 to take the necessary decisions before a meeting of the Privy Council at the Palace. Wilson says that he tried to find Brown but without success. Brown says that he was at the Commons or his official residence in Carlton Gardens. There was no attempt to call the Cabinet together.

Rumours were sweeping through Whitehall and Westminster about what was happening, including the idea that a second devaluation was underway. By the time Wilson was on his way to the Palace Brown had convened his own *ad hoc* group of ministers in the Commons, none of whom knew what was going on. Eventually Brown spoke to Wilson on the telephone and demanded that he come down to the Commons and explain what was happening.

317

Wilson furiously accused Brown of forming a cabal and refused to be ordered to attend a meeting. Later the discontented ministers went to No 10 to see Wilson. Many like Stewart and Crosland were appalled at the way decisions were being taken but it was Brown who finally lost his temper, shouting at Wilson:

> Look, it's pretty obvious that you want my resignation, and, brother, if this is the way you are going to run affairs, you can have it . . . Well, you've asked for it, you've got it, and I'm going.[2]

He walked out of No 10 and pointedly sat on the back benches when a statement was made in the Commons at 3.20 am.

This sort of incident had happened many times before and no doubt Brown thought that once again differences would be patched up. The next day he wanted to withdraw his resignation and tried continually to get in touch with Wilson, who remained incommunicado. At 6 pm on 15 March he sent a letter to Wilson which the latter chose to interpret as a resignation letter and Brown finally quit at 10.30 that night. He says he resigned

> on a matter of fundamental principle . . . decisions were being taken over the heads and without the knowledge of Ministers.[3]

This decision to quit over the mechanics of government was just the action that Wilson needed to get rid of Brown in the most propitious circumstances. It was an issue that could not be exploited against Wilson in any coherent way and he was determined not to give Brown a second chance. But Brown too was ready to go. After the row over South African arms he knew that he had no political future, and he had enlisted the help of Vic Feather of the TUC to try and find him a job. Eventually Courtaulds offered up to £7500 a year for a 'consultancy'. His resignation came within a month of the offer.

When Brown resigned Wilson moved Michael Stewart to the Foreign Office for the second time. Stewart obtained a promise that he would not be moved again before the end of the administration and although Healey was to press very hard for the job, Wilson stuck to his promise. But Wilson was beginning to think of a major reconstruction of the government. His aim was clear:

> For the first time I can get rid of the people I took over in the Shadow Cabinet. When I became leader I only had one person in the Parliamentary Committee who had voted for me and when I formed my first Cabinet in 1964 it contained only two or three . . .

who were my supporters. The rest were opponents. Now I shall be strong and need not worry about any debt I owe to my enemies.[4]

Wilson's plan was to promote two of his old friends, Crossman and Castle, into key jobs. Crossman was to head a combined Ministry of Health and Social Security. He was also to take over the honorific title, previously held by George Brown, of First Secretary of State. Wilson was to give up his short-lived control of DEA, which would be left with Peter Shore, and Castle was to be in charge of a revamped Ministry of Labour that would take over the prices and incomes responsibilities of DEA. As Wilson put it: 'Barbara is to be the new inspiration . . . She's to make the whole difference by taking over relations with the trade unions.'[5] Castle was not enthusiastic about Wilson's idea of a new-style Ministry of Labour because it would not have enough status to ensure her place in any inner Cabinet. The problem was resolved when Crossman magnanimously agreed to give up the title of First Secretary. Castle was also worried about the consequences for her career:

> I am under no illusions that I may be committing political suicide. I have moved from the periphery of the whirlwind into its very heart.[6]

Castle's fears were proved by subsequent events to be better founded than Wilson's hopes.

Wilson then concentrated on other changes. Healey turned down a move to a combined Ministry of Technology and Power, and Ray Gunter moved under protest from Labour to Power. (He was never reconciled to leaving the Ministry of Labour and all his trade union friends, and he eventually resigned at the end of June.) Castle tried to get her deputy, the left-wing Stephen Swingler, promoted to Transport but Wilson refused because MI5 regarded him as a security risk. The dull but reliable Wilson supporter, Fred Peart, took over Crossman's job as Leader of the Commons and Wilson also got another long-time supporter, George Thomas, into the Cabinet as Welsh Secretary. The only casualty of the reshuffle was Gordon-Walker, who was sacked as Education Secretary. Wilson tried to pretend, using Crossman's phrase, that this was the Mark-II Wilson government. He had indeed begun with grandiose ideas about sacking his 'enemies' but had failed once again to be ruthless.

During the early stages of the reshuffle Wilson reassured his friends that he was going to create an 'inner Cabinet' to direct strategy. What emerged was the 'Parliamentary Committee' which first met at the end of April. It consisted of eight ministers (over a third of the Cabinet) – Wilson, Stewart, Gardiner, Healey, Jenkins, Peart, Castle and Crossman. It never functioned as a real 'inner Cabinet' and rarely discussed strategy, let alone directed it. It did meet regularly each week, though, but only to review relations with the parliamentary party and the NEC.

In the spring and summer of 1968 politics went very quiet. There were no great issues and no major developments after the government forced through the bill to withdraw the right of Kenyan Asians to enter Britain and introduced the March Budget. The government's standing, although still poor, began to improve slightly. Although the Conservatives gained Nelson and Colne in a by-election at the end of June, the swing was only 11%, half that of the dark days in March. The Caerphilly result in July showed that Labour could just hold the seat against the Plaid Cymru challenge and, although the nationalist vote had risen from 11% in 1966 to 40%, what seemed to be an inexorable rise after the Carmarthen by-election a year earlier was halted. This recovery continued through the summer (normally a good time for all governments with Parliament and politics in recess). By October the Conservative lead in the opinion polls was back into single figures. At the end of the month Labour held on to Bassetlaw by 740 votes (when a swing of just over 11% would have ensured defeat). Altogether the government could begin to feel that the worst might be over and that further recovery could be expected.

II. THE NADIR: NOVEMBER 1968–AUGUST 1969

Throughout 1968 the economic situation remained grim. By the autumn it was clear that the balance of payments deficit for the year would be about £300 million – the same as 1967. Before the Bassetlaw by-election at the end of October the Cabinet decided that more economic measures were required but agreed to postpone a package to a more propitious political date. It was announced at the end of November and included a scheme for import deposits together with even tougher hire purchase controls. The psychological impact was enormous. All the tough measures taken earlier in the year seemed to have had no effect. A year after devaluation the balance of payments was just as bad. The government's economic policy appeared to be leading nowhere.

The effect was to wipe out the tentative recovery in the government's standing. The Conservative lead in the opinion polls leapt from 7% to over 20% in a month and by early 1969 to 25%. Although this lead was to fall fairly steadily until the summer, it remained well over 10% until August. The same pattern was reflected in by-elections where swings of over 15% to the Conservatives became standard. The local elections in May (which were limited in scale) showed a slight Labour recovery from the depths of 1968 but they were still the second worst result since 1945.

The government's legislative programme was also soon in trouble. The centrepiece for the 1968–69 session was a bill to reform the House of Lords. The Conservatives refused to assist its passage, even though it incorporated the recommendations of an all-party committee, and an unholy alliance of left-wing Labour MPs who preferred total abolition and Conservative members who wanted no reform ensured that little progress was made in the Commons. By April 1969 the government accepted that it could not force the bill through. Instead it decided to withdraw it and concentrate on passing a bill to increase its powers to intervene in industrial relations. This led to a full-scale revolt by the trade unions, Labour MPs and eventually the Cabinet. The government was openly divided, with Jim Callaghan leading a fight against the proposals. It only ended in surrender by Wilson and Castle, the main architect of the proposals, and acceptance of the TUC's terms.

In 1960 Wilson had fought Gaitskell for the leadership on the basis of standing behind Labour Party Conference decisions. Yet in power Wilson failed to practise what he had once preached. His government was to see an unprecedented level of revolt against government policy by the party conference, and a whole series of conference votes were simply ignored by the government. The first signs of revolt were apparent in 1966 when the government lost a vote on the level of military expenditure and support for the United States on Vietnam. (The latter was repeated in 1967.) This was the first time a Labour government had been defeated on a defence or foreign policy issue at the conference. Further defeats followed on policy towards Greece after the Colonels' coup, on support for the Nigerian federal government in the civil war and also on Rhodesia. How far the government had drifted away from its supporters became evident in the last two years of its life when it suffered major defeats on a wide range of domestic policies. For example, in 1968 the government was defeated on wages policy, fuel policy, benefit policy and reintroduction of prescription charges. (The latter was on a show of hands with nobody prepared to support the government.)

Wilson and others in the government felt that there were electoral gains to be made if they ignored – and were seen to ignore – the party conference. Wilson was always inclined to appeal to the country as a national leader presenting Labour as the 'natural party of government'. To party supporters the picture was different. The optimistic mood of 1964 and 1966 was gone. They felt betrayed by the government they had worked to elect. Many thought that it was difficult to tell the difference between Labour government policies and those of the Conservatives. The long-term trend of falling individual membership of the party was accelerated in this period: numbers fell from 600,000 to 300,000 between 1964 and 1970.

A similar trend of rising anti-government feeling was apparent on the National Executive Committee by 1968. This was partly because the number of ministers on the Committee fell from fifteen in 1965 to ten in 1968, but it also reflected the feeling of disenchantment and sense of betrayal evident at the party conference. It was to reach its climax at the end of March 1969 when the NEC refused to support the government's policy on the trade .unions (with Callaghan voting against his own government and two junior ministers abstaining).

These internal disputes within the Labour movement helped to create a public image of division and strife. They were a high price to pay for the attempt to appear as a 'national' government, especially when that attempt was being undermined by real doubts about its competence and strategy.

The worst time for Wilson came at the end of April 1969 when the government was in acute difficulty. Labour MPs had been in open revolt over the bill to reform the Lords. That bill had just been abandoned but the government had decided instead to rush through before the summer recess a bill to reform industrial relations and impose legal penalties on the trade unions. Many in the Cabinet felt that this bill should be forced through in order to demonstrate that the government was in control. But the Whips were increasingly worried that backbench MPs would not support this legislation. A large section of the parliamentary party felt that Labour was going to lose the next election and saw no point in tearing the party apart when the Conservatives had plans to legislate in this area anyway. Discipline in the party was beginning to break down. After the refusal to support legislation to reform the Lords, fifty-five backbenchers voted against the White Paper on trade union reform (and forty abstained), and then forty abstained on the Defence White Paper. Many MPs were disillusioned with Wilson, whose deft political touch and tactical brilliance seemed to have deserted him totally. A group was collecting signatures to try and force a leadership vote in the parliamentary party. The Chairman of the PLP, Douglas Houghton, who was working closely with Callaghan in opposition to the Industrial Relations Bill, did little to stop moves to replace Wilson.

A large number of ministers felt that the government was in danger of disintegrating and Wilson with it. Even Wilson himself was talking in Cabinet as though the Conservatives would be in power in the early 1970s. On 29 April Crossman and Castle went to see him to discuss the menacing situation. He appeared to recognise its gravity, speaking of the 'disintegration' of the party. He even talked of introducing an 'Inner' Cabinet. He mentioned that John Silkin was going to be sacked as Chief Whip after the failure of his liberal attitude to internal party discipline but significantly did not tell them who was to replace him. That afternoon Bob Mellish, a tough working-class machine politician from Bermondsey, was appointed Chief Whip. This seemed to presage a new hard approach to force through the Industrial Relations Bill with the possibility of expulsion from the party for those who would not toe the line. Castle, who was in charge of the bill and a strong believer from her Bevanite days in a liberal disciplinary regime, was furious; both she and Crossman felt betrayed by Wilson. They realised that Wilson had known of Mellish's appointment but had not had the courage to tell them. Castle said bitterly: 'I'm through with Harold now . . . Henceforth I dedicate myself to his destruction' and they both agreed he had to go. But they had no positive solutions to suggest, as Castle put it: 'I am now looking for an excuse to extricate myself.' That evening Castle wrote a blistering letter that put her on the brink of resignation. She told Wilson:

> If the strategy is to railroad my Bill through Parliament by a Healey-type restrictive discipline of the Left, I will have no part of it.[7]

They met again the following day but there was no reconciliation because Castle remained convinced that Wilson had twice lied to her about Silkin's departure and Mellish's appointment. She remarked that 'I am now really frightened at Harold's state.'[8]

The next morning Wilson, for the only time in the government, was too ill to attend Cabinet. The explanations vary. Wilson says it was food poisoning, Castle thought it was psychosomatic and Crossman attributed it to a bad hangover. That evening Crossman and Castle were summoned to No 10. Crossman was shocked at what he saw:

for the first time since I have known him, Harold was frightened and unhappy, unsure of himself, needing his friends. The great india-rubber, unbreakable, undepressable Prime Minister was crumpled in his chair . . . he was injured, broken, his confidence gone, unhappy, wanting help.[9]

Wilson was in deep trouble. The Cabinet was split; Callaghan was leading a group opposed to the government's policies, and he was also doing little to stop speculation about his ambition to be Prime Minister. The backbenchers were in revolt and the prospect of Wilson being overthrown was openly discussed. Now by his own actions he had virtually alienated his two closest friends and colleagues. Crossman and Castle rallied round and spent the whole evening trying to convince him that he had to have a firm inner group in the Cabinet and that he must trust other ministers, particularly his friends, and stop trying to divide his colleagues against each other. They managed to raise Wilson's morale and he was soon able to make a joking reference in a speech – 'They say I'm going – well I'm going on.' There were difficult days ahead but Wilson's self-confidence was restored. However, the crisis did have a real impact. Wilson finally gave in and created an 'Inner Cabinet'. Apart from himself it consisted of Stewart, Jenkins, Crossman, Castle, Healey and Callaghan. The row over trade union reform led to Callaghan being excluded for a while, later Crosland and Benn were added. The way the government worked was fundamentally altered: a more 'collective' style of leadership was introduced and crucial decisions were genuinely taken by the inner group. Wilson was no longer the dominant figure he had been in the early years of the government.

III. RECOVERY: AUGUST 1969–JUNE 1970

From the spring of 1969 onwards it became increasingly clear that the balance of payments was at last beginning to improve. By the end of the year there was a huge surplus of £440 million. The government had staked virtually everything on putting the balance of payments right at whatever cost and their efforts were bearing fruit. Their political fortunes improved in line with better economic news. Perhaps surprisingly the internecine warfare in the Cabinet over the Industrial Relations Bill and the final acceptance of the TUC's position at the end of June had no effect on the government's standing. The first signs of a political recovery came in August and September when the Conservative lead in the opinion polls fell from around 20% to about 10%. By the end of the year their lead was well down into single figures. At the end of October five by-elections were held on the same day. The Inner Cabinet was braced for a series of Conservative gains but the average swing was held to 11% and there were none. Although there was obviously some way to go before an election victory looked possible ministers felt that the results were good enough to justify some optimism but not good enough to induce complacency. On that basis they were fairly happy.

At the end of July 1969 Wilson began to think about a final reshuffle before the election. His first idea was to move Barbara Castle from the Department of Employment and Productivity after the trauma of the battle with the TUC. Castle, her political reputation already badly bruised, wanted to stay on and not be seen to run away. Wilson then decided to put off any changes to the autumn. Two pressures were pushing him towards a reorganisation of the government and Whitehall. There was the influence of Sir William Armstrong, the Head of the Civil Service, who was a great believer in the virtues of large departments. And Wilson himself saw this as a useful way of removing people that he didn't like.

Wilson's original aim was to get rid of Callaghan, Crosland, Hart, Shore, Marsh and Greenwood. As usual his achievement was to fall short of his aspirations. Callaghan could not be sacked after his superficially successful handling of the Ulster problem in August. Crosland was eventually given the new ministry that combined Housing and Transport and was to form the embryo Department of the Environment. But he was left in a relatively powerless position and, as Wilson put it, 'It will stop him meddling so much in economics.'[10] The DEA was finally abolished but Shore was made minister without portfolio and not sacked. Judith Hart was moved out of the Cabinet to Overseas Development. Dick Marsh, by now disliked by many of his colleagues, was sacked. Greenwood stayed where he was but left the Cabinet and became one of Crosland's junior Ministers. One unintended casualty was Kenneth Robinson who remarked:

Harold explained to me that he expected Greenwood to resign when he was demoted but as he didn't I had to go.[11]

As the election approached ministers' minds were concentrated, as always, on winning votes. From 1969 example after example illustrates how far into policy making this effort percolated. The jurisdiction of the Ombudsman was extended and the Central Wales railway line was saved from closure. In July 1969 the Cabinet discussed BBC finances. The BBC needed an increase in the licence fee to start local radio and save all their orchestras. The Cabinet was not prepared to increase the licence fee so close to an election but didn't want any cutbacks either. The Cabinet's view was summarised by Crossman thus:

> Our crucial time-table as a Government was the next twelve months and we shouldn't let anybody else's dreams conflict with it . . . We would simply postpone the increase in the licence fee until 1971, after the election. Wilson was saying that we would demand that the BBC should do everything but we wouldn't give them the means to do it, and that was carried.[12]

In October the Cabinet had to decide on the legislative programme for the session before the election. The main items for the Queen's Speech were bills on pensions and nationalising the docks. The programme was deliberately overloaded, as one participant remarked:

> on the whole it is clear that we have got an electioneering speech. Things are being packed in that we can't possibly carry through even if we run into next October.[13]

In other areas it was necessary to put off difficult decisions. In November the Cabinet discussed the state of negotiations on entry to the EEC. The pace was slow but might have to be slower, as Wilson admitted:

> Anyway, we can ensure that the election comes first before anything gets embarrassing.[14]

In February 1970 it was the problem of pay for the armed forces, nurses, teachers and post office workers. All of the claims were inflationary and Jenkins was worried about the possibility of emergency economic measures in July upsetting the election timescale. Wilson insisted they look at the problem politically, as Barbara Castle described:

> Timing was the essence of our problem . . . we should aim to postpone the results of some of these claims as far as we could: he would rather win the Election and have a November Budget than have July measures and lose the Election . . . it was all pretty crude.[15]

326

After the rows in June over trade union reform ministers were now united, their minds concentrated on the task ahead. Unlike 1966 Wilson did not have the final say over election timing and tactics. His prestige had not recovered from the battering of the previous three years and all the crucial decisions were taken by the Inner Cabinet. Their first discussion came at the beginning of September 1969 at Chequers. No firm conclusions were drawn but ministers were optimistic, feeling that they could win and that the issue would turn on basic problems like prices, mortgages and unemployment. Although the economy was beginning to pick up there was general opposition to any expansionist pre-election boom. The feeling was that the government's reputation was so tied to sound finance, prudence and priority to the balance of payments that they couldn't suddenly change policy without looking too obviously opportunist. The discussion was resumed in the Inner Cabinet on 14 January. Jenkins was more optimistic about the state of the economy but the outlines of the Labour campaign were already clear and it was agreed that they would 'only be able to go to the country on a policy of sanity, steady recovery and moderation'.[16] This stance was made easier by the drift of the Conservative party towards a more abrasive, market-orientated economics exemplified at the Selsdon Park Conference at the beginning of the year.

Two months later on 8 March the Inner Cabinet discussed the situation again. Wilson first asked all of them to state a preference for a date, which was coming down to a choice between June and October. Five (Peart, Crossman, Stewart, Crosland and Castle) were firmly for October. Callaghan and Jenkins wanted to put the party organisation on notice for June but continue to plan for October. Healey and Benn preferred June but were happy to wait. Shore was the only one unequivocally in favour of June. Two months earlier Wilson had been strongly for October but now his views were beginning to change. He was worried about the possibility of a strong Conservative campaign in October or a run on the pound organised by the City. With the timing unresolved the group then discussed what would be their issues for the campaign. Jenkins said their main achievement was the balance of payments surplus and the image of competence. Callaghan, Crosland and Shore all agreed with this assessment. Others, in particular Castle and Crossman, had doubts about this approach and wanted some more attractive economic measures in the Budget. Wilson summed up in favour of Jenkins' line. The March Budget should be cautious to form a firm base for an election in June; if the election were

327

postponed until October then it might be possible to take some expansionary measures after the Budget.

At the end of March the Inner Cabinet was optimistic after the South Ayrshire by-election suggested there was nationally only a small gap between Labour and the Conservatives. The message from the local elections in London in April, however, was different. The Conservatives kept control of the GLC but their majority was reduced from sixty-four to thirty and Labour regained control of ILEA. The results suggested a swing to the Conservatives of about 7–10% since 1966, enough to give them an easy victory in a general election. A week later the Inner Cabinet had more or less decided that the election would be in October and backbench Labour MPs were also in favour of the later date.

Within three weeks there was a complete about turn and a hurried decision to go for a snap election. By the end of April Labour moved ahead in the opinion polls for the first time for three years. At the Inner Cabinet meeting on 29 April Wilson opened with a twenty-five-minute disquisition on possible dates, touching on the South African cricket tour, Wakes Weeks, Coventry shutdown week and the World Cup. His conclusion was that it had to be either the third week of June or else October. He was worried that Labour couldn't stay ahead until October and was attracted by June. Other members' views were changing too. Peart and Stewart now favoured June, Callaghan was confident of victory on either date but now he too favoured June. Crossman and Castle were becoming isolated as the only October supporters. Jenkins asked for another week to think. When discussion resumed on 4 May he saw little problem in going on until October and again no decision was taken.

The crucial factor in tipping the balance was the local elections on 9 May. Just as Wilson had predicted back in 1967, the large Conservative gains of that year were largely wiped out with Labour gaining 443 seats. This suggested a Labour majority at the election of about fifty. On 12 May Gallup gave Labour a 7% lead and the day after that the NOP poll showed a 3½% Labour lead. The Inner Cabinet met on 14 May to take the final decision. Wilson, who had already started to discuss ways of winding up the parliamentary session early, now claimed that he had favoured June for the last month. In his judgement the polls were satisfactory, the local election results better than anticipated and he expected to win with a majority of about twenty. He then went round the table forcing each member to state their views, saying he wanted no one to be able to claim they had favoured October if it all went wrong. There was no dissent from Wilson's analysis. The Inner Cabinet then agreed that no formal decision would be taken until after the joint Cabinet-NEC session on 17 May in order to avoid the NEC helping to write the manifesto. On 18 May the Cabinet agreed to a June election and an announcement was made immediately that polling would be on 18 June.

At its last meeting the Inner Cabinet decided their election campaign strategy. They agreed that any 'wild ideas' should be excluded from the manifesto and that 'it would be psychologically wrong to fight on new promises'.[17] As one participant put it, 'If we win this election we shall have a Government with no strategy at all and virtually no policy.'[18] Or as Harold Wilson said, 'We're really asking for a doctor's mandate.'[19] Labour was able to take this approach because the Conservatives had adopted a series of what were seen as more 'radical' ideas. Compared with the later Thatcherite policies they were fairly mild: Heath promised to reduce taxation by attacking the scale of public expenditure and waste in the public sector. Industrial policy was to be based on a less interventionist strategy with the clear implication that 'lame ducks' would be allowed to collapse. Industrial relations were to be regulated by a legal framework. Despite the vast number of advisory groups that had been working on new policies for the previous three years none of the proposals had been worked out in detail, but they did create the image that the Conservatives wanted to make a break with the past and try a new, more abrasive approach.

The Labour manifesto was presented largely as a catalogue of achievements with few promises for the future. It was defensive in tone and its title, 'Now Britain's Strong – Let's Make it Great to Live in', encapsulated its main themes. Pride of place was given to the achievement of a balance of payments surplus and the need to continue to build a strong economy. What proposals there were for legislation were almost entirely bills that were either in the programme before the election – the new pensions plan, nationalisation of the docks – or ones that had already been announced, such as that to make comprehensive education mandatory. The other proposals were essentially to continue with existing policies. It was dull but in line with the approach that the Inner Cabinet had decided the previous autumn. It contained no hint that there was any underlying philosophy or ideas about what to do during the next five years if Labour did win the election. The Labour campaign, with its emphasis on not selecting an unknown quantity, and playing safe with Labour and Harold Wilson, was to reflect the manifesto. It was a far cry from the hopes expressed in 1964 for radical reform.

20

Immigration, Gerrymandering and Ulster

In its last two years in office the government had to deal with three difficult problems in different areas of home affairs. The first, immigration control, was an emotive political issue where the government had to reconcile two conflicting forces: the political requirement to appease the prejudices of white voters and its desire to maintain a liberal image on racial matters. The second, parliamentary boundaries, was a self-imposed problem brought on by the government's determination to give itself the best chance of winning the 1970 election. The third, Ulster, was an unplanned response to an unexpected situation. All three problems affected the political reputation of Jim Callaghan as Home Secretary.

I. IMMIGRATION AND RACE RELATIONS

One of the immediate problems facing Callaghan on his move to the Home Office in November 1967 was what to do about the thousands of Kenyan Asians who as British passport holders might choose to exercise their automatic right of entry into the UK. The flow of black and Asian immigrants into Britain had been taking place since the late 1940s but it was only in the late 1950s that it first became a sensitive political issue. In 1962 the Conservative government had passed the Commonwealth Immigration Act, which set up a scheme of vouchers to regulate the rate of entry. The Labour party's position had been clear. In 1958 Hugh Gaitskell declared:

> The Labour party is opposed to the restriction of immigration as every Commonwealth citizen has the right as a British subject to enter this country at will. This has been the right of subjects of the Crown for many centuries and the Labour party has always maintained it should be unconditional.

Under increasing public pressure to limit entry this view changed so that by November 1963 Harold Wilson could say, in the Commons, that:

> We do not contest the need for the control of Commonwealth immigration into this country.

Nevertheless Labour was seen as the party that was sympathetic to immigrants and this had its effect in the 1964 election. Not only was Gordon-Walker defeated at Smethwick by a strongly anti-immigrant Conservative candidate (described by Wilson as a 'parliamentary leper') but Labour also lost Birmingham Perry Bar and Eton and Slough on the same issue.

Labour fought the 1964 election on a platform of keeping the 1962 act whilst they negotiated with Commonwealth governments for a system of controls in the country of origin. Accordingly Lord Mountbatten was sent off to India and Pakistan to see whether he could negotiate such an agreement. Ministers knew full well that it would be a nugatory visit but its failure would enable them to press on to the next stage – imposing their own controls. Ministerial discussions on immigration reveal two strong influences at work. The first was political, as the views expressed at the Cabinet Committee on Immigration illustrate:

> Ever since the Smethwick election it has been quite clear that immigration can be the greatest potential vote-loser for the Labour party if we are seen to be permitting a flood of immigrants to come in and blight the central areas in all our cities.[1]

The second factor was simply prejudice. The Home Secretary at this time was Frank Soskice and his view was:

> If we do not have strict immigration rules, our people will soon all be coffee-coloured.[2]

The Immigration Committee spent the first half of 1965 working out a new policy. In June they rejected the idea of a twelve-month moratorium on all immigration, including wives, dependants and children, only because of the problems it might cause at the end of the period. Their final proposals, agreed early in July with virtually no opposition, were published in a White Paper in August once parliament was in recess to try and limit the amount of opposition

331

within the parliamentary party. Unskilled workers without jobs would no longer receive vouchers, the total number of vouchers was to be reduced by 15%, the powers to repatriate immigrants were to be extended and the age for allowing in dependant children reduced from eighteen to sixteen.

In an attempt to try and balance these illiberal measures proposals were simultaneously published for a Race Relations Bill. This proved difficult to draft mainly because Soskice was opposed to any such legislation. The act, when eventually passed, outlawed restrictions on the transfer of rented property on the grounds of race and also outlawed discrimination on racial (but not religious) grounds in public places. The government had originally wanted to make these provisions part of the criminal law but under pressure from the Conservatives instead placed the emphasis on conciliation; only in the last resort could criminal proceedings be brought and then only by the Attorney-General. But whatever its limitations the act did establish the principle that racial discrimination was illegal and set up the Race Relations Board to monitor the situation.

When Kenya was granted independence the Asian minority had been given the right to opt for a British passport and therefore the automatic right of entry into Britain. In July 1965 ministers identified this as a problem but because of the political difficulties involved little detailed work took place. Immigration from Kenya was growing (partly induced by the threat of restrictions) and a campaign for the imposition of strict controls was ironically being run by Duncan Sandys, who as a minister had given the right to a British passport.

In October 1967 Jenkins put an inconclusive paper to the Home Policy Committee. Earlier in the month he had seen Crossman, as Leader of the Commons, to warn him he might need emergency legislation. On the one hand Jenkins' paper acknowledged the possibility of perhaps 50,000 Kenyan Asian immigrants a year (current figures were about 15,000 a year) but on the other it recognised they legally possessed British passports. Jenkins was instructed to work out possible legislation to withdraw the automatic right of entry by invalidating the passports.

Callaghan took over this work when he became Home Secretary at the end of November. Early in February 1968 he presented the draft Bill to the Immigration Committee, which agreed that it should be introduced within a week and pass rapidly through Parliament in an attempt to stop any last-minute rush of immigrants. The Bill (and the Act when passed) arbitrarily invalidated the right of a British passport holder to enter the UK (which, as the Cabinet was told, would have been unconstitutional in any democracy with a written constitution). The Act was also racially discriminatory in that automatic entry to the UK was only retained for British passport holders who had one parent or grandparent born in the UK. This neatly protected the position of most white Commonwealth citizens but excluded the Kenyan Asians, who would be subject to a strict quota on entries. The opportunity was also taken to tighten up other minor but important provisions, so that entry of dependants aged between sixty and sixty-five was prohibited as was entry of children joining single parents.

At the Cabinet there was opposition from George Brown and George Thomson. They reflected their department's advice that there should be at least the façade of consultation first. The Cabinet no doubt felt that it might marginally improve the presentation of the government's solution. The Cabinet agreed that Malcolm Macdonald, their roving High Commissioner in Africa, should go to Kenya for hurried talks. The next week, having heard that President Kenyatta refused any form of cooperation, they agreed to introduce the bill. Jenkins, who had started the process, was now unenthusiastic. He wanted a quota that limited immigration to what it had been before the recent rush to enter but Wilson insisted on a 25% cut below this level. In the Commons the bill produced a storm of protest. When it was rushed through Parliament on a three-line Whip in three days, thirty-five Labour MPs voted against the government. The whole episode badly damaged party morale both within Parliament and outside.

The government tried to make amends by introducing another Race Relations Act in April 1968. This prohibited discrimination in housing, commercial services and employment. It had been strongly opposed by the TUC, CBI and Ray Gunter as Minister of Labour. Its provisions were weak and reflected the lack of enthusiasm for the legislation within the government. In the first instance it relied on conciliation committees in each factory before any complaint could be made to the Race Relations Board. It also introduced the idea of 'racial balance', enabling firms with a high proportion of black employees not to hire any more. A Community Relations Council was established, although its role was unclear, its powers limited and with a budget of only £400,000 a year its activities circumscribed.

Under Callaghan the Home Office had produced much the same mixture as before: stricter controls on immigration and limited provisions to deal with racial discrimination in Britain. Ten years earlier the Labour party had favoured unrestricted immigration as a fundamental right. In power it passed draconian legislation to withdraw the legal entitlement of British passport holders to enter the country and increased the controls on immigration. Although the legislation on racial discrimination was very limited in scope and hardly 'balanced' the immigration proposals, it did at least establish the concept that discrimination could be an offence.

II. GERRYMANDERING PARLIAMENTARY BOUNDARIES

Towards the end of his period at the Home Office Callaghan had to deal with the report of the Commission set up in 1958, with all-party agreement, as an independent mechanism for reviewing and implementing changes to constituency boundaries every fifteen years. Under the 1958 legislation the government was legally bound immediately to lay orders before Parliament implementing the proposals. The Labour government knew, long before the report of the Commission, that its effect would be to benefit the Conservatives by about seventeen seats. (The Commission would abolish seats in the Labour areas of the inner cities as population fell and create new seats in the suburbs and counties.) And they were determined to avoid this outcome before the election. When in the autumn of 1965 Dick Crossman, as Local Government Minister, had come up with the idea of a Royal Commission on Local Government (to reorganise its functions and create entirely new authorities throughout the country) he gained approval from the Cabinet partly on the grounds that this would provide an excuse not to implement the recommendations of the Boundary Commission. The argument to be used in public would be that parliamentary boundaries should follow local government boundaries and this would be impossible if the latter were under review. In 1967, in a series of discussions Crossman, Wilson and Jenkins agreed that 'the right line to take is to let them complete their recommendations and then say that it is absurd to implement all of them pending the local government reform'.[3] Only the boundaries of the twenty or thirty largest seats would be redrawn.

On 12 June 1969 the Cabinet had before it the report of the Boundary Commission with its implications for Labour seats. They had to decide how to handle what one of them called 'this terribly dicey problem'. They decided to stick with their original idea of delaying implementation, clutching before them the fig leaf of the uncompleted work of the Royal Commission on Local Government. This ploy had the additional benefit of allowing implementation of new boundaries in both London and Scotland, where Labour expected to benefit, on the grounds that local government was not being examined there. Callaghan had inherited this scheme but Crossman paid tribute to his grasp of the presentational difficulties involved in the government's proposals:

> Even if we are looking out for party advantage, we want to combine this with moral rectitude and, as you might expect, Jim has done this very nicely.[4]

Callaghan accordingly introduced a bill to stop the implementation of the new boundaries, except the ones the government wanted, and forced it through the Commons on a three-line whip. The Conservatives, equally partisan in wanting the recommendations implemented, were happily able to pose as guardians of the constitution. In the Lords the Conservative majority effectively wrecked the bill by imposing a time limit of three months for the introduction of orders on all the new boundaries. On 24 July the Cabinet discussed how to get round this new obstacle. Callaghan proposed another idea: the Boundary Commission should be reactivated in 1972 to report in 1976 if there was good progress on local government reform; if not, the existing proposals would be introduced in 1972. This was done as one member commented 'as a device for placating the Lords and making us look a bit more respectable'.[5]

The Lords rejected this proposal and although the government could have forced the bill through in the next session, it decided to fall back on another option it had already discussed. Under the terms of the 1958 legislation the government was obliged to lay the orders implementing the new boundries before the Commons. However, the Attorney-General, Elwyn Jones, advised that the agreement did not bind the government to support the passage of the orders. They could therefore fulfil their legal obligation to lay the orders and then use their parliamentary majority to ensure that they were not passed, thereby maintaining the current constituencies. When the Cabinet gratefully accepted the idea Barbara Castle had her doubts:

> Everyone seemed to think this was a very ingenious solution though I am unhappy about the political morality of it.[6]

This was the shabby solution to their difficulties implemented by Callaghan in October 1969. The government therefore finally succeeded in its attempts to safeguard a handful of additional seats at the next election. But the way it had done so did nothing to improve its political reputation or that of the Home Secretary. It departed from an all-party agreement specifically designed to avoid gerrymandering and went to great lengths in its manoeuverings to retain its electoral advantage, including blatant flouting of the spirit if not the letter of the law.

III. ULSTER

Increasingly from the autumn of 1968 on the government was embroiled in the Ulster question, until in August 1969 it was to take the fateful decision to deploy British troops to maintain law and order. It was not a problem they had expected to meet and the Labour party had never developed any coherent policy on the province. The government's reaction to the developing crisis was one of *ad hoc* initiatives made worse by a lack of understanding of the problems they were facing. Ever since the partition of Ireland in 1922 and the establishment of a separate Parliament and government in Northern Ireland, every British government had studiously avoided involvement in the affairs of the province, apart from providing the bulk of the money and a small army garrison. Left to its own devices the Stormont government, which had been expressly set up to maintain the Protestant ascendancy, rapidly developed into a sectarian, oppressive and discriminatory regime. Westminster politicians preferred to avert their eyes from this unedifying spectacle as long as Ulster was reasonably quiet.

The situation began to change in 1967 with the formation of the Civil Rights Association, which was closely modelled on the black civil rights campaign in the United States. It was a movement of middle-class Catholics with only minimal IRA participation. Through a series of mass marches it publicised the state of affairs in the province and pressed its demands for a widespread reform of government, including:

- the end of gerrymandered boundaries that, for example, enabled the Protestants to elect 60% of the councillors in Londonderry, even though they were less than 40% of the population;
- one person, one vote in local elections through abolition of the business vote and enfranchisement of 250,000 people, mainly Catholics, who were excluded;

- laws against discrimination in local government where, for example, the Protestant-controlled Londonderry council employed over 80% Protestant workers;
- the end of the preferential allocation of better housing at lower rents to Protestants;
- repeal of the Special Powers Act which allowed ministers to order indefinite internment without trial, arrest for interrogation, curfews and the prohibition of newspapers and organisations;
- the disbanding of the police reserves known as the 'B-Specials', an all-Protestant force used to maintain control of the Catholic minority.

Although couched in reasonable terms, these demands were, given the peculiar nature of Ulster politics, an open attack on the Protestant ascendancy. The Protestants reacted with increasing violence against the civil rights marches and there was mounting disorder in the province. The Stormont government, under the vaguely liberal but ineffectual leadership of Prime Minister O'Neill, was caught in the middle of conflicting pressures. In 1965 he had begun the almost impossible task of trying to legitimise the Stormont government in the eyes of the Catholics by inviting the Prime Minister of the Irish Republic to a first-ever visit to the North. But every move he made in this direction only alienated more Protestants, both on the streets and in his own Cabinet.

Until 1968 O'Neill had had only four fairly formal discussions with Labour ministers but on 4 November that year came a crucial meeting with Wilson and Callaghan. Wilson was sympathetic to the demands of the Catholics and pushed hard for O'Neill to go further in the reform programme. In return they made their support for O'Neill plain and promised 'a very fundamental reappraisal' of relations if he were overthrown by the hardliners. At the end of the month O'Neill announced a package of reforms including the replacement of the Londonderry Council by a Development Commission, a local government Ombudsman, fairer procedures for allocating public housing and reform of the franchise for local elections.

These reforms proved too much for the extreme Protestants led by Ian Paisley and the Ulster Protestant Volunteers. At the end of November they stopped a civil rights march in Dungannon and in early January 1969 another march was viciously broken up. This led to disturbances in the Catholic Bogside district of Londonderry and the police responded with what was later officially described as a 'police riot'. When O'Neill set up a judicial enquiry into the disturbances a hardline member of his Cabinet, Brian Faulkner, resigned in protest. O'Neill called a general election in an attempt to reassert his authority but found he had miscalculated. A number of anti-O'Neill Unionists were elected and O'Neill himself only just defeated Paisley. Two months later at the end of April, after more riots and counter-violence from the police, O'Neill was ousted in a Cabinet coup and replaced as Prime Minister by Chichester-Clark. Despite the promises made the previous autumn London took no action. The annual Protestant marching season in July and August was now approaching, and the prospects for getting through this period without major civil strife were slim.

Ministers in London had begun to look at the Ulster situation seriously in the autumn of 1968 in a committee comprised of Wilson, Stewart, Callaghan and Healey. They agreed fairly rapidly that although it would be almost impossible to reject a request from the Stormont government to deploy troops to maintain law and order, they should try and avoid that position for as long as possible. (But they did not address how they were going to do this when they had no direct control over events in Ulster.) Ministers also agreed that if troops were deployed they should not be used to maintain the Protestant position or to stop civil rights marches. They were less clear about the rest of their policy in that event. They considered the possibility of an all-party conference and the imposition of direct rule from Westminster (a contingency bill had been drafted by March 1969) but no decisions were taken. Two desultory Cabinet meetings on the subject in late April and early May 1969 produced no clear idea about long-term aims.

One of the major problems facing ministers as they grappled with these problems was their almost complete ignorance of the complexities of Ulster politics. Northern Ireland was the nominal responsibility of the Home Office (as part of the divison that dealt with the Isle of Man and the Channel Islands) but until October 1968 they had not had one civil servant working full time on the subject. Even by the summer of 1969 they only had two. Ministers remained sublimely ignorant of the rituals of the two communities in Ulster. On 12 July 1969 there were large-scale riots in Londonderry after the Protestant marches to commemorate their victory at the Battle of the Boyne. One minister on the Northern Ireland committee commented:

> there had been commotions, on St Patrick's Day, it may have been.[7]

If ministers could not recognise one of the principal dates in the Protestant calendar they obviously had a lot to learn.

Major trouble was now expected during the Apprentice Boys March on 12 August. Wilson and Healey wanted to ban all marches. Callaghan disagreed on the basis that Chichester-Clark told him there would be no trouble, that he would fail if he tried to stop the marches and he didn't have enough police to do so anyway. So ministers braced themselves for trouble and agreed to the issue of CS gas to the RUC, though not the use of army helicopters. The Cabinet was clear about its objective, as Castle reported:

> Harold stressed that our aim must be to keep out the troops at all costs.[8]

But the Cabinet still had no idea how to achieve that aim apart from hoping for the best.

As expected the marches on 12 August produced wholesale civil disorder. It began in Londonderry when, after sporadic violence from the Catholics during the march, the police decided to enter the Bogside. This led to a three-day 'siege' with petrol bombs used against the police and CS gas against the Catholics. By 14 August the police were exhausted and the use of the B-Specials was threatening to turn into intercommunal violence. In the days before the march the Stormont government had negotiated with Callaghan over the conditions under which troops would be used. Stormont wanted them simply to maintain law and order whilst all the other arrangements for an independent government continued. Callaghan made it clear this was impossible and that any extended deployment meant the whole relationship between Stormont and Whitehall would change. No details were given because the government had not decided what it would do.

Late in the afternoon of 14 August Wilson and Callaghan agreed to the deployment of troops in Londonderry following a request from Stormont. Meanwhile rioting was spreading across the province. The worst outbreaks were in Belfast where, despite Chichester-Clark's promise to Callaghan that the police would not be armed, the situation got out of control. The RUC were using machine guns mounted on armoured cars to fire indiscriminately on rioters and the B-specials were also armed. It was the worst intercommunal violence for fifty years, leaving ten dead and 145 injured. British troops from the garrison were deployed on the afternoon of 15 August.

The very situation the government was so anxious to avoid had now occurred. It had to start from scratch and work out what its policy would be. As Callaghan recalled:

> there was not at that stage any real long-term planning: we were living from hand to mouth and making policy as we needed to.[9]

The first task on 19 August was to call hastily together those members of the Cabinet still in London to agree on the demands to be made of Chichester-Clark at a meeting taking place a couple of hours later. Ministers agreed that they would not raise the issue of London taking over direct control of Ulster, partly because they feared the reaction of the Conservatives with their Unionist connections. Instead they preferred to work through the Ulster government whilst making a few cosmetic changes. Wilson was keen to send a full-time minister to the province but Callaghan objected, since he wanted to maintain his own personal control over policy. It was agreed to send a few civil servants instead. Having been forced to deploy troops, now the hope was that they could return to barracks quickly, as Castle reported:

> we were all agreed on our political objectives: we were not going to underwrite a reactionary Government. We had agreed to put in troops to *restore* law and order but not to keep them there indefinitely to *maintain* it.[10]

That, as this and subsequent governments were to find, was easier said than done.

Immediately after the Cabinet meeting Wilson, Callaghan and Healey met Chichester-Clark and other Ulster ministers. Rapid agreement was reached on total control of security measures passing to Whitehall, with the RUC subordinate to the army. (The Protestants could accept this because it increased support for the status quo.) Chichester-Clark reluctantly accepted a new Chief Constable of the RUC from the mainland, and the disarming and disbandment of the B-Specials. But he proved obdurate over Callaghan's suggestion that the Ulster government should be broadened to include some Catholics. (Indeed Chichester-Clark was reluctant to deal with Shirley Williams, Callaghan's deputy at the Home Office, because she was a Catholic.)

At the end of August Callaghan visited Ulster for what, in public relations terms, was a successful visit. Underneath, the situation was still grim. On his return he told the Cabinet that the Ulster government was 'inert', unwilling to change and uncomprehending about the need for change. By 11 September Callaghan, despite his optimistic pronouncements in public, was even more pessimistic, telling his colleagues:

> the prospects were very bleak and he saw no hope of a solution. He had anticipated that the honeymoon wouldn't last very long and it hadn't . . . the only solutions would take years, if they could ever work at all.[11]

During the autumn the government secured small victories over Stormont in abolishing some of the worst features of the Protestant ascendancy. Although there was some amelioration of the Catholics' position, the basic structure of Unionist power remained intact. Indeed with no solution in sight British troops were increasingly seen by the Catholics as supporting Stormont power.

By April 1970 the first Catholic–army confrontations were taking place. In many ways Labour was lucky to lose power in June 1970 before it was obvious that its policy in Northern Ireland led nowhere, and before it had to meet the challenge of the Protestant marching season in July and August, and also contend with the increasing influence and power of the IRA. Within a year the Conservative government had introduced internment in a vain attempt to control the deteriorating security situation; in March 1972 direct rule was assumed from Whitehall.

The Labour government had never expected to be caught up in the tangled sectarian politics of Ulster. It is difficult to see how any government could have reacted differently and in August 1969 it had little alternative but to use the troops, given the scale of the disintegration in the province. Although the idea of abolishing Stormont was rejected, this was not a long-term solution as subsequent governments found. That they actually came out of the episode with their reputation enhanced was largely a matter of luck. The government was perceived as dealing well with the situation but it lost power before the inevitable deterioration took place. Callaghan's reputation too was increased by his public handling of the crisis in August 1969, whereas on both immigration and parliamentary boundaries he suffered some damage from carrying out government policy. The irony is that in both the latter areas his predecessor was closely involved in their preparation. Roy Jenkins' reputation as a liberal Home Secretary would have been severely tarnished if he had not had the good fortune to move to the Treasury at the end of 1967.

21

Patronage and Privilege: Reform of the House of Lords

The 1966 Labour manifesto promised legislation to ensure that the House of Lords lost its power to delay legislation. The Upper House had been stripped of its absolute veto over legislation by the Liberal government in 1911 and its powers of delay were reduced by the Labour government in 1949 to a maximum period of thirteen months. Although the composition of the Lords had been modified in the mid-1950s by the introduction of life peers (a combination of ageing politicians and safe establishment figures) appointed by the Prime Minister, it remained an anachronistic and indefensible institution with a built-in Conservative majority. The way in which that majority was used was subject to unwritten rules. Normally it would not oppose measures in the manifesto on which a Labour government was elected but on other proposals it felt freer to act. Nevertheless it had to use the powers circumspectly; any misuse of them was only likely to increase demands for radical change, or even abolition.

Implementing the manifesto commitment was a matter of political tactics. Any bill to strip the Lords of its remaining delaying powers would probably be defeated in the Lords and therefore take just over a year to become law. There was a risk that during this period the Lords might retaliate and delay key government legislation. Both of these factors pointed towards the need for early action in the session immediately after the election to resolve the situation quickly so that there was still time to pass the government's programme before the next election.

The first discussion in the Cabinet about Lords reform took place at the end of June 1966. Lords Gardiner and Longford submitted a paper arguing that not only should the powers of the Lords be reduced but also its composition should be changed. The idea of full-scale reform raised all sorts of difficult questions. What should happen to hereditary peers, should the government have a guaranteed majority and how should new peers be appointed? The majority of the Cabinet was firmly against any tampering with composition which it recognised as a potential political and constitutional minefield. It preferred to remove the remaining powers of the Lords to delay legislation and leave it as an indefensible but essentially powerless body.

The situation changed once Crossman, as Leader of the House of Commons, was put in charge. The original aim was to develop proposals with the idea of legislating in the 1967–8 session. In June he had backed the majority view in Cabinet but now his fertile brain was becoming obsessed by the idea of complete reform of the Lords. At a meeting with Wilson in April 1967 to discuss tactics he persuaded Wilson in five minutes that it would be best to go for wholesale reform, since it promised the more exciting piece of legislation. They agreed to set up a Cabinet committee (HL) chaired by Crossman. The committee took from June till September to come up with proposals, since many members (now with Lord Gardiner among them) were strongly opposed to altering the composition of the Lords. On 7 September 1967 the Cabinet was asked to reverse its decision taken in June 1966 not to touch composition. Most of the Cabinet were dubious in the extreme but with Wilson strongly backing Crossman, they went along with the proposal.

The committee had not come up with detailed proposals and the government now had to hurriedly decide between two basic proposals for reform for the legislation to be introduced later in the autumn. The first called for a House of Lords elected after each general election by a committee of the Commons to reflect the party balance in the Commons. The second retained hereditary peerages but removed their voting power and only allowed them to speak. Voting peers were to be created by Prime Ministerial patronage so as to give a small government majority over the opposition parties, although defeat would be possible if a number of the non-party cross-benchers voted against the government. An all-day meeting on the two schemes held at Chequers on 12 September ended in deadlock over the merits of the two options. To resolve the deadlock Crossman suggested announcing their intention to legislate and then trying to negotiate an agreed scheme of reform in an all-party conference. By early October the Cabinet reluctantly agreed to accept Crossman's tactics, though many preferred a simple solution on powers and others couldn't see the point of legislating at all. At the end of October the Queen's Speech announced forthcoming legislation to reduce powers and end the hereditary basis of the House of Lords (both options were compatible with this statement). Wilson subsequently explained in the Commons that the all-party discussions would be a real attempt to produce an agreed scheme but that legislation had to be passed that session.

At this point the government had taken eighteen months to produce proposals and still did not have a clear idea of what it wanted. It was now tied into inter-party negotiations. If successful, these could produce an agreed scheme which would presumably pass quickly through both the Commons and the Lords. If the talks failed, however, the government would have wasted even more time and made the prospect of contested legislation before the election more difficult to face.

The inter-party talks lasted from November 1967 until broken off in June 1968. Early agreement was reached on the main features of a reformed House of Lords. Hereditary peers were to lose the right to vote but in return the Lords would have a guaranteed minimum delaying period of six months. The new House would be composed of a small group of Liberals and roughly equal numbers of Labour and Conservative peers, although the government would normally have a majority of about ten over the other parties. There would also be about forty cross-bench peers, who would therefore be able to defeat the government.

When the Cabinet considered the scheme on 1 February 1968 considerable disquiet was expressed. Many members feared a new, reformed House of Lords would feel that it could legitimately defeat the government. The small government majority, the role of cross-benchers and the fact that peers would keep their title even if they changed allegiance seemed to offer no advantages over a straightforward abolition of the Lords' delaying powers. Many were doubtful about Crossman's role. As Barbara Castle commented:

> I am all the more suspicious of the proposals because Dick is now so sold on them. I know he has a fatal habit of getting carried away by short-term enthusiasms for a piece of work on which he is engaged.[1]

But Wilson was still keen on total reform and, having engaged in all-party talks, the government could hardly break them off at this stage. They decided to carry on. In the next couple of months discussion concentrated on the details of the new scheme: the role of the bishops, whether hereditary peers should vote in committees and whether nominated peers held their title for life or just for a single Parliament or even a single session. Finally only one crucial issue remained – the date when the scheme should come into operation. The Conservatives insisted it should not happen until after the election. This meant that if they won the scheme would never be implemented. They argued that the government's increasing unpopularity, which had reached unprecedented levels early in 1968, meant they no longer had a mandate for reform.

The Conservative peers were showing signs of rebellion and seemed ready to defeat the annual resolution renewing sanctions against Rhodesia. On 15 June Roy Jenkins warned in a speech that if the sanctions resolution were defeated then the all-party talks would be broken off. Two days later an alarmed Crossman found Wilson in a determined mood:

> 'Now there can be no question of any more talks. We must break them off and force through a Bill taking away the powers of the Lords.' I said, 'For God's sake, Harold, are you mad?' and he replied, 'That speech of Roy's . . . was deliberately intended to put me in my place. I must show that I am stronger than him.'[2]

Crossman was in a terrible state because his reform was to be thrown away. On 18 June the Lords defeated the renewal of Rhodesian sanctions and the government broke off the all-party talks. Although the talks seemed to be near agreement there must be doubts about whether the Conservatives ever intended to agree a scheme of reform. Their best tactics were to drag out the process of consultation to make it more difficult for the government to legislate before the election. This they had succeeded in doing; after nine months of negotiation the government was no nearer a solution and time was running out. They could not legislate until the next session starting in the autumn of 1968. The legislation was bound to be rejected by the Lords in their current mood, which meant that the bill could not become law before the 1969–70 session and could not be fully operational before the election. Meanwhile the Lords might decide to hold up other government legislation.

The day after the Lords' vote there was a meeting at No 10. Wilson had tried to keep Crossman out but he simply forced his way in. Wilson now wanted a bill just to end the delaying powers. Crossman objected that this would still leave the Lords plenty of opportunity to extend debate endlessly and delay legislation. He argued for dealing with powers and composition together. The next day at Cabinet Wilson had changed his mind yet again and now supported Crossman. The Cabinet agreed to legislate in the autumn to deal with both powers and composition.

Another Cabinet Committee (PL) was set up to devise proposals. It was chaired by Lord Gardiner and composed almost entirely of those who had been involved in all the earlier discussions. The problem was that by this stage they were obsessed by the minutiae of reform and out of touch with their colleagues. Their first decision was to stick with the proposals agreed by the inter-party talks. Although this might have seemed the best way to proceed, it was a fundamental error of judgement, since it did nothing to ensure the passage of the legislation through Parliament. Although the Conservatives had agreed to work the scheme if it became law, they had not agreed to help pass it. Ministers should have paid more attention to their supporters in the Commons who had little enthusiasm for the agreed scheme and preferred either radical measures or the status quo. Within a month of breaking off the inter-party talks the Cabinet on 18 July accepted the committee's recommendation to introduce legislation to implement the scheme virtually agreed in those talks. Only Castle and Marsh opposed the idea. The rest of the summer was spent in producing fifteen drafts of a White Paper that was eventually published at the beginning of November after the Cabinet had spent just eight minutes discussing it. Wilson also agreed that Callaghan was to be given the responsibility of passing the legislation.

The first signs of trouble came in a two-day debate on the White Paper. At the end of the debate the White Paper was approved by 110 votes, but forty-seven Labour MPs voted against and forty abstained. The next day Wilson was once again beginning to lose his enthusiasm for the measure and insisted that the Second Reading of the bill be postponed till the New Year. He told Crossman:

> If we find things too difficult on the economic front and that our backbenchers are really difficult to carry, we may have to drop the whole thing.[3]

At the Cabinet meeting on 5 December the minister in charge, Callaghan, indicated his total lack of enthusiasm for the proposal. In his view it shouldn't be introduced, it would have to be fought line by line, there was no guarantee of support and the all-party agreement wasn't going to help, even though that was what the proposals were based upon. Indeed, on this occasion, apart from Wilson and Crossman there were only five supporters of the scheme left in the Cabinet. The majority felt that it had no alternative but to go unhappily on, because to turn back would mean unacceptable loss of face.

The second reading of the bill was fixed for 3 February 1969. Wilson was not confident about the outcome and was on the verge of yet another volte-face on the proposals. He told Crossman:

> Now look, if we lose this, Dick, and if we lose it because the Tories defeat the Bill, tomorrow we will put in a short Bill to deal with powers without composition.[4]

However the bill was approved by votes with a hardcore of twenty-five Labour MPs voting against. Now the real problems began. Because it was a constitutional measure it had to be taken by the whole House and not in a small committee. The Conservatives had agreed on a free vote for their MPs, so they gave no cooperation, and the 'usual channels' for the control of business in the House failed to operate. The leading opponents of the bill formed an unholy alliance. On one side was Enoch Powell who objected to any reform. On the other was Michael Foot who wanted abolition and objected to entrenching the position of the Lords. Together, through long speeches, points of order and other procedural devices, they managed to string out the debate. Because of the scale of the backbench revolt the government could not generate enough support to restrict debate. The government's aim had been to spend just five days in discussing the bill in the Commons. The extent of the opposition can be judged by the fact that after two months and twelve sessions only the preamble and five clauses had been discussed.

After the first day of discussion the government knew that it was in deep trouble and was searching desperately for a way out. Ministers considered the possibility of leaving implementation of the scheme until after the election if the opposition would agree to pass the bill and not obstruct other legislation. This was rejected by the Conservatives. After two more days even Crossman was prepared to admit that they had a real problem.

The Cabinet reviewed the situation at the end of February. Crossman argued that they had to go on. To give in to backbench pressure would set an undesirable precedent for the even more contentious bill on industrial relations. Callaghan, who had originally opposed the bill, now also wanted to go on, partly because he did not want to be associated with failure. The Cabinet agreed to continue with the bill, though nobody had any idea how it could actually be passed. On 4 March an informal group of ministers met to discuss the options. The first was to have perhaps another fifteen days of debates to get the bill through. That was rejected on the grounds that the parliamentary party would not stand for it. The second was to abandon the bill, which was also ruled out. This left the possibility of a guillotine motion to cut off debate. No minister thought this would be practicable but, clutching at straws, Callaghan was sent off to talk to the opposition. They contemptuously refused to cooperate and indeed threatened a three-line Whip against the motion which, with the Labour rebels, would ensure the defeat of the guillotine. Two days later the Cabinet had another discussion. Wilson floated yet again the idea of a short bill on powers, but everybody else thought that though it would get through the Commons the Lords would defeat it, it would take a year to pass it and meanwhile other government business would be in chaos. With no obvious way out of the dilemma the Cabinet agreed to fight on in the hope that MPs would be forced to accept the government's will, thereby re-establishing discipline in the party, even though it must have been clear that the process of passing the bill was actually undermining it.

The government had reached a dead end. To go on meant conflict, no guarantee of success in the Commons and inevitable defeat in the Lords. The whole process would be nugatory unless the government was prepared to go through the entire procedure again in the next session. The only alternative left was to give up, which seemed an admission of total failure. For another month the government trudged wearily on but with no chance of ultimate success. Eventually they came up with what they hoped would be a face-saving formula for dropping the bill. This revolved around a complex series of moves over proposals to reform the law on industrial relations, described in the next chapter. In brief the ministers most closely concerned – Castle, Crossman and Jenkins – agreed that instead of a long bill on industrial relations to be introduced in the autumn they would introduce a short bill containing all the main anti-trade union clauses and pass it rapidly before the summer recess. They convinced Wilson that this was the way to restore discipline in the party and as a consequence they could drop the bill to reform the Lords. This was accepted by the Cabinet on 16 April. It had now agreed that because of the breakdown of discipline on the Lords measure it would introduce an even more unpopular bill to restore discipline. This was to be a disastrous miscalculation.

The previous two non-Conservative majority governments in this century both passed measures to reform the House of Lords. The Wilson government failed miserably. Why? In the first place its aims and strategy were unclear. Any measure was bound to be controversial and might well disrupt other legislation. This made it vital to act decisively in the 1966–7 session immediately after the election. Because the government had no proposals ready and then wavered over how far-reaching the reform should be, eighteen months were wasted at the start. The simplest proposal would have been to abolish the Lords' powers to delay legislation, which would have left them a virtually powerless anachronism. That was the decision originally taken in June 1966. The next mistake was for Wilson to be swayed by Crossman's enthusiasm for wholesale reform. Without Wilson's support Crossman would never have overcome the well-founded doubts of his Cabinet colleagues about this alternative.

Then because it could not agree on a scheme the Cabinet was convinced by Crossman to go into inter-party talks which took up another nine months, making legislation in the 1967–8 session impossible. The decision to break off the talks, where the Conservatives gained far more than the government, left the government in a weak position. It was unpopular and had little time left in which to legislate. If a bill was to be introduced then a short bill to abolish the powers of delay at least had the merit of uniting Labour MPs and ensuring an easy passage through the Commons. The decision to stick with the compromise proposals agreed in the inter-party talks was the worst of all possible worlds. It divided Labour MPs but gave no guarantee of opposition support. The government could easily have ditched the inter-party proposals by arguing that Conservative actions in the Lords over Rhodesian sanctions had made cooperation impossible and demonstrated the need to abolish powers. Having started on the legislation it went on because it did not know how to get out without loss of face. But the long drawn-out battle only made the final climbdown even more humiliating.

This damaging fiasco resulted from a combination of the maverick influence of Dick Crossman, Wilson's indecisiveness, a Cabinet committee out of touch with its colleagues, and a Cabinet unable to agree on a clear and consistent line of policy. It meant a lost opportunity for fundamental constitutional reform. The clear impression is that by April 1969, when the sorry saga drew to a close, the Cabinet was so disoriented, as a result of its massive unpopularity in the country, internal dissent and revolt amongst the parliamentary party and trade unions, that it was losing its judgement about 'the art of the possible'. The consequences were to be catastrophic.

22

In Place of Strife

A Labour government couldn't survive giving itself statutory strike-breaking powers.

Barbara Castle, 28 July 1966

The Labour party was built upon its close relationship with the trade unions, the main paymasters of the party. This role was reflected in their domination of the party conference through the 'block vote' and their powerful position on the NEC. For most of the time of the Attlee government the unions had been an asset and in the early years of the Wilson government the links, whilst perhaps not quite so close, benefitted the government. Ministers like George Brown and Ray Gunter, with their close ties with the union movement, were able to exploit the relationship to create the voluntary prices and incomes policy, and to mediate in industrial disputes. Other ministers, such as Barbara Castle, exploited the links to the utmost in trying to force through aspects of government policy. The unions and the TUC were prepared to be helpful to a government which they believed was generally acting in the interests of their members. The first real signs of strain became apparent in the July 1966 crisis when the unions only reluctantly accepted the twelve-month wage freeze. The unions regarded the July measures as the last chance to put right the economic situation and, when it became clear they had failed, were unwilling to cooperate in further wage restraint. As other social and economic reforms were dropped by the government, the feeling of partnership and common purpose, evident in the early months of the new government, rapidly evaporated.

Increasingly the government was taking a more jaundiced view of the unions as they searched for a solution to Britain's economic difficulties. During the 1960s the unions were suffering from a bad image and a hostile press. There was a widespread feeling that the poor state of industrial relations, particularly the level of unofficial stoppages, was hampering Britain's economic performance and that the unions had to take a large part of the blame for this state of affairs. Between 1964 and 1969 the proportion of the population seeing trade unions as beneficial fell from 70% to 57% and the number viewing them unfavourably rose from 12% to 26%. The number seeing strikes as the main problem facing the unions rose from 11% in 1966 to 46% in 1969. There was still a considerable reservoir of good feeling towards the unions but alongside that was an increasing view that the government should intervene, particularly in unofficial strikes.

Against this background it is easy to see why the government might be attracted to the idea of taking action to replace strife with better ways of settling industrial disputes. It is far more difficult to understand why a Prime Minister with a reputation for adroit handling of awkward political issues and a minister well known for her left-wing sympathies ended up with an agreement with the TUC which even Wilson himself regarded as 'not worth the paper it was written on' and in the process caused the most bitter and damaging divisions yet in the party and the Cabinet.

The 1964 Labour manifesto contained no commitment to legislate on industrial relations or investigate the trade unions. Indeed during the 1964 election campaign it was the Conservatives who advocated a Royal Commission, whereas Wilson had been strongly opposed. At the TUC conference in September 1964 he described it as a solution 'which would take minutes and waste years'. However, at the beginning of January 1965 Ray Gunter, as Minister of Labour, proposed, and the Cabinet accepted without discussion, the idea of a Royal Commission on the trade unions. TUC agreement was only obtained by the appointment of the General Secretary, George Woodcock, to the Commission, which was chaired by a judge, Lord Donovan. The membership was a typical cross section of the 'Great and Good', the most influential individual being Hugh Clegg, Professor of Industrial Relations at the University of Warwick and a firm advocate of the British laissez-faire style of industrial relations.

Three years later the Donovan Commission produced an unspectacular report recommending little change. The majority report came down firmly against the idea of any legal framework for industrial relations:

> The British system of industrial relations is based on voluntarily agreed rules which, as a matter of principle, are not enforced by law . . . We do . . . not . . . think that the law could not in any circumstances assist in the reduction of unofficial strikes. It cannot do so in this country today – this is the point. To take steps in this direction today would not only be useless but harmful.

They identified the core problem as the disorder in factory and workshop relations, but felt that this could not be put right by national agreements between employers and unions. The main proposal was to create a Commission for Industrial Relations (CIR), which would be a voluntary body to prod the system into self-reform by disseminating ideas about good practice.

Having set up the Royal Commission the government had to react to its report. No doubt it might have hoped for a more radical report so as to enable it to enact more modest proposals as an acceptable compromise. As it was there was no real pressure for intervention that could not have been met by negotiating with the TUC and setting up the CIR with an agreed, albeit limited, series of reforms. There was, however, one political problem of which Wilson was acutely aware. A few months before the Donovan report the Conservatives had proposed their alternative under the title, 'Fair Deal at Work'. This strongly advocated a strict legal framework for industrial relations. Wilson was worried about the impact of these proposals because of Labour's close links with the unions. If Labour failed to act then the Conservatives would have a very strong issue to exploit at the election. If the government did legislate it could defuse the issue and remove it from politics. It was a tactic that Wilson had used before with some success over entry to the EEC and a possible settlement with the illegal regime in Rhodesia.

A Cabinet Committee set up in late 1967 to consider a response to the Commission had produced no ideas by the time the report was published in the summer of 1968. When Castle had to make a speech in the Commons debate on the report in the middle of July she admitted to herself that the government line was 'non-existent' and that 'I have no policy to declare'.[1] Her comments after meeting the TUC at the beginning of July, though, showed that she was at this stage well aware of the potential source of conflict:

> I can't see any revolutionary changes being carried through unless the Government is prepared to impose them on an unwilling TUC.[2]

By the late autumn of 1968 the need for a policy was becoming acute. The exact nature of the government's proposals was thrashed out at an extraordinary weekend conference at the Civil Service College at Sunningdale in the middle of November. It was extraordinary because of the mixture of people involved – some from the government plus an unrepresentative sample of outside opinion. From the government came Castle (in the chair), her junior ministers, her PPS (John Fraser) and Peter Shore, from the DEA. The outsiders were Professor Clegg (the sole representative of Donovan) and another academic, Professor Robinson from Glasgow. There were two industrialists, including Campbell Adamson, the President of the CBI. The TUC was not represented but two junior trade unionists were present. Aubrey Jones, head of the Prices and Incomes Board, was also invited. The balance was deliberately weighted against any purely voluntary approach to the problem. Although the group rejected the idea of legally enforceable collective bargains, they did recommend a series of legal arrangements and powers for the government. Castle's PPS reported that the PLP would accept legal enforcement if some of the pro-trade union measures were also legally enforceable (a serious misjudgement). The conference concluded that

> we would never get anything positive out of the TUC and that the Government would have to risk giving a lead.[3]

It was on the basis of this conference that Castle's White Paper, 'In Place of Strife', was written. She always claimed, rightly, that it contained a number of pro-trade union measures; indeed she even believed it was 'first and foremost a charter of trade union rights'. The provisions which reinforced this belief were those that would:

- make it unlawful for an employer to prevent an individual joining a trade union;
- enable the Commission on Industrial Relations (CIR) to recommend the recognition of a trade union;
- create a development fund, with government support, to assist union mergers;
- provide compensation or reinstatement for unfair dismissal.

The White Paper also rejected the idea that collective bargains should be legally enforceable and that unofficial strikers could be sued for any damages that they caused. But there were also a number of proposals that would give the government new powers and limit the scope of the unions to take industrial action. These meant that:

- in an unofficial dispute the government could order a return to work for twenty-eight days for a 'cooling-off' period (on conditions existing before the dispute so that workers did not have to accept new working practices);
- the government could order a ballot to be held before a strike if

they believed there was a serious threat to the economy or national interest and the government could also determine the form of the question on the ballot;

– inter-union disputes would be referred to the TUC and ultimately the CIR, and the government could issue an order to enforce a CIR decision with appropriate financial penalties if the order was not obeyed. (Individual trade unionists would not be sent to jail for failure to pay fines since they would be paid direct through attachment of earnings.)

While Castle's proposals did, in some respects, undoubtedly strengthen the position of the unions, at the same time they provided for an unprecedented degree of government power to intervene directly in industrial relations. How they were used would depend on the government. Even Castle was worried that the strike-ballot proposal could be abused by a Conservative government and she secretly hoped that the TUC would agree to negotiate so that she could persuade Wilson, who had insisted on its inclusion, that it should be dropped.

Castle realised that she would have a difficult job persuading her colleagues to endorse the proposals and at the beginning of December 1968 she had a strategy session with Wilson. He immediately saw the political attractions of defusing a strong Conservative campaign theme. As he told Marcia Williams, 'Barbara has not so much out-heathed Heath as outflanked him.'[4] Wilson and Castle agreed that with Callaghan's known opposition to the proposals the ministerial group set up to examine the Donovan report would have to be by-passed and a small 'leak-proof' group, excluding Callaghan and any other doubters, established. This committee (MISC 230) was chaired by Wilson and apart from Castle consisted of Elwyn-Jones (Attorney-General), Lord Gardiner, Jenkins, Lee and Peart. In two short meetings on a draft White Paper it made no alterations of any substance and then sent 'In Place of Strife' on to Cabinet. Meanwhile, after the first meeting of MISC 230, Castle had 'on an impulse' decided to tell George Woodcock of the TUC the details of the White Paper before it was approved by the Cabinet. He may not have understood the contents very clearly from her description because he gave her the highly misleading advice that 'he didn't think there was anything there that need alarm the trade union movement'.[5]

Wilson's intention was to have one Cabinet meeting on 3 January followed by publication of the White Paper on 9 January. The level of opposition he encountered was such that four meetings were required, fitted in around sessions of the Commonwealth Prime Ministers' Conference. The first lasted all day and by the end Castle and Wilson's idea of bouncing the Cabinet into agreement was in trouble. Opposition to the proposals came from two groups. The first led by Callaghan with support from Marsh, Crosland, Hart and others was opposed to legislation in principle. Their views were summed up by Callaghan when he told Castle during the meeting:

> I think it is absolutely wrong and unnecessary to do this. I think what you ought to do is set up the Commission, put the trade unions on their honour and do what you can.[6]

This was a minimalist position that would have provided some action on trade unions whilst not alienating the TUC and the Labour party. Wilson and Castle responded that this was not enough, that the public expected the government to do more.

The second group, led by Crossman and Jenkins, was opposed not to the philosophy behind the reforms but to the tactical way in which the issue was being handled. They argued that it would be disastrous to publish the White Paper with firm proposals in January but not legislate before late autumn. During the interval there would be time for a campaign to develop against the proposals and a long battle would have to be fought at every trade union conference in the early summer, followed by the TUC and Labour conferences in September and October. Legislation would then have to be passed in the months leading up to the election, which could be very damaging. They suggested two alternatives. One was to publish a White Paper that contained possibilities rather than firm proposals and to spend the time until the autumn in consultations. The other was to rush through a short bill before the summer and dispose of the issue quickly. To make room the bill to reform the House of Lords, already doomed, could be dropped. At the end of the meeting, all they could agree on was to set up a committee to look at alternatives.

Wilson and Castle kept up the pressure on their colleagues by briefing the press through the Lobby that agreement had been reached and publication of the White Paper would take place later that month. This made any real consideration of alternatives impossible. As Crossman gloomily mused:

> I've got no alternative to propose. There is no time to think of one. I may well be forced to toe the line and see us tearing ourselves to pieces all over again.[7]

The Committee only had time to consider a paper from Castle that outlined some of the alternatives and not surprisingly rejected them all. But the position of the TUC was made clear just before the next Cabinet meeting on 8 January when they gave Castle a twenty-eight-paragraph letter that in effect rejected all her proposals. This was the time to sit back and think out a clear strategy and consider all the implications if the TUC was going to oppose the government. Instead the Cabinet paid no attention to the TUC views and the majority in favour of proceeding with the White Paper regardless of opposition was sixteen to seven. The next two meetings were devoted to deciding whether the White Paper should provide for consultation over the proposals. Although the process had taken a little longer than Wilson and Castle had intended, there had been no real consideration of any alternatives or any different strategy.

The initial public reaction to the proposals set out in 'In Place of Strife', published on 16 January, was favourable, with opinion polls showing over 60% support. But already by the end of January the reaction of groups closer to the government was becoming clear. A meeting of the trade union group of sponsored Labour MPs showed little support for Castle and she recognised that they would follow the lead of their unions. The mood in the NEC was hostile and at the PLP meeting on 5 February, according to Castle, 'there were almost non-stop objections to the three proposals they dislike most: the strike ballot, the conciliation pause and the attachment of wages.'[8] Indeed so many MPs wanted to register their hostility that a second meeting had to be held. On 3 March, at the end of the Commons debate on the White Paper, fifty-five Labour MPs voted against the White Paper and about forty abstained. Castle was finding that, however hard she tried, it was impossible to present the proposals as being pro-trade union. It was Tony Crosland who summed up the views he found amongst Labour supporters:

> around the country nobody has read 'In Place of Strife', and they just think that Wilson has got a massive trade union bug in him and that Barbara has gone bonkers.[9]

Opposition amongst the trade unions was growing and this, combined with internal party dissent, came to a head at a NEC meeting on 26 March. The Executive voted sixteen to five in favour of a trade union resolution that they were 'unwilling to accept legislation based on all the proposals' in 'In Place of Strife' and also rejected a motion 'welcoming the government's readiness to consult'. It was virtually unprecedented for the NEC publicly to dissent from a Labour government in this way and it was a major defeat for the government, and in particular for Barbara Castle, who was effectively rejected by her old friends on the left of the party. It was made worse by the action of Jim Callaghan, who twice voted against the policy of his own government. Three junior ministers abstained.

Callaghan had broken the fundamental convention of collective responsibility of Cabinet ministers – after all he had not resigned in January when 'In Place of Strife' had been agreed. Tony Benn for one wanted him sacked. Wilson refused but told Castle, 'I intend to be very tough about it when I get back' (from Nigeria). Castle's reaction was, 'I'll believe that when it happens.'[10] Her scepticism was well justified by events at the Cabinet meeting on 3 April. In his memoirs Wilson says he gave Callaghan a 'constitutional homily' on the duties and responsibilities of a minister.[11] Others round the table failed to notice the homily, as Castle commented, 'I've never seen him so weak-kneed',[12] and the meeting broke up in confusion. Nevertheless the press was briefed that Callaghan had been on the receiving end of a 'dressing down' by Wilson which caused Castle to remark, 'Harold had clearly compensated to the lobby for what he failed to do in Cabinet.'[13]

The strength of opposition to the government's proposals among its own supporters was to cause a rethink of their strategy. In January a minority in the Cabinet had favoured introduction of a short bill in that session before opposition had time to develop. Then Castle had been bitterly against any such idea:

> I for one am not prepared to put forward a shorter Bill in which all the emphasis will be on the penal bits. I could not imagine anything more detrimental to my whole philosophy.[14]

Towards the end of March her views were changing and with her officials she was already thinking about what might go into a short bill. It was after Callaghan's public revolt at the NEC that she made up her mind, heavily influenced by the danger of allowing discussions with the unions to go on for months when, as she admitted, they showed no signs of being willing to negotiate about anything. At the beginning of April, after a series of meetings between Castle, Jenkins, Crossman and Wilson, the new strategy was gradually worked out. A short bill would be introduced immediately and passed that session before the summer recess.

Jenkins would announce this plan in the Budget speech and firmly link the necessity for it to Britain's economic recovery. But the plan had other motives too. The bill to reform the House of Lords was stuck in the Commons, looked unlikely to pass and a large number of backbenchers were in open revolt. The Cabinet was looking for an excuse to drop the bill but so far had not found one. Now the need to find room for the Industrial Relations Bill would provide a fig leaf of respectability for doing so. This group of ministers also hoped that a quick bill would force Callaghan to resign or stop his guerilla warfare against the proposals. Wilson was also convinced that discipline had to be reasserted within the party and felt the need to drive the unpopular Industrial Relations Bill through would provide the mechanism for doing this. But he was already beginning to lose touch with political reality and told the inner group of ministers:

> the Party must realise that, unless they accepted the package, they would be faced with an Election and a large number of them would lose their seats.

As Barbara Castle commented: 'It sounded a curious kind of threat to me.'[15]

The next problem was what to put in the short bill. Castle's officials were arguing that it should contain only the penal clauses against the unions on the basis that the state of the economy required these powers to be taken immediately. Castle was doubtful and wanted some pro-union measures included. Wilson insisted on including government-ordered strike ballots. The inner group eventually overrode Wilson and substituted provisions on inter-union disputes instead. They finally agreed that the package should include:

- a statutory right to join a union;
- power for the government to order an employer to recognise a union if recommended by the CIR;
- power for the government to impose a settlement in inter-union disputes after the TUC and CIR had failed to get a voluntary settlement;
- power for the government to order a twenty-eight-day 'conciliation pause' in unofficial disputes.

Both of the latter two powers were to carry the ultimate threat of fines on recalcitrant trade unions and individuals, although failure to pay fines was not to lead to jail sentences. Although the government again tried to present the proposals as a balanced package, in practice all the argument centred around the latter two proposals and the powers it would give the government to interfere in industrial disputes.

The Cabinet agreed the new strategy and proposals on 14 April. Callaghan was slightly more conciliatory after the dropping of compulsory strike ballots but still opposed to legislating in a hurry, as were Mason, Marsh and Crosland. The TUC was told of the government's modified intentions but its hostility to the ideas remained unaltered.

At the end of April attention within the government and at Westminster focused on the growing threats to Wilson's own position flowing from the unprecedented level of revolt within the Labour party. At one point, when he replaced Silkin with Mellish as Chief Whip, Wilson seemed on the point of collapse but he rapidly recovered and resolved to fight the battle with the TUC. Meanwhile officials were hastily drafting the necessary legislation ready for introduction in the Commons. Castle did not lower the political temperature when she told the Scottish TUC that the short bill would not be the end of the process and that the government still intended to introduce another bill in the autumn that would include the power for the government to order a compulsory ballot. The TUC's strength of feeling about the proposed new penal clauses was made clear when Vic Feather condemned them for seeking to 'introduce the taint of criminality into industrial relations'. Feather told Wilson and Castle at the beginning of May, 'In the end they [the unions] just won't take fines.'[16] Even Barbara Castle commented in the middle of April: 'I'm worried by the quietly stubborn hostility of the TUC.'[17]

Meanwhile Wilson was laying down the law to Labour MPs, stressing that the future of the government was at stake. He told them on 17 April that the bill was

> an essential component in ensuring the economic success of the Government . . . essential to our economic recovery, essential to the balance of payments, essential to full employment . . . the passage of this Bill is essential to the Government's continuance in office. There can be no going back on that.

Crossman was not impressed with Wilson's performance, which he described as 'a disastrous wind-up, a bumbling, fumbling, argumentative reply, devastating in its failure'. Wilson had failed to convince his opponents, as Crossman described:

There was no attempt whatsoever to give people a vision of our policy or to indicate our new line in terms of a broad strategy. He just plunged in saying, 'You will bloody well have an Industrial Relations Act.'[18]

At the next PLP meeting on 7 May Douglas Houghton, the Chairman and long-time friend of Callaghan, opened by saying that nothing the bill could do would 'redeem the harm we can do to our movement and to the nation by the disintegration or defeat of the Labour party'. The rest of the meeting reflected this mood. Wilson's close supporters were convinced that Houghton and Callaghan were acting in concert to replace Wilson. Crossman was provoked into a furious outburst at the Cabinet meeting the next morning:

> the plotters had better realise that it wouldn't work: 'four of the inner heart of the Cabinet couldn't and wouldn't serve' under the supplanter. We would sink or swim together. 'Sink or sink,' interposed Jim. Dick rounded on him: how could he work with the rest of us when he believed the next Election was already lost? . . . 'If my colleagues want me to go, I will,' murmured Jim unctuously. Dick flashed back at him, 'Why don't you go? Get out!'[19]

Wilson, secretly pleased at the outburst, intervened to calm things down. But the position of Callaghan on the Inner Cabinet that Wilson had been forced to set up at the beginning of May was becoming embarrassing. On 12 May Castle was opposed to dropping Callaghan from the Inner Cabinet which she thought would just make him a martyr and Wilson favoured a collective rebuke. It was Jenkins and Crossman who insisted and said they couldn't operate with a 'spy' in their midst. The next day Callaghan was dropped.

The TUC was trying to create the impression of movement and willingness to compromise while not conceding any issue of principle. It was totally opposed to the government taking powers to intervene in industrial relations but had decided to produce its own alternative plan, which involved some limited changes to TUC rules. Individual unions were willing to make some cosmetic changes but they were never prepared to allow the TUC to become a body capable of imposing discipline (including expulsion) on the unions. The TUC proposals were to be discussed at a special congress on 5 June. If the government was to legislate before the recess, time was already short and once negotiations started with the TUC there was no guarantee when the process would stop.

After the PLP meeting and the bitter row in the Inner Cabinet on 8 May the 'inner' group of Wilson, Castle, Jenkins and Crossman decided that afternoon that they were not in a sufficiently strong position to ignore the TUC and introduce the bill immediately. They decided to wait until after the TUC special congress and meanwhile to open negotiations. But the very willingness to negotiate illustrated the weakness of the government's position. They were already doubtful about whether they could force through their own solution, yet negotiations were likely to take them a long way from their original aims.

On 12 May the TUC produced its alternative to the government's proposals. It was willing to change its procedures to be followed in unofficial strikes so that it would be able to intervene and give its 'considered opinion and advice'. In inter-union disputes there would be no stoppage until the TUC had considered the problem and the unions involved would be under an 'obligation' to try and get a resumption of work. This represented a slight strengthening of the existing voluntary arrangements but clearly fell a long way short of the government's proposals. The TUC emphasised that any action by the government on penal powers would stop any internal TUC reforms. There were three inconclusive meetings between Wilson and Castle and the TUC during May. At the first, Wilson made it clear that if legislation was to be avoided then the TUC was expected to introduce sanctions against member unions which did not discipline their members over unofficial disputes or failed to settle inter-union disputes without industrial action. At the next two meetings there was no substantive change in the position. The TUC was only prepared to offer slightly different wording in the rule changes they had proposed. On 21 May it was agreed to adjourn the talks until after the special TUC congress.

On 20 May the Inner Cabinet discussed its tactics and there was tacit agreement that there should be further concessions to the TUC. The option of postponing the bill was unanimously rejected and discussion centered on two possibilities. The majority (including Wilson and Castle) backed legislation, including penal powers, but deferring introduction of the conciliation pause. Mellish (Chief Whip) stated categorically that the penal clauses on the conciliation pause would never be supported by the backbenchers. He and Crossman wanted the conciliation pause dropped altogether and the powers on inter-union disputes included but not to come into effect immediately. Castle too was beginning to have doubts as to whether the Cabinet could be persuaded to go along with the strategy which she and Wilson favoured. Her doubts were confirmed two days later when the Cabinet did show increasing hesitation. There was the expected opposition from the long-time opponents – Callaghan, Crosland and Marsh – but now others, such as Shore, Hughes and Shackleton, were dubious about the wisdom of going on with the bill, and both Benn and Greenwood were expressing caution about the confrontational strategy adopted with the TUC. Wilson simply said that a full discussion would take place after the TUC congress.

Both Wilson and Castle knew that they were engaged in a dangerous game with the TUC. The main problem for them was psychological. They increasingly felt that their own credibility was at stake in the negotiations and that victory over the TUC was required in order not to lose face. As Wilson told the Inner Cabinet, 'Brinkmanship is essential; we have to push it right up to the edge.'[20] But as Castle recognised, with the reputation of the government at stake, it might all go wrong:

> Of course, we shall do our best to get an agreement with the TUC
> . . . But we may, in spite of ourselves, take us all over the brink – it
> is a risk we must take if we are not to destroy the total credibility of
> the Government.[21]

Wilson realised that he was in a difficult position. Far from seeing the threat of the bill as a means to push the TUC to an agreement (as he claims in his memoirs), he thought that his reputation and leadership were at stake, and that he could not credibly accept anything less than the government proposals. He told Castle privately on 21 May what he expected to happen:

> He astonished me by saying cheerfully that he didn't see how we
> could get a settlement with the TUC, but he and I were now too
> committed to back down. He therefore intended to make this an
> issue of confidence in *him* and, if he were defeated, he would stand
> down from the leadership.[22]

Ten days later Wilson spoke to Castle about the likely motion to introduce the guillotine in order to ensure the passage of the Industrial Relations Bill through the Commons as an issue of confidence in him and if he were defeated he would resign immediately. Castle saw this attitude as part of his wider disillusionment with his political position and plans for staging a personal recovery:

I believe he is positively looking forward to being free to bid for the recapture of the leadership in opposition. It is clear to me that . . . he is himself resigned to our election defeat and is preoccupied with how he can outmanoeuvre Jim and thwart his ambitions.[23]

After the 21 May meeting with the TUC Castle and Crossman, with their families, went off on holiday on Charles Forte's yacht off the coast of Italy. But Castle had to interrupt her holiday for a secret meeting at Chequers, at which Vic Feather of the TUC insisted Wilson and Castle should talk to Jack Jones and Hugh Scanlon, the two main opponents of the government. Feather wanted to bring out just how big a gap there was between the two sides and he succeeded. Jones describes Castle as 'shrewish' throughout and says, 'She poured scorn on any ideas that did not involve legal enforcement'.[24] Jones and Scanlon made it clear that they only supported the TUC reforms in order to avoid government legislation and would have have preferred no action at all but that there was no way in which they would support government intervention in industrial relations. The meeting did serve to demonstrate that the situation was reaching stalemate and could only be resolved by one side backing down. With the TUC determined and united, Labour MPs unwilling to legislate against the wishes of the TUC and increasing numbers in the Cabinet unwilling to do so either, all the signs pointed to Wilson and Castle as the ones who would sooner or later have to surrender.

The special TUC Conference went ahead on 5 June. The TUC's own proposals on the modifications to their rules were agreed by eight million votes to 800,000 and any strengthening of those proposals was rejected. 'Unalterable opposition' to financial penalties was approved by a majority of eight million but 'certain proposals' in the White Paper (presumably those strengthening the position of the unions) were welcomed with a similar majority. The press reaction was surprisingly favourable, emphasising that the TUC had moved a considerable way towards meeting the government.

Wilson, however, was worried by this mood and wanted, regardless of the doubts of his colleagues, to set out a tough government position before the negotiations with the TUC started again. Without consulting Castle he issued a statement, in her name, rejecting the TUC proposals, particularly those on unofficial strikes, as inadequate. Indeed he suggested to Castle that they should go further and introduce some new government proposals. He now wanted a system whereby a union would be obliged to discipline members who failed to obey an order to end an unofficial dispute. If the union did not do this he wanted the TUC to discipline them, possibly leading to expulsion from the TUC, together with the withdrawal of legal immunities from any union who failed to act so that they could be sued for damages by an employer in a subsequent dispute. These would have been draconian proposals going far beyond anything the Conservatives had proposed. After a bitter row with Castle these ideas were not sent to the TUC, although officials started work on how to implement such a scheme.

On the evening of Sunday 8 June the Inner Cabinet considered their tactics for a meeting the next morning with the TUC. Healey, Jenkins and Crossman all indicated that they were impressed by how far the TUC had moved (even though little had changed from the 12 May proposals) and thought their latest proposals should now be accepted. The meeting with the TUC was amicable but largely went over old ground. Wilson did, however, make one proposal which represented yet another concession by the government. He now firmly offered to drop the penal clauses if the TUC would change its rules along the lines the government wanted so that the congress became a body capable of disciplining the trade union movement. This proposal was to dominate the last days of negotiation. Wilson saw it as a way of putting the onus back on the TUC to reject a reasonable proposal. If they did reject it Wilson wanted immediate legislation. But the Cabinet, when they considered the state of the negotiations, would not go so far. They only agreed that the penal clauses would not have immediate effect – giving the TUC more time to act.

On 12 June, after a meeting that broke up just before midnight, deadlock was reached. The TUC refused to make the amendment to their rules that Wilson and Castle wanted. Instead they offered a separate advisory circular. Both Wilson and Castle were clear that this was inadequate. Castle had earlier told the Inner Cabinet that: 'a rule change was the minimum for my credibility' and during the negotiations Wilson had told Castle: 'This amendment to rule or we break.' When the talks broke down Wilson and Castle remained cheerful:

> 'We've done very well tonight,' said Harold jubilantly. I myself believed that Cabinet and the PLP must be prepared to back us now that what everyone believed was a generous offer had been turned down.[25]

The two sides agreed to meet again on 18 June when the TUC would be told how the government intended to proceed.

The next few days would be crucial in deciding how the government would react. Could Wilson and Castle win the backing of an increasingly worried Cabinet to legislate against the wishes of the TUC? Even if they could, would Labour MPs support such a bill? On 16 June Douglas Houghton sent a letter to Wilson telling him that the PLP would not support penal sanctions. This was an ultimatum designed to try and make the government draw back. But Wilson still seems to have hoped that if the TUC refused to move then enough of the backbenchers would fall into line and support the government when there was no alternative. Houghton had been working closely with Callaghan and they had agreed that if the Cabinet did support the penal clauses then Callaghan would resign. He would then be in a very strong position, with the TUC and the PLP behind him, to challenge for the leadership as the candidate to unite the party against the divisive Wilson. A great deal would turn on the Cabinet meeting on 17 June. Would the Cabinet now back Wilson against the TUC and the Parliamentary Party?

For Barbara Castle 17 June was 'the most traumatic day of [her] political life'. It began with a meeting with Wilson at 9 am at which she floated an idea that individual strikers would not be fined, only the union organisation. They were both keen on the idea but when the Inner Cabinet met at 10.30 they were dubious, realising that the TUC would not accept it and that anyway it was irrelevant to the main issue. Wilson and Castle now had only Michael Stewart to support them on the Inner Cabinet, with Jenkins unable to decide what to do, and no decisions were taken before the full Cabinet met from 11.15 to 12.30.

Wilson and Castle made their position clear. They wanted the Cabinet to agree to introduce a bill involving penal clauses (with their implementation delayed for a few months) if the TUC failed to agree to change their rules as the government required. The only immediate support they received was from Michael Stewart, who said the TUC proposals were inadequate. Wilson's opponents opened by simply asking whether the penal clauses bill could actually be passed. Mellish intervened to say, 'If the TUC rejected our proposals the PLP would not support the Government.' The long-standing opponents, Crosland, Callaghan and Marsh then argued strongly for a settlement. The crucial intervention came from Peter Shore, who was not known for making strong speeches in Cabinet. In the autumn he had helped Castle draft the proposals. Now he argued that the TUC had come a long way and that the exercise was not, as Wilson and Castle thought it was, a matter of securing a victory over the TUC. He wanted the best deal that could be agreed with the TUC but no threats. When the meeting adjourned no decisions had been taken but the overwhelming desire for compromise was clear.

The Cabinet reassembled at 4.30 for their final discussion. Just before, Jenkins, who had been one of the main supporters of the proposals in April, told Castle that he no longer thought the battle worthwhile and they should get the best terms they could from the TUC. The meeting, which lasted for two and a half hours, was described by Crossman as 'the most devastating Cabinet meeting I have attended'. For the first time ministers firmly committed themselves to one side or the other. Wilson and Castle found that they had only five supporters, none of any weight apart from Michael Stewart. Ranged against them were the other sixteen members of the Cabinet and the Chief Whip. Wilson demanded that the Cabinet authorise him to tell the TUC that either they changed their rules in the way the government wanted or the penal-clauses bill would go forward. The Cabinet refused. Wilson, in an increasingly agitated and emotional state (according to Castle he consumed three double brandies in the last half-hour of the meeting), shouted at his colleagues:

> You're soft, you're cowardly, you're lily-livered . . . I won't negotiate on your terms. If you order me to go back to the TUC and say I'm to accept a declaration of intent I refuse to do it, because a declaration would not be worth the paper it is written on. I insist on getting the change of rules or on standing for the penal clauses. You can't deny me this.

But the Cabinet did deny him. Wilson and Castle were left to get the best terms they could without threatening the TUC with legislation.[26]

Wilson and Castle were defeated; their whole strategy lay in ruins. Earlier in the month Wilson was clear that in these circumstances he would quit and fight for the leadership again in opposition. That evening he spent a long time with Bob Mellish, and talked of defeating the rest of Cabinet and getting rid of Callaghan but by the next day he told Mellish: 'I'm not going to resign. They won't chase me out. I'm going to stay.'

The talks with the TUC on 18 June were an anti-climax. Wilson had no cards left in his hand. The TUC, eager for final agreement, made another offer. There would be no change to their rules but instead they would provide a 'solemn and binding' undertaking. This would have the same standing as the Bridlington Declaration of 1939 on inter-union disputes (it was not part of the rules of the TUC but was normally treated as equally binding). But the wording of the undertaking, however 'solemn and binding', was weak. On unofficial disputes if the TUC thought it was 'unreasonable' to order a return to work they would 'give an opinion', otherwise they would 'place an obligation' on the union concerned 'to take energetic steps' to obtain an immediate return to work. This was a long way from the TUC acting as a disciplinary body. Wilson and Castle grasped at this straw and settled.

While they were talking with the TUC the rest of the Cabinet were waiting at No 10 to hear the outcome, concerned by what would happen if Wilson refused the TUC's terms. If he did they expected him to resign. Jenkins was agonising over whether he should go together with Wilson and Castle, since he had been so involved in devising the strategy that had failed. Crossman had no such worries. He had no intention of resigning (he had told Castle at the beginning of the month that he would reluctantly resign with her), and he was trying to persuade Jenkins to stay and lead the fight against Callaghan for the leadership.

All such preparations were in vain because shortly after 5 pm Wilson and Castle returned to announce the deal with the TUC. News of a settlement was greeted with great relief by their colleagues and later that evening by Labour MPs. It was relief mainly generated by the thought that at last the whole bruising battle was over. Wilson soon cheerfully washed his hands of responsibility for the whole affair, remarking to Sir William Armstrong:

> Poor Barbara. She hangs around like someone with a still-born child. She can't believe it's dead.[27]

After a six-month battle the government achieved none of its original aims, and the process left it battered and divided with its reputation badly damaged. What had gone wrong?

The rising tide of concern about industrial relations, together with the publication of what the government regarded as the disappointing Donovan report and Conservative proposals for a completely new legal framework for industrial relations, meant that some action by the government was almost inevitable. The ideas behind 'In Place of Strife' were conceived in an atmosphere dominated by interventionist thinking and with no attempt to consult the TUC. An alternative approach would have been to build on the voluntary approach in Donovan, set up the Commission on Industrial Relations, and introduce a programme of legislation agreed with the TUC. Properly handled this would have avoided splitting the Labour movement and, with adroit public relations work, could have been presented as a coherent approach to the problem. But Wilson was determined to 'steal the Conservatives' clothes' by introducing Labour's own tough proposals and thereby defuse the whole question as an election issue. He also believed that the government would reap major benefits by being seen as a 'national' government, not tied to one interest group, and legislating in the interests of the community as a whole. In doing this he seriously underestimated the problems of carrying his supporters with him.

Once set on this course Wilson and Castle committed a series of tactical blunders. First, the Cabinet was manipulated into agreeing the proposals without any proper consideration of the alternatives. This may have limited the scope for opposition from Callaghan and his supporters but it also meant that the sound advice from Wilson's own supporters, who were dubious about the proposals, was ignored. The second mistake was to publish a White Paper in January and defer legislation till the autumn. This could not have been better arranged, as Crossman and others pointed out, for a campaign against the proposals to develop. There were two alternative courses. One was to publish a White Paper but to leave large areas open to negotiation before the government was ready to legislate in the autumn. The other was to introduce a short bill immediately after publication before the opposition had time to organise.

In the end the government finished up with the worst of all worlds by publishing the White Paper with no room for negotiation, giving time for opposition to mount, and then suddenly changing course twice: first, announcing an immediate bill containing nearly all the most controversial proposals; second, deferring it and entering into negotiations with the TUC. None of the aims underlying the changes in strategy and tactics – the need to appease opposition in the party, the attempt to deal with Callaghan or restore discipline in the party after the fiasco of the House of Lords reform – were achieved. These swift changes cast real doubt on whether the government had ever thought out a clearly defined strategy and confirmed their inability to maintain a consistent policy. The episode also demonstrates that its political touch was disintegrating under pressure.

By contrast the TUC remained consistent throughout. Once negotiations began in May the TUC stubbornly maintained its position of no legislation and no changes to its rules, only cosmetic adjustments to its existing procedures. The government had no mechanism for persuading the TUC to change its mind, and the TUC only saw the negotiations as a way of trying to persuade Wilson and Castle to back down. In these circumstances the negotiations achieved little and mainly consisted of a series of government concessions aimed at tempting the TUC to reciprocate but with no result. One of Wilson's problems was that the further he went in the battle with the TUC the more he lost sight of the real objective and the more he saw his aim as to defeat the TUC. The rhetoric that the measure was needed to ensure Britain's economic recovery never seemed convincing.

Wilson and Castle were not defeated by the TUC, although the unions' hostility to change provided an essential ingredient for the defeat. They were defeated by their own backbench MPs and Cabinet colleagues. By April Labour MPs were openly discontented with Wilson's leadership, and the decision to go for the short bill that session was the last straw. Many could not see why they were being asked to have the battle with the TUC. They expected to lose the next election and that the Conservatives would then pass their own legislation. Why, they argued, should the Labour party tear itself apart on the issue when at least they could go into the election united? In the end enough MPs were opposed to the bill, as Houghton and Mellish told Wilson, for the legislation not to be passed.

In the Cabinet there were those opposed to the legislation – Callaghan, his loyal lieutenant Crosland, Marsh and Mason. But the doubters went along with the proposals. As the opposition mounted, more and more members of the Cabinet gradually realised that any likely gains at the end would not be worth the battle. It took Peter Shore to remind his colleagues at the crucial meeting that the aim of the proceedings was not to defeat the TUC. In the end Wilson and Castle were left isolated to make the best terms they could with the TUC. Terms just as good, if not better, could have been obtained by negotiating with the TUC in the first place. But for Wilson the terms were better than resignation and the probable end of his career.

The episode had major repercussions for a number of political careers. For Wilson the episode finally wrecked the remaining parts of his dwindling reputation. For almost three years after 1964 he had seemed to be invincible, the supreme political tactician.

Devaluation soured that idea and continuing economic difficulties and the failure of much else in the government's programme further battered his image. By April 1969 large parts of the parliamentary party were in almost open revolt against his leadership which seemed to be leading to inevitable defeat at the polls. Even his close friends, Castle and Crossman, deserted him over the way he ran the government and he was forced to establish a more collective style of leadership. It was never to be 'glad, confident morning' again for Wilson.

Castle was under no doubt about the importance of the industrial relations issue for her own political future. As early as January 1969 she wrote in her diary:

> I'm under no illusions that Donovan may be the political end of me with our own people. I'm taking a terrific gamble and there is no certainty that it will pay off. My only comfort is that I am proposing something I believe in.[28]

Castle's gloomy prognostications were proved correct; her reputation never recovered and her career had reached its height. Wilson remained friendly and told her a week after the defeat:

> You and I must keep together. I am the only friend you have and you are the only friend I have. I'm like the elephant: I may appear to forget but I never do.[29]

Wilson didn't forget. In 1974 he made her Secretary of State for Social Services. But Callaghan didn't forget either and the moment he became Prime Minister in 1976 he sacked her.

Ever since his decision to run for Treasurer of the Labour party and his volte-face over incomes policy, Callaghan had been moving closer to the unions. His opposition to the proposals was to be expected. But he chose to stay in the Cabinet and then vote against his own government at the NEC. Wilson did not have the strength to sack him and Callaghan knew this. Callaghan was clearly playing for high stakes. Throughout he was close to the TUC and to Douglas Houghton who, as chairman of the PLP, was close to the Labour MPs opposed to the legislation and who also made his opposition to 'In Place of Strife' public. Had Wilson either failed to carry the Cabinet and resigned or failed to get the legislation through the Commons, then the obvious successor would have been Callaghan. His stand would have been vindicated, and he would have appeared as the man to reunite the party and the unions before the election. If Wilson had gone, it is very unlikely, despite his brave words in private, that he, as a discredited leader, would have been able to make a comeback. When the crunch came Wilson knew this and decided to accept humiliation at the hands of the TUC rather than quit. Callaghan's bid to replace Wilson failed in the short term and he had to wait another seven years before he became Prime Minister.

The ultimate irony is that neither the TUC nor Callaghan were long-term winners either. The inability of the TUC to control the unions, or the unions their members, during the 'Winter of Discontent' in 1978–79 aided the Conservative election victory and the legislation that was greatly to reduce the role and influence of the unions. And it was Callaghan as Prime Minister who was brought down by the unions.

23

Two Years' Hard Slog

After devaluation in November 1967, the subsequent major public expenditure cuts and the most deflationary Budget ever introduced in peacetime, the government took a simple decision with profound implications. The creation of a surplus on the balance of payments was to be its overriding objective and it was content to be judged politically against this one criterion. The problem for the government was that it was not clear how a surplus was to be created. In practice it relied on massive deflation – a blunt instrument which took a long time to work. The promise was the traditional one of 'light at the end of the tunnel' but it did not expect to have to struggle for two years to get there. It was to take until the second half of 1969 before the balance of payments turned round. Despite the bold public front, culminating in an election campaign fought on the issues of recovery and competence, the story of these years viewed from behind the scenes looks very different. Fearing another overwhelming crisis, the government embarked amid great secrecy on desperate and potentially devastating contingency measures for another devaluation. Worried about the effects of wage settlements, it tried very hard to go for sweeping new powers over prices and incomes. In late 1968 it was starting to lose its nerve and political judgement with yet another round of deflation. By the time an election was called the government could claim it had achieved its primary objective – a large surplus on the balance of payments – but away from the public gaze its private assessment of Britain's economic propsects told a much less successful story.

Whilst hoping for the best the government spent much of 1968 preparing for the worst. Within a month of devaluation Wilson was telling the Cabinet that it had not worked, that the foreign exchange reserves were low and money was not flowing back into the country. After the further round of public expenditure cuts in January 1968 Jenkins was confirming privately that virtually no money had flowed back into the reserves and if the Budget failed then another devaluation would be necessary, which he expected to lead to the fall of the government. At the height of the gold crisis in March 1968 the government closed both the gold and foreign exchange markets to try and reduce speculation against the pound. Jenkins told the Cabinet that without the excuse given by the United States to close the foreign exchanges (the US had only asked for the gold market to be closed) there could have been a catastrophic run on the pound leading to devaluation.

The Chancellor also told the Cabinet at the height of this crisis that the new international arrangements would mean the end of the sterling area and the role of sterling as a reserve currency. This was a blow to the prestige of the City but it was the long-term solution to the inherent weakness of the pound. It would take time to negotiate and until an international agreement was in place the pound would, Jenkins admitted, be in a precarious situation. The Basle agreements that implemented this new structure were not completed until July 1968 with a $2-billion medium-term loan facility to fund the rundown of sterling. Even with the agreements in place there were a series of short-term panics about the pound.

It was in these circumstances that the government began early in 1968, in great secrecy, to plan for another devaluation. The work was carried out in a specially established small Cabinet committee (MISC 205) composed of Wilson, Jenkins, Crosland, Shore and Castle. The basic problem was, as Jenkins told the committee early in June 1968, that foreign exchange reserves were so low that they would be inadequate to stop a run on the pound before devaluation could work. If there was to be another crisis the group agreed that a range of measures (known as 'Plan Brutus') would be required. The unusual feature of this plan, agreed in June 1968, is that it did not rely on the traditional Treasury deflationary package but instead provided for a much more directly interventionist approach of controls over capital transactions and imports. Exchange controls would be imposed on all countries so that all the sterling balances held by foreign governments in Britain would be frozen. Import quotas would be imposed on all items except raw materials and 'basic' foodstuffs, there would be crash cuts in defence expenditure and all overseas aid to the Third World would be tied to purchases of British goods. In addition there was 'Operation Bootstrap' which involved the compulsory acquisition by the government of all privately held overseas securities (a measure only previously adopted in wartime). It was thought that these measures would so undermine international confidence that the pound would have to be left to float (downwards). Ministers realised this package would lead to a major increase in unemployment, austerity at home and a serious disruption to world trade, and were worried about the political consequences for themselves. But they felt they had no choice but to prepare for the worst. The Treasury was told to be ready to implement the plan at seven to ten days' notice.

After the November 1968 crisis and the introduction of import deposits Plan Brutus was slightly modified by the Treasury but at the end of the month MISC 205 reaffirmed that it was still the option for another crisis. Early in February 1969, with no improvement in the balance of payments in sight, the classically trained Treasury mandarins came up with an alternative to Brutus. This was 'Plan Hecuba', so secret that only one copy was made which had to be read by members of MISC 205 at No 10 before their meeting. If things continued to go badly the floating of the pound might be preferable to further borrowing from the IMF with the attendant restrictions on domestic economic policy. In that case 'Hecuba' would apply. It was the usual Treasury deflationary package but the severity of the measures envisaged ranged from a wages' freeze to immediate cuts in public expenditure and major increases in taxation. Ministers made no decision as to whether they preferred Brutus or Hecuba and both were left as contingency plans.

The last sterling crisis under the Labour government came in May 1969 when floating of the pound was still on the agenda. Jenkins told MISC 205 on 12 May that the foreign exchange reserves were falling because of rumours of a Deutschmark revaluation. He was negotiating for a standby credit of $1 billion and although floating was ruled out for the moment, 'It might be forced on us during the summer.' Eight days later foreign exchange losses were still mounting, and Jenkins told his colleagues that he did not rule out a complete review of strategy and a different economic policy. Indeed he had 'seriously considered' floating the pound. But short-term support for the pound eased the crisis and within a few months the improvement in the balance of payments that was to lead to a huge surplus of £440 million for the year was apparent. With this improvement the position of the pound was secure in the short term.

In the event there was no need to implement the contingency planning or to decide between Plans Hecuba and Brutus. Further devaluation was avoided by a combination of luck, the diminishing role of sterling as a reserve currency, an improvement in the reserves and a healthier balance of payments. But the very existence of these plans indicates that the economic situation was far worse than ministers were prepared to admit in public. If the plans had had to be implemented the political consequences would have been catastrophic after all the previous measures; as Jenkins told his colleagues it could have meant the fall of the government.

Although by early 1968 the government had agreed major public expenditure cuts and a tough Budget was in prospect, they were still not sure that they had done enough to restore or maintain confidence in the international financial markets. They were concerned that the level of wage increases, running at about 6½% a year, was too high. The non-statutory 'zero norm' adopted in 1967 was due to expire in July 1968, and the Cabinet had to decide how to replace it. By now they had three years' experience of prices and incomes policy in various guises. None had made much impact, although the July 1966 freeze had slightly reduced the rate of growth in incomes.

The initial work was done in a small committee, chaired by Wilson and containing also Jenkins, Shore, Crosland and Gunter. In their view the maximum that could be afforded was a 5% wage rise and they wanted to set a new 'norm' of 3½%. Despite the bruising experience of the previous year, when proposals to take extensive powers to control both prices and incomes had not been put forward in the face of fierce opposition from the TUC, this group still hankered after comprehensive statutory powers to control all wage settlements. They proposed that all wage, price and dividend increases would have to be notified. The government would have powers to order price reductions and to order employers not to pay increases over 3½% (and retrospectively to stop payments over the norm) as well as to impose a twelve-month gap between wage settlements. To ensure enforcement they also envisaged monitoring wage increases at every factory and plant throughout the country. The scheme was drawn up quickly and with no consultation on its feasibility. Aubrey Jones, the head of the Prices and Incomes Board, only heard about the proposals just before the Cabinet met to discuss them on 29 February. He told ministers that the powers they envisaged simply couldn't work.

At that Cabinet meeting the ministers concerned made a strong plea for the powers, with Jenkins calling them 'absolutely essential'. A large proportion of the Cabinet was worried. Marsh was opposed in principle to the new powers, whereas Crosland and Callaghan (working together as usual) were more sceptical, arguing that if wages were going to go up by about 5–6% it was not really worth all the effort and political cost to bring this down by a percentage point or so. Others too thought that there would be real problems with Labour MPs in getting the powers through the

Commons. Peter Shore was sent off to talk to the CBI and TUC to gauge their reactions. When the Cabinet returned to the subject on 7 March Shore reported that the CBI didn't like the ceiling and that although the TUC hadn't taken a firm view, their opposition was evident. The Attorney-General produced a paper on the legal problems involved, particularly on the proposals to make retrospective reductions in wage increases and powers for the government to make binding legal orders without reference to the Prices and Incomes Board, which held all the statutory powers. Jenkins repeated his view that the controls were essential in the short term and, in an assessment of the economic situation so gloomy that it was not recorded in the minutes, he spoke of another devaluation and the fall of the government within months if the confidence of the international financial community in Britain was not restored. But Callaghan, supported by Brown, Marsh, Greenwood and Crossman, argued that the government could not control wages in detail at plant and factory level, that the Civil Service was incompetent to judge the validity of wage claims and that:

> Strong measures of this kind may bring the opposite effect to what we require. Don't let us forget the seamen's strike. We thought it bold and brave to stand out then, but it was catastrophic.[1]

In the end Peter Shore was told to think again about the idea of detailed wage control by the government.

Five days later Shore reported that he had finally talked to Aubrey Jones of the Prices and Incomes Board and had given up the idea of detailed control of wages by the government. Instead he proposed to control only the total wages bill for each company and any excess over $3\frac{1}{2}\%$ would be reported to the Board not the government. The government's role would be limited to ordering a standstill of up to eleven months where an increase was referred to the Board and to ordering price reductions if recommended by the Board. These scaled-down proposals were acceptable to the rest of the Cabinet and the debate then centered on the length of time for which the new powers should be taken. Shore had originally proposed that they should run from July 1968 until October 1970. But as Wilson quickly pointed out this would entail either trying to pass a replacement or explaining why one was not being passed in the immediate run-up to the election. He thought it would be far better for the act to expire at the end of 1969 and if the government wanted to renew the powers it could be done through the annual

Expiring Laws Continuance Act, which would be difficult for rebel Labour MPs to oppose.

Labour backbenchers saw through Wilson's ploy and by May 1968 he had been forced by the level of opposition to drop the idea of slipping through the renewal of powers at the end of 1969. But there were almost universal doubts within the Cabinet about whether a prices and incomes policy could be kept going after the end of 1969, given the level of opposition within the trade unions and amongst Labour MPs. By the autumn of 1968 most of the Cabinet were not prepared to fight to maintain the policy. As Barbara Castle, the minister responsible for the detailed implementation of the policy, wrote after talking to Crosland and Jenkins:

> It is clear that he and Roy are getting ready to back out of it and certainly they would not dig in their heels to the tune of risking a major strike. This leaves me carrying an immense can. I have got to go on justifying a policy which three-quarters of the Cabinet no longer believe in, and pending its winding up I am being publicly bullied into enforcing it on the weaker brethren.[2]

During 1969 there were a few desultory discussions of prices and incomes policy. In March a small group of six ministers discussed what powers to take for 1970 onwards. Most accepted that an incomes policy only made about 1% difference to the rate of increases, and that therefore it wasn't worth all the effort and disputes that it generated, particularly with the economic situation improving and an election approaching. They agreed just to take powers to hold up increases for three months while the Prices and Incomes Board investigated. They rejected Castle's bid to keep the more draconian powers introduced in 1968 to reduce price increases. The government had now moved full circle and reverted to the limited powers it had first taken in 1965. In the autumn of 1969 the Cabinet agreed Castle's proposal to amalgamate the Prices and Incomes Board with the Monopolies Commission to create a Commission for Industry and Manpower. The aim was entirely political. The Conservatives were committed to abolish the Prices and Incomes Board, and Castle hoped to make it more difficult for them to do so after the amalgamation. A large part of the Cabinet was dubious about the proposal, and, as Castle admitted, the government powers to control prices and incomes after 1969 would be 'purely symbolic'. As Crossman summed up the debate:

We would have no effective Government powers . . . and it is clear that the prices and incomes policy is in fact in ruins but here was an Industrial Commission to put in its place.[3]

In the event the necessary legislation was not passed before the election and the Board was abolished by the Conservatives.

In November 1969 there was a discussion of what 'norm' should be adopted for the next year. Jenkins said he was happy to settle for increases of 6% and therefore wanted a 3½% norm. After a long debate in committee and in Cabinet, they eventually settled for a range of 2½-4½%. But it was all academic, since the government had no powers to enforce the norm. In fact, for political reasons, with the election approaching, the government was quite happy for wages to rise rapidly to create a sense of prosperity in the electorate. In practice this is what happened. Wage and salary increases in 1969 were nearly 8% higher than in 1968, and in 1970 they were 13% above the 1969 figure.

Despite all the tough measures the balance of payments showed no sign of improvement as 1968 passed. By June Jenkins was already telling his colleagues that given the high level of imports and large capital outflows a deficit for the year of nearly £300 million, the same as 1967, was likely (an accurate forecast). A linked problem was that the deflationary measures were having their expected effect and unemployment was rising again. By the autumn Jenkins was forecasting 3% unemployment for 1969 and only a 2% growth in output. Inflation was also picking up and earnings in the first half of the year were 8% up on a year earlier. At the beginning of November Shore produced the first draft of a White Paper entitled 'The Economic Assessment up to 1972'. This gave 'absolute priority' to obtaining a £500 million surplus on the balance of payments and forecast only a slight drop in unemployment before 1971. The general gloomy tenor of the document so appalled his colleagues that he was forced to withdraw it and rewrite it. The idea of publishing the assessment was dismissed out of hand and in its rewritten form it was only issued as a working paper for officials at the National Economic Development Office.

The government feared that publication of bad trade figures in mid-July 1968 might start another run on the pound. MISC 205 discussed what to do. Plan Brutus was kept in reserve and it was agreed that import quotas would take too long to implement and a surcharge was out, for international reasons, after the reaction in 1964. Jenkins therefore suggested a scheme for import deposits, under which importers would have to deposit with the government

378

a sum equal to half the value of the imports they wished to make. MISC 205 agreed that contingency planning should start. The expected run on the pound did not take place, but neither did any improvement in the balance of payments. By the end of October the position appeared to be as bad as it had been a year earlier on devaluation.

Jenkins was arguing strongly in MISC 205 for stronger measures. On 23 October he wanted an immediate increase in hire purchase controls on cars and durable goods. His colleagues decided to wait another week, then agreed on 29 October to go ahead. Later the same morning the Cabinet was invited to ratify that decision. It was Denis Healey who pointed out that the crucial Bassetlaw by-election was to be held on 31 October and they hurriedly agreed to postpone announcing the measures until after polling. This crude political judgement had its desired effect when Labour held the seat by just 740 votes. On 13 November Crosland warned MISC 205 that the October trade figures were dreadful and that, if the November figures were equally bad, they should prepare to introduce import quotas in December.

Within five days there was an international financial crisis following pressure on a weak franc, where devaluation was expected together with revaluation of the Deutschmark. On the evening of 18 November Jenkins told an emergency meeting of MISC 205 that the French were resisting devaluation but the pressure on both the franc and sterling was such that a further 15% devaluation of the pound looked inevitable, unless Germany decided to revalue the Deutschmark. The outlook for the British economy was poor. Jenkins expected only a small balance of payments surplus to be achieved by the end of 1969 with no real improvement in 1970. He wanted to introduce higher purchase tax and tighter hire-purchase controls immediately, although at this stage he did not favour import deposits. It was Castle and Shore who argued that concentrating solely on domestic restraint would be catastrophic politically. Ministers were agreed on the need to deal with the domestic crisis, and the crisis on the foreign exchanges provided a suitable opportunity to introduce the measures necessary for domestic reasons, while claiming in public that they were caused by the international situation.

On 19 November Jenkins accepted that import deposits should form part of the package. The international situation was still difficult with Germany refusing to revalue to take the pressure off the franc and the pound. That evening the German Ambassador was summoned to No 10 and told by Wilson and Jenkins that if the

Germans did not revalue then in the next economic crisis Britain would seriously consider completely withdrawing all British forces in Germany. Over the next two days international bankers meeting in Bonn devised a package for an 11% devaluation of the franc together with credit facilities. De Gaulle rejected the deal on 23 November and instead introduced an austerity package the next day.

In London the government quickly went ahead with its own package regardless, while the international situation still provided suitable cover. (Indeed had the government waited for the November trade figures to be published in December – showing a major fall in the deficit from £68 million in October to £16 million – much of the rationale for the package would have disappeared.) There was no time to work out anything in detail. On the morning of 22 November the Cabinet had to agree on the package to be announced by the Chancellor that afternoon. Crossman described the scene:

> Perhaps the most remarkable thing was that when we asked about the details and machinery of the import deposit scheme no one knew. Tony Crosland was in Vienna, the PM didn't know, neither did Jack Diamond [Chief Secretary] nor Barbara. The inner group of six who had prepared the package didn't know what goods were covered by the scheme . . . It is fantastic that in this particular case there was no bit of paper giving the package or the reasons for it. It was all told to us verbally and we have serious doubts whether a clear-cut plan had ever been worked out.[4]

The package had been introduced in exactly the same way as in every previous crisis – an ill-planned set of measures rushed through at the last moment without any discussion of either the details or alternative strategies.

The November package was both unnecessary and damaging, the product of a panic. Ministers lost their nerve waiting for the expected upturn and even a slight delay would have showed a rapid improvement in the balance of payments. The total impact of import deposits was a saving of about £60 million worth of imports in 1969. As the total current account of the balance of payments surplus for the year was £440 million, the effect of introducing import deposits was merely to increase an already large surplus. Domestically its effects were to further deflate an already stagnant economy.

Although the trade figures started to improve at the turn of

1968–69 there was no steady rate of progress or upsurge in ministerial morale. Figures for February 1969 were very bad with a deficit of £50 million, causing yet another outbreak of panic which led to a further bout of deflation. The 1969 Budget increased Corporation Tax, Selective Employment Tax and Purchase Tax, and reduced demand in the economy by about £250 million. But gradually during 1969 it became clear that a major surplus on the balance of payments for the year would be achieved. By July even Jenkins was optimistic in Cabinet and in October ministers agreed to reduce import deposits from 50% to 40% at the end of the year and to phase them out by the end of 1970.

One of the major consequences of the improved situation was a decrease in the number of ministerial discussions about economic policy. Here, Jenkins remained supreme and a few inchoate attempts in the autumn of 1968 by Castle, Shore, Crossman and a few others to discuss an alternative economic policy were easily swept aside. When in 1969 the policies seemed to bear fruit there was even less debate about alternatives. The level of public expenditure too generated little controversy after the major cuts in January 1968. Although the annual reviews involved reductions in the planned levels, this was done during 1968–69 without major policy changes.

The last important policy decision before the election was the content of the 1970 Budget. Because of the imminent election all ministers accepted that Budget policy would be determined by electoral considerations and the debate focused on what tactics to adopt. In the middle of 1969 some ministers hankered after the traditional bout of economic expansion in the run-up to an election. At the Inner Cabinet meeting on 30 June Castle argued for a more radical policy and Crossman for a more cynical policy, asking why the government should not 'do a Maudling' and go for a quick burst of growth to give the illusion of prosperity. Jenkins was opposed, not on principle, but because he thought the chances of bringing it off were slight. By the autumn of 1969, with the balance of payments at last in healthy surplus, the political factors argued in favour of making a virtue out of necessity, and standing on a record of prudent stewardship of the economy and success in the one area the government had made central to its strategy. The Inner Cabinet accordingly accepted Jenkins' advice in September 1969 not to go for an expansionist policy and again in January it agreed that it would be disastrous politically to have a 'giveaway' Budget. Jenkins even went so far as to tell the Cabinet on 12 February that he 'would rather lose the election than jeopardise our economic success.'[5] But in personal political terms Jenkins could afford to lose the election because he would then be in a strong position to challenge a defeated Wilson for the leadership. Indeed by late February Wilson was telling his friends that he was worried by Jenkins' too cautious approach to the Budget and expressing his own desire for something more expansionary. In the April 1970 Budget Jenkins, convinced it was psychologically vital not to have any tax increases, even managed a small decrease in income tax by raising personal allowances. Apart from that it was essentially a standstill Budget but optimistic in tone, based on a successful recovery.

Behind the public optimism what were ministers' real views about the state of the economy? On 19 January SEP considered a paper by Jenkins for the government to submit to NEDC on the prospects for the economy in the early 1970s. It was Peter Shore who pointed out the politically disastrous nature of the assessment. Top priority was still given to achieving a balance of payments surplus of about £300 million a year but the price to be paid in the rest of the economy was substantial. Growth at 2.9% a year was the lowest projection ever published by any government and compared with the 4% a year expected in the rest of Europe. No reduction was expected in unemployment which would remain between 500,000–750,000. Regional policies showed no signs of success. All the other members of the committee were similarly critical about publishing such a dismal forecast, and Wilson instructed that the assessment should be withdrawn and a more optimistic picture substituted.

From October 1964 the government had always given high priority to the balance of payments and preserving the value of sterling. For this reason devaluation was inevitably seen as a major failure. From November 1967 the sole criterion for economic success was a sizeable surplus on the balance of payments. This was so for political just as much as economic reasons. Only by achieving this surplus could the government argue that devaluation had not been a failure after all and demonstrate that their economic policy was bearing fruit. By 1970 that single aim had been achieved but at what cost?

None of the measures taken between 1967 and 1970, apart from import deposits and some cuts in overseas defence expenditure, acted directly on the balance of payments. The general policy was once again to deflate the economy through increased taxation and reduced government expenditure, in the hope that this would in turn reduce demand for imports and increase the scope for exports.

In total the 1968 and 1969 Budgets diverted 4% of national wealth away from consumption, and this shift of resources was reinforced by reductions in public expenditure. The consequences of devaluation took far longer to take effect than the government expected and it was not until well into 1969 that there was some degree of certainty that a major improvement had in fact taken place. They misjudged the situation in the autumn of 1968 and introduced further deflation and import deposits, which only ensured that the surplus in 1969 was even bigger than it would otherwise have been. But this criticism can be applied to the totality of the measures taken in the two years after devaluation. The government achieved a far greater surplus than was required either on political or economic grounds. (It reached £735 million in 1970, the highest for twenty years, at a cost of domestic deflation far greater than necessary.)

In parallel with this highly conventional economic policy the government also adopted an even more conventional policy on debt repayment and the funding of government expenditure. Outstanding official borrowing abroad rose by over 500% between 1964 and 1968. Jenkins then embarked on a massive repayment exercise, which cut the debt in half by 1970. This was complemented in domestic financing by the rapid decline in the public sector borrowing requirement from £2 billion in the financial year 1967–68 to £450 million in 1968–69 to a surplus of £500 million in 1969–70. This was the only year until the late 1980s that the government was not a borrower, and indicated the extent to which expenditure had been cut and taxation increased to fund that expenditure. These policies were in line with the agreements reached with the IMF, and reflected Jenkins' own determination to do better than those commitments by reducing borrowing and cutting expenditure. Although these policies may have satisfied international bankers, the additional public expenditure cuts and higher taxation required at home, with their deflationary effect and direct impact on individual income, must have affected Labour's political support. The 'slog' was far harder and longer than it needed to be.

Jenkins' achievement in balancing the budget and producing a balance of payments surplus in the short term have been overrated; these policies did not produce a British 'economic miracle'. The underlying problems of the economy remained unresolved. Devaluation and deflation could do no more than buy time to make the necessary structural adjustments but these were not forthcoming. British industry remained uncompetitive (despite the short-term price advantage given by devaluation) and productivity remained low compared with other industrialised nations. Despite the prices and incomes policy wages continued to grow faster than productivity. By 1970 they were rising 9% faster than productivity. Inflation too was picking up at an annual rate of 6½% (compared with 2½% in 1967). Unemployment at over 550,000 in 1970 was 10% higher than in 1967 and showed no sign of falling. Growth in output was only just over 1½% in both 1969 and 1970.

When it sought re-election in June 1970 the government had little choice but to stand on its record on the improvement in the balance of payments. After all the earlier hopes for the revitalis-ation of the British economy this was all it could offer. It remained to be seen whether this produced a sufficient level of confidence in the government's overall performance and prospects to guarantee success at the general election.

PART
FIVE

ASSESSMENT

24
Defeat:
The 1970 Election

The General Election was announced on 18 May, with polling day on 18 June. The government fought the campaign on an essentially conservative stance. Having 'put the economy right', they were seeking a mandate to continue in much the same way for the next five years. The manifesto had no major policy initiatives to suggest and during the campaign Labour was content, as ministers had agreed months before, to depict the Conservatives as the radicals trying to upset a safe and established way of running the country. To some extent the Conservatives were willing to accept that designation and campaign on a basis of upsetting what they argued was a dangerous complacency about the state of the nation.

These general factors were reflected in the style of each campaign. Wilson, relaxed and casual, gradually developed an informal 'walkabout' as his main activity for each day. He was content to portray an avuncular, reassuring, pipe-smoking, family-doctor image in the style of Stanley Baldwin. Heath was more strident as he fought to save his political career from a second defeat and probable removal from the leadership. He spoke mainly to all-ticket, all-Conservative rallies and concentrated on major themes in an attempt to put across the message, which he summarised on 13 June as: 'I have to say to the British people, "For Heaven's sake, wake up."' The Labour campaign had been put together at the last minute and was run largely by Wilson's staff from No 10, whereas the Conservative campaign was well organised and planned long in advance. Whether this made much difference to the outcome is doubtful.

There were few live issues in the campaign. Wilson had successfully defused EEC entry and Rhodesia as subjects for much interparty debate and although Enoch Powell played up the race and immigration issue, neither Heath nor Wilson showed any inclination to get drawn into that particular quagmire. The state of the economy – whether the 'recovery' was soundly based or not, the prospects for future inflation and Britain's relative economic decline – was the main issue. The campaign itself was uneventful; public attention was focused on the superb weather and England's progress in the World Cup in Mexico, leading to the unexpected 3–2 defeat by West Germany on the Sunday before polling. The only events of note during the campaign were the government's request to the Cricket Council to call off the tour by South Africa due to start at the beginning of June because of likely crowd trouble from anti-apartheid demonstrators, their rejection of a recommended pay award for doctors and a short strike in Fleet Street. None seems to have had an impact on the polls.

The 1970 election will be remembered as the one that the opinion polls got wrong. Throughout the campaign they showed a steady Labour lead, of nearly 10% at one point, a week before polling. Two-thirds of the electorate expected Labour to win, compared with nearly 60% in January who had expected the Conservatives to win. The polls did show a declining Labour lead in the last days of the campaign but only ORC, published on polling day, detected a small Conservative lead. This movement reflected a sudden surge of doubts about the reality of the government's claims about economic recovery. On 9 June the balance of payments figures for the 1969–70 financial year were published, showing a substantial surplus of £606 million. Yet the figures that had the greatest impact were those published on the Monday before polling, which revealed a trade deficit for May of £31 million. As it turned out, these were freak figures (in a year that produced the highest balance of payments surplus for twenty years) but taken in isolation at a critical time they seemed to support the Conservative argument that the economy was still weak and fragile. Then on polling day itself the unemployment figures were announced giving a record high June total.

The first signs that Labour might not win the election came shortly after polling closed when the first ever exit poll suggested a 4.4% swing to the Conservatives. This was confirmed by the first result at Guildford, recording a 6% swing. The final result was a Conservative lead of nearly 3½%, giving them 330 seats – a majority over Labour of forty-three and an overall majority of thirty. The average swing to the Conservatives was 4.8% giving them a net gain of sixty-six seats. Altogether eighty-eight seats changed hands, the most since 1945. The only Cabinet Minister to lose his seat was Jack Diamond at Gloucester, although George Brown was defeated at Belper and Jennie Lee at Cannock. The Liberals had a disastrous election, losing seven of their thirteen MPs, and polling a million votes less than in 1964. Plaid Cymru lost

388

its only seat at Carmarthen, as did the SNP at Hamilton (although they won Western Isles).

The results were hardly a massive endorsement of the Conservatives. Turnout, at 72%, was the lowest for thirty-five years, though this partly reflected the holiday season. Perhaps the most telling statistic was that from a NOP survey which showed that only 29% of the electorate cared 'very much' who won the election. If the result was only a half-hearted show of enthusiasm for the Conservatives, why did Labour lose?

The Labour recovery, as reflected in opinion polls, was not soundly based. For over two years they had suffered from a record degree of unpopularity in the opinion polls. From the summer of 1969 they began to close the gap. Not until May 1970 did the polls indicate the first Labour lead, a lead confirmed by the local election results. The Inner Cabinet, although increasingly confident of victory during the spring of 1970 on the basis of the polls, remained uncertain and divided about the relative merits of a June or October poll. It was this sudden surge of support that convinced them to make a quick dash to the polls in the hope of securing another five years of power before the fragile position collapsed. For most of the campaign they seemed likely to succeed. The Conservative message about the poor state of the economy was only making slow headway before the trade and unemployment figures were published in the last week of the campaign. These seemed to confirm what the Conservatives were saying. But that message could not have been successful unless there was already a well of suspicion about the reality of economic recovery and the competence of the Labour government to handle the economy. It needed little to revive memories of repeated economic failure from July 1966 to devaluation and 'two years' hard slog'. When the crunch came too many people could remember past failures and were not prepared to give a vote of confidence. Instead they preferred a largely unknown alternative that seemed to promise a new departure and at least a chance of improved performance. That alternative too was to prove ultimately unsuccessful, leading to the miners' strike, the three-day week, the collapse of the Conservative government in February 1974 and the return of a minority Labour government, headed by Harold Wilson.

25
Breach of Promise

On 25 October 1951, two days after their defeat in the general election, Clement Attlee and Hugh Dalton were at Chequers reminiscing about what they had achieved in government over the previous six years. They were proud of their record:

> We've done all that now; written the first chapter of the Socialist story, in law and administration. What next? The younger people must write the second chapter.[1]

The next generation of Labour politicians had to wait thirteen years, far longer than they expected, for the opportunity to write that second chapter of the story. The long period of waiting made it all the more important for the Labour government under Harold Wilson to seize the opportunity before them in 1964 and again in 1966, and use it to the full. It was only the second majority Labour government in history and only the third time this century that a non-Conservative government had obtained a majority. How then should the record of the 1964–70 government be judged?

Undoubtedly there were many achievements in the field of social reform. A series of measures were passed which were, on a smaller scale, successors to the major institutional reforms of the Attlee government, and which had a significant impact on social attitudes and the lives of ordinary individuals. Into this category falls the creation of the Open University, a truly imaginative idea that gave a second chance to hundreds of thousands of people who had missed out on educational opportunities earlier in their lives. The Equal Pay Act of 1970 for the first time established the concept of equal pay for equal work and was an important step on the long path towards equality for women. The introduction of redundancy pay benefitted thousands of workers and established the principle that they did have a right to be compensated for the loss of their job. The two Race Relations Acts were a start in combating some of the worst aspects of racism in Britain, and in accepting the important principle that the state did have the right and duty to intervene to control this sort of behaviour. The introduction of rent tribunals, the concept of a 'fair rent' and, most importantly, protection from eviction, brought major improvements for tenants, particularly those at the lowest end of the private-rented sector. The Ombudsman did provide at least some redress against incompetence, and worse, in the bureaucracy.

In an indirect way the government was also responsible for the introduction of other measures that were to have profound effects on social life over the next decades. It helped to pass, with varying degrees of enthusiasm, backbench legislation that abolished the death penalty (of enormous symbolic importance), legalised homosexuality between consenting adults, provided easier abortion and easier divorce, and abolished theatre censorship. Despite some of the criticism of these changes in recent years they were a major step towards a more tolerant and 'civilised' society.

Attempts at institutional reform were less successful. Although some new bodies were established, the results were both disappointing and short-lived. The Land Commission and the Ministry of Land and Natural Resources were hamstrung from the start, and never had a chance of making any impact. The attempt to bring about change within existing institutions in Britain was for the most part a half-hearted affair with few tangible results. The Law Commission, though it did some useful work tidying up legislation, did not bring about any major change in the operation of the law. The attempt to reform the Civil Service ended in almost complete failure.

The government had a good record on one of the most important areas for any Labour administration – economic equality. More might have been done had it been able to devise effective methods of acting directly on the distribution of earned income. The idea of an 'incomes guarantee' that had been favoured before 1964 proved impracticable and little action was taken on a national minimum wage. Incomes policy – directed primarily at controlling all wages across the board – provided only a marginal benefit to the lower paid and even this was swept away in the wages explosion of the last year of the government. What fiscal measures it did introduce were equally ineffective. Although a special surcharge was introduced for the highest paid in 1968, this was only for one year and Capital Gains Tax (introduced in 1965) had so many exemptions (including owner-occupied houses) that it only slowed down the rate at which the wealth of the richest accumulated. They had no interest in going any further and considering a wealth tax. Where the government was able and willing to act was through the provision of benefits and other state spending, and this had the greatest impact on the less well off. (In total one in seven of the population was dependent on state benefits in one form or the other in the 1960s.) This impact was achieved through increases in pensions, supplementary benefit and family allowances. Family allowances, for example, were doubled between 1964 and 1970, although most of this increase did not come up until 1968 and the introduction of 'clawback' to stop the better off benefitting from the extra payments. In addition new benefits such as rate rebates were important. By the end of the 1960s one million households were receiving this benefit. Apart from these direct payments and concessions government expenditure also provided benefits in kind. Public expenditure had been rising under the Conservatives but the Labour government increased the rate during the first three years of its life: as a proportion of Gross Domestic Product it went up from 34% in 1964–5 to 40% in 1967–68. Even after the post-devaluation cuts took effect (when public expenditure actually fell for two years) in 1969–70 it still took up nearly 38% of GDP. Within this overall pattern expenditure on social services rose from 16% of national wealth in 1964 to 23% in 1970. Similarly spending on health rose from 3.9% to 4.9% and on education from 4.8% to 6.1%. The impact of all these measures taken together was significant. When the broadest measure of disposable income (after taxation but including benefits) is considered, the period 1964–69 showed an average decline of 16%. But those individuals on the highest incomes suffered a fall of 33%, whereas those on the lowest incomes went up by 104%.

However, these extra benefits could only be paid for at a price – increased taxation. The share of national income collected in taxes rose from 32% to 43% during the period of the Labour government. Income tax was raised by 2½p in the pound in the November 1964 Budget and not subsequently reduced. Although over the life of the government the increases were greatest for the highest paid, all income groups finished up paying more. In total, taxes on personal income rose from an average of 10% of total personal income in 1964 to 14% in 1970. There were similar increases in indirect taxation with the main increases on wine (108%) and purchase tax on luxuries (120%), and the lowest increases in duty on beer and tobacco (30–40%), and purchase tax on clothing and furniture (38%).

In the field of social reform, equality and redistribution of income the government's record is all the more commendable, since it was achieved in the face of an awful economic legacy, economic difficulties throughout the period, and considerable opposition from the Treasury and Jim Callaghan. Those difficulties meant that many aspirations had been abandoned – for example, the much-vaunted housing programme never achieved the grandiose targets of the 1964 and 1966 manifestos and the raising of the school leaving age to sixteen was postponed in 1968. The major reform of benefits and pensions never took place because the government delayed work, and had not thought through its legislative priorities. Yet enough remained for a creditable achievement even if it fell short of what many in 1964 had hoped to attain.

The economic difficulties were part-inherited and part-self-imposed, and the government's overall management of the economy is central to any assessment of its record. In 1970 Labour fought the election very largely on what it saw as its major achievement – the transformation of a balance of payments deficit of about £700 million in 1964 into a surplus of the same size in 1970. This was not what it set out to do but what it set its sights on producing after 1967. But this recovery in one aspect of economic performance was only achieved at a substantial cost elsewhere. Unemployment rose from an average of 350,000 in 1964 to 555,000 in 1970 – an increase of nearly 60%. At the same time inflation almost doubled from an average of 3.3% in 1964 to 6.4% in 1970. The funding of the balance of payments deficit and the defence of the value of the pound also resulted in a major increase in Britain's foreign indebtedness. By 1967 Britain had total debts of £6.5 billion, the largest government foreign debt per head of the population anywhere in the world, although this debt was halved by 1970.

To a large extent many of the problems with the British economy were not of the government's making. They had proved impossible for its predecessors to cure and its successors were to be equally unsuccessful. The Labour government was faced with a low growth economy steadily losing ground, relative to its competitors. Low investment, wages rising faster than productivity growth and the handicap of a large number of declining industries (and an over-valued pound) lay at the root of Britain's economic problems. Already in the late 1960s the twin problems that were to bedevil the 1970s – simultaneously rising unemployment and inflation – were becoming apparent. In 1964 the government promised answers to these problems. It wanted to place the emphasis on action to improve the 'real' economy through the National Plan, regional planning and the greater use of technology. Later more dubious initiatives, such as SET, were also tried. None of the ideas was particularly successful in practice. The Department of Economic Affairs was not able fundamentally to alter economic policy and it never replaced the Treasury as the key ministry in policy formulation. Regional policy had some limited successes but the National Plan never had a chance even before it was abandoned in July 1966. At the crucial moment the government gave priority to the defence of sterling. The targets were hopelessly over-optimistic but the real failure lay in the fact that no preparatory work had been done on how 'indicative' planning should work or what mechanisms were required to ensure that the aims of the plan were the dominant influence in economic policy. (The episode leaves unresolved doubts as to whether an essentially free-market economy, strongly linked into the international system, could be 'planned' in any meaningful sense without draconian powers that no government could take in peacetime.) The emphasis on 'technology' provided a convenient slogan but developing a coherent policy proved far more difficult. Half the government's expenditure on Research and Development continued to go into the arms industry, an inefficient use of limited resources, while a large percentage of the rest was swallowed up by a few high-technology, high-risk projects, such as Concorde and nuclear power. The new Ministry of Technology was never anything more than a 'ministry for industry', involved in the day-to-day problems of a piecemeal collection of declining industries. The fashionable policy of merging uncompetitive firms proved equally fruitless as a revitalising measure. The renationalising of steel implemented a promise that had survived from the early 1950s but it was unclear how it would enable the industry to cope with a difficult future of overcapacity, low productivity and investment.

Although it had some new ideas, the Labour government was unable to alter the long-term trends affecting the British economy which seemed to lie too deep for any government to control. Throughout the 1960s the dismal catalogue of statistics continued. Britain's share of world exports, having fallen from 21% in the early 1950s to 16% in the early 1960s, reached 11% by the end of the decade. Similarly Britain's share of world exports of manufactures fell from 12.7% in 1960 to 8.6% in 1970, whilst major competitors such as Germany, Italy and Japan were increasing their share. Economic growth under the Labour government remained around 2% a year (the National Plan was based on 4% per year), whereas all Britain's competitors had higher rates throughout the 1960s: Germany (3.3%), France (5%), Italy (4.7%) and Japan (10%). Manufacturing output continued to grow more slowly than among major competitors, as did output per person (the nearest guide to productivity). Britain's inflation rate was also higher. The only bright spot was investment, which reached an all-time high in the late 1960s. However, even this achievement has to be judged against the fact that at these historically high levels investment was still below the levels achieved by Britain's competitors.

Against this background the original decision to defend the value of the currency and the timing of the subsequent decision to devalue lies at the core of the government's economic, and political, performance. For three years the government fought desperately to avoid devaluation and this battle involved major costs. The economy was deflated in all three Budgets from 1965 to 1967, there were rises in Bank Rate, tougher hire purchase controls, increased taxation, cuts in government spending plans, increased purchase tax, and the two special 'packages' in July 1965 and July 1966. In addition the government incurred massive debts to maintain the value of the pound and accepted major constraints on its policy to obtain American backing in the summer of 1965. Yet the economic measures did not act directly on the balance of payments but sought instead simply to reduce demand and therefore reduce imports. This was nothing new: deflation had been the basis of all the Treasury packages over the previous ten years to try and cope with recurrent balance of payments problems. They had not worked in the past and there was no evidence that they would work on these occasions.

Why did the government embark on such a long drawn-out and ultimately futile course, one which they had heavily criticised when in opposition? Certainly Wilson, and at the start of the government Brown and Callaghan too, were strongly opposed to devaluation and believed that it was not the solution to Britain's economic problems. To an extent Wilson was right. Devaluation would not by itself put right the underlying malaise of underperformance and the relative decline in the British economy, as the experience after 1967 demonstrated. But the government's other economic policies showed no sign of doing so either. This attitude also neglected the fact that British export prices had become increasingly uncompetitive because of the overvalued pound. Without devaluation the British economy could not even begin to compete on world markets. The serious constraint that was not tackled until after devaluation was the sterling balances. These were one of the prime causes of the weakness of the pound because of the inadequate reserves available to cope with speculation or the threat of withdrawal.

There was therefore a strong argument for using the international resources that were available (exhausted in an effort to simply support sterling) to fund the rundown of the balances, as was eventually done in 1968. If this move had been made earlier many problems would have been avoided.

Once the government had decided not to devalue, Wilson increasingly saw the whole prestige of the government staked on the value of the pound. This led to his disastrous refusal even to discuss devaluation as a rational policy option until it was too late. The reluctance of the politicians was reinforced by the institutional forces surrounding them. The Treasury, the Bank of England, the City, the international financial community and the United States government were all opposed to devaluation and a rundown of the sterling balances for various reasons. They saw it as a betrayal of Britain's obligations and a direct threat to the world financial system. In addition a great deal of national pride and prestige was bound up with the urge to maintain the value of the pound and its role as a reserve currency.

Under these pressures, and with its tiny parliamentary majority, it is easy to appreciate why the government did not devalue in the autumn of 1964. It is also easy to see why devaluation took place in November 1967. By then there was little alternative; the economy was in recession, no improvement seemed likely in the balance of payments, the reserves were as low as they had been for the previous three years and external assistance was only available at major political cost. That the situation was so bad in November 1967 and that no fundamental improvement had occurred since 1964 despite all the measures taken by the government is the most damning indictment possible of its economic policy, and an illustration of the fact that it had been moving down a cul-de-sac for three years. The crucial question therefore is why devaluation did not take place after the March 1966 election and in particular during the July crisis of that year.

In retrospect the decision to deflate rather than devalue in July 1966 was the historic moment in the fortunes of the government: it was then that it took the wrong turning. Its parliamentary position was secure and it had a full term ahead. It was by then aware of the sort of penalties in terms of its domestic priorities and its freedom of action overseas that its previous action had entailed. Deflation could only be justified if it offered a fundamental solution to economic problems. This it clearly did not, as previous 'stop-go' policies had demonstrated. The July 1966 measures meant only more of the same, and they also used up two precious commodities

– the cooperation of the trade unions and time. Although the government faced a problem in that the trade unions were more 'left-wing' and antagonistic than the unions during the Attlee government, until July 1966 relations between the two had been reasonably good and the government had obtained strong cooperation over its incomes policy. The twelve-month freeze introduced as part of the crisis package was sold to the unions as part of the solution to Britain's economic problems. When they realised it was not, they were less willing to cooperate over later incomes policies or over the consequences of devaluation. That sacrifice by the unions could and should have been held in reserve for the crucial measures to try and make devaluation work. July 1966 was also the time to devalue politically. Never an easy option (despite what some members of the Cabinet seem to have thought), it would necessarily involve a measure of deflation to try and limit the effects of a rise in import prices and move more resources into exports. If the pound had been devalued in July 1966, then the consequences would have had time to work through by about the end of 1968, giving the government time to demonstrate that it was on the road to economic recovery before the election. As it was, devaluation at the end of 1967 did not leave it enough time to recover before the 1970 election. The reason why devaluation did not occur in July 1966 is that, in spite of Brown's support for the measure and Callaghan's wavering, Wilson remained strongly opposed personally. It was his choice to stick to the deal he had made with the Americans a year earlier, and this was the point when the real price had to be paid for that deal. US support for the pound in return for no devaluation, deflation at home and the maintenance of external commitments was still dominating British policy.

The secret deal struck with the Americans in the summer of 1965, while it served its short-term purpose of getting the government through to the election, tied them to an ultimately unsustainable strategy. It stringently limited the room for manoeuvre on domestic economic policy, by giving the Americans a major say in that policy and ensuring that the dominating elements were defence of the pound, deflation and incomes policy. It also seriously affected strategic policy. Had the British presence in the Far East not become a bargaining counter, then the government might have taken a more realistic view of Britain's military commitments. As it was, from 1964 until 1968 there was a last-gasp effort to keep Britain's world role by maintaining virtually all the commitments in the Far East and in addition the Gulf. Even though the government decided in 1967 on ultimate withdrawal from the Far East, and in 1968 decided to accelerate the withdrawal timetable and pull-out from East of Suez, altogether the actual impact on defence expenditure of that belated decision was limited. (Planned defence expenditure was reduced but actual expenditure showed little change and fell by just 2.3% over the life of the government.) As the Americans recognised, the economic and strategic elements were linked. When the balance of payments figures for the late 1960s are examined in detail they throw an interesting light on British policy. Throughout the period the private-sector balance of payments, taking account of visible and invisible trade, showed a healthy, positive balance in every year. Visible exports were less than imports but this was easily offset by heavy surpluses on invisible trade. The real problem came in the government sector. Here net spending abroad, almost entirely on military commitments, ran at well over £400 million a year: it was the major single cause of the balance of payments difficulties. This figure did not fall during the life of the Labour government, and therefore most of the weight of the effort to cope with the deficits and the effects of devaluation had to be taken by the private domestic economy. Britain's failure to bring its military commitments into line with what it could afford was a fundamental cause of its economic problems, as it had been ever since 1945. By maintaining its forces in the Far East under American pressure the government was only making its difficulties worse.

In the long perspective the decisions to make the final withdrawal from East of Suez, to devalue and to end the role of sterling as a reserve currency (all taken in the year after July 1967) can be seen as the last step in the painful withdrawal from Empire, the end of the illusion that Britain could maintain a worldwide military presence without the economic base to support such an effort and the end of the idea that Britain was still a lynchpin of the world economic order. Although the Labour government did not really articulate, even to themselves, the full consequences of these decisions (and many illusions still survive), the United States government recognised that this period marked the end of the phase when Britain could be anything more than just another medium-sized ally. But despite strong American pressure for Britain also to reduce its role in the nuclear field the Labour government clung to the 'independent' deterrent: Wilson proved just as keen as his predecessors and successors on keeping absolute British control over the system, and just as willing to authorise spending large sums to keep it fully modernised.

If the government's overall economic and defence strategy was flawed, the same criticism can be made of its central political strategy after the March 1966 election. In the period between October 1964 and the election the government played its cards well and kept its nerve in some tricky situations. It had squarely (and rightly) put the blame for its dreadful economic inheritance on the Conservatives and it kept the initiative politically so as to dictate the timing of the election and secure a major triumph. The period after the election gave them an opportunity for a fresh start but there was no rethink of government strategy, no attempt to consider a plan for a five-year parliament in which the Labour party had received its second biggest majority ever. Instead an incoherent programme of legislation was reintroduced after the election and work on important reforms (the House of Lords and a new state pension scheme) went ahead at a snail's pace. Without a strategy, or a clear programme of reforming legislation, the government drifted from one issue to another without stamping its authority on events. These problems were made worse by economic failure apparent from July 1966 onwards until its loss of direction was confirmed by devaluation and the consequent massive cuts in public expenditure, the stiff 1968 Budget and further crisis measures in the autumn of 1968.

In parallel with these blows the government developed a penchant for self-inflicted wounds – the D-Notice affair, the row over arms sales to South Africa, the failure to reform the House of Lords and, worst of all, the ill-fated attempt to regulate industrial relations. In addition the government took other decisions that damaged its reputation – for example, the refusal to implement the agreed parliamentary boundary changes. In 1964 Harold Wilson had said: 'The Labour party is a moral crusade or it is nothing.' In office it seemed anything but a moral crusade. It gave a low priority to moral issues as a matter of clear political choice. The aid programme was ruthlessly cut on the grounds that the state of the economy, and particularly the balance of payments, ruled out doing more. Yet at the same time the government decided to spend £700 million in scarce dollars to buy American military aircraft rather than British alternatives and also to maintain worldwide military commitments. The population of Diego Garcia could be expelled from their homes in order to provide a military base for the United States. The Kenyan Asians could have their right to settle in Britain removed the moment they seemed likely to exercise that right. And in a policy of outrageous hypocrisy it could secretly connive at the breaking of its own sanctions against Rhodesia by the oil companies whilst continuing to lecture others on the need to do more to defeat the illegal Smith regime.

Overall the general impression of the record of the government is one of a series of lost opportunities and broken promises. The roots of that failure go back to the twin threads of policy and personality running through the experience of the Labour party in opposition after 1951. Political pragmatism has a part to play in any government but the history and fate of this government reveal its lack of a clear intellectual and theoretical structure to help it define long-term goals and provide a justification for its actions. Since 1918 the Labour party had, theoretically, been committed to attaining a 'socialist' solution in Britain. It had never worked out what 'democratic socialism' meant in practice. It settled instead, perhaps inevitably, for a series of short-term programmes. Whether the sum of these parts amounted to 'socialism' is another question and it was easier to fall back on Herbert Morrison's comforting dictum that 'Socialism is what a Labour government does.' This had certainly been the case from 1945–51 when a programme of full employment, nationalisation, social security and a free health service (all major programmes amounting to a substantial achievement) became synonymous with 'socialism'. And when the Conservatives broadly accepted the work of the Attlee government, it formed the basis of a new framework in British politics. The subsequent question was fundamental. Was the role of the Labour party to keep within that framework, whilst operating it to try and secure a marginally more egalitarian result; or was it to pursue more fundamental change in the distribution of wealth and power?

This question was never answered before 1964, although the party had drifted towards working within the existing structure. The theoretical analysis that supported this approach was contained in Tony Crosland's *The Future of Socialism*, with its emphasis on redistributing the benefits of economic growth through public expenditure so as to help the underprivileged. To some extent, as we have seen, the Labour government did try to do this. But with economic growth stuck in a rut at about 2% a year and with a perpetual atmosphere of economic crisis, the room for manouevre was limited. At the same time there were some ideas for more radical action, such as Crossman's state pension plan of 1957. As a fully funded scheme it would have accumulated vast assets, made private sector pensions unattractive and, by purchasing shares with its funds, would have altered fundamentally not just the distribution of wealth (by putting the poorest pensioners onto half-wages) but also the ownership of wealth. In office the will to implement such a radical scheme was missing.

In opposition Wilson had steered well clear of developing any theoretical basis for the work of a future government. After the long, divisive rows of the 1950s and early 1960s Wilson adopted vague general themes, such as 'modernisation' and 'science and technology', as a way of unifying the party. In the short term he succeeded, as he demonstrated in the run-up to the 1964 election. But this approach brought real problems once in office. The government had a programme of sorts on which it had been elected but, once this slightly vague set of promises had been implemented, it had little idea what it wanted to do next or what its priorities were when it came under pressure and was forced to take difficult decisions. All governments tend to get swept along or sidetracked by external events to some extent but in this case the intellectual vacuum produced a sense of drift after only a short period in office.

Another serious handicap for the government was that it was unable to put aside or transcend the personality clashes and political rivalries inherited from thirteen years in opposition. The Labour party had always been divided but the peculiar intensity of the battles in the 1950s between the Bevanites, Gaitskell's supporters, the unilateralists and the group around Wilson left lasting wounds. Trust and mutual respect between the groups were missing, so that almost every move was regarded with suspicion and at the top of the party there was persistent rivalry. Such activity is to some extent a normal and inevitable part of political life but between Wilson, Brown and Callaghan (and later on Jenkins) these rivalries had a major impact on policy making, as they manoeuvred for position and power. In the July 1966 crisis George Brown's decision to treat the episode as a way of undermining and possibly replacing Wilson was one of the major factors in the eventual outcome. It helped ensure that there was never a sensible debate about policy, as many of those who wanted devaluation preferred Wilson as leader and no devaluation to Brown and devaluation. The semi-public battle over the sale of arms to South Africa was similarly about the possible replacement of Wilson by a new leader from the right of the party. In 1969 the row over industrial relations was stoked up by Callaghan's ambition to replace Wilson.

Wilson must take some of the blame for this state of affairs. Although in many ways kind (few others would have put up with George Brown so long) and unwilling to sack his colleagues, he was also a man with a deeply insecure personality. He constantly saw threats and plots against his position. Sometimes he was right to do so but on many occasions he was his own worst enemy. His suspicion of his colleagues and his preference for covert action helped to create an atmosphere of conspiracy and mistrust within the government. Differences over policy became attempted coups. Douglas Jay, who served in both the Wilson and Attlee governments, compared the two:

> The Wilson Government was an unhappy one, in which unease and suspicion festered, in contrast to the sense of purpose and achievement which buoyed us up even in the most arduous moments in 1945–51.[2]

Wilson seems to have lacked the self-confidence to realise that as Prime Minister he was virtually unassailable, barring complete catastrophe. Only two Prime Ministers this century (Asquith and Chamberlain) have lost the confidence of their own parties and had to resign, and both of those were in wartime. Wilson's use of the press may have been adroit for some purposes but his habit of 'briefings', often at the expense of his colleagues, created distrust. Not surprisingly they often replied in kind. Although admired for his tactical skill, Wilson did not inspire confidence in his colleagues. As Tony Crosland put it:

> The trouble with Harold is one hasn't the faintest idea whether the bastard means what he says even at the moment he speaks it.[3]

Crosland was never a friend of Wilson but even one of his closest supporters, Tony Benn, came sadly to the same conclusion:

> In the end, the tragedy of Wilson was that you couldn't believe a word he said.[4]

There was an even more serious flaw in Harold Wilson's leadership. Ultimately more harmful than the lack of trust and fraternal feeling was the political and intellectual vacuum, already mentioned, at the centre of government. It is impossible to find out what Harold Wilson really believed, as opposed to what he said and did, about the policy issues the government had to face. For example, on entry to the EEC he manoeuvered the issue through Cabinet and obtained a decision to apply for entry, yet it remains unclear whether Wilson believed that entry was the right policy for

Britain. Similarly it is impossible to establish Wilson's real views about Britain's possession of a nuclear deterrent.

By 1964 Wilson's life had been devoted to politics for twenty years. His earlier career suggests that what fundamental beliefs he had had long disappeared. As a student he was a Liberal but in 1943 he decided to go into politics in the Labour party. As a minister he turned out to be safe and unexciting, and his main achievement was to dismantle central control over the economy. He was clearly on the 'non-ideological' centre-right of the party. His rapid conversion to the cause of Nye Bevan in 1951 had the desired effect of establishing his credentials with the left-wing party activists for the period of opposition that was in prospect and gave him an identity separate from his rival, Hugh Gaitskell. Wilson's career as a Bevanite was short-lived and certainly ended when he replaced Bevan on the NEC. He further enhanced his reputation as being on the left of the party by his decision to oppose Gaitskell for the leadership in 1960, although his attitude to the main issue involved – unilateral nuclear disarmament – was studiously ambiguous. Although Wilson was content to draw support from the left he showed no signs of any strong personal support for its causes. Indeed in opposition his reputation was built on effective performances in the House of Commons based on clever criticisms of the Conservative government but showing few signs of any clear alternative approach.

While Wilson's pragmatic approach and lack of a strong personal political message was a considerable asset in electoral terms in 1964, and also within the complex, faction-ridden internal politics of the Labour party, it was ultimately to prove a damaging liability in government. He saw all issues in straight political terms, and his aim was to exploit them tactically and achieve a 'politically' successful conclusion. For him, playing the game of politics was everything and success was judged solely by electoral popularity, clever parliamentary tactics and good media coverage. The achievement of particular policy goals was incidental to this process. Wilson was driven by intense personal ambition but once he had obtained power he tended to enjoy it for its own sake. His memoirs give the impression of a man obsessed with the trappings of power – the protocol of receptions in Washington, the use of communications at No 10, Chequers or on an RAF flight, the special security briefings and access to highly classified information. This same trait was demonstrated in his love of personal diplomacy – his meetings with President Johnson or Ian Smith and his interventions in the Vietnam war and the Nigerian civil war.

Wilson, as an ex-civil servant, also loved the Whitehall system. He admired its superficial efficiency in producing papers and moving work smoothly through a hierarchy of committees, and tended to believe that this was equivalent to dealing with and resolving real problems. Wilson would certainly have made a better permanent secretary than Prime Minister. Dick Crossman, one of Wilson's oldest confidants, gained this impression very clearly in September 1968:

> I realised for the first time that he doesn't feel himself representing the Labour movement, really caring about the trade unions or feeling great loyalty to the party. He cares about being PM, about politics, about power. He has become de-partied to a great extent, an occupant of Downing Street who adores running things well.[5]

This impression that Wilson had become 'de-partied' is confirmed by his approach to a host of political questions. One of his main aims was not to project and argue for new or radical Labour policies but instead to defuse potential Conservative policies or arguments. His bid to enter the EEC was bound to fail, given de Gaulle's opposition. But Wilson seems to have regarded the effort as a useful way of demonstrating that Heath's great aim was unattainable and thus irrelevant as an election issue in 1970. Similarly his attempts to negotiate with Smith, in the *Tiger* and particularly the *Fearless* talks, were designed to ensure that he could not be accused by the Conservatives of being unwilling to try and reach a settlement. The disastrous attempt to legislate on industrial relations also started out as a move to foil Conservative attempts to exploit the issue.

Wilson's view of politics was essentially negative; he wanted to remove as many issues as possible from the political arena. He justified this view by arguing that the majority of the electorate were not interested in politics, and merely wanted somebody in office who would run the country quietly and competently. Hence the obsession with his image as the pipe-smoking, Baldwinesque 'family doctor'. In 1970 this low-key approach dominated the Labour campaign with its lack of policy commitments, its emphasis on continuity and conservatism, and 'playing safe' with Labour.

Wilson's style, and his lack of conviction and commitment, set the tone for the whole administration. The overall impression is that there is little that Wilson wanted to achieve in policy terms and conversely little that he would not do if it were politically advantageous. With no radical drive from the top, no desire to achieve anything in particular, it is not surprising that so little was achieved and that the government seemed to be the prisoner of events outside its control. This approach was combined with a dogged refusal to discuss key issues, such as devaluation, and an obsession with others, such as trade union reform, which gravely damaged the government. The final judgement on Wilson must therefore be essentially negative and the blame for the government's overall failure has to rest largely with him.

Perhaps Wilson was one of the few leaders who could have kept the Labour party reasonably united, although this is easier when the party is in office as Wilson was to discover after 1970. But long-term problems were building up. Many Labour party supporters and activists were acutely disappointed by the record of the government. At the time this showed up in a 50% drop in individual membership, and an unwillingness to canvass and work for candidates at local and national elections. Later the sense of dissatisfaction or even betrayal led to a debate about how to prevent a repetition of the events of 1964–70, how to ensure that a Labour government would be true to the more radical demands of many of its members. The 1964–70 government sowed the seeds of much of the grassroots revolt in the 1970s with its demands for greater accountability within the party. The unpopularity of the government for much of its life also dragged down many local Labour councils, particularly in 1967–68, and when the electoral pendulum swung back again many of the new Labour councillors were to the left of those they had replaced – another portent of trouble for the future. Wilson's strategy can also be criticised because it was not even successful in its own terms. He was unable to stem the long-term decline in the Labour party vote. Its share of the total electorate reached an all-time high of nearly 41% in 1951 and fell to 34½% by 1964, and continued downwards to 31½% in 1970. The slight rise in 1966 was a mere blip in a remorseless decline. This decline in support for a 'socialist' or 'social democratic' party is unique in Europe and Harold Wilson, like other leaders before and after him, failed to come up with an answer to the problem.

The criticism that the government was too conservative raises the intriguing question of what would have been different if the Conservatives had won the 1964 election. Much of the social legislation would not have been passed and the poorest groups in society might not have been protected from the worst effects of tough economic measures (though spending on health and education would have continued to rise). On the economic front the

Conservatives would have had to deflate after the 1964 election (as they were already planning to do) and in the absence of devaluation they too would have been forced to take a series of measures to protect the pound. 'Confidence' in sterling might have been higher after a Conservative victory, thus easing some of the pressure on the foreign exchanges, but it is doubtful whether the Conservatives could have got to the end of the decade without devaluing. The long-term trend has been for a fall in the value of the pound against the dollar, and in the 1960s sterling was overvalued and devaluation at some stage inevitable. (It was a Conservative government that eventually 'floated' the pound in the early 1970s.) It is likely that a Conservative government would also have adopted a 'corporatist' approach to economic policy, trying to involve the trade unions in some form of 'planning' and incomes policy. The Conservatives might well have tried to legislate on industrial relations and if it was anything like the legislation passed in the early 1970s it would probably have come to the same disastrous conclusion. The Conservatives also had no answer to the long-term problems facing the British economy, as their record between 1970 and 1974 demonstrated.

On defence policy the Conservatives would have continued the Polaris programme in exactly the way that the Labour government did. They too would have been obliged to withdraw from East of Suez, simply because they could not have found the money to sustain the policy. Indeed there were many in the Conservative party who advocated a more rapid withdrawal than the Labour government envisaged. On Vietnam a Conservative government would have adopted the same friendly support for the American position whilst stopping short of military commitment. The Conservatives under Heath were strongly in favour of entry into the EEC but it is difficult to see how they could have succeeded, given de Gaulle's opposition. On Rhodesia it is unlikely that they could have stopped an intransigent regime declaring UDI as long as they stuck to the 'Five Principles'. Although they might not have imposed such wide-ranging sanctions as the Labour government, since the latter was unable and unwilling to enforce sanctions this would have made little difference. The Conservatives would have tried hard to settle with Smith but again adherence to the Five Principles (in particular the fifth on acceptability to all Rhodesians) would have aborted that effort, as their attempt in the early 1970s failed.

If, apart from some social legislation and some measures aimed at greater equality, the election of the Labour government made such little difference in broad terms, was an alternative strategy available? It is difficult to argue against the essentially tactical approach adopted between October 1964 and March 1966, although from a strategic point of view more work could have been put in hand on longer-term reforms so that they would have been ready immediately if Labour were re-elected. It is the period after March 1966 that is crucial. Early action on major measures, such as the new state pension scheme and reform of the House of Lords, would have ensured that they were in place well before the next election. And the July 1966 crisis was the time to adopt a different strategy. That was the moment to devalue the pound and start the rundown of the sterling area. Although deflation would have been necessary there would have been time for the benefits of a lower pound to work through before the election. July 1966 was also the time to link this new policy with withdrawal from East of Suez on the timescale eventually adopted in 1968, so that it would have been completed before the election. This would have saved money and reduced the strain on the balance of payments, and would therefore have helped make devaluation work with less drastic impact on the domestic economy.

The question remains, however, as to whether a more radical policy was possible. In all major areas of policy the approach of the 1964–70 government was backward looking: it accepted the consensus established by the end of the Attlee government which the Conservatives too had, by and large, left unaltered. What might the Labour government have done to move beyond that consensus and establish a new one in its turn? Given the work of the Attlee government in introducing a mixed economy, the health service and social security, the key area to be tackled was the distribution of wealth and power. Here options were available to the 1964–70 government but not used. The 1957 pension plan, if properly implemented, would have had fundamental, long-term effects in redistributing wealth, yet no attempt was made to implement it. A wealth tax, as found in other 'socialist' countries such as Sweden, featured only on the fringes of discussion and was never seriously considered. A major programme of new benefits was also possible, particularly if they were funded through a 'clawback' mechanism to preserve the universal principle whilst ensuring that the benefits did not go to those on above-average incomes. New departures were also possible in defence and foreign affairs. Cancellation of Polaris was feasible in 1964 or, if this was seen as too great a blow to British prestige, permanent assignment to NATO as advocated by the Americans was an alternative. A more detached relationship with the Americans could have been adopted without jeopardising important institutions such as NATO. EEC entry was not an automatic choice and some in the Cabinet, particularly Dick Crossman, favoured a more independent role for Britain – a 'little England' policy that would give greater scope to develop Labour party policy and move Britain towards a more Scandinavian-style society. At all levels, therefore, different options were available but they usually remained unconsidered as the government, without ever taking a conscious decision to do so, seemed content to stay within the existing political consensus. The point of identifying alternative courses and policies is not to argue that some or all of them should have been adopted or that they would necessarily have transformed the outlook for the country or the Labour party. They simply illustrate that alternatives were available but not chosen.

In retrospect it is difficult to see the government as other than a comparative failure; not just because it failed to make radical changes but because, even with the limited aims it set itself, it was unable to produce results. Compared with the records of the other non-Conservative majority governments this century – that of the Liberal government from 1906 and of the 1945–51 Attlee government – the achievements of the Wilson government from 1964–70 were limited and outweighed by the failures. It proved unable to write an enduring and significant contribution to the second chapter of the socialist story. The promise remained unfulfilled.

Appendix

KEY CABINET COMMITTEES

EDC	Economic Development
EN	Economic Policy
EPC	Economic Planning
H	Home Policy
HL	House of Lords Reform
I	Immigration Policy
IP	Industrial Policy
L	Legislation
NPC	Nuclear Policy
OPD	Overseas Policy and Defence
P	Pensions Policy
PESC	Public Expenditure Survey
PI	Prices and Incomes Policy
P(L)	Parliamentary Reform (Lords)
QL	Queen's Speech and Legislative Programme
R/RX	Rhodesia
SEP	Strategic Economic Policy
SS	Social Services
ST	Science and Technology
MISC 205	Financial and Monetary Policy

Notes

References to 'Wilson' are to *The Labour Government 1964–70*, to 'Crossman' to the relevant volume of *The Diaries of a Cabinet Minister*, to 'Castle' to *The Castle Diaries 1964–70* and to 'Benn' to *Out of the Wilderness: Diaries 1963–67*.

CHAPTER 1: POLICIES AND PERSONALITIES 1951–64

1 Crossman, *Backbench Diary*, p 726 (18.12.58)
2 Hugh Dalton, *Diary*, p 700 (13.7.60)
3 *Ibid*
4 Quoted in Andrew Roth, *Sir Harold Wilson: The Yorkshire Walter Mitty*, p 271
5 Crossman, Vol 3, p 375 (20.2.69)
6 Benn, p 131 (17.7.64)
7 Crossman, *Backbench Diary*, p 980 (15.2.63)

CHAPTER 2: THE POLITICS OF TIGHTROPE WALKING

1 Crossman, Vol 1, p 50 (9.11.64)
2 Castle, p 3; Crossman, Vol 1, p 139 (26.1.65)
3 Crossman, Vol 1, p 211 (6.5.65)
4 Castle, p 30 (7.6.65)
5 Wilson, p 101
6 Crossman, Vol 1, pp 213–5 (10.5.65)
7 *Ibid*, p 243 (3.6.65)
8 *Ibid*, p 306 (5.8.65)
9 Castle, p 29 (13.4.65)
10 Wilson, p 94
11 Castle, p 34 (31.5.65)
12 Cecil King, *Diary*, p 38 (14.10.65)
13 Crossman, Vol 1, pp 136–7 (22.1.65)
14 *Ibid*
15 *Ibid*
16 Cecil King, *Diary*, p 19 (12.7.65)
17 Castle, pp 79–80 (21.12.65)
18 *Ibid*
19 Cecil King, *Diary*, p 39 (15.10.65)
20 Crossman, Vol 1, p 358 (21.10.65)
21 *Ibid*, p 432 (23.1.66)
22 *Ibid*
23 *Ibid*, p 461 (19.2.66)

CHAPTER 3: THE AMERICAN CONNECTION

1 Henry Kissinger, *White House Years*, p 91
2 Bruce to State Dept, 8.5.67: Johnson Library, *NSF Countries UK*, Vol 2
3 Rusk to Johnson, 24.10.64: Johnson Library, *NSF Countries Europe and USSR: UK Walker Visit Briefing Book*
4 UK Ambassador (Dean) to Bundy, 14.5.65: Johnson Library, *NSF Memos to the President from Bundy*, Vol 10, 4/15–5/31/65
5 Davis to Rusk, 9.7.65: Johnson Library, *NSF Countries Europe and USSR: UK UK Memos*, Vol VI, 7/65–9/65
6 Heller to Johnson, 30.3.65: Johnson Library, *WH Central File, Confidential File F1–9*
7 Stewart (UK Embassy) to Rusk, 18.11.66: Johnson Library, *NSF Countries Europe and USSR: UK UK Memos*, Vol IX, 8/66–1/67
8 Klein to Bundy, 1.6.65: Johnson Library, *NSF Countries UK Trendex*, 4/65–8/65
9 Bundy to Johnson, 28.6.65 (8.45 am): Johnson Library, *NSF Memos to the President from Bundy*, Vol 11, June 1965
10 Bundy to Johnson, 28.7.65 (8.45 pm): Johnson Library, *NSF Memos to the President from Bundy*, Vol 12, July 1965
11 Agenda for White House Meeting, 28.7.65 (6 pm), by Bator: Bator to Bundy, 29.7.65: Johnson Library, *NSF Countries UK Trendex*, 4/65–8/65
12 Gardner Ackley to Johnson, 29.7.65: Johnson Library, *NSF Countries UK Balance of Payments Crisis, 1965*
13 Bator to Bundy, 29.7.65: Johnson Library, *NSF Countries UK Trendex*, 4/65–8/65
14 Bundy to Johnson, 2.8.65 (1.45 pm): Johnson Library, *NSF Memos to the President from Bundy*, Vol 13, August 1965
15 *Ibid*
16 George Ball to Johnson, 6.8.65: Johnson Library, *NSF Countries UK Trendex*, 4/65–8/65
17 *Ibid*
18 Ackley to Johnson, 9.8.65: Johnson Library, *WH Central File, Confidential File CO 305*
19 Bundy to Johnson, 10.9.65 (5 pm): Johnson Library, *NSF Memos to the President from Bundy*, Vol 14, 9/1–9/22/65
20 Crossman, Vol 1, pp 455–6 (14.2.66)
21 *Ibid*, p 418 (21.12.65)
22 Bator to Johnson, 14.7.66 (9.30 pm): Johnson Library, *NSF Memos to the President from Rostow*, Vol 8, 7/1–15/7/66, No 6
23 Cecil King, *Diary*, p 78 (16.7.66–conversation of 15.7.66)
24 Fowler to Johnson, 14.7.66: Johnson Library, *NSF Countries Europe and USSR: UK UK Memos*, Vol VIII, 1/66–7/66
25 Crossman, Vol 1, p 574 (18.7.66)
26 Bator to Johnson, 1.6.67: Johnson Library, *NSF Countries UK, Visit of PM Wilson*, 6/67
27 Crossman, Vol 2, pp 645–8; Castle, pp 353–6 (12.1.68)
28 Summary notes of 587th NSC Meeting: Johnson Library, *NSC Meetings*, Vol 5, Tab 69, 6/9/68
29 Wilson, p 755
30 Kissinger, *op cit*, p 417
31 *Ibid*, p 89

CHAPTER 4: DEFENDING THE POUND

1 House of Commons, 16.4.58
2 Crossman, Vol 1, p 26 (22.10.65)
3 Lord Wigg, *George Wigg*, p 310
4 Crossman, Vol 1, p 69 (23.11.64)
5 *Ibid*, p 97 (13.12.64)
6 *Ibid*, p 71 (24.11.64)
7 Note by US Treasury June 1965, 'The Issue of Further Financial Assistance to the UK': Johnson Library, *NSF Countries UK Trendex*, 4/65–8/65
8 Tel, US Embassy London–State Department, 26.10.64: Johnson Library, *NSF Countries UK*, Vol 1
9 Martin to Johnson, 30.3.65: Johnson Library, US Treasury Files
10 Castle, pp 10–11 (10.2.65)
11 *Ibid*, pp 35–6; Crossman, Vol 1, p 242 (3.6.65)
12 Summers to Hinton, US Treasury Memorandum, 21.6.65: Johnson Library, *NSF Countries UK Balance of Trade Crisis, 1965*
13 Minutes of meeting, George Ball–UK Ambassador, 22.6.65: Johnson Library, *NSF Countries UK*, Vol 6
14 Fowler to Johnson, 28.6.65: Johnson Library, *NSF Countries UK*, Vol 3
15 US Treasury Memorandum, 25.6.65 (sent to White House): Johnson Library, *NSF Countries UK*, Vol 8
16 US Treasury Department note, 12.7.65: US National Archives, Office of Treasury Secretary, ES Box 73, Weekly Reports
17 Castle, pp 46–7 (8.7.65)
18 Crossman, Vol 1, pp 268–9 (6.7.65)
19 Tel, US Embassy London–State Department, 26.7.65: Johnson Library, *NSF Countries UK*, Vol 6
20 Crossman, Vol 1, p 290 (27.7.65)
21 Castle, pp 52–3 (27.7.65)
22 Crossman, *op cit*
23 *Ibid*
24 Fowler to President Johnson, 28.6.65: *op cit*
25 Crossman, Vol 1, p 321 (12.9.65)
26 *Ibid*, pp 316–7 (1.9.65)
27 Castle, p 103 (11.2.66)
28 Bundy to Trend, 16.8.65: Johnson Library, *NSF Countries UK Trendex*, 4/65–8/65
29 US Treasury Memorandum, 21.6.65: *op cit*
30 James Callaghan, *Time and Chance*, p 189
31 Castle, p 724 (3.11.69)
32 Castle, pp 58–9 (1.9.65); see also Crossman, Vol 1, pp 315–6
33 Bundy to Trend 16.8.65: *op cit*
34 US Treasury Memorandum to President Johnson, 10.9.65: Johnson Library, *NSF Memos to the President from Bundy*, Vol 14, 9/1–9/22/65

CHAPTER 5: A NEW DEFENCE POLICY?

1 *Guardian*, 26.10.60

2 Minutes of meeting, Wilson–McNamara, 2.3.64: Johnson Library, *NSF Countries Europe and USSR: UK UK Meetings/Wilson*, 3/2/64
3 Minutes of meeting, Healey–McNamara, 25.3.64, Mulley–William P. Bundy, 17.2.64: Johnson Library, *NSF Countries UK*, Vol 1
4 Minutes of meeting, Gordon-Walker–Rusk and McNamara and others, 27.10.64: Johnson Library, *NSF Countries UK Walker Visit Briefing Book*, 10/26–27/64
5 Castle, p 356 (12.1.68)
6 Ball to Johnson, 5.12.64, 'The Wilson Visit': Johnson Library, *NSF Countries UK, PM Wilson Visit*, 12/6–7/64
7 Meeting of Dept of State (Ball) and White House Staff (Bundy/Neustadt), 19.11.64: Johnson Library, *NSF MLF Memcons*
8 State Department Memorandum, 19.11.64: Johnson Library, *NSF MLF Memcons*
9 Minutes of meeting, Mulley–William P. Bundy, 17.2.64: Johnson Library, *NSF Countries UK*, Vol 1
10 *Ibid*
11 For example, visit by Neustadt and Ball, end of November 1964; Tel, State Dept–US Embassy London, 23.11.64; Tel, Bundy–Ball and Neustadt, 29.11.64: Johnson Library, *NSF Countries Europe and USSR: UK UK Memos*, Vol II, 10/64–2/65
12 Quoted in Reed and Williams, *Denis Healey and the Politics of Power*, p 173
13 Wilson, p 44
14 Bundy to Johnson, 16.12.65 (9.30 am): Johnson Library, *NSF Memos to the President from Bundy*, Vol 17; Container #5, Bundy to Johnson, 12.1.65 (3.30 pm): Johnson Library, *NSF Countries UK, PM Wilson Visit*, 12/17/65
15 Rusk to Johnson, brief on 'Nuclear Sharing in the Alliance': Johnson Library, *NSF Countries UK, PM Wilson Visit*, 12/17/65
16 Tel, State Dept–US Embassy London, 28.12.64: Johnson Library, *NSF Countries UK*, Vol 2
17 Crossman, Vol 1, pp 152–3 (8.2.65)
18 *Ibid*, pp 190–1 (1.4.65)
19 Confidential Report by McNamara, 'Military Export Sales Programme–UK': Johnson Library, *NSF Countries UK*, Vol 6
20 Message Johnson–Wilson, 3.3.66: Johnson Library, *WH Central File, Confidential File CO 301, WH CO 305 (UK)*, 1966
21 House of Commons, 16.12.64, *Hansard*, cols 423–4
22 Chapman Pincher, *Inside Story*, p 227
23 Minutes of meeting, Mulley–William P. Bundy, 17.2.64: Johnson Library, *NSF Countries UK*, Vol 1
24 Minutes of meeting, Wilson–McNamara, 2.3.64: Johnson Library, *NSF Countries Europe and USSR: UK UK Meetings/Wilson*, 3/2/64
25 Quoted in Roth, *op cit*
26 Johnson Library, *NSF Countries UK, PM Wilson Visit*, 12/15–19/65, 'UK Defense Review'
27 *Times*, 3.2.66
28 Briefing document, 'UK Military Expenditure Overseas': Johnson Library, *NSF Countries UK, PM Wilson Visit*, 12/7–8/65
29 Johnson to Wilson, 26.8.65: Johnson Library, *NSF NSC Histories Trilateral Negotiations and NATO 1966–67*, Book 1, Tabs 1–9

30 *Ibid*, 6.10.66
31 *Ibid*, 15.11.66
32 Background paper, 'British Forces in Germany': Johnson Library, *NSF Countries UK, Visit of Foreign Secretary Brown*, 10/14/66
33 Johnson to Wilson, 15.11.66: *op cit*
34 Rostow to Johnson (undated but mid-November, just before 15.11 message): Johnson Library, *WH Central File, Confidential File FO 4-1, FO 3-2-1*
35 Johnson to Wilson, 19.11.66: Johnson Library, *NSF NSC Histories Trilateral Negotiations and NATO 1966–67*, Book 1, Tabs 26–44
36 Crossman, Vol 2, p 145 (2.12.66)
37 Bator to Johnson, 17.3.67: *NSC Histories*, *op cit*, Book 2, Tabs 53–71; text of agreed final minute of trilateral talks, *NSC Histories*, Book 2, Tabs 72–98
38 Johnson Library: *Secret Administrative History of the State Department*, Chapter 3, Europe Section D
39 *Ibid*
40 *Ibid*

CHAPTER 6: ECONOMIC PLANNING?

1 Susan Crosland, *Tony Crosland*, p 173
2 Cmnd 2764
3 Sir Leo Pliatzky, *Getting and Spending*, p 63
4 Crossman, Vol 1, pp 300–1; Castle, pp 54–5 (3.8.65)
5 Crossman, Vol 1, p 321 (12.9.65)
6 *Ibid*, Vol 3, pp 443–4, 448–9, 452–3 (17/21/24.4.69)

CHAPTER 7: A BETTER SOCIETY

1   Crossman, Vol 1, pp 153–5; Castle, pp 11–12 (11.2.65)
2   Crossman, Vol 1, p 131 (15.1.65)
3   *Ibid*, p 303 (4.8.65)
4   *Ibid*, pp 348–50 (14.10.65)
5   *Ibid*, p 25 (22.10.64)
6   *Ibid*, p 126 (11.1.65)
7   Mary Craig, *Longford: A Biographical Portrait*, p 149
8   George Brown, *In My Way*, p 175
9   Crossman, Vol 2, pp 252–3; Castle, pp 222–3 (23.2.67)
10 Crossman, Vol 2, p 277; Castle, p 234 (14.3.67)

CHAPTER 8: THE SHADOW OF THE PAST: RHODESIA

1 Quoted in Lord Blake, *A History of Rhodesia*, p 358
2 Castle, p 17 (5.3.65)

3   *Ibid*, pp 60–1 (7.10.65)
4   *Ibid*; Crossman, Vol 1, p 344
5   Castle, pp 71–2; Crossman, Vol 1, pp 393–4 (29.11.65)
6   Johnson Library: *Secret Administrative History of the State Department*, Chapter 10, Sections C, D and E
7   State Dept–US Embassy London, 23.9.65; US Embassy–State Dept, 30.9.65; Komer to Bundy, 30.9.65; State Dept–US Embassy, London, 4.12.65: Johnson Library, *NSF Countries, UK*, Vol 1, Rhodesia, Vol 1
8   State Dept–US Embassy London, 28.11.65: Johnson Library, *UK Cables*, Vol VII, 10/65–1/66
9   Castle, p 78; Crossman, Vol 1, p 418 (21.12.65)
10 Castle, p 81 (22.12.65)
11 Cecil King, *Diary*, pp 47–8 (24.12.65)
12 Castle, p 90 (3.1.66)
13 Thomas C. Mann (State Dept) to President Johnson, 22.12.65: Johnson Library, *WH Central File, Confidential File CO 250*

CHAPTER 10: THE POLITICS OF DRIFT

1   Crossman, Vol 2, p 348 (9.5.67)
2   Castle, pp 79–80 (21.12.65)
3   *Ibid*, p 165
4   Michael Stewart, *Life and Labour*, p 190
5   Crossman, Vol 1, pp 608–9 (10.8.66)
6   *Ibid*, Vol 2, p 410 (5.7.67)
7   Douglas Jay, *Change and Fortune*, p 407
8   Benn, p 436 (21.6.66)
9   *Ibid*, p 456 (18.7.66)
10 Crossman, Vol 2, p 51 (25.9.66)
11 *Ibid*, p 159 (8.12.66)
12 *Ibid*, p 160 (8.12.66)
13 Joe Haines, *The Politics of Power*, pp 157–9
14 Benn, p 345 (2.11.65)
15 Wilson, p 373
16 *Ibid*, p 375
17 Crossman, Vol 2, p 410

CHAPTER 11: JULY 1966: ECONOMIC CRISIS AND POLITICAL PLOT

1   Crossman, Vol 1, pp 510–11 (2.5.66)
2   Castle, pp 125–6 (12.5.66)
3   Crossman, Vol 1, p 529 (26.5.66)
4   *Ibid*, pp 537–8 (14.6.66)
5   Castle, p 136 (16.6.66)
6   *Ibid*, p 136 (20.6.66)
7   *Ibid*, (21.6.66)
8   Jay, *op cit*, p 342

9   Crossman, Vol 1, pp 567–8 (12.7.66)
10 Wilson, p 253
11 Fowler to Johnson, 14.7.66: Johnson Library, *NSF Countries Europe and USSR: UK Memos*, Vol VIII, 1/66–7/66
12 Cecil King, *Diary*, p 78 (16.7.66 – conversation of 15.7.66)
13 Wilson, p 256
14 Castle, p 145 (14.7.66)
15 *Ibid*, p 146 (18.7.66)
16 Benn, p 454 (16.7.66)
17 Castle, p 147 (18.7.66)
18 Crossman, Vol 1, p 574; Castle, p 148 (18.7.66)
19 Benn, pp 456–7 (18.7.66)
20 Crossman, *op cit*
21 Castle, p 149 (19.7.66)
22 Jay, *op cit*, pp 345–6
23 Crossman, Vol 1, p 578 (20.7.66)
24 Quoted in Foot, *The Politics of Harold Wilson*, p 168
25 Quoted in Alexander and Watkins, *The Making of the Prime Minister 1970*, p 22
26 Benn, p 455 (17.7.66)

CHAPTER 12: EUROPE: THE COLD ANTE-CHAMBER

1   Quoted in Butler and King, *The British General Election of 1964*, p 79
2   Crossman, Vol 1, p 513 (9.5.66)
3   Richard Marsh, *Off the Rails*, p 96
4   Quoted in Reed and Williams, *op cit*, p 223
5   *Guardian*, 23.2.63
6   Brown, *op cit*, p 220
7   Crossman, Vol 2, p 323 (21.4.67)
8   Castle, p 214 (2.2.67)
9   Wilson, p 387
10 Johnson Library: *Secret Administrative History of the State Department*, Chapter 3, Europe Section C
11 Castle, p 247 (27.4.67)
12 *Ibid*, pp 244–5 (25.4.67)

CHAPTER 13: PEACE AND WAR

1   Cmnd 2736, *Overseas Development: The Work of the New Ministry*
2   Bundy to President Johnson, 17.2.65: Johnson Library, *NSF Memos to the President from Bundy*, Vol 8, 1/1–2/28/65
3   House of Commons, 1.4.65
4   Johnson Library: *NSF Countries UK, PM Wilson Visit*, 7/29/66 (background paper, 'British Attitudes on Vietnam')
5   *Hansard*, 17.5.66

6   Conversation Rusk–Dean, 22.6.65: Johnson Library, *NSF Countries UK*, Vol 6
7   Tel, US Embassy London–Washington, 1.7.66: Johnson Library, *NSF Countries UK*, Vol 8
8   *Hansard*, 23.6.66, cols 918–922
9   *Ibid*, 30.6.66, col 324
10 Rostow to Johnson, 14.7.66: Johnson Library, *NSF Countries Europe and USSR: UK UK Memos*, Vol VIII, 1/66–7/66
11 Conversation Rusk–Dean and Waller, 15.6.65: Johnson Library, *NSF Countries Europe and USSR: UK UK Memos*, Vol VII, 7/65–9/65
12 Castle, p 41 (18.6.65)
13 Crossman, Vol 1, p 255 (27.6.65)
14 *Ibid*, Vol 2, pp 237–8; Castle, p 220 (14.2.67)
15 Johnson Library: *Oral History Collection: Interviews with Chester Cooper AC 74–200*
16 *Ibid*
17 *Ibid*
18 Wilson, p 365
19 *Ibid*
20 Johnson Library: *NSC Histories*, 'The Middle East Crisis 12 May–19 June 1967', Vol 9, Appendix P
21 Minutes of National Security Meeting, 24.5.67: *NSC Histories*, Vol 1, Tabs 21–30
22 Castle, pp 257–8 (23.5.67)
23 *Ibid*
24 State Department Memo Hinton to Battle: *NSC Histories*, Vol 3, Tabs 96–110
25 Joint Chiefs of Staff Memorandum to Secretary of State for Defense: *JCSM-310-67, NSC Study*, Vol 3, Tabs 81–95
26 Minutes of meeting, Burke Trend and others–Dean Rusk, McNamara and others, 2.6.67: Johnson Library, *NSF Countries UK*, Vol 11
27 *Hansard*, 17.7.69
28 *Ibid*, 19.11.69
29 Stewart, *op cit*
30 Crossman, Vol 3, pp 415–6 (14.3.69)
31 *Ibid*
32 Johnson Library: *NSF Briefing Book, Visit of British Foreign Secretary Stewart*, 21–24.3.65 (Indian Ocean Islands)
33 Johnson Library: *NSF Countries Europe and USSR: UK Walker Visit Briefing Book* (talking points paper by State Department, 'Indian Ocean Islands')
34 Castle, pp 56–7 (31.8.65)
35 Johnson Library: *NSF Briefing Book, PM Wilson Visit*, 29/7/66 (Indian Ocean Projects);
    Johnson Library: *NSF UK Defence Review*, 1/27/66 (position paper, 'Indian Ocean Base Plans')
36 Quoted in Minority Rights Group Report No 54, 'Diego Garcia'

CHAPTER 14: NEGOTIATIONS AND SANCTIONS: RHODESIA 1966–70

1   Castle, p 159 (8.8.66)
2   Wilson, p 277
3   Crossman, Vol 2, pp 114–15 (8.11.66)
4   Castle, pp 190–2 (28.11.66)
5   Crossman, Vol 2, pp 141–2 (30.11.66)
6   *Ibid*, pp 146–9 (4.12.66)
7   Castle, pp 391–2 (7.3.68)
8   Wilson, p 317
9   Castle, pp 281–2 (22.7.67)
10 Wilson, p 567
11 Crossman, Vol 3, pp 215–17 (8.10.68)
12 Castle, pp 525–6 (6.10.68)
13 *Ibid*, p 601 (6.1.69)
14 Bingham Report, para 6.33
15 *Ibid*, p 257, para 7 of Commonwealth Office minutes of meeting, 21.2.68
16 House of Commons, 27.3.68, *Hansard*, col 1668
17 Bingham Report, p 269, para 7 of FCO minutes of meeting, 6.2.69
18 House of Lords, 9.11.78, *Hansard*, cols 735–7
19 House of Commons, 7.11.78, *Hansard*, cols 735–57
20 House of Lords, 9.11.78, *Hansard*, cols 464–74

CHAPTER 15: A MODERN AND CIVILISED SOCIETY

1   Crossman, Vol 2, p 150 (5.12.66)
2   *Ibid*, Vol 3, p 587 (22.7.69)
3   *Ibid*, p 103 (20.6.68)
4   *Ibid*, p 107 (25.6.68)
5   Castle, pp 74–5 (5.12.65)
6   Crossman, Vol 2, pp 47–8 (22.9.66)
7   *Ibid*, p 97 (27.10.66)
8   *Ibid*, p 468 (7.9.67)

CHAPTER 16: THE 'WHITE HEAT' OF REVOLUTION

1   Marsh, *op cit*, p 79
2   Crossman, Vol 2, p 254 (18.10.67)
3   Castle, pp 738–9 (10.12.69)
4   *Ibid*, p 625 (24.3.69)
5   Crossman, Vol 3, p 486 (12.5.69)

CHAPTER 17: DOWNHILL TO DEVALUATION

1 Crossman, Vol 1, pp 590–2; Castle, pp 154–5 (28.7.66)
2 Crossman, Vol 1, p 603 (4.8.66)
3 *Ibid*, Vol 2, p 280 and pp 286–7 (16/22.3.67)
4 *Ibid*, Vol 1, p 595 (31.7.66)
5 *Ibid*, Vol 1, p 607; Castle, p 160 (10.8.66)
6 Castle, p 186 (15.11.66)
7 Wilson, p 379
8 Crossman, Vol 2, p 310 (12.4.67)
9 *Ibid*, p 463 (5.9.67)
10 Crossman, Vol 2, pp 436–7; Castle, pp 280–3 (22.7.67)
11 Rostow and Fowler to Johnson, 19.10.67: Johnson Library, *NSF NSC Histories*, 'The Balance of Payments Program', Tabs 1–3
12 Crossman, Vol 2, pp 561–2 (8.11.67)
13 Callaghan to Fowler, 10.11.67: Johnson Library, *WH Central File, Confidential File FO 3-2-1, FO 4*, 'Financial Reactions'
14 Crossman, Vol 2, p 569 (13.11.67)
15 Castle, p 323 (14.11.67)
16 *Ibid*, pp 325–6 (16.11.67)

CHAPTER 18: CONFLICT, CRISIS AND CUTS

1 Wilson, p 470
2 Castle, p 313 (23.10.67)
3 Johnson Library: *NSF Countries UK*, Vol 8, 1978: 257A
4 Castle, pp 338–40 (15.12.67)
5 Crossman, Vol 2, pp 477–9 (14/15.9.67)
6 *Ibid*, p 598 (12.12.67)
7 Castle, pp 336–7 (13.12.67)
8 Crossman, Vol 2, p 601 (13.12.67)
9 Castle, pp 338–40; Crossman, Vol 2, pp 603–5 (15.12.67)
10 Castle, pp 340–1 (16.12.67)
11 Crossman, Vol 2, pp 606–7 (17.12.67)
12 *Ibid*, pp 607–9; Castle, pp 341–2 (18.12.67)
13 Castle, p 322 (13.11.67)
14 Susan Crosland, *op cit*, pp 194–6
15 *Ibid*
16 Crossman, Vol 2, pp 645–8; Castle, pp 353–6 (12.1.68)

CHAPTER 19: THE POLITICS OF DISASTER AND RECOVERY

1 Castle, p 379 (23.2.68)
2 Brown, *op cit*, p 178
3 *Ibid*
4 Crossman, Vol 2, pp 721–3 (19.3.68)
5 *Ibid*, pp 746–7 (28.3.68)

6 Castle, p 423 (4.4.68)
7 *Ibid*, pp 640–1; Crossman, Vol 3, pp 463–5 (29.4.69)
8 Castle, p 641 (30.4.69)
9 Crossman, Vol 3, pp 470–1 (1.5.69)
10 Castle, p 720 (15.10.69)
11 Crossman, Vol 3, p 677 (12.10.69)
12 *Ibid*, p 602; Castle, p 696 (30.7.69)
13 Crossman, Vol 3, p 683 (14.10.69)
14 *Ibid*, p 719 (6.11.69)
15 Castle, pp 761–3 (12.2.70)
16 Crossman, Vol 3, p 780 (14.1.70)
17 Castle, p 800 (15.5.70)
18 Crossman, Vol 3, p 916 (11.5.70)
19 Castle, *op cit*

CHAPTER 20: IMMIGRATION, GERRYMANDERING AND ULSTER

1 Crossman, Vol 1, pp 149–50 (5.2.65)
2 George Thomas, *George Thomas, Mr Speaker*, p 91
3 Crossman, Vol 2, p 202 (18.1.67 – see also entry for 19.9.67)
4 *Ibid*, Vol 3, pp 515–6 (12.6.69)
5 *Ibid*, pp 590–2 (24.7.69)
6 Castle, p 719 (14.10.69)
7 Crossman, Vol 3, p 570 (15.7.69)
8 Castle, p 696 (30.7.69)
9 James Callaghan, *A House Divided*, p 70
10 Castle, pp 699–700 (19.8.69)
11 Crossman, Vol 3, p 636 (11.9.69)

CHAPTER 21: PATRONAGE AND PRIVILEGE: REFORM OF THE HOUSE OF LORDS

1 Castle, p 365 (1.2.68)
2 Crossman, Vol 3, p 97 (17.6.68)
3 *Ibid*, p 267 (21.11.68)
4 *Ibid*, p 356 (3.2.69)

CHAPTER 22: IN PLACE OF STRIFE

1 Castle, pp 486–7 (15/16.7.68)
2 *Ibid*, p 477 (2.7.68)
3 *Ibid*, pp 549–51 (15/16.11.68)

4   *Ibid*, p 566 (4.12.68)
5   *Ibid*, p 574 (19.12.68)
6   *Ibid*, pp 582–3 (3.1.69)
7   Crossman, Vol 3, p 308 (4.1.69)
8   Castle, p 601 (5.2.69)
9   Crossman, Vol 3, p 457 (27.4.69)
10 Castle, pp 625–6 (26.3.69)
11 Wilson, p 640
12 Castle, pp 630–1 (3.4.69)
13 *Ibid*, pp 631–2 (4.4.69)
14 *Ibid*, pp 582–3 (3.1.69)
15 *Ibid*, pp 629–30 (2.4.69)
16 *Ibid*, pp. 644–5 (5.5.69); Wilson, p 647
17 Castle, pp 636–7 (16.4.69)
18 Crossman, Vol 3, pp 444–5 (17.4.69)
19 Castle, p 647 (8.5.69)
20 *Ibid*, pp 655–6; Crossman, Vol 3, pp 497–8 (20.5.69)
21 *Ibid*
22 Castle, pp 657–8 (21.5.69)
23 *Ibid*, pp 660 (1.6.69)
24 Jack Jones, *Union Man*, p 205
25 Castle, pp 669–71 (12.6.69)
26 Castle, pp 672–6; Crossman, Vol 3, pp 520–5 (17.6.69)
27 Susan Crosland, *op cit*, p 204
28 Castle, pp 584–5 (7.1.69)
29 *Ibid*, p 680 (24.6.69)

CHAPTER 23: TWO YEARS' HARD SLOG

1   Castle, pp 392–3 (7.3.68)
2   *Ibid*, p 521 (25.9.68)
3   Crossman, Vol 3, pp 654 (24.9.69 – meeting on 25.9.69)
4   *Ibid*, pp 269–71 (22.11.68)
5   *Ibid*, pp 815–6 (12.2.70)

CHAPTER 25: BREACH OF PROMISE

1   Ben Pimlott, *Hugh Dalton*, p 606
2   Jay, *op cit*, p 411
3   Susan Crosland, *op cit*, p 184
4   *Guardian*, 3.10.87
5   Crossman, Vol 3, p 180 (4.9.68)

Bibliography

PRIMARY SOURCES

President Lyndon B. Johnson Papers, Johnson Library, Austin, Texas
US State Department Papers, US National Archives, Washington DC
US Treasury Department Papers, US National Archives, Washington DC
Anthony Crosland Papers, British Library of Political and Economic Science, London
James Griffiths Papers, National Library of Wales, Aberystwyth

The following collections are only partially open for research:
Desmond Donnelly Papers, National Library of Wales, Aberystwyth
George Brown Papers, Bodleian Library, Oxford
Anthony Greenwood Papers, Bodleian Library, Oxford

OFFICIAL PAPERS

Cmnd 2577	Machinery of Prices and Incomes Policy
Cmnd 2592	Statement on the Defence Estimates
Cmnd 2639	Prices and Incomes Policy
Cmnd 2736	Overseas Development: The Work of the New Ministry
Cmnd 2739	Immigration from the Commonwealth
Cmnd 2764	The National Plan
Cmnd 2767	The Parliamentary Commissioner for Administration
Cmnd 2808	Prices and Incomes Policy: An 'Early Warning System'
Cmnd 2874	Investment Incentives
Cmnd 2922	University of the Air
Cmnd 3006	A Plan for Polytechnics and Other Colleges
Cmnd 3150	Prices and Incomes Standstill: Period of Severe Restraint
Cmnd 3171	Rhodesia: Documents relating to a Proposal for a Settlement
Cmnd 3235	Prices and Incomes Policy after 30 June 1967
Cmnd 3438	Fuel Policy
Cmnd 3590	Productivity, Prices and Incomes in 1968 and 1970
Cmnd 3638	The Civil Service
Cmnd 3883	National Superannuation and Social Insurance: Proposals for Earnings Related Social Security
Cmnd 3888	In Place of Strife
Cmnd 4237	Productivity, Prices and Incomes Policy after 1969
Cmnd 532	Disturbances in Northern Ireland
Cmnd 566	Violence and Civil Disturbances in Northern Ireland in 1969

Foreign and Commonwealth Office   Report on the Supply of Petroleum and petroleum products to Rhodesia (Bingham Report) 1978

BIBLIOGRAPHY

SECONDARY SOURCES

I. Diaries, Memoirs and Autobiographies

Benn, Tony, *Out of the Wilderness: Diaries 1963–7*, London, Hutchinson, 1987

Brockway, Fenner, *Towards Tomorrow*, London, Hart-Davis, 1977

Brown, George, *In My Way: The Political Memoirs of Lord George-Brown*, London, Gollancz, 1971

Callaghan, James, *Time and Chance*, London, Collins, 1987

Castle, Barbara, *The Castle Diaries 1964–70*, London, Weidenfeld and Nicolson, 1984

Crossman, Richard, *The Diaries of a Cabinet Minister*
 Vol 1: Minister of Housing 1964–66
 Vol 2: Lord President of the Council and Leader of the House of Commons 1966–68
 Vol 3: Secretary of State for Social Services 1968–70
 London, Hamish Hamilton and Jonathan Cape, 1975, 1976 and 1977

Davenport, Nicholas, *Memoirs of a City Radical*, London, Weidenfeld and Nicolson, 1974

Driberg, Tom, *Ruling Passions*, London, Jonathan Cape, 1977

Elwyn Jones, Lord, *In My Time*, London, Weidenfeld and Nicolson, 1983

Griffiths, James, *Pages from Memory*, London, Dent, 1969

Hailsham, Lord, *The Door Wherein I Went*, London, Collins, 1975

Haines, Joe, *The Politics of Power*, London, Jonathan Cape, 1977

Jay, Douglas, *Change and Fortune: A Political Record*, London, Hutchinson, 1980

Johnson, Lyndon B., *The Vantage Point: Perspectives of the Presidency 1963–1969*, London, Weidenfeld and Nicolson, 1972

Jones, Jack, *Union Man*, London, Collins, 1986

King, Cecil, *The Cecil King Diary 1965–1970*, London, Jonathan Cape, 1972

Kissinger, Henry, *The White House Years*, London, Weidenfeld and Nicolson, 1979

Lee, Jenny, *My Life with Nye*, London, Jonathan Cape, 1980

MacDougall, Donald, *Don and Mandarin: Memoirs of an Economist*, London, John Murray, 1987

Macmillan, Harold, *Pointing the Way 1959–1961*, London, Macmillan, 1972

Macmillan, Harold, *At the End of the Day 1961–63*, London, Macmillan, 1973

Marsh, Richard, *Off the Rails*, London, Weidenfeld and Nicolson, 1978

Maudling, Reginald, *Memoirs*, London, Sidgwick and Jackson, 1978

Mayhew, Christopher, *A Time To Remember*, London, Hutchinson, 1987

Morgan, Janet (ed), *The Backbench Diaries of Richard Crossman*, London, Hamish Hamilton and Jonathan Cape, 1981

O'Neill, Lord, *The Autobiography of Terence O'Neill*, London, Hart-Davis, 1972

Pimlott, Ben (ed), *The Political Diary of Hugh Dalton 1918–40, 1945–60*, London, Jonathan Cape, 1986

Pincher, Chapman, *Inside Story*, London, Sidgwick and Jackson, 1978

Redcliffe Maud, J. P. R., *Experiences of an Optimist*, London, Hamish Hamilton, 1981

Robens, Lord, *Ten Year Stint*, London, Cassell, 1972

Stewart, Michael, *Life and Labour*, London, Sidgwick and Jackson, 1980

BIBLIOGRAPHY

Thomas, George, *George Thomas, Mr Speaker: The Memoirs of The Viscount Tonypandy*, London, Century Publishing, 1985
Wigg, Lord, *George Wigg*, London, Michael Joseph, 1972
Williams, Marcia, *Inside No 10*, London, Weidenfeld and Nicolson, 1972
Williams, P. M. (ed), *The Diary of Hugh Gaitskell 1945–56*, London, Jonathan Cape, 1983
Wilson, Harold, *The Labour Government 1964–70: A Personal Record*, London, Weidenfeld and Nicolson, 1971
Wilson, Harold, *Memoirs Vol 1: The Makings of a Prime Minister 1916–64*, London, Weidenfeld and Nicolson, and Michael Joseph, 1986
Wyatt, Woodrow, *Confessions of an Optimist*, London, Collins, 1985

II. Biographies

Bartram, P., *David Steel: His Life and Politics*, London, W. H. Allen, 1981
Campbell, J., *Roy Jenkins*, London, Weidenfeld and Nicolson, 1983
Campbell, J., *Nye Bevan and the Mirage of British Socialism*, London, Weidenfeld and Nicolson, 1987
Chester, L., Linklater, M. and May, D., *Jeremy Thorpe: A Secret Life*, London, Fontana, 1979
Craig, M., *Longford: A Biographical Portrait*, London, Hodder and Stoughton, 1978
Crosland, S., *Tony Crosland*, London, Jonathan Cape, 1982
Donoghue, B. and Jones, G. W., *Herbert Morrison: Portrait of a Politician*, London, Weidenfeld and Nicolson, 1973
Fisher, N., *Iain Macleod*, London, André Deutsch, 1973
Foot, M., *Aneurin Bevan:*
  Vol 1: 1897–1945, London, Macgibbon and Kee, 1962
  Vol 2: 1945–1960, London, Davis-Poynter, 1973
Foot, P., *The Politics of Harold Wilson*, Harmondsworth, Penguin, 1968
Goodman, G., *The Awkward Warrior, Frank Cousins: His Life and Times*, London, Davis-Poynter, 1979
Hoggart, S. and Leigh, D., *Michael Foot: A Portrait*, London, Hodder and Stoughton, 1981
Jenkins, R., *Tony Benn*, London, Writers and Readers, 1980
Kay, E., *Pragmatic Premier*, London, Leslie Frewin, 1967
Kellner, P. and Hitchen, C., *The Road to Number Ten*, London, Cassell and Co, 1976
Pimlott, B., *Hugh Dalton*, London, Jonathan Cape, 1985
Reed, B. and Williams, G., *Denis Healey and the Policies of Power*, London, Sidgwick and Jackson, 1971
Roth, A., *Sir Harold Wilson: The Yorkshire Walter Mitty*, London, Macdonald and Jane's, 1977
Smith, D., *Harold Wilson: A Critical Biography*, London, Hale, 1964
Smith, L., *Harold Wilson: The Authentic Portrait*, London, Hodder and Stoughton, 1964
Snow, P. A., *Stranger and Brother: A Portrait of C. P. Snow*, London, Macmillan, 1982
Williams, P., *Hugh Gaitskell*, London, Jonathan Cape, 1979

III. Politics

Alexander, A. and Watkins, A., *The Making of the Prime Minister 1970*, London, Macdonald, 1971

Budge, I., Robertson, D. and Head, D. J. (ed), *Ideology, Strategy and Party Change*, Cambridge, Cambridge University Press, 1987

Bruce-Gardyne, J. and Lawson, N., *The Power Game: An Examination of Decision-Making in Government*, London, Macmillan, 1976

Butler, D. E. and King, A., *The British General Election of 1964*, London, Macmillan, 1965

Butler, D. E. and King, A., *The British General Election of 1966*, London, Macmillan, 1966

Butler, D. E. and Pinto-Duschinsky, M., *The British General Election of 1970*, London, Macmillan, 1971

Butler, D. E. and Sloman, A., *British Political Facts 1900–1979*, London, Macmillan, 1980

Callaghan, J., *A House Divided: The Dilemma of Northern Ireland*, London, Collins, 1973

Callaghan, J., *The Far Left in British Politics*, Oxford, Basil Blackwell, 1987

Cook, C. and Ramsden, J. (ed), *By-Elections in British Politics*, London, Macmillan, 1973

Craig, F. W. S., *British Electoral Facts 1832–1980*, Chichester, Parliamentary Research Services, 1981

Craig, F. W. S., *British General Election Manifestos 1900–1974*, London, Macmillan, 1975

Donnelly, D., *Gadarene 68: The Crimes, Follies and Misfortunes of the Wilson Government*, London, William Kimber, 1968

Gordon-Walker, P., *The Cabinet*, London, Jonathan Cape, 1970

Haseler, S., *The Gaitskellites: Revisionism in the British Labour Party 1951–64*, London, Macmillan, 1969

Hedley, P. and Aynsley, C., *The D-Notice Affair*, London, Michael Joseph, 1967

Hennessy, P., *The Great and the Good: An Inquiry into the British Establishment*, London, Policy Studies Institute, 1986

Hennessy, P. and Seldon, A., *Ruling Performance*, Oxford, Basil Blackwell, 1987

Howard, A. and West, R., *The Making of the Prime Minister*, London, Jonathan Cape, 1965

Howell, D., *British Social Democracy: A Study in Development and Decay*, London, Croom Helm, 1980

Jackson, R. J., *Rebels and Whips: An Analysis of Dissension, Discipline and Cohesion in British Political Parties*, London, Macmillan, 1968

James, R. R., *Ambitions and Realities: British Politics 1964–70*, London, Weidenfeld and Nicolson, 1972

Jenkins, M., *Bevanism: Labour's High Tide*, Nottingham, Spokesman, 1979

Jenkins, P., *The Battle of Downing Street*, London, Charles Knight, 1970

Kavanagh, D. (ed), *The Politics of the Labour Party*, London, Allen and Unwin, 1982

Keith-Lucas, B. and Richards, P. G., *A History of Local Government in the Twentieth Century*, London, Allen and Unwin, 1978

McKie, D. and Cook, C., *The Decade of Disillusion: British Politics in the Sixties*, London, Macmillan, 1972

Mellows, C., *The British MP: A Socio-Economic Study of the House of Commons*, Farnborough, Saxon House, 1978

Minkin, L., *The Labour Party Conference*, Manchester, Manchester University Press, 1980

Morgan, J. P., *The House of Lords and the Labour Government 1964–70*, Oxford, Oxford University Press, 1975

Morgan, K. O., *Labour People: Leaders and Lieutenants: Hardie to Kinnock*, Oxford, Oxford University Press, 1987

Norton, P., *Dissension in the House of Commons 1945–74*, London, Macmillan, 1976

Pinto-Duschinsky, M., *British Political Finance 1830–1980*, London, American Enterprise Institute, 1981

Pollitt, C., *Manipulating the Machine: Changing the Pattern of Ministerial Departments 1960–83*, London, Allen and Unwin, 1984

Richards, P. G., *Parliament and Conscience*, London, Allen and Unwin, 1970

Roth, A., *Heath and the Heathmen*, London, Routledge and Kegan Paul, 1972

Rush, M., *The Cabinet and Policy Formation*, London, Longman, 1984

Shrimsley, A., *The First Hundred Days of Harold Wilson*, London, Weidenfeld and Nicolson, 1965

Stacey, F., *The British Ombudsman*, Oxford, Oxford University Press, 1971

Sunday Times 'Insight' Team, *Ulster*, London, André Deutsch, 1972

Walker, J., *The Queen Has Been Pleased: The British Honours System at Work*, London, Secker and Warburg, 1986

Wyatt, W., *Turn Again Westminster*, London, André Deutsch, 1973

IV. Economic and Social

Beckerman, W. (ed), *The Labour Government's Economic Record: 1964–70*, London, Duckworth, 1972

Bogdanov, V. and Skidelsky, R. (eds), *The Age of Affluence 1951–1964*, London, Macmillan, 1970

Cohen, C. D., *British Economic Policy 1960–69*, London, Butterworths, 1971

Cox, A., *Adversary Politics and Land: The Conflict over Land and Property Policy in Post-War Britain*, Cambridge, Cambridge University Press, 1984

Davies, W., *Three Years Hard Labour: The Road to Devaluation*, London, André Deutsch, 1968

Dunleavy, P., *The Politics of Mass Housing in Britain 1945–75*, Oxford, Oxford University Press, 1981

Gamble, A. M. and Walkland, S. A., *The British Party System and Economic Policy 1945–83: Studies in Adversarial Politics*, Oxford, Oxford University Press, 1984

Godsen, P., *The Education System since 1944*, Oxford, Martin Robertson and Co, 1983

Hall, T., *Nuclear Politics: The History of Nuclear Power in Britain*, Harmondsworth, Penguin, 1986

Levin, B., *The Pendulum Years: Britain and the Sixties*, London, Jonathan Cape, 1970

Middlemas, K., *Power, Competition and the State: Vol 1: Britain in Search of Balance 1940–61*, London, Macmillan, 1986

Pliatzky, Sir L., *Getting and Spending: Public Expenditure, Employment and Inflation*, Oxford, Basil Blackwell, 1982

Pollard, S., *The Development of the British Economy 1914–80* (3rd edition), London, Edward Arnold, 1983

Solomon, R., *The International Monetary System 1945–1976: An Inside View*, New York, Harper & Row, 1974

Stewart, M., *Politics and Economic Policy in the UK since 1964: The Jekyll and Hyde Years*, Oxford, Pergamon, 1978

Strange, S., *Sterling and British Policy: A Political Study of an International Currency in Decline*, London, Oxford University Press/Royal Institute of International Affairs, 1971

Williams, R., *The Nuclear Power Decisions: British Policies 1953–78*, London, Croom Helm, 1980

V. Defence and Foreign Policy

Aitken, J., *Officially Secret*, London, Weidenfeld and Nicolson, 1971

Bailey, M., *Oilgate: The Sanctions Scandal*, London, Coronet, 1979

Bartlett, C. J., *The Long Retreat: British Defence Policy 1945–1970*, London, Macmillan, 1972

Baylis, J., *Anglo-American Defence Relations 1939–84* (2nd edition), London, Macmillan, 1984

Blake, R., *A History of Rhodesia*, London, Eyre Methuen, 1977

Buteux, P., *The Politics of Nuclear Consultation in NATO 1965–1980*, Cambridge, Cambridge University Press, 1983

Chalmers, M., *Paying for Defence*, London, Pluto, 1985

Darby, P., *British Defence Policy East of Suez 1947–1968*, London, Oxford University Press, 1973

Flower, K., *Serving Secretly*, London, John Murray, 1987

Good, R. C., *UDI – The International Politics of the Rhodesian Rebellion*, London, Faber and Faber, 1973

Herring, G. C., *America's Longest War: The United States and Vietnam 1950–1975*, New York, John Wiley and Sons, 1979

Johnson, F. A., *Defence by Ministry: The British Ministry of Defence 1944–74*, London, Duckworth, 1980

Karnow, S., *Vietnam: A History*, London, Century Publishing, 1983

Kirk-Greene, A. H. M., *Crisis and Conflict in Nigeria* (2 Vols), London, Oxford University Press, 1971

Lewy, G., *America in Vietnam*, New York, Oxford University Press, 1978

Maclear, M., *Vietnam: The Ten Thousand Day War*, London, Eyre Methuen, 1981

Madeley, J., *Diego Garcia: A Contrast to the Falklands*, Minority Rights Group Report No 54

Meredith, M., *The Past is Another Country: Rhodesia 1890–1979*, London, André Deutsch, 1979

Morgan, D. J., *The Official History of Colonial Development: Vol 4: Changes in British Aid Policy 1951–1970*, London, Macmillan, 1980

Morgan, D. J., *The Official History of Colonial Development: Vol 5: Guidance Towards Self-Government in British Colonies 1941–1971*, London, Macmillan, 1980

Nailor, P., *Denis Healey and Rational Decision-Making in Defence* (in Beckett and Gooch (eds), *Politicians and Defence: Studies in the Formulation of British Defence Policy 1845–1970*, Manchester, Manchester University Press, 1981)

de St Jorre, J., *The Nigerian Civil War*, London, Hodder and Stoughton, 1972

Williams, G. (ed), *Crisis in Procurement: A Case Study of the TSR 2*, London, Royal United Services Institute, 1969

Wright, P., *Spycatcher*, New York, Viking, 1987

Index

FOR THE BEST IN PAPERBACKS, LOOK FOR THE 🐧

In every corner of the world, on every subject under the sun, Penguin represents quality and variety – the very best in publishing today.

For complete information about books available from Penguin – including Puffins, Penguin Classics and Arkana – and how to order them, write to us at the appropriate address below. Please note that for copyright reasons the selection of books varies from country to country.

In the United Kingdom: Please write to *Dept E.P., Penguin Books Ltd, Harmondsworth, Middlesex, UB7 0DA*.

If you have any difficulty in obtaining a title, please send your order with the correct money, plus ten per cent for postage and packaging, to *PO Box No 11, West Drayton, Middlesex*

In the United States: Please write to *Dept BA, Penguin, 299 Murray Hill Parkway, East Rutherford, New Jersey 07073*

In Canada: Please write to *Penguin Books Canada Ltd, 2801 John Street, Markham, Ontario L3R 1B4*

In Australia: Please write to the *Marketing Department, Penguin Books Australia Ltd, P.O. Box 257, Ringwood, Victoria 3134*

In New Zealand: Please write to the *Marketing Department, Penguin Books (NZ) Ltd, Private Bag, Takapuna, Auckland 9*

In India: Please write to *Penguin Overseas Ltd, 706 Eros Apartments, 56 Nehru Place, New Delhi, 110019*

In the Netherlands: Please write to *Penguin Books Netherlands B.V., Postbus 195, NL–1380 AD Weesp*

In West Germany: Please write to *Penguin Books Ltd, Friedrichstrasse 10–12, D–6000 Frankfurt/Main 1*

In Spain: Please write to *Longman Penguin España, Calle San Nicolas 15, E–28013 Madrid*

In Italy: Please write to *Penguin Italia s.r.l., Via Como 4, I-20096 Pioltello (Milano)*

In France: Please write to *Penguin Books Ltd, 39 Rue de Montmorency, F-75003 Paris*

In Japan: Please write to *Longman Penguin Japan Co Ltd, Yamaguchi Building, 2–12–9 Kanda Jimbocho, Chiyoda-Ku, Tokyo 101*

A CHOICE OF PENGUINS

The Secret Lives of Trebitsch Lincoln   Bernard Wasserstein

Trebitsch Lincoln was Member of Parliament, international spy, right-wing revolutionary, Buddhist monk – and this century's most extraordinary conman. 'Surely the final work on a truly extraordinary career' – Hugh Trevor-Roper. 'An utterly improbable story ... a biographical coup' – *Guardian*

Out of Africa   Karen Blixen (Isak Dinesen)

After the failure of her coffee-farm in Kenya, where she lived from 1913 to 1931, Karen Blixen went home to Denmark and wrote this unforgettable account of her experiences. 'No reader can put the book down without some share in the author's poignant farewell to her farm' – *Observer*

In My Wildest Dreams   Leslie Thomas

The autobiography of Leslie Thomas, author of *The Magic Army* and *The Dearest and the Best*. From Barnardo boy to original virgin soldier, from apprentice journalist to famous novelist, it is an amazing story. 'Hugely enjoyable' – *Daily Express*

The Winning Streak   Walter Goldsmith and David Clutterbuck

Marks and Spencer, Saatchi and Saatchi, United Biscuits, GEC ... The UK's top companies reveal their formulas for success, in an important and stimulating book that no British manager can afford to ignore.

Bird of Life, Bird of Death   Jonathan Evan Maslow

In the summer of 1983 Jonathan Maslow set out to find the quetzal. In doing so, he placed himself between the natural and unnatural histories of Central America, between the vulnerable magnificence of nature and the terrible destructiveness of man. 'A wonderful book' – *The New York Times Book Review*

Mob Star   Gene Mustain and Jerry Capeci

Handsome, charming, deadly, John Gotti is the real-life Mafia boss at the head of New York's most feared criminal family. *Mob Star* tells the chilling and compelling story of the rise to power of the most powerful criminal in America.

FOR THE BEST IN PAPERBACKS, LOOK FOR THE

A CHOICE OF PENGUINS

The Assassination of Federico García Lorca   Ian Gibson

Lorca's 'crime' was his antipathy to pomposity, conformity and intolerance. His punishment was murder. Ian Gibson – author of the acclaimed new biography of Lorca – reveals the truth about his death and the atmosphere in Spain that allowed it to happen.

Between the Woods and the Water   Patrick Leigh Fermor

Patrick Leigh Fermor continues his celebrated account – begun in *A Time of Gifts* – of his journey on foot from the Hook of Holland to Constantinople. 'Even better than everyone says it is' – Peter Levi. 'Indescribably rich and beautiful' – *Guardian*

The Hunting of the Whale   Jeremy Cherfas

'*The Hunting of the Whale* is a story of declining profits and mounting pigheadedness ... it involves a catalogue of crass carelessness ... Jeremy Cherfas brings a fresh eye to [his] material ... for anyone wanting a whale in a nutshell this must be the book to choose' – *The Times Literary Supplement*

Metamagical Themas   Douglas R. Hofstadter

This astonishing sequel to the bestselling, Pulitzer Prize-winning *Gödel, Escher, Bach* swarms with 'extraordinary ideas, brilliant fables, deep philosophical questions and Carrollian word play' – Martin Gardner

Into the Heart of Borneo   Redmond O'Hanlon

'Perceptive, hilarious and at the same time a serious natural-history journey into one of the last remaining unspoilt paradises' – *New Statesman*. 'Consistently exciting, often funny and erudite without ever being overwhelming' – *Punch*

When the Wind Blows   Raymond Briggs

'A visual parable against nuclear war: all the more chilling for being in the form of a strip cartoon' – *Sunday Times*. 'The most eloquent anti-Bomb statement you are likely to read' – *Daily Mail*

A CHOICE OF PENGUINS

Better Together   Christian Partnership in a Hurt City
David Sheppard and Derek Warlock

The Anglican and Roman Catholic Bishops of Liverpool tell the uplifting and heartening story of their alliance in the fight for their city – an alliance that has again and again reached out to heal a community torn by sectarian loyalties and bitter deprivation.

Fantastic Invasion   Patrick Marnham

Explored and exploited, Africa has carried a different meaning for each wave of foreign invaders – from ivory traders to aid workers. Now, in the crisis that has followed Independence, which way should Africa turn? 'A courageous and brilliant effort' – Paul Theroux

Jean Rhys: Letters 1931–66
Edited by Francis Wyndham and Diana Melly

'Eloquent and invaluable … her life emerges, and with it a portrait of an unexpectedly indomitable figure' – Marina Warner in the *Sunday Times*

Among the Russians   Colin Thubron

One man's solitary journey by car across Russia provides an enthralling and revealing account of the habits and idiosyncrasies of a fascinating people. 'He sees things with the freshness of an innocent and the erudition of a scholar' – *Daily Telegraph*

They Went to Portugal   Rose Macaulay

An exotic and entertaining account of travellers to Portugal from the pirate-crusaders, through poets, aesthetes and ambassadors, to the new wave of romantic travellers. A wonderful mixture of literature, history and adventure, by one of our most stylish and seductive writers.

The Separation Survival Handbook   Helen Garlick

Separation and divorce almost inevitably entail a long journey through a morass of legal, financial, custodial and emotional problems. Stripping the experience of both jargon and guilt, marital lawyer Helen Garlick maps clearly the various routes that can be taken.

The Russian Album Michael Ignatieff

Michael Ignatieff movingly comes to terms with the meaning of his own family's memories and histories, in a book that is both an extraordinary account of the search for roots and a dramatic and poignant chronicle of four generations of a Russian family.

Beyond the Blue Horizon Alexander Frater

The romance and excitement of the legendary Imperial Airways East-bound Empire service – the world's longest and most adventurous scheduled air route – relived fifty years later in one of the most original travel books of the decade. 'The find of the year' – *Today*

Getting to Know the General Graham Greene

'In August 1981 my bag was packed for my fifth visit to Panama when the news came to me over the telephone of the death of General Omar Torrijos Herrera, my friend and host...' 'Vigorous, deeply felt, at times funny, and for Greene surprisingly frank' – *Sunday Times*

The Search for the Virus Steve Connor and Sharon Kingman

In this gripping book, two leading *New Scientist* journalists tell the remarkable story of how researchers discovered the AIDS virus and examine the links between AIDS and lifestyles. They also look at the progress being made in isolating the virus and finding a cure.

Arabian Sands Wilfred Thesiger

'In the tradition of Burton, Doughty, Lawrence, Philby and Thomas, it is, very likely, the book about Arabia to end all books about Arabia' – *Daily Telegraph*

Adieux: A Farewell to Sartre Simone de Beauvoir

A devastatingly frank account of the last years of Sartre's life, and his death, by the woman who for more than half a century shared that life. 'A true labour of love, there is about it a touching sadness, a mingling of the personal with the impersonal and timeless which Sartre himself would surely have liked and understood' – *Listener*